Materials Development in Language Teaching

CAMBRIDGE LANGUAGE TEACHING LIBRARY

A series covering central issues in language teaching and learning, by authors who have expert knowledge in their field.

For a complete list of titles please visit: www.cambridge.org/elt/cltl

A selection of recent titles in this series

Materials Development in Language Teaching (Second Edition)
Edited by Brian Tomlinson

Values, Philosophies, and Beliefs in TESOL
Making a Statement
Graham Crookes

Listening in the Language Classroom
John Field

Lessons from Good Language Learners
Edited by Carol Griffiths

Teacher Language Awareness
Stephen Andrews

Language Teacher Supervision
A Case-Based Approach
Kathleen M. Bailey

Conversation
From Description to Pedagogy
Scott Thornbury and Diana Slade

The Experience of Language Teaching
Rose Senior

Learners' Stories
Difference and Diversity in Language Learning
Edited by Phil Benson and David Nunan

Task-Based Language Teaching
David Nunan

Rules, Patterns and Words
Grammar and Lexis in English Language Teaching
Dave Willis

Language Learning in Distance Education
Cynthia White

Group Dynamics in the Language Classroom
Zoltán Dörnyei and Tim Murphey

Testing for Language Teachers (Second Edition)
Arthur Hughes

Motivational Strategies in the Language Classroom
Zoltán Dörnyei

The Dynamics of the Language Classroom
Ian Tudor

Using Surveys in Language Programs
James Dean Brown

Approaches and Methods in Language Teaching (Second Edition)
Jack C. Richards and Theodore S. Rodgers

Teaching Languages to Young Learners
Lynne Cameron

Classroom Decision Making
Negotiation and Process Syllabuses in Practice
Michael P. Breen and Andrew Littlejohn

Establishing Self-Access
From Theory to Practice
David Gardner and Lindsay Miller

Collaborative Action Research for English Language Teachers
Anne Burns

Affect in Language Learning
Edited by Jane Arnold

Developments in English for Specific Purposes
A Multi-Disciplinary Approach
Tony Dudley-Evans and Maggie Jo St John

Language Learning in Intercultural Perspective
Approaches through Drama and Ethnography
Edited by Michael Byram and Michael Fleming

Materials Development in Language Teaching

Second Edition

Edited by
Brian Tomlinson 2011

CAMBRIDGE
UNIVERSITY PRESS

CAMBRIDGE UNIVERSITY PRESS
Cambridge, New York, Melbourne, Madrid, Cape Town,
Singapore, São Paulo, Delhi, Tokyo, Mexico City

Cambridge University Press
The Edinburgh Building, Cambridge CB2 8RU, UK

www.cambridge.org
Information on this title: www.cambridge.org/9780521157049

First published 1998
Second edition 2011

Printed in the United Kingdom at the University Press, Cambridge

A catalogue record for this publication is available from the British Library

Library of Congress Cataloguing in Publication data
Materials development in language teaching / edited by Brian Tomlinson. – 2nd ed.
   p.   cm. – (Cambridge language teaching library)
   Includes bibliographical references and index.
   ISBN 978-0-521-15704-9
   1. Language and languages – Study and teaching.   2. Teaching – Aids and devices.
   I. Tomlinson, Brian.   II. Title.   III. Series.
   P53.15.M38   2010
   418.0071–dc22   2010035789

ISBN 978-0-521-15704-9 Paperback
ISBN 978-0-521-76285-4 Hardback

Contents

Contents

Part C The process of materials evaluation

Part D The electronic delivery of materials

Part E Ideas for materials development

Preface

Brian Tomlinson

This is a book of original chapters on current issues in materials development written by well-known contributors to the fields of applied linguistics and TEFL, most of whom have made presentations at MATSDA conferences.

MATSDA (The Materials Development Association) is an international materials development association founded in 1993 by Brian Tomlinson to contribute to the development of quality materials for learners of second and foreign languages. It aims to bring together teachers, researchers, materials writers and publishers in a joint endeavour to stimulate and support principled research, innovation and development. It does this by holding conferences, running workshops, providing consultants, publishing a journal (*Folio*) and stimulating books like this one.

For further information about MATSDA and for application forms for membership contact Brian Tomlinson, President of MATSDA, brianjohntomlinson@gmail.com, or go to the MATSDA website at www.matsda.org.uk. The main aim of this book is to further the work of MATSDA in providing information, ideas and stimulus which will facilitate the application of current thinking and research to the practical realities of developing and exploiting classroom materials. It also aims to stimulate further experimentation and innovation and thus to contribute to the continuing development of quality materials.

More and more applied linguistics and teacher development courses are including components on materials development (there are even MA courses focusing on L2 materials development at the International Graduate School of English in Seoul and at Leeds Metropolitan University), and more and more presentations at ELT conferences are focusing on issues related to the writing and exploitation of materials. And yet until 1998 few books had been published which investigated these issues. *Materials Development for Language Teaching* filled this gap by providing an opportunity for researchers, teachers, writers and publishers to communicate their informed views and suggestions to an audience seeking to gain new insights into the principles and procedures which were informing the current writing and exploitation of L2 materials. This revised edition of *Materials Development for Language Teaching* aims to retain the insights of the 1998 edition whilst adding new ideas and information related to developments since its initial publication. It includes five new chapters, two extra chapters on making use of new technologies in materials development and three replacement chapters on the pre-use evaluation of materials by publishers, on making use of corpora in published materials and on the post-use evaluation of tasks. The other chapters are revised and updated versions of chapters published in the 1998 edition.

Glossary of basic terms for materials development in language teaching

Brian Tomlinson

The following terms are used frequently in this book. Unless they are differently defined by the author(s) of the chapter, they are used with the meanings given below.

Authentic task (or real world task)

A task which involves learners in using language in a way that replicates its use in the 'real world' outside the language classroom. Filling in blanks, changing verbs from the simple past to the simple present and completing substitution tables are, therefore, not authentic tasks. Examples of authentic tasks would be answering a letter addressed to the learner, arguing a particular point of view and comparing various holiday brochures in order to decide where to go for a holiday.
See **pedagogic task**.

Authentic text

A text which is not written or spoken for language-teaching purposes. A newspaper article, a rock song, a novel, a radio interview, instructions on how to play a game and a traditional fairy story are examples of authentic texts. A story written to exemplify the use of reported speech, a dialogue scripted to exemplify ways of inviting and a linguistically simplified version of a novel would not be authentic texts.
See **simplified texts; text**.

CLIL

Content and Language Integrated Learning – an approach in which students acquire a second or foreign language whilst focusing on learning new content knowledge and skills (e.g. about science, about composing music, about playing football).
See **experiential learning**.

Communicative approaches

Approaches to language teaching which aim to help learners to develop communicative competence (i.e. the ability to use the language effectively for communication). A **weak communicative approach** includes overt teaching of language forms and functions in order to help learners to develop the ability to use them for communication. A **strong communicative approach** relies on providing learners with experience of using language as the main means of learning to use the language. In such an approach learners, for example, talk to learn rather than learn to talk.

Communicative competence

The ability to use the language effectively for communication. Gaining such competence involves acquiring both sociolinguistic and linguistic knowledge and skills (or, in other words, developing the ability to use the language fluently, accurately, appropriately and effectively).

Concordances (or concordance lines)

A list of authentic samples of language use each containing the same key word or phrase, for example:

> The bus driver still didn't have **any** change so he made me wait.

> I really don't mind which one. **Any** newspaper will do.

> I just know what they are saying. **Any** teacher will tell you that it's

Concordances are usually generated electronically from a corpus. See **authentic text; corpus.**

Corpus

A bank of authentic texts collected in order to find out how language is actually used. Often a corpus is restricted to a particular type of language use, for example, a corpus of newspaper English, a corpus of legal documents or a corpus of informal spoken English, and it is usually stored and retrieved from electronically.

See **text.**

Coursebook

A textbook which provides the core materials for a language-learning course. It aims to provide as much as possible in one book and is designed so that it could serve as the only book which the learners necessarily use during a course. Such a book usually includes work on grammar, vocabulary, pronunciation, functions and the skills of reading, writing, listening and speaking.

See **supplementary materials**.

Discovery activity

An activity which involves learners in investing energy and attention in order to discover something about the language for themselves. Getting learners to work out the rules of direct speech from examples, asking learners to investigate when and why a character uses the modal 'must' in a story and getting learners to notice and explain the use of ellipsis in a recorded conversation would be examples of discovery activities.

ELF

English as a lingua franca – the English used by non-native speakers or the use of English by non-native speakers to achieve communication with each other. Some applied linguists consider ELF to be a variety of English whereas others consider it to be a way of using English.

See **World English**.

Experiential learning

Referring to ways of learning language through experiencing it in use rather than through focusing conscious attention on language items. Reading a novel, listening to a song and taking part in a project are experiential ways of learning language.

Foreign language

A language which is not normally used for communication in a particular society. Thus English is a foreign language in France and Spanish is a foreign language in Germany.

Global coursebook

A coursebook which is not written for learners from a particular culture or country but which is intended for use by any class of learners in the specified level and age group anywhere in the world.

Language awareness approaches

Approaches to teaching language which emphasise the value of helping learners to focus attention on features of language in use. Most proponents of language awareness approaches emphasise the importance of learners gradually developing their own awareness of how the language is used through discoveries which they make for themselves.

See **discovery activity**.

Language data

Instances of language use which are used to provide information about how the language is used. Thus a corpus can be said to be made up of language data.

See **corpus**.

Language practice

Activities which involve repetition of the same language point or skill in an environment which is controlled by the framework of the activity. The purpose for language production and the language to be produced are usually predetermined by the task or the teacher. The intention is not to use the language for communication but to strengthen, through successful repetition, the ability to manipulate a particular language form or function. Thus, getting all the students in a class, who already know each other, repeatedly to ask each other their names would be a practice activity.

See **language use**.

Language use

Activities which involve the production of language in order to communicate. The purpose of the activity might be predetermined but the language which is used is determined by the learners. Thus, getting a new class of learners to walk around and introduce themselves to each other would be a language use activity; and so would getting them to complete a story for which they have been given the beginning.

See **language practice**.

Learning styles

The way(s) that particular learners prefer to learn. Some language learners have a preference for hearing the language (auditory learners), some for seeing it written down (visual learners), some for learning it in discrete bits (analytic learners), some for experiencing it in large chunks (global or holistic or experiential learners), and many prefer to do something physical whilst experiencing the language (kinaesthetic learners). Learning styles are variable and people often have different preferences in different learning contexts.

Lexical approaches

These are approaches which focus on the use of vocabulary and especially on the choices available to users of English when wanting to communicate particular meanings in particular contexts for particular purposes.

Lexical chunks

These are phrases in which a group of words are used with only one meaning (e.g. 'have no option but'). They can be fixed terms in which the words never change (e.g. 'at the end of the day') or they can be routines in which one of the elements can change (e.g. 'All the best for the future/next week/exam/interview', etc.).

L2

A term used to refer to both foreign and second languages.

See **foreign language; second language**.

Materials

Anything which is used to help language learners to learn. Materials can be in the form, for example, of a textbook, a workbook, a cassette, a CD-ROM, a video, a photocopied handout, a newspaper, a paragraph written on a whiteboard: anything which presents or informs about the language being learned.

Materials adaptation

Making changes to materials in order to improve them or to make them more suitable for a particular type of learner. Adaptation can include reducing, adding, omitting, modifying and supplementing. Most teachers adapt materials every time they use a textbook in order to maximise the value of the book for their particular learners.

Materials evaluation

The systematic appraisal of the value of materials in relation to their objectives and to the objectives of the learners using them. Evaluation can be pre-use and therefore focused on predictions of potential value. It can be whilst-use and therefore focused on awareness and description of what the learners are actually doing whilst the materials are being used. And it can also be post-use and therefore focused on evaluation of what happened as a result of using the materials.

Multimedia materials

Materials which make use of a number of different media. Often they are available on a CD-ROM which makes use of print, graphics, video and sound. Usually such materials are interactive and enable the learner to receive feedback on the written or spoken language that they produce.

New technologies

A term used to refer to recently developed electronic means of delivering language-learning materials or of facilitating electronic communication between learners. It includes the Internet, as a resource as well as emails, YouTube, chat rooms, blogs, Facebook, video conferencing and mobile phone technology.

Pedagogic task

A task which does not replicate a real world task but which is designed to facilitate the learning of language or of skills which would be useful in a real world task. Completing one half of a dialogue, filling in the blanks in a story and working out the meaning of ten nonsense words from clues in a text would be examples of pedagogic tasks. Pedagogic tasks can, however, require the use of real world skills. A task requiring a group to reproduce a diagram which only one member of the group has seen, for example, involves the use of visualisation, giving precise instructions and asking for clarification. It is arguable that such tasks, despite not being real world tasks, are in fact authentic.

PPP

An approach to teaching language items which follows a sequence of presentation of the item, practice of the item and then production of the item. This is the approach still currently followed by most commercially produced coursebooks. Some applied linguists prefer, however, an experiential PPP approach in which production comes before presentation and practice.

See **language practice; SLA; language use**.

Second language

The term is used to refer to a language which is not a mother tongue but which is used for certain communicative functions in a society. Thus, English is a second language in Nigeria, Sri Lanka and Singapore, and French is a second language in Senegal, Cameroon and Tahiti.

See **foreign language**.

Self-access materials

Materials designed for learners to use independently (i.e. on their own without access to a teacher or a classroom). They are normally used by the learner at home, in a library or in a self-study centre and can be paper-based or electronic.

Simplified texts

These are texts which have been made simpler so as to make it easier for learners to read them. The usual principles of simplification involve reduction in length of the text, shortening of sentences, omission or replacement of difficult words or structures, omission of qualifying clauses and omission of non-essential detail. Some applied linguists prefer to simplify texts by adding examples, by using repetition and paraphrase and by increasing redundant information. In other words, by lengthening rather than shortening the text, by elaboration rather than reduction.

SLA

This is an abbreviation for Second Language Acquisition and is normally used to refer to research and theory related to the learning of second and foreign languages.

Supplementary materials

Materials designed to be used in addition to the core materials of a course. They are usually related to the development of the skills of reading, writing, listening or speaking rather than to the learning of language items, but also include dictionaries, grammar books and workbooks.

See **coursebook**.

Tasks

These are activities in which the learners are asked to use the target language in order to achieve a particular outcome within a particular context (e.g. solving a problem; planning a meeting; selecting candidates for an interview).

Task-based approaches

This refers to materials or courses which are designed around a series of authentic tasks which give the learners experience of using the language in ways in which it is used in the 'real world' outside the classroom.

They usually have no pre-determined language syllabus and the aim is for learners to learn from the tasks the language that they need for successful participation in them. Examples of such tasks would be working out the itinerary of a journey from a timetable, completing a passport application form, ordering a product from a catalogue and giving directions to the post office.

See **authentic task.**

Text

Any extended sample of a language presented to learners of that language. A text can be written or spoken and could be, for example, a poem, a newspaper article, a passage about pollution, a song, a film, a live conversation, an extract from a novel or play, a passage written to exemplify the use of the past perfect, a recorded telephone conversation, a scripted dialogue or a speech by a politician.

Text-based approaches

Approaches in which the starting point is a text rather than a teaching point. The learners first of all experience and respond to the text before focusing attention on salient language or discourse features of it.

See **experiential learning.**

Workbook

A book which contains extra practice activities for learners to work on in their own time. Usually the book is designed so that learners can write in it and often there is an answer key provided in the back of the book to give feedback to the learners.

World English

A variety of English which is used for international communication.
See **ELF.**

For definitions of other terms frequently used in EFL and applied linguistics see:

Crystal, D. 1985. *A Dictionary of Linguistics and Phonetics*, 2nd edn. Oxford: Basil Blackwell.

Glossary of basic terms

Davies, A. 2005. *A Glossary of Applied Linguistics*. Edinburgh: University of Edinburgh Press.

Ellis, R. 1994. 'Glossary'. In *The Study of Second Language Acquisition*. Oxford: Oxford University Press, pp. 692–729.

Johnson, K. and H. Johnson, H. 1999. *The Encyclopedic Dictionary of Applied Linguistics: A Handbook for Language Teaching*. Oxford: Wiley-Blackwell.

Richards, J. and R. Schmidt, H. Platt and M. Schmidt. 2010. *Longman Dictionary of Language Teaching & Applied Linguistics*, 4th edn. Harlow: Longman.

Tomlinson, B. 1984. 'A glossary of basic EFL terms'. In A. Cunningsworth, *Evaluating and Selecting EFL Teaching Materials*. London: Heinemann, pp. 80–102.

Acknowledgements

The author is grateful to Jane Walsh of Cambridge University Press for her insights, suggestions and support, and to Freda Mishan, Jaya Mukundan and Ivor Timmis for their very helpful reviews of the draft version of the book.

The authors and publishers acknowledge the following sources of copyright material and are grateful for the permissions granted. While every effort has been made, it has not always been possible to identify the sources of all the material used, or to trace all copyright holders. If any omissions are brought to our notice, we will be happy to include the appropriate acknowledgements on reprinting.

p. 39, fig. 2, Davies, Mark. (2008-) The Corpus of Contemporary American English (COCA): 410+ million words, 1990-present. Available online at http://www.americancorpus.org; pp. 42–43, figs. 2.3, 2.4, Michigan Corpus of Upper-level Student Papers. (2009). Ann Arbor, MI: The Regents of the University of Michigan; p. 53, fig 3.1, *Collins Cobuild data sheets* Concordance for 'any', 1986. Collins Cobuild; p. 79. Nunan, D. and Lockwood, J. 1991. *The Australian English Course*. Cambridge University Press; pp. 79–80, Burns, A. Joyce, H. and Gollin, S. 1996. *'I see what you mean.' Using Spoken Discourse in The Classroom: A Handbook for Teachers*. NCELTR, Macquarie University (Sydney); pp. 192–195, Littlejohn, A. and Hicks, D. 2008. *Primary Colours Pupil's Book 5*. Cambridge University Press; pp. 284–289, Goodey and Goodey. 2005. *Messages*. Cambridge University Press; p. 307, fig. 12.2 © Oxford University Press 2008; p. 333, fig. 13.2, screenshot reproduced with permission; p. 333, fig. 13.3, Screenshot reproduced courtesy of Languagelab.com; p. 399–400, McGinley, P. *"The Adversary"* from *Times Three*. Martin Secker & Warburg; p. 400, Thomas, R. S. 1963 *"Sorry"* from *The Bread of Truth* HarperCollins Publishers Ltd.; p. 401, Leon Leszek Szkutnik, *"He Never Sent me Flowers"*. (Warsaw); pp. 423–424, Gordimer, N. 1991. *My Son's Story*. Reproduced with permission of A P Watt Ltd on behalf of Felix Licensing BV.

The publisher has used its best endeavours to ensure that the URLs for external websites referred to in this book are correct and active at the time of going to press. However, the publisher has no responsibility for the websites and can make no guarantee that a site will remain live or that the content is or will remain appropriate.

1 Introduction: principles and procedures of materials development

Brian Tomlinson

1.1 Introduction

This book concerns itself with what we could do in order to improve the quality of materials which are used for the teaching and learning of second languages. I would like to start the book by considering some of the steps which I think we could take and at the same time introducing issues which are dealt with in the various chapters of the book. I should stress that although the contributors to this book are basically like-minded in their approach to the development of L2 materials, many of the issues raised are controversial and some of the stances taken in the book are inevitably contradictory. In such cases we hope you will be informed, stimulated and able to make up your own mind by relating the authors' stances to your own experience.

I am going to argue that what those of us involved in materials development should do is to:

1. Clarify the terms and concepts commonly used in discussing materials development.
2. Carry out systematic evaluations of materials currently in use in order to find out to what degree, how and why they facilitate language learning.
3. Consider the potential applications for materials development of current research into second language acquisition and into language use.
4. Consider the potential applications of what both teachers and learners believe is valuable in the teaching and learning of a second or foreign language.
5. Pool our resources and bring together researchers, writers, teachers, learners and publishers in joint endeavours to develop quality materials.

1.2 Terms and concepts

Let me start by clarifying some of the basic terms and concepts which you will frequently encounter in this book.

1.2.1 *Materials*

Most people associate the term 'language-learning materials' with coursebooks because that has been their main experience of using materials. However, in this book the term is used to refer to anything which is used by teachers or learners to facilitate the learning of a language. Materials could obviously be videos, DVDs, emails, YouTube, dictionaries, grammar books, readers, workbooks or photocopied exercises. They could also be newspapers, food packages, photographs, live talks by invited native speakers, instructions given by a teacher, tasks written on cards or discussions between learners. In other words, they can be anything which is deliberately used to increase the learners' knowledge and/or experience of the language. Keeping this pragmatic concept of materials in mind can help materials developers to utilise as many sources of input as possible and, even more importantly, can help teachers to realise that they are also materials developers and that they are ultimately responsible for the materials that their learners use. It can also be useful to keep in mind that materials 'can be instructional in that they inform learners about the language, they can be experiential in that they provide exposure to the language in use, they can be elicitative in that they stimulate language use, or they can be exploratory in that they facilitate discoveries about language use' (Tomlinson 2001: 66).

1.2.2 *Materials development*

'Materials development is both a field of study and a practical undertaking. As a field it studies the principles and procedures of the design, implementation and evaluation of language teaching materials' (Tomlinson 2001: 66). As a practical undertaking it refers to anything which is done by writers, teachers or learners to provide sources of language input, to exploit those sources in ways which maximise the likelihood of intake and to stimulate purposeful output: in other words the supplying of information about and/or experience of the language in ways designed to promote language learning. Ideally the 'two aspects of materials development are interactive in that the theoretical studies inform and are informed by the development and use of classroom materials' (Tomlinson 2001: 66).

Materials developers might write textbooks, tell stories, bring advertisements into the classroom, express an opinion, provide samples of language use or read a poem aloud. Whatever they do to provide input, they do so ideally in principled ways related to what they know about how languages can be effectively learned. All the chapters in this book concentrate on the three vital questions of what should be provided for the learners, how it should be provided and what can be done with it to promote language learning.

Although many chapters in this book do focus on the development of coursebook materials (e.g. Jan Bell and Roger Gower in Chapter 6, Hitomi Masuhara in Chapter 10 and Frances Amrani in Chapter 11), some focus on electronic ways of delivering materials (e.g. Gary Motteram in Chapter 12 and Lisa Kervin and Beverly Derewianka in Chapter 13), a number of others focus on teacher development of materials (e.g. David Jolly and Rod Bolitho in Chapter 5 and Rod Ellis in Chapter 9), and some suggest ways in which learners can develop materials for themselves (e.g. Jane Willis in Chapter 3 and Alan Maley in Chapter 15).

1.2.3 Materials evaluation

This term refers to attempts to measure the value of materials. In many cases this is done impressionistically and consists of attempts to predict whether or not the materials will work, in the sense that the learners will be able to use them without too much difficulty and will enjoy the experience of doing so. A number of chapters in this book challenge this vague, subjective concept of evaluation and advocate more systematic and potentially revealing approaches. For example, Frances Amrani in Chapter 11 reports ways of reviewing materials prior to publication which can improve the quality of the materials, Andrew Littlejohn in Chapter 8 proposes a more objective, analytical approach to evaluation and Rod Ellis in Chapter 9 argues the need for whilst-use and post-use evaluation of materials in order to find out what the actual effects of the materials are. Other recent publications which propose systematic approaches to the evaluation of language-learning materials include McGrath (2002), McDonough, Shaw and Masuhara (2011), Rubdi (2003) and Tomlinson (2003a).

All the chapters in this book implicitly accept the view that for materials to be valuable, the learning points should be potentially useful to the learners and that the learning procedures should maximise the likelihood of the learners actually learning what they want and need to learn. It is not necessarily enough that the learners enjoy and value the materials.

1.2.4 Language teaching

Most people think of teaching as the overt presentation of information by teachers to learners. In this book the term 'teaching' is used to refer to anything done by materials developers or teachers to facilitate the learning of the language. This could include the teacher standing at the front of the classroom explaining the conventions of direct speech in

3

English, it could include a textbook providing samples of language use and guiding learners to make discoveries from them, it could include a textbook inviting learners to reflect on the way they have just read a passage or it could include the teacher providing the vocabulary a learner needs whilst participating in a challenging task. Teaching can be direct (in that it transmits information overtly to the learners) or it can be indirect (in that it helps the learners to discover things for themselves). It can also be pre-emptive (in that it aims to prevent problems), facilitative (in that it aims to help the learners do something), responsive (in that it responds to a need for language when it occurs) or remedial in that it aims to remedy problems. Most chapters in this book focus on indirect teaching as the most effective way of facilitating the learning of a language. For example, in Chapters 2 and 3 Randi Reppen and Jane Willis suggest ways in which learners can be helped to make discoveries about language use by analysing samples of language in use, in Chapter 16 Grethe Hooper Hansen looks at ways in which learners can be helped to learn from information which is actually peripheral to the task they are focusing on, and in Chapter 17 Brian Tomlinson proposes procedures which could enable self-access learners to learn for and about themselves.

1.2.5 Language learning

Learning is normally considered to be a conscious process which consists of the committing to memory of information relevant to what is being learned. Whilst such direct learning of, for example, spelling rules, conventions of greetings and vocabulary items can be useful to the language learner, it is arguable that much language learning consists of subconscious development of generalisations about how the language is used and of both conscious and subconscious development of skills and strategies which apply these generalisations to acts of communication. Language learning can be explicit (i.e. the learners are aware of when and what they are learning) or it can be implicit (i.e. the learners are not aware of when and what they are learning). Language learning can also be of declarative knowledge (i.e. knowledge about the language system) or of procedural knowledge (i.e. knowledge of how the language is used). Most of the chapters in this book take the position that communicative competence is primarily achieved as a result of implicit, procedural learning. But most of them also acknowledge that explicit learning of both declarative and procedural knowledge is of value in helping learners to pay attention to salient features of language input and in helping them to participate in planned discourse (i.e. situations such as giving a presentation or writing a story which allow time for

4

planning and monitoring). Consequently many of the chapters view the main objectives of materials development as the provision of the meaningful experience of language in use and of opportunities to reflect on this experience. This is the position taken by Ronald Carter, Rebecca Hughes and Michael McCarthy in Chapter 4, in which they argue for the need to expose learners to spoken English as it is actually used. It is also the position taken by Brian Tomlinson in Chapter 14 in which he proposes experiential ways of helping learners to transfer the high level skill of visualisation from their L1 reading process, by Grethe Hooper Hansen in Chapter 16 when she advocates multi-level experience of language in use and by Brian Tomlinson in Chapter 17 when he suggests an experiential approach to self-access learning of language.

1.3 Systematic evaluation of materials

In Chapter 7 Philip Prowse gets a number of well-known materials writers to reveal how they set about writing materials. The remarkable thing is that most of them follow their intuitions rather than an overt specification of objectives, principles and procedures. Obviously these intuitions are informed by experience of what is valuable to learners of a language and in many cases they lead to the development of valuable materials. But how useful it would be if we were able to carry out long-term, systematic evaluations of materials which are generally considered to be successful. I know of a number of famous textbook writers who do sit down and identify the popular and apparently successful features of their competitors so that they can clone these features and can avoid those features which appear to be unpopular and unsuccessful. Doing much more than this sort of ad hoc impressionistic evaluation of materials would involve considerable time and expenditure and would create great problems in controlling such variables as learner motivation, out-of-class experience and learner–teacher rapport. But longitudinal, systematic evaluations of popular materials could be undertaken by consortia of publishers, universities and associations such as MATSDA, and they could certainly provide empirically validated information about the actual effects of different types of language-learning materials. Such research is carried out by publishers, but it tends to focus on what makes the materials popular rather than on what effect the materials have on language acquisition, and most of this research is understandably confidential (see Chapter 11 by Frances Amrani for information about this type of research).

A number of chapters in this book try to push the profession forward towards using more systematic evaluation procedures as a means of informing materials development. In Chapter 8 Andrew Littlejohn exemplifies procedures for achieving thorough and informative analysis of what materials are actually doing, in Chapter 11 Frances Amrani reports on systematic evaluations of materials carried out by publishers prior to the publication of materials, and in Chapter 5 David Jolly and Rod Bolitho propose ways in which learner evaluations of materials feed into the development process. In Chapter 9 Rod Ellis insists that we should stop judging materials by their apparent appeal and start evaluating them by observing what the learners actually do when using the materials and by finding out what they seem to learn as a result of using them.

1.4 Second language acquisition research and materials development

> It seems clear that researchers cannot at present agree upon a single view of the learning process which can safely be applied wholesale to language teaching. (Tarone and Yule 1989)

> no second language acquisition research can provide a definitive answer to the real problems of second language teaching at this point. ... There is no predetermined correct theory of language teaching originating from second language acquisition research. (Cook 1996)

The quotations above are still true today and it is also still true that we should not expect definitive answers from second language acquisition (SLA) research, nor should we expect one research-based model of language acquisition to triumph over all the others. We must therefore be careful not to prescribe applications of unsubstantiated theories. But this should not stop us from applying what we *do* know about second and foreign language learning to the development of materials designed to facilitate that process. What we do know about language learning is a result of thousands of years of reflective teaching and of at least a century of experimental and observational research. If we combined the convincing anecdotal and empirical evidence available to us, we could surely formulate criteria which could contribute to the development of successful materials. From the reports of many of the writers in this volume it would seem that they rely on their intuitions about language learning when they set out to write textbooks. This also seems to be true of many of the authors who have contributed reports on their processes for materials development to a book called *Getting Started: Materials Writers on Materials Writing* (Hidalgo, Hall and Jacobs 1995). The validity of their intuitions is demonstrated by the quality of their materials. But intuitions are only useful if they are informed by recent and relevant classroom experience and by knowledge of the findings of recent second language acquisition research. And all of us could benefit from more explicit guidelines when setting out to develop materials for the classroom.

What I am arguing for is a compilation of learning principles and procedures which most teachers agree contribute to successful learning plus a compilation of principles and procedures recommended by most SLA researchers. A marriage of the two compilations could produce a list of principles and procedures which would provide a menu of potentially profitable options for materials developers from the classroom teacher adapting a coursebook unit to the author(s) setting out to develop a series of commercially published textbooks for the global market. Such a list should aim to be informative rather than prescriptive and should not give the impression that its recommendations are supported by conclusive evidence and by all teachers and researchers. And, of course, it needs to be supplemented by information about how the target language actually works (for ways of gaining such information, see, for example, Chapter 2 in this book by Randi Reppen, Chapter 3 by Jane Willis and Chapter 4 by Ronald Carter, Rebecca Hughes and Michael McCarthy). My own list of basic principles is as follows:

1. A prerequisite for language acquisition is that the learners are exposed to a rich, meaningful and comprehensible input of language in use.
2. In order for the learners to maximise their exposure to language in use, they need to be engaged both affectively and cognitively in the language experience.
3. Language learners who achieve positive affect are much more likely to achieve communicative competence than those who do not.
4. L2 language learners can benefit from using those mental resources which they typically utilise when acquiring and using their L1.
5. Language learners can benefit from noticing salient features of the input and from discovering how they are used.
6. Learners need opportunities to use language to try to achieve communicative purposes.

For a justification of these principles and a discussion of ways of applying them to materials development see Tomlinson (2010). See also McGrath (2002), McDonough, Shaw and Masuhara (2011) and Tomlinson (2008) for discussion of the application of learning principles to materials development.

Of course, one problem is that there is considerable disagreement amongst researchers about some of the main issues relevant to the teaching and learning of languages. Some argue that the main prerequisite for language acquisition is comprehensible input (i.e. being exposed to language you can understand); others argue that the main prerequisite is opportunity for output (i.e. situations in which you have to actu-ally use the language). Some researchers argue that the best way to acquire a language is to do so naturally without formal lessons or con-scious study of the language; others argue that conscious attention to distinctive features of the language is necessary for successful language learning. Try skimming through an overview of second language acqui-sition research (e.g. Ellis 2008) and you will soon become aware of some of the considerable (and, in my view, stimulating) disagreements amongst SLA researchers. Such disagreements are inevitable, given our limited access to the actual mental processes involved in the learning and using of languages, and often the intensity of the arguments pro-voke additional and illuminating research. However, I believe that there is now a sufficient consensus of opinion for SLA research to be used as an informative base for the formulation of criteria for the teaching of languages. The following is a summary of what I think many SLA researchers would agree to be some of the basic principles of second language acquisition relevant to the development of materials for the teaching of languages.

1.4.1 Materials should achieve impact

Impact is achieved when materials have a noticeable effect on learners, that is when the learners' curiosity, interest and attention are attracted. If this is achieved, there is a better chance that some of the language in the materials will be taken in for processing.

Materials can achieve impact through:

(a) novelty (e.g. unusual topics, illustrations and activities);
(b) variety (e.g. breaking up the monotony of a unit routine with an unexpected activity; using many different text-types taken from many different types of sources; using a number of different instruc-tor voices on a CD);
(c) attractive presentation (e.g. use of attractive colours; lots of white space; use of photographs);
(d) appealing content (e.g. topics of interest to the target learners; top-ics which offer the possibility of learning something new; engaging stories; universal themes; local references);
(e) achievable challenge (e.g. tasks which challenge the learners to think).

One obvious point is that impact is variable. What achieves impact with a class in Brazil might not achieve the same impact with a class in Austria. And what achieves impact with ten learners in a class might not achieve impact with the other five. In order to maximise the likelihood of achieving impact, the writer needs to know as much as possible about the target learners and about what is likely to attract their attention. In order to achieve impact with most of the learners, the writer also needs to offer choice. The more varied the choice of topics, texts and activities, the more likely is the achievement of impact.

1.4.2 Materials should help learners to feel at ease

Research has shown ... the effects of various forms of anxiety on acquisition: the less anxious the learner, the better language acquisition proceeds. Similarly, relaxed and comfortable students apparently can learn more in shorter periods of time. (Dulay, Burt and Krashen 1982)

Although it is known that pressure can stimulate some types of language learners, I think that most researchers would agree that most language learners benefit from feeling at ease and that they lose opportunities for language learning when they feel anxious, uncomfortable or tense (see, for example, Oxford 1999). Some materials developers argue that it is the responsibility of the teacher to help the learners to feel at ease and that the materials themselves can do very little to help. I disagree.

Materials can help learners to feel at ease in a number of ways. For example, I think that most learners:

- feel more comfortable with written materials with lots of white space than they do with materials in which lots of different activities are crammed together on the same page;
- are more at ease with texts and illustrations that they can relate to their own culture than they are with those which appear to them to be culturally alien;
- are more relaxed with materials which are obviously trying to help them to learn than they are with materials which are always testing them.

Feeling at ease can also be achieved through a 'voice' which is relaxed and supportive, through content and activities which encourage the personal participation of the learners, through materials which relate the world of the book to the world of the learner and through the absence of activities which could threaten self-esteem and cause humiliation. To me the most important (and possibly least researched) factor is that of the 'voice' of the materials. Conventionally, language-learning materials are de-voiced and anonymous. They are usually written in a semi-formal style and reveal very little about the personality, interests and experiences of the writer. What I would like to see materials writers do is to chat to the learners casually in the same way that good teachers do and to try to achieve personal contact with them by revealing their own preferences, interests and opinions. I would also like to see them try to achieve a personal voice (Beck, McKeown and Worthy 1995) by ensuring that what they say to the learners contains such features of orality as:

- informal discourse features (e.g. contracted forms, informal lexis);
- the active rather than the passive voice;
- concreteness (e.g. examples, anecdotes);
- inclusiveness (e.g. not signalling intellectual, linguistic or cultural superiority over the learners).

1.4.3 Materials should help learners to develop confidence

Relaxed and self-confident learners learn faster (Dulay, Burt and Krashen 1982).

Most materials developers recognise the need to help learners to develop confidence, but many of them attempt to do so through a process of simplification. They try to help the learners to feel successful by asking them to use simple language to accomplish easy tasks such as completing substitution tables, writing simple sentences and filling in the blanks in dialogues. This approach is welcomed by many teachers and learners. But in my experience it often only succeeds in diminishing the learners. They become aware that the process is being simplified for them and that what they are doing bears little resemblance to actual language use. They also become aware that they are not really using their brains and that their apparent success is an illusion. And this awareness can even lead to a reduction in confidence. I prefer to attempt to build confidence through activities which try to 'push' learners slightly beyond their existing proficiency by engaging them in tasks which are stimulating, which are problematic, but which are achievable too. It can also help if the activities encourage learners to use and to develop their existing extra-linguistic skills, such as those which involve being imaginative, being creative or being analytical. Elementary-level learners can often gain greater confidence from making up a story, writing a short poem or making a grammatical discovery than they can from getting right a simple drill. For more discussion of the value of setting learners achievable challenges see de Andres (1999) and Tomlinson (2003b, 2006).

The value of engaging the learners' minds and utilising their existing skills seems to be becoming increasingly realised in countries that have decided to produce their own materials through textbook projects rather than to rely on global coursebooks, which seem to underestimate the abilities of their learners. See Tomlinson (1995) for a report on such projects in Bulgaria, Morocco and Namibia, and Popovici and Bolitho (2003) for a report on a project in Romania. See Tomlinson *et al.* (2001)

and Masuhara *et al.* (2008) for evaluations of global coursebooks, and Tomlinson (in press) for a discussion of the importance of engagement.

1.4.4 What is being taught should be perceived by learners as relevant and useful

Most teachers recognise the need to make the learners aware of the potential relevance and utility of the language and skills they are teaching. And researchers have confirmed the importance of this need. For example, Stevick (1976) cites experiments which have shown the positive effect on learning and recall of items that are of personal significance to the learner. And Krashen (1982) and Wenden (1987) report research showing the importance of apparent relevance and utility in language acquisition.

In ESP (English for specific purposes) materials it is relatively easy to convince the learners that the teaching points are relevant and useful by relating them to known learner interests and to 'real-life' tasks, which the learners need or might need to perform in the target language. In general English materials this is obviously more difficult; but it can be achieved by narrowing the target readership and/or by researching what the target learners are interested in and what they really want to learn the language for. An interesting example of such research was a questionnaire in Namibia which revealed that two of the most important reasons for secondary school students wanting to learn English were so they would be able to write love letters in English and so that they would be able to write letters of complaint for villagers to the village headman and from the village headman to local authorities.

Perception of relevance and utility can also be achieved by relating teaching points to interesting and challenging classroom tasks and by presenting them in ways which could facilitate the achievement of the task outcomes desired by the learners. The 'new' learning points are not relevant and useful because they will help the learners to achieve long-term academic or career objectives, but because they could help the learners to achieve short-term task objectives now. Of course, this only works if the tasks are begun first and the teaching is then provided in response to discovered needs. This is much more difficult for the materials writer than the conventional approach of teaching a predetermined point first and then getting the learners to practise and then produce it. But it can be much more valuable in creating relevance and utility for the teaching point; and it can be achieved by, for example, referring learners to 'help pages' before and/or after doing sub-tasks or by getting learners to make decisions about strategies they will use in a task and then referring them to 'help pages'. So, for example, learners could be asked to choose from (or add to) a list of project tasks and then to decide on strategies for achieving their project targets. Those learners who decide to research local documents could be referred to a section in the book which provides advice on scanning, whereas those learners who decide to use question-naires could be referred to a section which deals with writing questions.

Obviously providing the learners with a choice of topic and task is important if you are trying to achieve perception of relevance and util-ity in a general English textbook.

1.4.5 Materials should require and facilitate learner self-investment

Many researchers have written about the value of learning activities that require the learners to make discoveries for themselves. For example, Rutherford and Sharwood-Smith (1988) assert that the role of the classroom and of teaching materials is to aid the learner to make efficient use of the resources in order to facilitate self-discovery. Similar views are expressed by Bolitho and Tomlinson (1995); Bolitho *et al.* (2003), Tomlinson (1994a, 2007) and Wright and Bolitho (1993).

It would seem that learners profit most if they invest interest, effort and attention in the learning activity. Materials can help them to achieve this by providing them with choices of focus and activity, by giving them topic control and by engaging them in learner-centred discovery activi-ties. Again, this is not as easy as assuming that what is taught should be learned, but it is possible and extremely useful for textbooks to facilitate learner self-investment. In my experience, one of the most profitable ways of doing this is to get learners interested in a written or spoken text, to get them to respond to it globally and affectively and then to help them to analyse a particular linguistic feature of it in order to make discover-ies for themselves (see Tomlinson 1994a for a specific example of this procedure). Other ways of achieving learner investment are involving the learners in mini-projects, involving them in finding supplementary materials for particular units in a book and giving them responsibility for making decisions about which texts to use and how to use them (an approach I saw used with great success in an Indonesian high school in which each group in a large class was given responsibility for selecting the texts and the tasks for one reading lesson per semester).

1.4.6 Learners must be ready to acquire the points being taught

Certain structures are acquired only when learners are mentally ready for them. (Dulay, Burt and Krashen 1982)

Meisel, Clahsen and Pienemann (1981) have put forward the Multi-dimensional Model in which learners must have achieved readiness in order to learn developmental features (i.e. those constrained by developing speech-processing mechanisms – e.g. word order) but can make themselves ready at any time to learn variational features (i.e. those which are free – e.g. the copula 'be'). Pienemann (1985) claims that instruction can facilitate natural language acquisition processes if it coincides with learner readiness, and can lead to increased speed and frequency of rule application and to application of rules in a wider range of linguistic contexts. He also claims that premature instruction can be harmful because it can lead to the production of erroneous forms, to substitution by less complex forms and to avoidance. Pienemann's theories have been criticised for the narrowness of their research and application (restricted mainly to syntax, according to Cook 1996), but I am sure most teachers would recognise the negative effects of premature instruction as reported by Pienemann.

Krashen (1985) argues the need for roughly tuned input, which is comprehensible because it features what the learners are already familiar with, but which also contains the potential for acquiring other elements of the input which each learner might or might not be ready to learn (what Krashen refers to as i + 1 in which i represents what has already been learned and 1 represents what is available for learning). According to Krashen, each learner will only learn from the new input what he or she is ready to learn. Other discussions of the need for learner readiness can be found in Ellis (1990) (see especially pp. 152–8 for a discussion of variational and developmental features of readiness) and in Ellis (2008).

Readiness can be achieved by materials which create situations requiring the use of variational features not previously taught, by materials which ensure that the learners have gained sufficient mastery over the developmental features of the previous stage before teaching a new one, and by materials which roughly tune the input so that it contains some features which are slightly above each learner's current state of proficiency. It can also be achieved by materials which get learners to focus attention on features of the target language which they have not yet acquired so that they might be more attentive to these features in future input.

But perhaps the most important lesson for materials developers from readiness research is that we cannot expect to select a particular point for teaching and assume that all the learners are ready and willing to learn it. It is important to remember that the learner is always in charge and that 'in the final analysis we can never completely control what the learner does, for HE [*sic*] selects and organises, whatever the input' (Kennedy 1973: 76).

1.4.7 Materials should expose the learners to language in authentic use

Krashen (1985) makes the strong claim that comprehensible input in the target language is both necessary and sufficient for the acquisition of that language provided that learners are 'affectively disposed to "let in" the input they comprehend' (Ellis 1994: 273). Few researchers would agree with such a strong claim, but most would agree with a weaker claim that exposure to authentic use of the target language is necessary but not sufficient for the acquisition of that language. It is necessary in that learners need experience of how the language is typically used, but it is not sufficient because they also need to notice how it is used and to use it for communicative purposes themselves.

Materials can provide exposure to authentic input through the advice they give, the instructions for their activities and the spoken and written texts they include. They can also stimulate exposure to authentic input through the activities they suggest (e.g. interviewing the teacher, doing a project in the local community, listening to the radio, etc.). In order to facilitate acquisition, the input must be comprehensible (i.e. understandable enough to achieve the purpose for responding to it). This means that there is no point in using long extracts from newspapers with beginners, but it does not mean that beginners cannot be exposed to authentic input. They can follow instructions intended to elicit physical responses, they can listen to dramatic renditions of stories, they can listen to songs, they can fill in forms.

Ideally materials at all levels should provide frequent exposure to authentic input which is rich and varied. In other words the input should vary in style, mode, medium and purpose and should be rich in features which are characteristic of authentic discourse in the target language. And, if the learners want to be able to use the language for general communication, it is important that they are exposed to planned, semi-planned and unplanned discourse (e.g. a formal lecture, an informal radio interview and a spontaneous conversation). The materials should also stimulate learner interaction with the input rather than just passive reception of it. This does not necessarily mean that the learners should always produce language in response to the input; but it does mean that they should at least always do something mentally or physically in response to it.

See in particular Chapters 1, 2, 3, 4, 12, 13, 14, 15 and 17 of this book for arguments in favour of exposing learners to authentic materials, and also see Gilmore (2007) and Mishan (2005).

1.4.8 The learners' attention should be drawn to linguistic features of the input

There seems to be an agreement amongst many researchers that helping learners to pay attention to linguistic features of authentic input can help them to eventually acquire some of those features. However, it is important to understand that this claim does not represent a back-to-grammar movement. It is different from previous grammar teaching approaches in a number of ways. In the first place the attention paid to the language can be either conscious or subconscious. For example, the learners might be paying conscious attention to working out the attitude of one of the characters in a story, but might be paying subconscious attention to the second conditionals which the character uses. Or they might be paying conscious attention to the second conditionals, having been asked to locate them and to make a generalisation about their function in the story. The important thing is that the learners become aware of a gap between a particular feature of their interlanguage (i.e. how they currently understand or use it) and the equivalent feature in the target language. Such noticing of the gap between output and input can act as an 'acquisition facilitator' (Seliger 1979). It does not do so by immediately changing the learner's internalised grammar but by alerting the learner to subsequent instances of the same feature in future input. So there is no immediate change in the learners' proficiency (as seems to be aimed at by such grammar teaching approaches as the conventional Presentation–Practice–Production approach). There is, however, an increased likelihood of eventual acquisition provided that the learners receive future relevant input.

White (1990) argues that there are some features of the L2 which learners need to be focused on because the deceptively apparent similarities with L1 features make it impossible for the learners to otherwise notice certain points of mismatch between their interlanguage and the target language. And Schmidt (1992) puts forward a powerful argument for approaches which help learners to note the gap between their use of specific features of English and the way these features are used by native speakers. Inviting learners to compare their use of, say, indirect speech with the way it is used in a transcript of a native speaker conversation would be one such approach and could quite easily be built into coursebook materials.

Randi Reppen in Chapter 2 of this book and Jane Willis in Chapter 3 exemplify ways of helping learners to pay attention to linguistic features of their input. Kasper and Roever (2005) and Schmidt (2001) also discuss the value of noticing how the language is actually used.

1.4.9 Materials should provide the learners with opportunities to use the target language to achieve communicative purposes

Most researchers seem to agree that learners should be given opportunities to use language for communication rather than just to practise it in situations controlled by the teacher and the materials. Using language for communication involves attempts to achieve a purpose in a situation in which the content, strategies and expression of the interaction are determined by the learners. Such attempts can enable the learners to 'check' the effectiveness of their internal hypotheses, especially if the activities stimulate them into 'pushed output' (Swain 1985) which is slightly above their current proficiency. They also help the learners to automatise their existing procedural knowledge (i.e. their knowledge of how the language is used) and to develop strategic competence (Canale and Swain 1980). This is especially so if the opportunities for use are interactive and encourage negotiation of meaning (Allwright 1984: 157). In addition, communicative interaction can provide opportunities for picking up language from the new input generated, as well as opportunities for learner output to become an informative source of input (Sharwood-Smith 1981). Ideally teaching materials should provide opportunities for such interaction in a variety of discourse modes ranging from planned to unplanned (Ellis 1990: 191).

Interaction can be achieved through, for example:

- information or opinion gap activities which require learners to communicate with each other and/or the teacher in order to close the gap (e.g. finding out what food and drink people would like at the class party);
- post-listening and post-reading activities which require the learners to use information from the text to achieve a communicative purpose (e.g. deciding what television programmes to watch, discussing who to vote for, writing a review of a book or film);
- creative writing and creative speaking activities such as writing a story or improvising a drama;
- formal instruction given in the target language either on the language itself or on another subject:

> We need to recognise that teaching intended as formal instruction
> also serves as interaction. Formal instruction does more than teach
> a specific item: it also exposes learners to features which are not the
> focus of the lesson. (Ellis 1990)

The value of materials facilitating learner interaction is stressed in this book by Alan Maley in Chapter 15 and by Brian Tomlinson in Chapter 17. See Swain (2005) for an overview of the literature on the Output Hypothesis and its insistence that output is not just the product of language learning but part of the process of language learning too.

1.4.10 Materials should take into account that the positive effects of instruction are usually delayed

Research into the acquisition of language shows that it is a gradual rather than an instantaneous process and that this is equally true for instructed as well as informal acquisition. Acquisition results from the gradual and dynamic process of internal generalisation rather than from instant adjustments to the learner's internal grammar. It follows that learners cannot be expected to learn a new feature and be able to use it effectively in the same lesson. They might be able to rehearse the feature, to retrieve it from short-term memory or to produce it when prompted by the teacher or the materials. But this does not mean that learning has already taken place. I am sure most of you are familiar with the situation in which learners get a new feature correct in the lesson in which it is taught but then get it wrong the following week. This is partly because they have not yet had enough time, instruction and exposure for learning to have taken place.

The inevitable delayed effect of instruction suggests that no textbook can really succeed if it teaches features of the language one at a time and expects the learners to be able to use them straightaway. But this incremental approach is popular with many publishers, writers, teachers and learners as it can provide a reassuring illusion of system, simplicity and progress. Therefore, adaptation of existing approaches rather than replacement with radical new ones is the strategy most likely to succeed. So, for example, the conventional textbook approach of PPP (Presentation–Practice–Production) could be used to promote durable learning if the objective of the Production phase was seen as reinforcement rather than correct production and if this was followed in subsequent units by more exposure and more presentation relating to the same feature. Or the Production phase could be postponed to another unit which is placed after further exposure, instruction and practice have been provided. Or the initial Production phase could be used to provide output which would enable the learners to notice the mismatch between what they are doing and what proficient speakers typically do.

In my view, in order to facilitate the gradual process of acquisition, it is important for materials to recycle instruction and to provide frequent and ample exposure to the instructed language features in communicative use. This is particularly true of vocabulary acquisition, which requires frequent, spaced and varied recycling in order to be successful (Nation 2003, 2005; Nation and Wang 1999). It is equally important that the learners are not forced into premature production of the instructed features (they will get them wrong) and that tests of proficiency are not conducted immediately after instruction (they will indicate failure or an illusion of success).

Ellis (1990) reports on research revealing the delayed effect of instruction and in Chapter 9 of this book he argues the need for post-use evaluation of materials to find out what learners have eventually learned as a result of using them.

1.4.11 Materials should take into account that learners differ in learning styles

Different learners have different preferred learning styles. So, for example, those learners with a preference for studial learning are much more likely to gain from explicit grammar teaching than those who prefer experiential learning. And those who prefer experiential learning are more likely to gain from reading a story with a predominant grammatical feature (e.g. reported speech) than they are from being taught that feature explicitly. This means that activities should be variable and should ideally cater for all learning styles. An analysis of most current coursebooks will reveal a tendency to favour learners with a preference for studial learning and an apparent assumption that all learners are equally capable of benefiting from this style of learning. Likewise an analysis of the teaching and testing of foreign languages in formal education systems throughout the world will reveal that studial learners (who are actually in the minority) are at an advantage.

Styles of learning which need to be catered for in language-learning materials include:

- visual (e.g. learners prefer to see the language written down);
- auditory (e.g. learners prefer to hear the language);
- kinaesthetic (e.g. learners prefer to do something physical, such as following instructions for a game);
- studial (e.g. learners like to pay conscious attention to the linguistic features of the language and want to be correct);
- experiential (e.g. learners like to use the language and are more concerned with communication than with correctness);
- analytic (e.g. learners prefer to focus on discrete bits of the language and to learn them one by one);
- global (e.g. learners are happy to respond to whole chunks of language at a time and to pick up from them whatever language they can);
- dependent (e.g. learners prefer to learn from a teacher and from a book);
- independent (e.g. learners are happy to learn from their own experience of the language and to use autonomous learning strategies).

I think a learner's preference for a particular learning style is variable and depends, for example, on what is being learned, where it is being learned, whom it is being learned with and what it is being learned for. For example, I am happy to be experiential, global and kinaesthetic when learning Japanese out of interest with a group of relaxed adult learners and with a teacher who does not keep correcting me. But I am more likely to be analytic and visual when learning French for examination purposes in a class of competitive students and with a teacher who keeps on correcting me. And, of course, learners can be helped to gain from learning styles other than their preferred style. The important point for materials developers is that they are aware of and cater for differences of preferred learning styles in their materials and that they do not assume that all learners can benefit from the same approaches as the 'good language learner' (see Ellis 1994: 546–50).

See Oxford and Anderson (1995) for an overview of research into learning styles. See also Anderson (2005) and Oxford (2002).

1.4.12 Materials should take into account that learners differ in affective attitudes

> the learner's motives, emotions, and attitudes screen what is presented in the language classroom … This affective screening is highly individual and results in different learning rates and results. (Dulay, Burt and Krashen 1982)

Ideally language learners should have strong and consistent motivation and they should also have positive feelings towards the target language, their teachers, their fellow learners and the materials they are using. But, of course, ideal learners do not exist and even if they did exist one day, they would no longer be ideal learners the next day. Each class of learners using the same materials will differ from each other in terms of long- and short-term motivation and of feelings and attitudes about the language, their teachers, their fellow learners and their learning materials, and of attitudes towards the language, the teacher and the materials. Obviously no materials developer can cater for all these affective variables, but it is important for anybody who is writing learning materials to be aware of the inevitable attitudinal differences of the users of the materials.

One obvious implication for the materials developer is 'to diversify language instruction as much as possible based upon the variety of cognitive styles' (Larsen-Freeman and Long 1991) and the variety of affective attitudes likely to be found amongst a typical class of learners. Ways of doing this include:

- providing choices of different types of text;
- providing choices of different types of activities;
- providing optional extras for the more positive and motivated learners;
- providing variety;
- including units in which the value of learning English is a topic for discussion;

- including activities which involve the learners in discussing their attitudes and feelings about the course and the materials;
- researching and catering for the diverse interests of the identified target learners;
- being aware of the cultural sensitivities of the target learners;
- giving general and specific advice in the teacher's book on how to respond to negative learners (e.g. not forcing reluctant individuals to take part in group work).

For reports on research into affective differences see Arnold and Brown (1999), Dörnyei and Ushioda (2009), Ellis (1984: 471–83) and Wenden and Rubin (1987).

For specific suggestions on how materials can cater for learner differences see Tomlinson (1996, 2003b, 2006) and Chapter 15 by Alan Maley in this book.

1.4.13 Materials should permit a silent period at the beginning of instruction

It has been shown that it can be extremely valuable to delay L2 speaking for beginners of a language until they have gained sufficient exposure to the target language and sufficient confidence in understanding it. This silent period can facilitate the development of an effective internalised grammar which can help learners to achieve proficiency when they eventually start to speak in the L2. There is some controversy about the actual value of the silent period and some learners seem to use the silence to avoid learning the language. However, I think most researchers would agree that forcing immediate production in the new language can damage the reluctant speaker affectively and linguistically and many would agree with Dulay, Burt and Krashen that:

> communication situations in which students are permitted to remain silent or respond in their first language may be the most effective approach for the early phases of language instruction. This approach approximates what language learners of all ages have been observed to do naturally, and it appears to be more effective than forcing full two-way communication from the very beginning of L2 acquisition. (1982: 25–6)

The important point is that the materials should not force premature speaking in the target language and they should not force silence either. Ways of giving learners the possibility of not speaking until they are ready include:

- starting the course with a Total Physical Response (TPR) approach in which the learners respond physically to oral instructions from a teacher or CD (see Asher 1977; Tomlinson 1994b, Tomlinson and Masuhara in press);

- starting with a listening comprehension approach in which the learners listen to stories in the target language, which are made accessible through the use of sound effects, visual aids and dramatic movement by the teacher;
- permitting the learners to respond to target language questions by using their first language or through drawings and gestures.

A possible extension of the principle of permitting silence is to introduce most new language points (regardless of the learners' level) through activities which initially require comprehension but not production. This is an approach which I call TPR Plus and which we used on the PKG Project in Indonesian secondary schools. It usually involved introducing new vocabulary or structures through stories which the learners responded to by drawing and/or using their first language, and through activities in which the whole class mimed stories by following oral instructions from the teacher (see Barnard 2007; Tomlinson 1990, 1994b).

For discussion of research into the silent period see Ellis (2008); Krashen (1982); Saville-Troike (1988).

1.4.14 Materials should maximise learning potential by encouraging intellectual, aesthetic and emotional involvement which stimulates both right- and left-brain activities

A narrowly focused series of activities which require very little cognitive processing (e.g. mechanical drills; rule learning; simple transformation activities) usually leads to shallow and ephemeral learning unless linked to other activities which stimulate mental and affective processing. However, a varied series of activities making, for example, analytic, creative, evaluative and rehearsal demands on processing capacity can lead to deeper and more durable learning. In order for this deeper learning to be facilitated, it is very important that the content of the materials is not trivial or banal and that it stimulates thoughts and feelings in the learners. It is also important that the activities are not too simple and that they cannot be too easily achieved without the learners making use of their previous experience and their brains.

The maximisation of the brain's learning potential is a fundamental principle of Lozanov's Suggestopedia, in which 'he enables the learner to receive the information through different cerebral processes and in different states of consciousness so that it is stored in many different parts of the brain, maximising recall' (Hooper Hansen 1992). Suggestopedia does this through engaging the learners in a variety of left- and right-brain activities in the same lesson (e.g. reciting a dialogue, dancing to instructions, singing a song, doing a substitution drill, writing a story). Whilst not everybody would accept the procedures of Suggestopedia, most researchers seem to agree on the value of maximising the brain's capacity during language learning and the best textbooks already do contain within each unit a variety of different left- and right-brain activities.

For an account of the principles of Suggestopedia see Lozanov (1978) and Chapter 16 in this volume by Grethe Hooper Hansen. See also Tomlinson (2003b) for a discussion of the need to humanise materials, Tomlinson and Avila (2007a, 2007b) for a discussion of the value of developing materials which help the learners to make full use of their mental resources whilst learning and using an L2, and Tomlinson (in press) for suggestions for ways of engaging L2 learners cognitively, affectively, aesthetically and kinaesthetically.

1.4.15 Materials should not rely too much on controlled practice

It is interesting that there seems to be very little research which indicates that controlled practice activities are valuable. Sharwood-Smith (1981) does say that 'it is clear and uncontroversial to say that most spontaneous performance is attained by dint of practice', but he provides no evidence to support this very strong claim. Also Bialystok (1988) says that automaticity is achieved through practice but provides no evidence to support her claim. In the absence of any compelling evidence most researchers seem to agree with Ellis, who says that 'controlled practice appears to have little long term effect on the accuracy with which new structures are performed' (Ellis 1990: 192) and 'has little effect on fluency' (Ellis and Rathbone 1987). See De Keyser (2007) on language practice and also Ellis (2008).

Yet controlled grammar practice activities still feature significantly in popular coursebooks and are considered to be useful by many teachers and by many learners. This is especially true of dialogue practice, which has been popular in many methodologies for the last 30 years without there being any substantial research evidence to support it (see Tomlinson 1995). In a recent analysis of new low-level coursebooks I found that nine out of ten of them contained many more opportunities for controlled practice than they did for language use. It is possible that right now all over the world learners are wasting their time doing drills and listening to and repeating dialogues. See Tomlinson *et al.* (2001) and Masuhara *et al.* (2008) for coursebook reviews which also report a continuing dominance of practice activities.

1.4.16 Materials should provide opportunities for outcome feedback

Feedback which is focused first on the effectiveness of the outcome rather than just on the accuracy of the output can lead to output becoming a profitable source of input. Or in other words, if the language that the learner produces is evaluated in relation to the purpose for which it is used, that language can become a powerful and informative source of information about language use. Thus a learner who fails to achieve a particular communicative purpose (e.g. borrowing something, instructing someone how to play a game, persuading someone to do something) is more likely to gain from feedback on the effectiveness of their use of language than a learner whose language is corrected without reference to any non-linguistic outcome. It is very important, therefore, for materials developers to make sure that language production activities have intended outcomes other than just practising language.

The value of outcome feedback is focused on by such writers on task-based approaches as Willis and Willis (2007) and Rod Ellis in Chapter 9 in this volume. It is also stressed by Brian Tomlinson in Chapter 17 of this volume.

To find out more about some of the principles of language learning outlined above, you could make use of the index of one of the following books:

Cook, V. 2008. *Second Language Learning and Second Language Teaching*, 4th edn. London: Edward Arnold.

Ellis, R. 2008. *The Study of Second Language Acquisition*, 2nd edn. Oxford: Oxford University Press.

Larsen-Freeman, D. and M. Long. 1991. *An Introduction to Second Language Acquisition Research*. London: Longman.

1.5 What teachers and learners believe and want

I have argued above that materials developers should take account of what researchers have told us about language acquisition. I would also argue that they should pay more attention to what teachers and learners believe about the best ways to learn a language and also to what they want from the materials they use (even though this would often contradict the findings of SLA researchers).

Teachers spend far more time observing and influencing the language-learning process than do researchers or materials developers. Yet little research has been done into what teachers believe is valuable for language learning and little account is taken of what teachers really want. In this book Hitomi Masuhara argues in Chapter 10 for the need to find out what teachers really want from coursebooks and she puts forward suggestions for how this information could be gained and made use of. Also Frances Amrani in Chapter 11 describes how attempts have been made to find out exactly what teachers think and feel about trial versions of coursebooks so that their views can influence the published versions. David Jolly and Rod Bolitho in Chapter 5 propose a framework which could help teachers to adapt materials and to write materials themselves; and Rod Ellis in Chapter 9 outlines a way in which teachers can improve materials as a result of whilst-use and post-use evaluation of them. Also Saraceni (2003) focuses on learner involvement in adapting materials.

There have been attempts to involve learners in the evaluation of courses and materials (see Alderson 1985 for an interesting account of post-course evaluations which involved contacting the learners after their courses had finished) and a number of researchers have kept diaries recording their own experiences as learners of a foreign language (e.g. Schmidt and Frota 1986). But little systematic research has been published on what learners actually want their learning materials to do (see Johnson 1995 for an account of what one adult learner wants from her learning materials).

One exceptional example of trying to make use of both learner and teacher beliefs and wants was the Namibia Textbook Project. Prior to the writing of the Grade 10 English textbook, *On Target* (1995), teachers and students all over the country were consulted via questionnaires. Their responses were then made use of when 30 teachers met together to design and write the book. The first draft of the book was completed by these teachers at an eight-day workshop and it was then trialled all over the country before being revised for publication by an editorial panel. Such consultation and collaboration is rare in materials development and could act as a model for textbook writing. See Tomlinson (1995) for a description of this and other similar projects.

1.6 Collaboration

The Namibian Textbook Project mentioned above is a classic example of the value of pooling resources. On page iv of *On Target* (1995) 40 contributors are acknowledged. Some of these were teachers, some were curriculum developers, some were publishers, some were administrators, some were university lecturers and researchers, some were examiners, one was a published novelist and all of them made a significant contribution to the development of the book. This bringing together of expertise in a collaborative endeavour is extremely rare and, as one of the contributors to the Project, I can definitely say it was productive. Too often in my experience researchers have made theoretical claims without developing applications of them, writers have ignored theory and have followed procedural rather than principled instincts, teachers have complained without making efforts to exert an influence, learners have been ignored and publishers have been driven by considerations of what they know they can sell. We all have constraints on our time and our actions, but it must be possible and potentially valuable for us to get together to pool our resources and share our expertise in a joint endeavour to develop materials which offer language learners maximum opportunities for successful learning. This bringing together of different areas of knowledge and expertise is the main aim of MATSDA and it is one of the objectives of this book. The contributors to *Materials Development in Language Teaching* include classroom teachers, researchers, university lecturers, teacher trainers, textbook writers and publishers, and we hope that our pooling of knowledge and ideas will help you to use, adapt and develop materials in effective ways.

1.7 New directions in materials development

Since *Materials Development in Language Teaching* was first published in 1998, there have been some new directions in materials development. The most obvious one is the increase in quantity and quality of language-learning materials delivered through new technologies. Whilst some new technology programmes and courses have been rightly criticised for simply reproducing activity and task types from paper sources, others have been praised for exploiting the interactive possibilities of new technologies such as video conferencing, emails, YouTube, Facebook, Twitter, blogs and mobile phones. See Chapter 12 by Gary Motteram, Chapter 13 by Lisa Kervin and Beverly Derewianka, Chapter 15 by Alan Maley and Chapter 17 by Brian Tomlinson in this volume for discussion of the possibilities offered to materials developers by new technologies. See also Reinders and White (2010).

Other new directions in materials development include materials for text-driven approaches, for task-based approaches and for Content and Language Integrated Learning (CLIL) approaches. Brian Tomlinson in Chapters 14 and 17 of this volume refers to approaches in which a potentially engaging text drives a unit of materials instead of a pre-determined teaching point, and Tomlinson (2003c) details a flexible framework for developing text-driven materials which has been used on materials development projects in, for example, Bulgaria, Ethiopia, Morocco, Namibia, Singapore and Turkey. Task-based approaches (in which an outcome-focused task drives the lesson) have received a lot of attention recently, but much of it has focused on the principles and procedures of task-based teaching. However, Rod Ellis in Chapter 9 of this volume gives attention to task-based materials, as do Ellis (2003), Van den Branden (2006), Nunan (2004), Samuda and Bygate (2008) and Willis and Willis (2007). CLIL has been commanding a lot of attention recently and it has been used as a means of teaching English and a content subject at the same time in primary, secondary and tertiary institutions in Europe (Eurydice 2006), as well as an approach in which a content area which engages the learner is used to help them improve their English (Tomlinson and Masuhara 2009). Most of the literature on CLIL so far has focused on the theory of CLIL and on its integration into curricula in educational institutions. However, there is a chapter on materials for CLIL in Coyle *et al.* (2010).

I hope that the chapters in this book will provide a theoretical and practical stimulus to help materials developers and teachers to produce quality materials for learners using the 'new' approaches referred to above, as well as to continue to develop innovative and effective materials for the more established approaches.

References

Alderson, J. C. 1985. 'Is there life after the course?' *Lancaster Practical Papers in English Language Evaluation*. University of Lancaster.

Allwright, R. 1984. 'Why don't learners learn what teachers teach? The interaction hypothesis'. In D. Singleton and D. Little (eds.), *Language Learning in Formal and Informal Contexts*. Dublin: IRAAL.

Anderson, N. J. 2005. 'L2 learning strategies'. In E. Hinkel (ed.), *Handbook of Research in Second Language Learning*. Mahwah, NJ: Lawrence Erlbaum.

De Andres, V. 1999. 'Self-esteem in the classroom or the metamorphosis of butterflies'. In J. Arnold (ed.), *Affect in Language Learning*. Cambridge: Cambridge University Press.

Arnold, J. and H. D. Brown. 1999. 'A map of the terrain'. In J. Arnold (ed.), *Affect in Language Learning*. Cambridge: Cambridge University Press.

Asher, J. 1977. *Learning Another Language Through Actions: The Complete Teacher's Guidebook*. Los Gatos, CA: Sky Oak Productions.

Barnard, E. S. 2007. 'The value of comprehension in the early stages of the acquisition and development of Bahasa Indonesia by non-native speakers'. In B. Tomlinson (ed.), *Language Acquisition and Development: Studies of First and Other Languages*. London: Continuum.

Beck, I. L., M. G. McKeown and J. Worthy. 1995. 'Giving a text voice can improve students' understanding'. *Research Reading Quarterly*, 30(2). University of Commerce: Institute of Economic Research.

Bialystok, E. 1988. 'Psycholinguistic dimensions of second language proficiency'. In W. Rutherford and M. Sharwood-Smith (eds.), *Grammar and Second Language Teaching*. Rowley, MA: Newbury House.

Bolitho, R. and B. Tomlinson. 1995. *Discover English*, 2nd edn. Oxford: Heinemann.

Bolitho, R., R. Carter, R. Hughes, R. Ivanic, H. Masuhara and B. Tomlinson. 2003. 'Ten questions about language awareness'. *ELT Journal*, 57(2): 251–9.

Canale, M. and M. Swain. 1980. 'Theoretical bases of communicative approaches to second language teaching and testing'. *Applied Linguistics*: 11–47.

Cook, V. 1996. *Second Language Learning and Second Language Teaching*, 2nd edn. London: Edward Arnold.

　2008. *Second Language Learning and Second Language Teaching*, 4th edn. London: Edward Arnold.

Coyle, D., P. Hood and D. Marsh. 2010. *CLIL: Content and Language Integrated Learning*. Cambridge: Cambridge University Press.

Dörnyei, Z., and E. Ushioda (eds.). 2009. *Motivation, Language Identity and the L2 Self*. Bristol: Multilingual Matters.

Dulay, H., M. Burt and S. Krashen. 1982. *Language Two*. New York: Oxford University Press.

Ellis, R. 1984. *Classroom Second Language Development*. Oxford: Pergamon.

　1990. *Instructed Second Language Acquisition*. Oxford: Basil Blackwell.

　1994. *The Study of Second Language Acquisition*. Oxford: Oxford University Press.

　2003. *Task-Based Language Learning and Teaching*. Oxford: Oxford University Press.

　2008. *The Study of Second Language Acquisition*, 2nd edn. Oxford: Oxford University Press.

Ellis, R. and M. Rathbone. 1987. *The Acquisition of German in a Classroom Context*. London: Ealing College of Higher Education.

Eurydice. 2006. *Content and Language Integrated Learning (CLIL) at School in Europe*. Brussels: Eurydice.

Gilmore, A. 2007. 'Authentic materials and authenticity in foreign language learning'. *Language Teaching*, 40: 97–118.

Hidalgo, A. C., D. Hall and G. M. Jacobs. 1995. *Getting Started: Materials Writers on Materials Writing*. Singapore: SEAMO.

Hooper Hansen, G. 1992. 'Suggestopedia: a way of learning for the 21st century'. In J. Mulligan and C. Griffin (eds.), *Empowerment Through Experiential Learning*. London: Kogan Page.

Johnson, J. 1995. 'Who needs another coursebook?' *FOLIO*, 2(1): 31–5.

Kasper, G. and C. Roever. 2005. 'Pragmatics in second language learning'. In E. Hinkel (ed.), *Handbook of Research in Second Language Learning*. Mahwah, NJ: Lawrence Erlbaum.

Kennedy, G. 1973. 'Conditions for language learning'. In J. Oller and J. Richards (eds.), *Focus on the Learner*. Rowley, MA: Newbury House.

De Keyser, R. (ed.). 2007. *Practice in a Second Language*. Cambridge: Cambridge University Press.

Krashen, S. 1982. *Principles and Practice in Second Language Acquisition*. Oxford: Pergamon.

1985. *The Input Hypothesis*. London: Longman.

Larsen-Freeman, D. and M. Long. 1991. *An Introduction to Second Language Acquisition Research*. London: Longman.

Lozanov, G. 1978. *Suggestology and Outlines of Suggestopedy*. London: Gordon and Breach.

Masuhara, H., M. Haan, Y. Yi and B. Tomlinson. 2008. 'Adult EFL courses'. *ELT Journal*, 62(3): 294–312.

McDonough, J., C. Shaw and H. Masuhara. 2011. *Materials and Methods in ELT*. Oxford: Blackwell.

McGrath, I. 2002. *Materials Evaluation and Design for Language Teaching*. Edinburgh: University of Edinburgh Press.

Meisel, J., H. Clahsen and M. Pienemann. 1981. 'On determining developmental stages in natural second language acquisition'. *Studies in Second Language Acquisition*, 3: 109–35.

Mishan, F. 2005. *Designing Authenticity into Language Learning Materials*. Bristol: Intellect.

Nation, P. 2003. 'Materials for teaching vocabulary'. In B. Tomlinson (ed.), *Developing Materials for Language Teaching*. London: Continuum.

2005. 'Teaching and learning vocabulary'. In E. Hinkel (ed.), *Handbook of Research in Second Language Teaching and Learning*. Mahwah, NJ: Erlbaum.

Nation, P. and K. Wang. 1999. 'Graded readers and vocabulary'. *Reading in a Foreign Language*, 12: 355–80.

Nunan, D. 2004. *Task-based Language Teaching*. Cambridge: Cambridge University Press.

On Target. 1995. Grade 10 English Second Language Learner's Book. Windhoek: Gamsberg Macmillan.

Oxford, R. 1999. 'Anxiety and the language learner'. In J. Arnold (ed.), *Affect in Language Learning*. Cambridge: Cambridge University Press.

2002. 'Sources of variation in language learning'. In R. B. Kaplan (ed.), *The Oxford Handbook of Applied Linguistics*. New York: Oxford University Press.

Oxford, R. L. and N. J. Anderson. 1995. 'A crosscultural view of learning styles'. *Language Teaching*, 28: 201–15.

Pienemann, M. 1985. 'Learnability and syllabus construction'. In K. Hyltenstam and M. Pienemann (eds.), *Modelling and Assessing Second Language Acquisition*. Clevedon, Avon: Multilingual Matters.

Popovici, R. and R. Bolitho. 2003. 'Personal and professional development through writing: the Romanian Textbook Project'. In B. Tomlinson (ed.), *Developing Materials for Language Teaching*. London: Continuum.

Reinders, H. and C. White. 2010. 'The theory and practice of technology in materials development and task design'. In N. Harwood (ed.), *English Language Teaching Materials: Theory and Practice*. Cambridge: Cambridge University Press.

Rubdi, R. 2003. 'Selection of materials'. In B. Tomlinson (ed.), *Developing Materials for Language Teaching*. London: Continuum.

Rutherford, W. and M. Sharwood-Smith (eds.). 1988. *Grammar and Second Language Teaching*. Rowley, MA: Newbury House.

Samuda, V. and M. Bygate. 2008. *Tasks in Second Language Learning*. Basingstoke: Palgrave MacMillan.

Saraceni, C. 2003. 'Adapting courses: a critical view'. In B. Tomlinson (ed.), *Developing Materials for Language Teaching*. London: Continuum.

Saville-Troike, M. 1988. 'Private speech: evidence for second language learning strategies during the "silent period"'. *Journal of Child Language*, 15: 567–90.

Schmidt, R. 1992. 'Psychological mechanisms underlying second language fluency'. *Studies in Second Language Acquisition*, 14: 357–85.

2001. 'Attention'. In P. Robinson (ed.), *Cognition and Second Language Instruction*. New York: Cambridge University Press.

Schmidt, R. and S. Frota. 1986. 'Developing basic conversational ability in a second language: a case study of an adult learner of Portuguese'. In R. Day (ed.), *Talking to Learn: Conversation in Second Language Acquisition*. Rowley, MA: Newbury House.

Seliger, H. 1979. 'On the nature and function of language rules in language teaching'. *TESOL Quarterly*, 13: 359–69.

Sharwood-Smith, M. 1981. 'Consciousness raising and the second language learner'. *Applied Linguistics*, 2: 159–69.

Stevick, E. 1976. *Memory, Meaning and Method*. Rowley, MA: Newbury House.

Swain, M. 1985. 'Communicative competence: some roles of comprehensible input and comprehensible output in its development'. In S. Gass and C. Madden (eds.), *Input in Second Language Acquisition*. Rowley, MA: Newbury House.

2005. 'The output hypothesis: theory and research'. In E. Hinkel (ed.), *Handbook of Research in Second Language Learning*. Mahwah, NJ: Lawrence Erlbaum.

Tarone, E. and G. Yule. 1989. *Focus on the Language Learner*. Oxford: Oxford University Press.

Tomlinson, B. 1990 'Managing change in Indonesian high schools'. *ELT Journal*, 44(1): 25–37.

1994a. 'Pragmatic awareness activities'. *Language Awareness*, 3 & 4: 119–29.

1994b. 'TPR materials'. *FOLIO*, 1(2): 8–10.

1995. 'Work in progress: textbook projects'. *FOLIO*, 2(2): 26–31.

1996. 'Choices'. *FOLIO*, 3(1): 20–3.

2001. 'Materials development'. In R. Carter and D. Nunan (eds.), *The Cambridge Guide to Teaching English to Speakers of Other Languages*. Cambridge: Cambridge University Press.

2003a. 'Materials evaluation'. In B. Tomlinson (ed.), *Developing Materials for Language Teaching*. London: Continuum.

2003b. 'Humanizing the coursebook'. In B. Tomlinson (ed.), *Developing Materials for Language Teaching*. London: Continuum.

2003c. 'Developing principled frameworks for materials development'. In B. Tomlinson (ed.), *Developing Materials for Language Teaching*. London: Continuum.

2006. 'Developing classroom materials for teaching to learn'. In J. Mukundan (ed.), *Focus on ELT Materials*. Petaling Jaya: Pearson Malaysia.

2007. 'Teachers' responses to form-focused discovery approaches'. In S. Fotos and H. Nassaji (eds.), *Form Focused Instruction and Teacher Education: Studies in Honour of Rod Ellis*. Oxford: Oxford University Press.

2008. 'Language acquisition and language learning materials'. In B. Tomlinson (ed.), *English Language Teaching Materials: A Critical Review*. London: Continuum.

2010. 'Principles of effective materials development'. In N. Harwood (ed.), *English Language Teaching Materials: Theory and Practice*. Cambridge: Cambridge University Press.

In press. 'Engaged to learn: ways of engaging L2 learners'. In J. Mukundan (ed.), *Readings on ELT Materials V*. Petaling Jaya: Pearson Longman.

Tomlinson, B. and J. Avila. 2007a. 'Seeing and saying for yourself: the roles of audio-visual mental aids in language learning and use'. In B. Tomlinson (ed.), *Language Acquisition and Development: Studies of Learners of First and Other Languages*. London: Continuum, pp. 61–81.

2007b. 'Applications of the research into the roles of audio-visual mental aids for language teaching pedagogy'. In B. Tomlinson (ed.), *Language Acquisition and Development: Studies of Learners of First and Other Languages*. London: Continuum, pp. 82–9.

Tomlinson, B. and H. Masuhara. 2009. 'Engaging learners of English through football'. In V. P. Vasquez and J. A. Lopez (eds.), *Aplicaciones Didacticas Para La Ensananza Integreda De Lenguay Contenidos*. Universidad de Cordoba.

In press. 'Playing to learn: how physical games can contribute to second language acquisition'. *Simulation and Gaming: An Interdisciplinary Journal of Theory, Practice and Research*. Anniversary Issue.

Tomlinson, B., B. Dat, H. Masuhara and R. Rubdy. 2001. 'EFL courses for adults'. *ELT Journal*, 55(1): 80–101.

Van den Branden, K. (ed.). 2006. *Task-Based Language Education: From Theory to Practice*. Cambridge: Cambridge University Press.

Wenden, A. 1987. 'Conceptual background and utility'. In A. Wenden and J. Rubin (eds.), *Learner Strategies in Language Learning*. Hemel Hempstead: Prentice Hall.

Wenden, A. and J. Rubin (eds.). 1987. *Learner Strategies in Language Learning*. Hemel Hempstead: Prentice Hall.

White, L. 1990. 'Implications of learnability theories for second language learning and teaching'. In M. Halliday, J. Gibbons and H. Nicholas (eds.), *Learning, Keeping and Using Language, I*. Amsterdam: John Benjamins.

Willis, D. and J. Willis. 2007. *Doing Task-Based Teaching*. Oxford: Oxford University Press.

Wright, T. and R. Bolitho. 1993. 'Language awareness: a missing link in language teacher education'. *ELT Journal*, 47(4).

Part A Data collection and materials development

2 Using corpora in the language classroom

Randi Reppen

2.1 Introduction

Since the mid 1990s, dictionaries based on corpora (collections of naturally occurring texts) have been widespread in English as a second language (ESL) classrooms. These dictionaries, based on large collections of natural language, not only provide learners with information about word meanings, but also provide important information about word use. As a natural extension of using dictionaries based on corpora, teachers have become increasingly interested in using information from corpora to inform and create language-learning materials. In the 1990s resources such as Johns (1994) and Tribble and Jones (1997) provided teachers with some ideas and guidelines for ways to use corpus information in the classroom. Now, with more and more corpus-informed or corpus-based teaching resources becoming available (such as: *Focus on Vocabulary* (Schmitt and Schmitt 2005); the *Touchstone* series (McCarthy, McCarten and Sandiford 2006/2006); and *Real Grammar* (Conrad and Biber 2009)), this interest has continued to grow and has even expanded to teachers themselves wanting to bring corpora into language classrooms. Using corpora in the language classroom can provide teachers and students with several advantages. Corpora can provide a rich source of authentic material, and, therefore, examples of the language students will encounter outside the language classroom. Corpora can also provide students with many examples of the target feature (e.g. a vocabulary item or grammatical structure) in a concentrated manner, to help them better understand the feature and its contexts and cotexts of use.

Before discussing some ways to bring corpora into a classroom, a word about corpora and corpus linguistics is in order. A corpus is a collection of naturally occurring texts that is usually stored on a computer (see Biber, Conrad and Reppen 1998 for more on the characteristics of corpora). If the texts are stored on a computer, it is possible to search texts for particular features. A number of tools are available for searching corpora (e.g. AntConc, MonoConc, WordSmith – see the Appendix for more information). It is also important to note that the term 'text' is used to refer to either spoken or written discourse. The spoken texts are usually transcribed into a written version, and in most cases the audio files are not available.

Corpus linguists have used a variety of corpora to describe many aspects of language use, ranging from characteristics of English across different registers (e.g. informal conversation, academic prose, newspapers), to exploring language change over time (Atkinson 1999; Fitzmaurice 2003), to specific lists of vocabulary that are found in academic English (Coxhead 2000), to describing and comparing different world Englishes (Balasubramanian 2009; Schmied 2006), to exploring language use in specialised settings (Connor and Upton 2004; Friginal 2009). The information from these studies, along with the rich descriptions of English provided in the Longman Grammar of Spoken and Written Language (Biber *et al.* 1999) and the Cambridge Grammar of English (Carter and McCarthy 2006), helps to provide a picture of the language that students will encounter, and therefore can be of great value in helping teachers plan what to teach and as a resource for developing teaching materials (O'Keeffe, McCarthy and Carter 2007; Reppen 2010).

2.2 Ways to use corpora in the classroom

This chapter will discuss three ways for teachers to provide learners with hands-on corpus activities. First, teachers can bring in material from corpus searches and have students work with the teacher-prepared material. Secondly, teachers can use some of the online corpora that are available. This section will focus on four available corpora that are very user-friendly (COCA, Time, MICASE and MICUSP). Thirdly, teachers can bring in existing corpora or create specialised corpora for their class (e.g. a corpus from readings or from student papers) and have students interact with the corpora. These three ways are described in the sections that follow. Each has certain advantages and, of course, the ideas can be used in combination. For example, a teacher might bring in some prepared concordance lines (i.e. samples of the use of a particular language feature) to introduce new vocabulary, and then later have students search an online corpus to see more examples of the words in context, in order to provide students with greater exposure to the different senses of the target word. This type of exposure to language can help learners get a better idea of the patterns of use and the words that co-occur with the new vocabulary.

2.2.1 Using teacher-prepared corpus material

In many places classes may not have easy access to computers, or may not be able to access the computer lab during class time. Teachers can still use corpus activities without having computers available for students (see Chapter 3 by Jane Willis). Instead of the students interacting with the corpus, the teacher will explore the corpus and bring the results into the classroom in the form of teacher-prepared material. For example, teachers can bring in word frequency lists or concordance lines that feature target vocabulary. There are several advantages of teacher-prepared corpus material for learners. One major advantage is that teachers can control the material. Since the teachers search the corpus for the students, and then bring in those results, teachers can make sure that the vocabulary load is not too great, and that the students are exposed to the target form in a way that is meaningful and relevant for the students. This is a definite advantage in beginning courses where vocabulary load is an issue. In a lower level class the teacher might decide to delete the second-to-last and last lines of the examples of the verb concordance in Figure 2.1, since these contain difficult discipline-specific vocabulary (e.g. *foot pounds*, *erg*, *j*, *N*). Removing these lines does not impact the authenticity of the material; rather, it helps provide lower level students with meaningful and non-distracting input. Teacher-prepared concordance lines allow teachers to check that the content is appropriate for their learners. Prepared concordance material is also an ideal way to introduce students to reading concordance lines, something that can be distracting or confusing at first since sentences are often not complete (see Figure 2.1).

Figure 2.1 *An example of concordance output for the target word* **show** *from a corpus of textbooks and class lectures (T2K-SWAL corpus, Biber et al., 2002).*

```
        ... that Mister Rogers is the best show on TV. But just because someone ...
   ... playmate: "Mister Rogers" is the best show on TV; and if you don't ...
      ... the week. present a current events show on a daily or weekly basis ...
                ... look like a real T.V. show. Our, um, our guest speaker ...

            ... they need to be able to show that this data set is in ...
   ... the plaintiff. The plaintiff must now show that the reason offered by the ...
      ... particular emotion. In this section I show that even if this enterprise were ...
             ... We added them up. And we show that, in the limit, there's no ...
            ... foot pounds. It is easy to show that 1 j equals 107 erg ...
        ... remainder of this section we will show that this is true, but only ...
        ... that the savings ratio is (formula). show that, for reasonable values of N ...
```

Data collection and materials development

Teachers can also use concordance output or KWICs (key word in context) like those shown in Figure 2.1 to begin a discussion of how a word can belong to different parts of speech (e.g. both as a noun and a verb) and to help students see patterns that are associated with the different forms. For example, in Figure 2.1 the teacher has grouped the target form *show* by part of speech (i.e. noun vs. verb) to help students see patterns. Looking at the KWICs in Figure 2.1 highlights that, as a verb, *show* is often followed by *that*, thus exposing students to a strong pattern that is found in academic writing. Or, the teacher could ask students to discover clues to help them to know that *show* is being used as a noun (e.g. use of an article). By first introducing students to KWICs that are brought into the classroom and guiding them to engage ways to discover patterns of language use, students will be less overwhelmed when interacting with corpora on their own. In addition, they will be practising valuable analytical skills and will become familiar with some of the processes for discovering patterns of language use that can help them to become more autonomous language learners.

2.2.2 Using web corpora

For teachers whose students are fortunate enough to have access to computers, online corpora are a useful resource. The availability of corpora with web interfaces is something that has changed drastically over the past five years. Although interacting with a corpus on the Web can limit some research options, it provides a wealth of options for language teachers and learners. This section will present examples from four online corpora that have very friendly user interfaces that can be used to address a range of different language-learning situations. The Appendix also lists other corpus resources that might be of interest to teachers and learners.

The first two corpora in this section are the Time corpus and COCA (Corpus of Contemporary American English); both were developed by Mark Davies and have the same user interface and both of these corpora can be useful for teaching. Amongst other uses, the COCA can be a useful tool for raising student awareness of differences of language use in speech and writing, whilst the Time corpus can provide accessible examples of writing. In addition to providing KWICs, the interfaces of these two corpora allow users to search the corpus specifying a part of speech. Search results can be displayed in either a list or chart (e.g. bar graph).

The bar graph display in the COCA can be a useful tool to raise learners' awareness of differences between forms that are frequently used in speech but not in writing. Figure 2.2 shows the results of a search on the word *get*. The bar graph provides students with a powerful visual

Figure 2.2 Screen shot from COCA for get

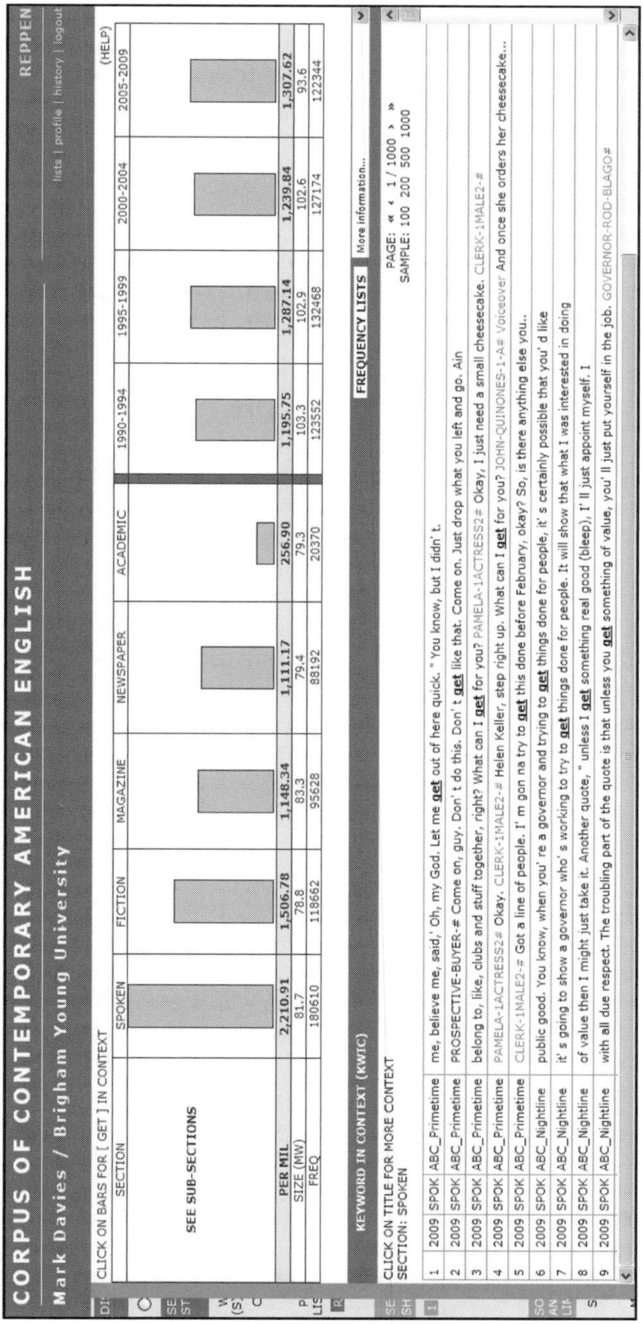

of how frequent *get* is in speech, and how infrequently it is used in academic writing. Students could then be asked to think of other words to use instead of *get* when writing papers for class.

Since the Time corpus is a written collection from a news magazine, it is a rich resource for looking at academic writing that is not discipline-specific, and which has vocabulary that is accessible to advanced learners. In addition to vocabulary, one of the ways that the Time corpus can be used to help advanced writers is to look at the use of various transitions. Teachers could either give individual students lists of transition words to explore in the corpus, or students could work in teams to explore certain transitions and then report their findings to the class.

The next two corpora were created by the English Language Institute (ELI) of the University of Michigan: MICASE (Michigan Corpus of Academic Spoken English) and MICUSP (Michigan Corpus of Upper Level Student Papers). MICASE is a 1.8 million word corpus of spoken academic language from a variety of university contexts (e.g. lectures, study groups, advising sessions) across a range of disciplines. In addition to the transcripts, sound files are also available. The sound files are linked to the transcripts, thus allowing teachers and students a variety of options to enhance academic listening skills and to create focused listening activities. Users can filter searches by many criteria including: discipline, speaker gender, academic level, interactivity of the interaction, and native language of the participants. The home page for the MICASE corpus also offers teachers and students many valuable ideas and resources for interacting with the corpus.

The recently launched MICUSP site is a corpus of about 2.6 million words from 829 university student papers that have received a grade of A or A–. As with MICASE, users can search the corpus by discipline and student level. In addition, users can also target particular types of writing (e.g. argumentative, creative, research report) and particular features of writing (graphs, abstracts, methods sections). A clear bar graph displays the results of searches. In addition to the generous context that is provided in the KWICs, users can view complete papers. This new corpus will be a tremendous resource for intermediate and advanced writing courses. In addition, MICUSP can be used in both native and non-native disciplinary writing courses, providing ESP (English for Specific Purposes) classes with an amazing teaching tool. For example, both native and non-native English-speaking biology students can see how successful writers refer to charts in the text of research papers. Students tackling academic papers for the first time can see many examples of how citations are used and also see a variety of ways to use citations. Students can see many examples of well-written abstracts as used in student papers, rather than only from published research articles, thus providing a more realistic target for their writing. Figure 2.3 shows the search results for the word *claim* as it occurs with the textual feature 'Reference to sources' across disciplines and levels, whilst Figure 2.4 shows the results for the word *find* with the same search values. Not only can the user immediately see that *find* is used across more disciplines, but it is also evident that *claim* is strongly preferred by students writing papers for philosophy courses.

The goal of such an activity is not to prescribe that using *claim* when writing philosophy papers will result in a better grade, but to examine the KWICs and see how the words *claim* and *find* are used in different disciplines and to become aware of some of the subtleties of these two words. Additionally, when looking through the texts to see how successful student papers reference sources, students will hopefully add to their variety of resources for referring to sources.

2.2.3 Creating corpora for classroom use

Whilst using existing online corpora is much easier than creating corpora in the classroom, the available online corpora may not meet specific needs of certain language classes. Additionally, using corpora and corpus search tools in the classroom can provide teachers and learners with information that is not available from the online corpora. For example, in beginning reading classes, knowing the amount of unknown words in a text is extremely useful. In this case teachers can use the word frequency lists from corpus search tools such as MonoConc, AntConc or WordSmith to quickly assess the amount of new vocabulary students will encounter in a reading. Teachers can have students scan the frequency list of words in a text and note where they begin to encounter unknown words. The teacher can then make an informed decision as to the difficulty of the text. If too many words are unknown, the teacher immediately knows that the text is too challenging, and can select another reading. Or, if only some words are unknown, depending on how many and which words are unknown, the teacher could use a variety of activities to help students discover the meanings of the unfamiliar words. For example, students could work in teams and use KWICs from the text to discover the word meanings. Discovery approaches, or focused noticing activities, help learners not only to become autonomous learners, but also help them to learn target forms (vocabulary or grammar) more effectively (Ellis 2005; VanPatten and Williams 2007).

In a reading class or a content-based class, creating an electronic version or mini corpus of the readings can offer a variety of activities for interacting with the texts. Donely and Reppen (2001) describe how a content-based course for intermediate and advanced English language

Figure 2.3   Screen shot from MICUSP showing the results of a search for claim used in reference to sources.

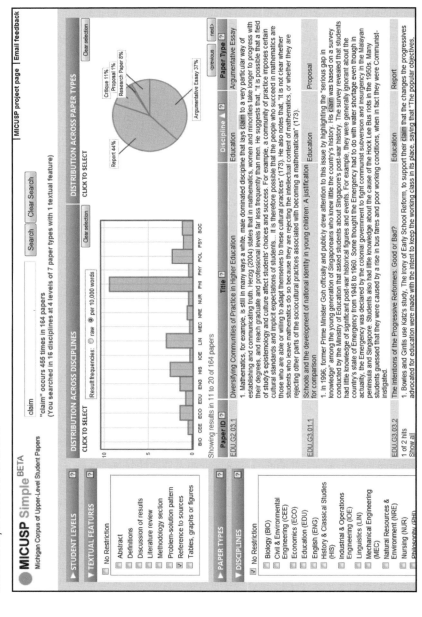

Figure 2.4   Screen shot from MICUSP showing the results of a search for find *used in reference to sources.*

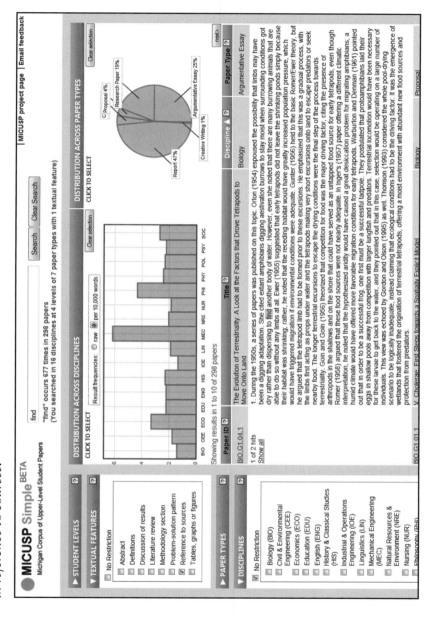

learners used a corpus of class readings to learn specialised vocabulary associated with a unit on anthropology. With this specialised corpus the teacher was also able to reinforce the non-content-specific academic words that were in the readings. The specific content terms (e.g. anthropology, matrilineal) were defined in the readings, whilst the more 'invisible' academic words were assumed to be known by the readers, which is often not the case in ESL settings.

Another example of a specialised class corpus is building a corpus of student papers. The teacher could then use this class corpus to guide students in comparing features found in their writing with features found in the MICUSP corpus. By filtering the searches in MICUSP, the comparisons between the student writing corpus and MICUSP can be made even more meaningful by selecting the student level (e.g. junior level or graduate level) and/or discipline (biology, philosophy, political science) that matches the students in the class.

In the case of an advanced writing course for ESP students, or an interdisciplinary writing course, students could create their own mini corpora. These corpora could then be used to explore the patterns found in the writing of their discipline. For example, in an interdisciplinary writing class a biology major who is required to write lab reports could assemble a corpus of lab reports, whilst a business major in the same class could assemble a corpus of business case studies to explore the type of writing tasks that are expected in that discipline. By having students create specialised corpora, they will be able to independently explore the language that is used in their specific fields and also become familiar with the different types of writing tasks that are common in their area of study.

2.3 Conclusion

The many ways to bring hands-on corpus use into the language classroom are as varied as the classes themselves. Will using corpora or corpus-informed material address all the challenges of teaching a language? No, but it will add to the options and resources available for teachers and encourage learner autonomy. For example, Friginal (2006) reports on an ESP writing course for forestry, where students worked with a specialised class corpus. Even after the course students reported that they continued to use the specialised corpus to check word choices and also the structures that they were using in their class papers. Additionally, corpora provide a rich source of material that reflects the real language use that students will encounter outside the classroom. Using corpora in the classroom is a good example of bringing authentic material into classes where previously this was much more of a challenge.

As corpora and corpus tools become more available, and as teachers become better trained and more comfortable with using corpus resources (O'Keeffe, McCarthy and Carter 2007; Reppen 2010), the ways in which corpora will be used for language learning will continue to expand. One aspect that will not change is the need to match learner goals and teaching resources and to use appropriate resources to accomplish teaching and learning goals. Corpora are one more tool toward that goal.

References

Atkinson, D. 1999. *Scientific Discourse in Sociohistorical Context: The Philosophical Transactions of the Royal Society of London*. Hillsdale, NJ: Lawrence Erlbaum.

Balasubramanian, C. 2009. *Register Variation in Indian English*. Amsterdam: John Benjamins.

Biber, D., S. Conrad and R. Reppen. 1998. *Corpus Linguistics: Investigating Language Structure and Use*. Cambridge: Cambridge University Press.

Biber, D., S. Conrad, R. Reppen, P. Byrd and M. Helt. 2002. 'Speaking and writing in the university: a multi-dimensional comparison'. *TESOL Quarterly*, 36: 19–48.

Biber, D., S. Johansson, G. Leech, S. Conrad and E. Finegan. 1999. *The Longman Grammar of Spoken and Written English*. London: Longman.

Carter, R. and M. McCarthy. 2006. *The Cambridge Grammar of English*. Cambridge: Cambridge University Press.

Connor, U. and T. Upton. 2004. 'The genre of grant proposals: a corpus linguistic analysis'. In U. Connor and T. Upton (eds.), *Applied Corpus Linguistics: A Multidimensional Perspective*. Amsterdam: Rodopi.

Conrad, S. and D. Biber. 2009. *Real Grammar*. Harlow: Pearson Longman.

Coxhead, A. 2000. 'A new Academic Word List'. *TESOL Quarterly*, 34(2): 213–38.

Donley, K. M. and R. Reppen. 2001. 'Using corpus tools to highlight academic vocabulary in SCLT'. *TESOL Journal*, 12: 7–12.

Ellis, N. 2005. 'At the interface: dynamic interactions of explicit and implicit language knowledge'. *Studies in Second Language Acquisition*, 27: 305–52.

Fitzmaurice, S. 2003. 'The grammar of stance in early eighteenth-century English epistolary language'. In P. Leistyna and C. Meyer (eds.), *Corpus Analysis: Language Structure and Language Use*. Amsterdam: Rodopi.

Friginal, E. 2006. 'Developing technical writing skills in forestry using corpus-informed instruction and tools'. Paper presented at the American Association of Applied Corpus Linguistics Conference, Flagstaff, Arizona.

2009. *The Language of Outsourced Call Centers: A Corpus-Based Study of Cross-Cultural Interaction*. Amsterdam: John Benjamins.

Johns, T. 1994. 'From printout to handout: grammar and vocabulary teaching in the context of data-driven learning'. In T. Odlin (ed.), *Perspectives on Pedagogical Grammar*. Cambridge: Cambridge University Press.

McCarthy, M., J. McCarten and H. Sandiford. 2004/2006. *Touchstone 1–4*. Cambridge: Cambridge University Press.

O'Keeffe, A., M. McCarthy and R. Carter. 2007. *From Corpus to Classroom*. Cambridge: Cambridge University Press.

Reppen, R. 2010. *Using Corpora in the Language Classroom*. Cambridge: Cambridge University Press.

Schmied, J. 2006. 'East African Englishes'. In B. Kachru, Y. Kachru and C. Nelson (eds.), *The Handbook of World Englishes*. Basingstoke: Blackwell.

Schmitt, D. and N. Schmitt. 2005. *Focus on Vocabulary*. Harlow: Longman.

Tribble, C. and G. Jones. 1997. *Concordances in the Classroom*. Houston: Athelstan.

VanPatten, B. and J. Williams (eds.). 2007. *Theories in Second Language Acquisition: An Introduction*. Mahwah, NJ: Lawrence Erlbaum.

West, M. 1953. *A General Service List of English Words*. London: Longman.

Appendix: Examples of useful corpus sites and tools

AntConc

www.antlab.sci.waseda.ac.jp/software.html

This freeware program can create word frequency lists, and KWICs. This easy-to-use program also identifies n-grams of 2–6 words.

AWL Highlighter

www.nottingham.ac.uk/~alzsh3/acvocab/awlhighlighter.htm

This site allows the user to input texts and highlights the words from the Academic Word List (AWL). It also has links to a gap-making program for fill-in-the-blank exercises, and to other useful sites.

British National Corpus (BNC)

www.natcorp.ox.ac.uk

A 100-million word multi-register corpus of spoken and written British English, searchable by word or phrase. In addition to information about the BNC, the site has links to many resources. Note: accessing the BNC through Mark Davies's site, http://view.byu.edu/BNC, allows a few more search options.

Business Letter Concordancer (BLC)

http://someya-net.com/concordancer/index.html

This site links users to a concordancer that accesses several corpora including a corpus of business letters, personal letters and letters of historic figures (e.g. Thomas Jefferson, Robert Louis Stevenson).

Collins Cobuild Corpus Concordance Sampler

www.collins.co.uk/Corpus/CorpusSearch.aspx

This site allows the user to search a 56-million word corpus. Forty concordance lines are provided for each search.

Collocate

www.athelstan.com

This reasonably priced program identifies, collocates and generates n-grams (aka word clusters) and provides some statistics (e.g. mutual information, t scores).

Compleat Lexical Tutor

www.lextutor.ca

In addition to access to various corpora and tools, this site allows you to input texts for vocabulary analysis based on the academic word list and the General Service Word List (West 1953). The site also has many useful articles on corpora and language teaching, and tests for assessing vocabulary.

Corpus.BYU.edu

http://corpus.byu.edu

This site links to the many corpora (e.g. COCA and TIME) that are searchable through an interface developed by Mark Davies. The format for searches is the same regardless of the corpus. The interface is user-friendly and also allows for part-of-speech and wildcard searches. This site has one of the best interfaces with the BNC for word and phrase searches that include graphs and tables of search results by register.

Corpus of Contemporary American English (COCA)

www.americancorpus.org

An online, searchable 400+ million word corpus of American English arranged by register, including news, spoken and academic texts. The texts in this corpus are from 1990 to the present. This site allows the user also to search by part of speech (POS).

Data collection and materials development

Corpus of Spoken Professional American English (CSPAE)

www.athel.com/cspa.html

A two-million word corpus of professional spoken language (meetings, academic discussions, and White House press conferences). A 42,722 word sample is available for free.

ICAME – International Computer Archive of Modern and Medieval English

http://icame.uib.no

A site with links to information and corpus resources.

ICE – International Corpus of English

www.ucl.ac.uk/english-usage/ice/index.htm

This site has information about the availability of several spoken and written one-million word corpora of various world Englishes. The corpora of the various world Englishes follow the same format and provide a rich resource for cross comparisons.

KfNgram

www.kwicfinder.com/kfNgram/kfNgramHelp.html

A site that has online concordance and collocation resources. This site allows users to input and search corpora.

Michigan Corpus Linguistics

www.elicorpora.info

This site links users to many valuable corpora and corpus resources. In addition to the two corpora mentioned below, there is also a corpus of Generation 1.5 writing and a corpus of conference presentations. Teachers can find activities for using the suite of corpora from this site along with pre-made worksheets. Language researchers and students will also find useful materials on this well-designed site.

MICASE – Michigan Corpus of Academic Spoken English

This free, online, searchable corpus of academic spoken language is a valuable resource. The online concordancer is user-friendly and has a number of search options. In addition to the transcripts, the sound files are also available. The corpus is available for purchase for a modest fee (use from the website is free). There are links to lesson material that has been prepared based on MICASE. There is also a free shareware program for transcription that can be downloaded.

MICUSP – Michigan Corpus of Upper Level Student Papers

This free, online, searchable corpus of student papers from a variety of disciplines provides teachers and students with many useful resources. The searches can be designed to target specific disciplines, types of writing, and/or parts of papers (e.g. conclusions, citations). The bar graph that displays results provides an easy-to-interpret visual. The first launched beta version will be upgraded to include more search features.

MonoConc

www.athelstan.com/mono.html

This affordable and easy-to-use concordancing package provides concordances, frequency lists and collocate information.

Paul Nation's webpage

www.victoria.ac.nz/lals/staff/paul-nation/nation.aspx

This page has many links to information about vocabulary. It also has a download of a free program, Range, to compare target texts with two word lists (the General Service List and the Academic Word List).

Scottish Corpus of Texts and Speech

www.scottishcorpus.ac.uk/corpus/search/

A Scottish corpus of spoken and written texts and a search tool.

Time Corpus

http://corpus.byu.edu/time/

This online corpus of *Time Magazine* from 1923 up to 2006 is searchable through Mark Davies's user-friendly interface. The *Time* corpus allows interesting explorations of how language changes over a relatively short period of time. It is also a useful resource for looking at written academic language that is accessible for language learners. This site allows the user also to search by part of speech (POS).

Data collection and materials development

University of Lancaster

Centre for Computer Corpus Research on Language

http://ucrel.lancs.ac.uk

This site is a rich resource of information about corpora and corpus linguistics.

VOICE – Vienna–Oxford International Corpus of English

www.univie.ac.at/voice/

VOICE is a one-million word corpus of English as a lingua franca (ELF). The corpus is available online and includes over 1,250 speakers of mostly European languages interacting in English in a variety of settings. Free registration allows users to search the corpus in a variety of ways and to see complete transcripts.

WebCONC

www.niederlandistik.fu-berlin.de/cgi-bin/web-conc.cgi?art=google&sprache=en

This online software produces KWICs in many languages.

Web Concordancer

www.edict.com.hk/concordance/

A free concordancing program and links to several corpora including Brown and Lancaster Oslo Bergen (LOB). This site also allows users to input and search a corpus.

WordSmith

www.lexically.net/wordsmith/

A concordancing program that, in addition to creating concordance lines, provides other information (e.g. frequency, key words, mutual information scores, word length, etc.). A powerful tool for searching a corpus.

3 Concordances in the classroom without a computer: assembling and exploiting concordances of common words

Jane Willis

3.1 Introduction

In recent years there has been growing interest in corpus linguistics, corpora in the language classroom and using concordances for language learning. Mauranen (2004), O'Keeffe, McCarthy and Carter (2007), Römer (2006), Sinclair (2004) and Chapter 2 in this volume all bear this out. And it is not just linguists and lexicographers, grammarians and materials writers who stand to gain from new insights into language use through these developments, but teachers and learners as well. In 1991 Tim Johns published his seminal paper 'Should you be persuaded – two samples of data-driven learning materials', illustrating how learners can benefit from becoming language investigators in their own right:

> The use of the concordancer can have a considerable influence on the process of language learning, stimulating enquiry and speculation on the part of the learner, and helping the learner also to develop the ability to see patterning in the target language and to form generalisations to account for that patterning.

This inductive data-driven approach, with its element of 'challenge and discovery' (*ibid.*), is in itself a valuable educational experience and one for which, as I go on to show, computers are not essential.

Later in this chapter I illustrate five different ways in which teachers can exploit sets of concordance lines that their learners have assembled by hand, without a computer. This Do It Yourself (DIY) approach is suitable for all classrooms as it engages learners (from beginners upwards) in collecting and analysing language data for themselves. It is especially applicable to classroom situations where people do not have access to technology, though it can be enhanced by use of hi-tech back-up, if available, outside class.

3.2 From corpus to concordances

How do researchers set about the task of describing language? Let us imagine that a researcher wishes to study the language of three-year-old children to see if there is any difference between the language of boys and girls at that age. Usually the first step is to gather a corpus (which can be stored electronically), a body of the relevant language, in this case the language of three-year-old boys and girls. This is an obvious step, but it is not an easy one. Decisions must be taken as to the size of the corpus, and care must be taken to see that the corpus is as representative as possible. But in principle the task is a manageable one. Once a researcher has assembled an appropriate corpus, that corpus can be used to answer relevant research questions.

Increasingly nowadays corpora are used in this way to help researchers analyse and describe the grammar and lexis of the language. A study may be directed at a particular genre of language – spoken as opposed to written, say, or the language of television chat shows or of research articles in medical journals. Corpora can also be used to provide a picture of the language as a whole, but if this is the aim, then a very large corpus running into many millions of words is required. One of the earliest and best known large corpora of this kind is The Bank of English. This corpus, assembled in the 1980s and named the **Collins and Birmingham University International Language Database** (hence COBUILD), provided the basis for the *Collins Cobuild English Dictionary, The Collins Cobuild Student's Grammar, The Collins Cobuild English Course* and many other reference books. COBUILD set a trend and was soon followed by a number of other corpus-building projects directed at learners of English, such as the British National Corpus (BNC) and the many others listed in the Appendix to Chapter 2. These in turn led to more corpus-informed reference books and grammars such as *The Cambridge Grammar of English* (2005) and *The Longman Student Grammar* (2002).

The process of gathering a corpus of this kind is extremely complex. Once the corpus has been assembled, however, and has been stored in computer memory, the process of examining it is relatively simple.

If lexicographers wish to analyse and define a particular word, they can use a computer program called a concordancer to generate a number of concordance lines of that word. Even a limited number of concordances can provide us with some useful insights, as the small set of concordance lines for the word *any* in Figure 3.1 shows. These lines were carefully selected to give a tiny but representative sample from the original COBUILD corpus. Pedagogic grammars and coursebooks often give the rule that *any* is used in negatives and questions, and *some* is used in statements. As you read down through this set of concordances, try to think of what the word *any* actually means. In how many cases do the lines here conform to the commonly given rule?

Figure 3.1

```
        are interesting to observe. Any child under two is given a bottle
        so the young men went for any job they could rather than a farm job
state of affairs could not go on any longer. Someone had to act soon
      they hadn't dared to strike any more matches - they were just
  the longest open tradition of any of the English link that have
   complicated. The closing of any of them would be a major engineering
       We work more overtime than any other country in Europe, even
         dry. I don't think there was any rain all summer long, was there?
     just won't come out. Have we any stain remover? . . . I thought there
   at Steve's house. just turn up any time after 12. It'll go on all afternoon
         hard pressed. there was never any time for standing back and appraising
```

Source: Cobuild data sheets, 1986

These concordance lines suggest that the rule does not hold up very well. Around half the examples show *any* used in positive statements. In fact, in all its uses *any* seems to carry a general non-specific meaning of '*It doesn't matter which*' (which is maybe why it is used commonly in questions and negatives where there is often nothing to be specific about). A far larger set of concordances would be needed if we wished to identify common collocations, patterns and pragmatic uses. But this small sample does accurately reflect the balance of uses of the word *any* from the research corpus, which in turn reflects typical everyday usage.

The corpus research process, then, involves isolating a particular linguistic feature, a word or a pattern, and studying that feature in detail. From this organised study of the language, researchers are able to produce a description of the language – its grammar and lexis, its typical patterns, collocations, meanings and uses.

Once we begin to view the process of language description in this way, it is a short step to applying the process pedagogically. Teachers want to make language description accessible to students. Students need to discover and internalise regularities in the language they are studying. If we can place students in the position of researchers (as suggested by Johns 1991 and 2002, and illustrated in Willis and Willis 1996), this will accomplish these goals neatly and economically and could well increase the self-esteem and confidence of the students.

This process of language analysis will inevitably lead to particular aspects of the language becoming salient, which is the first aim of any kind of awareness-raising activity. A rationale for such an approach is outlined in Brian Tomlinson's Chapter 1, the Introduction to this book. Schmidt (1990) and others argue that 'noticing' features of the target language is a necessary initial stage in the learning process. Ellis (1991: 241, fleshed out in Ellis

(2003: 163)), argues that 'consciousness-raising constitutes an approach to grammar teaching which is compatible with current thinking about how learners acquire L2 grammar'. Rather than rely on a diet of 'practice activities' which restrict input and expect immediate accuracy in the 'production' of small items of language, we should be giving learners plenty of opportunities to discover language and systematise it for themselves before expecting them to proceduralise their knowledge and put it to use. In support of this, Willis (2003) illustrates numerous practical ways to draw learners' attention to different aspects of language – from words to lexical phrases and pattern grammar. Later in this chapter I show how different kinds of analysis activities based on concordance lines for the most frequent words can highlight a rich array of language features. These activities help students both to recognise and memorise useful patterns and recurrent chunks (fixed phrases, such as *a matter of fact, Know what I mean?*) as well as to analyse and make useful generalisations about grammar.

3.3 The need for a 'pedagogic corpus'

So far we have been talking about building large corpora for research purposes – a 'research corpus'. However, concordance lines from a research corpus will inevitably be drawn from unfamiliar contexts and will often contain lexis that learners do not know. For maximum benefit, learners need to work with a relatively small corpus of familiar texts, written and spoken, all of which are at an appropriate level – a 'pedagogic corpus' (Willis and Willis 2007: 187–9). This will normally be made up of some or all of the texts and transcripts of recordings from the coursebook that learners have read or listened to before, and other supplementary materials they are already familiar with.

The important thing is that this corpus must provide sufficient illustrative examples of the language we want our students to learn. It is obviously advantageous if this corpus is made up of 'authentic' texts, that is, not texts written for language-teaching purposes to illustrate a specific language point, or simplified to the point of distorting natural language use. Texts such as these should not be included in a pedagogic corpus; there is little point in learners studying language that is unnatural or untypical of the language they will meet in real life. If we can achieve the aim of providing a suitably representative pedagogic corpus, we can then design a series of language analysis exercises based on that corpus, exercises which have the potential to help students, in the role of researchers, to discover typical features of the language for themselves.

The purpose of this chapter is first to explore how far this aim is feasible. It is certainly more readily achievable in an environment which offers ready access to computer hardware and software, but we will look beyond that to see how far the aim can be achieved by a resourceful teacher or materials writer without easy access to computers. Learners can also be given the useful experience of choosing texts which interest them and compiling a corpus for themselves; for example, ESP learners might like to choose extracts from their favourite professional journals.

3.4 Preparations for concordancing by hand

It is preferable to base language analysis activities on texts familiar to learners, that is, ones they have already read or listened to for some communicative purpose. Having already processed the texts for meaning, students stand to gain more from the study of the forms that carry those meanings. This is a major pedagogic advantage of pedagogic corpora over concordances from computer-generated corpora. So the first step is to take stock of the texts (both spoken and written) from the learners' own pedagogic corpus, which is made up of texts that they are currently using or have already used. These are the texts to use for concordancing.

The next step is to identify which words appear with some frequency in these current texts and to select one or two to study in depth. Knowing which words are amongst the most frequent helps here, and this knowledge can be gained from an appropriate word frequency list.

As we saw in Chapter 2, frequency lists that have been computer generated are now generally available for the use of materials writers and teachers. Appendix A in this chapter contains lists of the top 150 word forms of spoken English and written English. These were compiled from The Bank of English, a large research corpus of over 200 million words of general (non-specialist) English. The most frequent 50 word forms actually account for 36 per cent of text (see Table 3.3 in Appendix B), so these highly frequent words make useful starting points for detailed study of a text. These are the words that it is possible to concordance by hand, simply because they are so frequent that examples of them are easy to find. Then, through analysis of the assembled concordance lines, senses of words, typical collocations, grammar patterns, pragmatics and phraseology and so on can be explored.

It is, however, worth remembering that not all words will be equally frequent in all discourse types, that is, not every text will have the same frequency patterns. For example, in spoken English the words *so, well, think, mean, things* and obviously *yes* and *no* are far more frequent than in written English (see Chapter 4 in this book by Ronald Carter, Rebecca Hughes and Michael McCarthy). Similarly, some words and phrases will be more common in spontaneous discourse than in planned discourse, for example vague language such as *that kind of thing*; *and stuff like that*. Words will typically occur in different senses and patterns depending on the genre of text. And of course specialist or topic words will also appear with higher frequency in a particular text than they would in a general corpus frequency count. But frequency lists can give us a rough indication of words worth looking out for. Better still would be frequency lists giving a breakdown of the common meanings and uses of each word in frequency order, such as the data sheets used in drawing up and implementing the lexical syllabus for the (now out-of-print) Collins Cobuild English Course, as exemplified in Willis (1990: 55–6).

Most corpus-derived learners' dictionaries do now give this kind of frequency information, together with natural examples and grammatical information for each meaning of a word. All of the most frequent words have several different meanings and uses, and for each main meaning there will be typical patternings. The **dictionary entries** for the most common words should contain a lot of useful information and give some indication of what to look out for in concordance lines once they are assembled. They can be used by teachers and materials writers before preparing activities based on concordances, and by students, selectively, after doing such activities, to consolidate their knowledge of aspects of the word under study.

There are, then, three essentials: the texts themselves, frequency information and a good dictionary.

3.5 Assembling and investigating concordances: sample class activities

In this section I will describe five sessions where hand-concordancing was used. Each session was based on a different type of text, involved a variety of analytic procedures, and illustrates the kinds of insights that can be gained from using these procedures. The procedures and steps taken will then be summarised.

3.5.1 Sample session 1: a focus on **as** for ESP students

I was once invited to a university ESP department in a developing country to lead a workshop on the lexical syllabus and the design of language analysis activities. There was little access to computers but, working with the texts the teachers had brought in, we successfully concordanced, by hand, a number of common words, to see what insights could be gained by doing so. Four teachers had brought in texts on the topic of farm animal nutrition that they were currently using with students studying English for agriculture. After a quick initial glance through these texts, I selected the word *as*, which ranks sixteenth in the general written frequency lists. Whilst other subject teachers were reading the texts to gain some idea of their subject matter, the four agricultural specialists split up sections of the texts between them and simply wrote up on the board all the examples of *as* they could find in their section, positioning the word *as* in the centre. This took around five minutes. The result looked something like Figure 3.2.

We began by identifying the actual phrases containing the word *as*, that is, deciding where the phrases began and ended. This was harder than it sounds since it involved making decisions relating to semantic units and clause or phrase boundaries. In the case of Example 1 (the first line), for instance, most people intuitively felt that the chunk needed to include both verbs: *are decreased proportionately as productivity rises* – to keep the semantic balance. In Example 6 (the sixth line) some pairs argued that *as is explained later* should not be separated from the first half of the sentence; when asked why, they were forced to reflect on and try to explain this meaning of *as*. Very few examples were as straightforward as *in the same way as … as a result of …* In fact, the whole process of identifying the boundaries of the *as* phrases stimulated both pair and class discussion of meanings and clause relations. Being asked to justify their decisions concerning where phrases with *as* began and ended often forced participants to make explicit things they had only felt subconsciously before. This kind of activity refines and deepens their understanding of a very useful word and is exactly what is meant by the term awareness-raising activity.

Figure 3.2

```
Maintenance costs are decreased proportionately as productivity rises
        complex activity which includes such actions as the search for food
            of blood constituents have been suggested as possible signals including
            . . . which receives signals from the body as a result of consumption of food
some agent associated with energy storage acts as a signal fot the long term . . .
that signal are received directly from the crop as is explained later.
                A variety of aromatic substance such as dill, aniseed , coriander and . . .
    intake and energy requirement suggests that, as with energy, intake should vary
    to environment temperature in the same way as monogastric animal, in that
                        This can be considered as an aspect of energy balance in
                Digestibility here is expressed as the coefficient for food energy
appears to be relatively unimportant in grazing as animals will graze in the dark
```

The second task was to try to classify the uses and meanings of the phrases with *as* and to find how many different ways these could be classified. After some discussion, mostly focusing on the meanings and functions of *as*, pairs generally grouped the phrases into around five or six categories, thus:

- referring to time (1)
- introducing examples (2, 7) (Students would know *such as*, but probably not the pattern such + noun + *as*)
- meaning similar to/same (8, 9 and possibly 6?)
- after verbs such as *suggested, acts, considered, expressed* (which also express similarity or something parallel)
- expressing a reason (12)
- left-over phrases: *as a result*

For each of these categories, pairs were then asked to suggest a further example that they had met before. They came up with phrases such as *functioned as, as you know, As a child, I lived in …*

They then felt they wanted to consult a dictionary to find whether their categories were similar to those in the dictionary and to find more parallel examples that might be useful. They did this in groups and then told each other their useful phrases. They particularly liked phrases such as *saving as little as £10 per week, as a consequence of …* and those with a more colloquial flavour: *as things stand*, and *as it turned out*.

It was noticeable that two categories of *as* were absent in this set of concordances: the phrase *as if* and the pattern *as X as*. Maybe these are simply less common in this genre of academic text; it would be interesting to take a bigger sample to find out if indeed this was the case.

So far these activities had involved a fair amount of repetition of phrases with *as* (helpful for learners who learn best by memorising) and discussion about the various meanings, functions and uses of *as* (helpful to learners with a more cognitive approach). All this was leading to a general broadening of understanding of how and when they and their students could use such expressions. In addition to the word *as*, many other useful words and phrases had been focused on.

An important effect of concordance lines is that they enable us to take a more objective look at the language. They are like tiny snapshots of a linguistic landscape. Just as when looking at a photograph of a familiar scene you often notice something you had not realised was there before, concordance lines taken from their familiar surroundings seem to make it more likely that we notice new things.

These new things may not just be related to the central word. So once learners have begun to look at a set of concordance lines with an analytical mindset, it is often useful to extend the area of study. In this particular session, as a final supplementary activity, we moved the focus of attention outwards from the central word and looked to see what useful grammatical insights we could gain from looking at other words and phrases in the concordance lines on the board. I thought that this activity might last another two or three minutes, but it proved extremely fruitful. After ten minutes or so the board looked like Figure 3.3.

The noun groups (underlined in Figure 3.3) could be further subdivided into those consisting of noun + noun, and those with adjective + noun:

maintenance costs	*complex activity*
blood constituents	*possible signals*
energy storage	*aromatic substances*
food intake	*environmental temperature*
energy requirement	*monogastric animals*
food energy	*energy balance*

Participants then went back to the texts themselves to see if they could find more noun + noun phrases, and came up with *body weight, production costs, control centres, blood glucose, heat increment.* They also recognised some of the concordance lines in their original context – a further deepening of their language experience. Identifying and exploring the structure and meaning of noun + noun phrases is a good way of focusing on the use of ESP topic lexis in many kinds of text. Noun

Figure 3.3

Maintenance costs are decreased proportionately as productivity rises
complex activity which includes such (actions) as the search for food
of blood constituents have been suggested as possible (signals) including
... which receives (signals) from the body as a (result) of consumption of food
some (agent) associated with energy storage acts as a signal fot the long term ...
that signals are received directly from the crop as is explained later.
A (variety) of aromatic substances such as dill, aniseed, coriander and ...
intake and energy requirement suggests that, as with energy, intake should vary
to environment temperature in the same way as monogastric animal, in that
This can be considered as (an aspect) of energy (balance) in
Digestibility here is expressed as the coefficient for food energy
appears to be relatively unimportant in grazing as animals will graze in the dark

phrases can be longer and more complex – look out for examples in medical and business text. They also feature commonly in newspaper headlines – try working out the possible meanings of the headline *Christmas Toy Trip Border Wrangle*.

Verbs and verb phrases (identified by dotted lines in Figure 3.3) that are not in themselves specialist agricultural terms, but which appear commonly in academic writing, were also noted by participants. These included *includes ..., have been suggested as ..., acts as ..., suggests that ..., can be considered as ..., appears to be ...*

Other features that could be focused on include:

- general nouns such as *aspect, variety, substances, signals, result, way, balance* (circled in Figure 3.3). These have very little specific meaning on their own and must be further explained, either beforehand, as in *energy balance*, or later, as in *signals from the body, result of consumption of food*.
- phrases with verbs ending in -ed: *are decreased, have been suggested as ..., associated with ...* . These can be further classified either structurally into passives or adjectival uses, or semantically into subject-specialist terms and academic discourse terms.
- nouns formed from common verbs: *maintenance, storage, consumption, digestibility, requirement*.
- adjectives formed from nouns: *aromatic, environmental*.

So, starting with concordance lines assembled by the class, this session stimulated a rich exploration of the meanings, uses and patterns associated with the word *as*, and, in addition, of many other features typical of that genre of text which had been captured by chance in the concordance lines.

None of these analysis activities requires much advance teacher preparation, since they are general enough to be valid for any text. Once a word has been identified for study, an initial look through a dictionary entry for the chosen word should be sufficient. Such sessions can always be supported by the use of dictionaries should queries arise or more examples be needed.

Summary of activities used

Assembling

- Learners identify lines containing the key word, and write them up (on the board, a wall poster or on an OHP transparency), with the key word in a central position. To save time, this can be prepared for homework.

Analysing

- Learners identify the boundaries of the phrases containing the key word.
- Learners classify the phrases according to their meaning or use, pattern or grammatical classes they appear to fit.
- Learners think of known examples parallel to those they have found and classified.

Extension and consolidation

- Learners use dictionaries to consolidate specific areas or uses of the key word (concentrating on the uses occurring in these lines) and share findings.
- Learners make a record of useful phrases and examples in their own notebooks.
- Learners look at other features that happen to occur in the concordance lines, look for more examples in the original text, and record examples of any useful items.

This first sample session has illustrated some very general, open analysis activities that can be done with any text and with minimal teacher guidance. The next sample session exemplifies some more specific analysis activities, based on categories of word meaning and use, identified in advance by the teacher, but with lines still assembled by the learners.

3.5.2 Sample session 2: common words in spontaneous spoken narrative

The activities in this session were based on hand-generated concordances assembled in advance by a class of 20 intermediate students who were completing a unit on an incident in an African game park. Recorded materials included an interview and a story about a family's encounter with a man-eating leopard which had been inadvertently released back into the game park. I did a quick scan through the transcripts to find ten words that all occurred quite frequently. These were: *at, had, I, in, of, one, so, that/that's, this, what/what's.* They were all fairly high on the spoken frequency list – most were above the 50 level.

Students had followed two or three task-based cycles, which entailed listening several times to the story and interview in order to complete the various tasks successfully. I then assigned each of the selected words to two students, and for homework they were asked to read through the transcripts again, searching for examples of the word assigned to them. They wrote out the concordance lines for their word on an OHP transparency and gave these to me a day ahead of the next class.

This allowed time for me to devise different kinds of consciousness-raising activities. With some words, for example *one*, I used a dictionary to help identify and describe useful categories. I actually wrote the instructions on the bottom of each OHP transparency, which I then photocopied for future use. Activities for three of the ten sets of concordances are illustrated in Figures 3.4, 3.5 and 3.6.

- In Figure 3.4 look at the verb phrases containing the word *I*. Can you divide them into two categories: those which actually tell the story and advance the action (e.g. *I got out of bed*), and those which do not (e.g. *I think*)? Try to find ways to classify the verbs in the second group.
- In Figure 3.5 find four examples of *this* which probably refer to the leopard.
- Look at the four other phrases with *this*. Which two refer to the time of the actual story and which two refer to the discourse itself (i.e. not the actual story)?
- Choose three phrases with *this* that you think you might find useful. Tell each other.

Figure 3.4

> son. He was just, on, I think about one at the time
>   And we er– I forget exactly where we went
> This is an important detail. I have to make it clear.
> first night we were there as I describe we went to
>   easily scared away. So, I got out of bed,
>   and   the   roof! So I lit a hurricane lamp
> as the animal came by, I switched the hurricane
> And er eventually and I don't exaggerate

Figure 3.5

> But erm – on **this** occasion er, we went to Tsavo
> connect with the ceiling. **This** is an important detail. I have
>   maybe kill – In fact **this** tig – this leopard that erm, we
>   In fact – this tig – **this** leopard that erm, we escaped
>   I don't exaggerate at **this** point – it started looking in at the
> How old was your son at **this** time? He was just one.
>   So, **this** one already had its er –
> And in the case of **this** one it had been kept in Nairobi

Figure 3.6

> Oh, I think about **one** at the time.
> Er. So eventually ... **One** of my plans
> just a bit less than **one**: Er. So
> we were in danger. **One** of my plans
> management, you know, if **one** area hasn't got enough
> and they mixed up **one** that had misbehaved
> they thought it was just **one** that they were
> they were moving from **one** area to another
> so this **one** already had its
> In the case of this **one**, it had been kept

- In Figure 3.6 find two examples where *one* probably refers to the son's age.
- Find four or five examples where *one* means one of two (or more).
- Find four cases where *one* refers to the leopard.
- Find four phrases where the word *one* is definitely part of a larger chunk.
- Which words do you think typically come after *one*? (There are two here.)
- In which single example could the word *one* be made plural (*ones*)?

The class did each set of activities quite quickly, in pairs, and discussed each set as a class before moving on to the next one. They wrote down any useful phrases and insights gained for each word. In the case of the first two sets, from *I* and *this*, we all gained several insights into the nature of spontaneous narrative – there is a lot of talk which is not directly telling the story, but relates to the discourse itself, for example emphasising a point (*I don't exaggerate at this point*) or expressing vagueness (*I forget exactly where*). The focus on *so* also drew attention to the way in which phases in the narrative can be signalled, as well as to the meaning of other uses of *so*. For this, a translation activity can work well: 'What word/s do you have for each use of *so* in your language?'

Many useful common lexical phrases were identified and practised: *in the case of this one*; *I have to make it clear that* ...; phrases with *of* such as *and all the rest of it*. Focusing on *in*, learners identified several 'new' phrases: *in an attempt to* ..., *in the (mistaken) belief that* ... . Some useful phrases occurred in more than one set of concordances and so were highlighted several times.

Summary of benefits of language analysis activities

From samples 1 and 2 we have seen that by working with concordance lines focusing on frequent words, learners can:

- become aware of the potential different meanings and uses of common words;
- identify useful phrases and typical collocations they might use themselves;
- gain insights into the structure and nature of both written and spoken discourse;
- become aware that certain language features are more typical of some kinds of text than others.

Some people think that this kind of activity is not practicable with elementary learners or near beginners. But it must always be useful to encourage learners to look critically at language, whatever their level. And it is quite possible to devise activities which enable beginners to do this, as the next section demonstrates.

3.5.3 Sample session 3: real beginners – a focus on *that*

As beginners will inevitably have a much more limited experience of English, the pedagogic corpus of texts and transcripts will initially be much smaller, and the texts and recordings shorter and briefer. But these will still contain a high proportion of common words. Beginners need to build up a deployable repertoire of useful words and phrases. Some of these can initially be memorised as fixed chunks – phrases they simply learn by heart without breaking them down grammatically. But noticing the part that common words play in such phrases will begin to give learners insights into the way the language works, and help them to see how to generate their own chunks for themselves (see Batstone 1994, N. Ellis 2003, Skehan 1994.)

Instead of asking beginners to write out complete concordance lines (which may introduce too many additional and possibly distracting features), learners can simply identify and list the chunks or phrases they find containing the key word.

In this early lesson with real beginners, learners first completed a teacher-led task brainstorming English words that were commonly used in their country (e.g. *football, hotel, disco*). They then heard a recording of four native speakers listing words of English that they thought would be understood internationally. Learners listened several times, identifying words they recognised, comparing the two lists of words, and then added more words to their own lists. Finally for the language focus activities they read the transcript of the task recording, firstly underlining all the 'international' words, and secondly circling all the phrases with the word *that*. These included:

Taxi? Oh yes, that's a good one.

Picnic. What about that?

Oh yes, that's a good one.

How about that?

Ah, we've done that one!

We've got that, sorry.

Got that!

That's a good one, yes!

Olympics? That's Greek!

Because the learners had completed a parallel task, they had probably heard or tried to express similar meanings themselves, so the meanings of these phrases were all fairly clear from the context. Having identified and practised pronouncing the phrases, learners were asked to classify them; for example, phrases starting with *that*, and phrases ending with *that* or *that one*. Some learners preferred to group the ones with similar words or patterns together, as shown in Figure 3.7.

The final classification is actually less important than the thought processes leading up to it, which involve learners in examining language, looking for patterns and trying to systematise what they find.

The phrases with *that* are all common phrases and useful for classroom communication, too. Initially they may well be learned and used as prefabricated chunks, much in the same way as people acquire language naturally (N. Ellis 2003). Teachers can show learners how to build new phrases from these patterns: *Pizza? That's Italian!* or *That's an interesting one.* Many phrases will be naturally recycled later, when the focus falls on another common word, such as *got* or *one*.

Figure 3.7

How about that.	We've done that one.	Oh Yes, that's a good one.
What about that.	We've got that.	That's a good one, yes.
	Got that	

3.5.4 Sample session 4: remedial beginners – a focus on the preposition *in*

This class of weak remedial beginners had completed several tasks about where they lived, and had read three short illustrated extracts from the *Guinness Book of Records* about the largest, the smallest and the most expensive houses in the world. After the reading task learners were asked to read the texts again and write the phrases with the word *in*. The analysis activity was 'Which phrases with *in* refer to place and which to time? Are there any phrases left over?' Note that this three-way classification activity (place, time and other) will work with any preposition.

The examples found in the texts being examined included:

Biltmore House in Asheville, USA

built in 1890

the most expensive house in the world

in 1922

a cottage in North Wales

built in the 19th century

the smallest house in Great Britain

In this first set of examples all the uses of *in* were either place or time. However, to give a broader picture of *in*, learners then were asked to look at examples from earlier texts and task-recording transcripts and to classify these:

Bridget lives in a small top floor flat in London

In fact there are more men in your family

Which room were these people in?

Come in!

Do you know the names of the letters in English?

Do this in groups.

In the second set of phrases, it can be deduced that *in* can also be used with groups of people, languages and fixed phrases such as *in fact*. It is also interesting for learners to note the examples of the adverbial use of *in* such as *Will you join in? Hand your books in* where *in* ends a sentence (this is rare in most other languages).

There is no reason why this kind of language analysis activity, with categories given, cannot be achieved with younger learners who can read. Children can be asked to find phrases with *in* in familiar story books and read them out or make a list, and then decide if they refer to place or time or something else. The teacher can begin by finding and reading out an example from each story just to get them started. The calling out and repetition of the phrases is useful practice; the process of classifying them helps learners to recognise typical patterns and memorise them.

This session exemplifies how one can begin an analysis activity using texts from the current lesson, and then go back over familiar texts used in previous lessons, both spoken and written. This search for more examples gives a broader picture of the uses of the common word and has the added advantage of recycling earlier texts. In other words, it is making full use of the pedagogic corpus so far covered by the learners, and is something that cannot be achieved working from a computer-generated corpus.

3.5.5 Sample session 5: revision activities based on course materials – intermediate learners

Here are two ways of using texts that learners have already covered and of encouraging learners to review and reread them.

Select the same number of common words as you have students in the class. Divide them up amongst the class, giving one word to each student, or two words to each pair of students. Ask students to assemble (on an OHP transparency if possible) concordance lines for their word from the texts and transcripts used so far that term.

Students then try to become experts for that word and other features found in its concordances, and set an analysis activity for the class to do in the next lesson. (These could all be written on sheets to be passed around or put on display round the walls.)

Alternatively, students display the concordance lines with a gap instead of the central word, for the class to guess the missing word.

Try the one in Figure 3.8 – the lines are taken from a well-known Intermediate textbook. Cover up the lines with a sheet of paper and then read them one by one. How many lines do you have to read before you are sure of what the missing word is? This works well if the lines are ordered so as to make this as difficult as possible – it makes learners think hard about what is typical and what is less common.

Here we find a greater number of uses of the target word than in the activity described in session 1, perhaps because these are taken from a wider variety of texts.

Figure 3.8

```
        I suddenly thought of it — eating an animal
           easier to imagine them — whole animals
    that's because I see rabbits — pets
                  It seems to me — if they can't make up their minds
           I want a kitten — I'd like its purring
                     It's not — if the animals are tortured or anything
  imitating meat which is nearly — bad as having the real thing
      Saturday I buy some cheese — a treat
                him to the funeral. — they went along the road, they passed
from a button phobia for as long — she could remember
    green leafy vegetables such — spinach, cabbage or lettuce
         cutting down on food such — hamburgers and sausages
```

In the same way, students can prepare their own test items. Groups of students (each with concordance lines for their assigned word) select a set of three or four cloze items to donate to a 'test item bank' kept by the teacher, who can select from the items to assemble a class test. This gives learners a sense of responsibility, as well as motivation to revise and reread, thereby gaining a deeper experience of language. For both the above activities the whole of the pedagogic corpus covered so far can be used.

3.6 Summary of types of concordance-based sessions

In the above section I have described five classroom sessions based on the analysis of concordance lines, focusing initially on one of the very common words of English. The words were all chosen by the teacher, but the students themselves were asked to find examples of phrases containing that word and, in all but one case, to write them up as concordance lines.

In session 1 the concordance lines were assembled in the session itself, and the analysis activities were carried out by students with relatively little teacher guidance.

In session 2 the students assembled the concordance lines in advance, allowing time for the teacher to investigate the concordances they had produced, and to set specific analysis activities for each word, based on given categories of the use of that particular word.

In session 3 the beginners listed phrases with *that* from the transcript of a spontaneous task recording, practised pronouncing these phrases, and tried two ways of classifying them.

In session 4 remedial beginners identified and classified phrases with *in* using categories generalisable to all prepositions (time, place, other). They worked first from the texts being studied at that time, and then went back to consider earlier examples from the textbook. In other words, they made full use of the examples that had already occurred in their pedagogic corpus.

We finally looked at gapped concordance lines taken from the course-book texts and recordings, prepared in advance by learners for an inter-mediate revision lesson. This gave us a slightly different picture of the word *as* from the one gained in the first sample session, which focused on *as* in an agricultural text. This shows that focusing on the same common word for a second (or even third) time but using different data will still give us many new insights into the use of that word and its typical phrases, and could lead into the study of other features typical of that genre of text.

With experience, the techniques illustrated here can be applied to concordance lines from any text, although specific language questions will vary according to the range of meanings, uses and patterns of the actual word being focused on.

3.7 Enhancing the process

This section looks at how the process of generating and exploiting hand-assembled concordances can be organised, systematised and varied.

3.7.1 Selecting words for concordancing

- Once you become familiar with your frequency lists, you will find it easier to scan a text and pick out suitable words. You will probably find that words from the top 50 or so frequency band are generally the most fruitful, but look out for others from the list too.
- If you are teaching ESP, try to find frequency lists for your special-ist area.
- Try to cover as many of the frequent words as you can; some words can be focused on several times, with different types of text, and learners can still make new discoveries.
- Keep a record (for each class you teach) of words covered, together with the meanings and uses of those words. The best way to do this is to print or copy out your frequency list, well spaced, and use it as a checklist; adding beside each word the meanings and patterns of that word and the date that you covered each one. By doing this you are, in fact, building up a *post hoc* lexical syllabus and ensuring balanced coverage – as it is easier to identify the gaps.

- Keep copies of the concordances and activities to use with other classes working with the same pedagogic corpus. You can also use them to develop test items.

If you can gain access to a computer and corpus software, for example AntConc, AWL Highlighter, WebCONC, WebConcordancer, WordSmith tools (for details see Chapter 2 Appendix), you can input your own pedagogic corpora. (Learners can be asked to help with this.) Look out for concordancing programs which also identify frequent phrases (e.g. 'n-grams' of 2–6 words). The concordancer can generate a word frequency list for each text or group of texts, so you can use that, together with its concordancing facility, to help you select words or phrases from those texts for students to focus on. Alternatively, you can simply print out the concordances for the class to analyse and classify.

3.7.2 Varying the focus and process

You can vary:

- the number of words you focus on in a session;
- the number of texts you investigate each time: single current text, recently used texts or the whole pedagogic corpus covered to date;
- the type of text: spoken, written or both;
- the types of word focused on each time: (prepositions, conjunctive items, adverbs, etc.) or parts of words (*-ing, -ed, -ly, -s, -er, -est*);
- student groupings: for example, the whole class collecting one word (from different texts), or groups responsible for different words, or on a rota basis, with each student responsible for a different word each week;
- method of display: 'word-sheets' round the walls – one for each word, to be added to (categories can be built up) as more texts are covered, or OHP transparencies with overlays presented to the class;
- timing: assembling concordances in a lesson or in advance of the lesson;
- the analysis activities set on the concordances: general or specific (see sessions 1 and 2 above) with or without given categories. (For more types of consciousness-raising activities see Willis 1990, 2003);
- extension and consolidation: with/without reference to dictionaries and grammars; students can be encouraged to build up their own phrase books or dictionaries, and/or to look for more examples in their outside reading or in other contacts with the language;
- testing activities: for example, blanking out common words in mixed sets of concordance lines from familiar texts; lines chosen by student or teacher or picked at random from an item bank built up by the class.

3.8 From pedagogic corpus to a balanced syllabus

It is essential that the data forming your learners' pedagogic corpus constitutes a representative sample of the language they will be using in their target discourse communities, in 'real life' situations. If the language of some of the texts and recordings from the class coursebook is over-simplified or unnatural (e.g. written to illustrate the use of one particular grammar structure), you should consider omitting these and supplementing your coursebook with reading texts and listening materials of a more authentic nature from other sources to balance your pedagogic corpus.

But how can teachers selecting supplementary materials ensure that these, together with appropriate coursebook texts and recordings, will offer a thorough and balanced coverage of the language features, words, meanings, patterns and uses their students need? How can materials writers ensure that their coursebook materials do offer a representative sample of language? If, say, you are assembling a general course on spoken English, how can you ensure that the recordings you use offer a balanced sample of spoken English?

A pedagogic corpus is inevitably quite small and needs to be selected in a principled manner. If, for example, you are teaching general English, you should ensure that there is not an overdue emphasis on planned, edited spoken monologue (e.g. radio documentary, rehearsed interviews) or purely transactional talk. There is a danger of including too much data of this kind (often because it is more easily accessible) at the expense of spontaneous spoken interaction, where turn-taking and topic-shifting is free and relatively unpredictable (see Chapter 4 in this book by Ronald Carter, Rebecca Hughes and Michael McCarthy).

Ideally what is needed is information derived from a larger research corpus, one that is representative of the type of language the learners will be needing. A large corpus (whether spoken or written, general or specialist) can give us information about the frequency of word forms and their typical patterns and uses. Armed with a checklist derived from a larger corpus, we can then aim to collect a pedagogic corpus which reflects these patterns and uses – a language 'microcosm'. If the pedagogic corpus can then be put on to a computer and analysed, the frequency lists can be compared, and typical examples of, say, the most frequent 2,000–3,000 words (as identified by the research corpus) can be selected from its concordances. If words or uses of words are found to be missing, we can try to select additional recordings/texts or design exercises that aim to fill the gaps. It is impossible to achieve a 100 per cent match between the pedagogic corpus and the research corpus, but a principled approach to corpus design is more likely to cover the language that students need than an approach which selects texts and language focus points in a more random fashion. See Willis and Willis (2007: 187–98) for more on the syllabus design process.

It is impossible for most language teachers and course designers to assemble their own research corpus for a particular group of learners, unless the learners' target discourse is a very narrow, well-defined area which is readily researchable. But there is a growing range of more specialist language corpora with frequency lists already assembled (see Chapter 2 Appendix for sources) and over the next few years more will be made available for public use. It is, however, possible to aim at assembling the learners' own pedagogic corpus, that is, one that reflects as far as possible their target language needs, even without the insights gained from a computational analysis of a research corpus.

The most frequent words, meanings and patterns are obviously going to be the most useful for learners and give the most efficient coverage of the target discourse. But in addition to the criterion of frequency, we need to take into account factors such as learnability and learners' immediate interests. Thus the syllabus might well include words that are similar in the two languages, and words from topic areas and types of text (e.g. sport, pop songs, magazine pieces) that students find motivating. Such texts would then become part of the pedagogic corpus, and would undoubtedly also serve to illustrate more common uses of common words.

To further increase their vocabulary and to extend their experience of language, individual learners should always be encouraged to read (and listen) more widely on their own, and to look out for more examples of specific features from outside data, but since this will be part of the individual learner's corpus, and unfamiliar to other learners, it would not form part of the pedagogic corpus available for concordance analysis.

3.9 Conclusion

I have attempted to show in this chapter that, even without access to an appropriate research corpus or computers of any kind, using hand-generated concordances to focus on common words can provide a wealth of effective learning opportunities for our learners. Even with the small samples of concordance lines illustrated here, learners would, for example, gain insights into the nature of academic text and spoken narrative – all useful for students wishing to write or to speak with more fluency and naturalness.

A full-length lexical syllabus derived from a suitable research corpus might comprise an inventory of, say, 2,000–3,000 words and their meanings and patterns. This could be used as a checklist, and would allow the teacher or materials writer to gain a far more reliable coverage of language that learners needed. But this is the ideal, and without computational facilities, it would take a long time to find and assemble suitable examples of all these words from the materials selected for the pedagogic corpus.

The benefits of focusing on a mere 50 or so very common words may at first sight have seemed somewhat limited in scope. However, because these words occur so frequently in all kinds of text and have so many different uses, they provide the cement for a huge number of fixed and semi-fixed expressions and grammatical patterns. Using these common words as 'bait', learners are likely to catch a wide variety of other useful words, phrases and patterns, and will inevitably gain insights into new aspects of the target language as exemplified by their pedagogic corpus.

The analysis activities encourage learners to process text more closely, to systematise their knowledge and to look out for similar examples in their own reading outside class. Once attention has been drawn to the meanings, uses and functions of common words in the target language, learners are more likely to notice and reflect on further occurrences of the language items that have been made salient through study of the concordances. This process should lead to the development of the learner's interlanguage. Analysis activities and awareness-raising procedures can also encourage learner independence and efficient dictionary use (especially with regard to the common words that students often think they know already and do not bother to look up). They help learners to recognise the parts played by collocation and lexical phrases and to realise there is more to language than just vocabulary and grammar.

Working directly from the data, searching for patterns, investigating and describing what is actually there, is a secure and relatively unthreatening activity. It is ideal for mixed-level classes since, being a learner-centred activity, it allows students to work at their own level, in their own time and in their own ways. It also provides solid benefits for teachers. I have constantly found that language analysis activities inform and enrich my own view of the language. Not only learners but also teachers are likely to gain from an investigative approach to language.

References

Batstone, R. 1994. 'Product and process: grammar in the second language classroom'. In M. Bygate, A. Tonkyn and E. Williams (eds.), *Grammar and the Language Teacher*. Hemel Hempstead: Prentice Hall International.

Ellis, N. 2003. 'Constructions, chunking, and connectionism: the emergence of second language structure'. In C. Doughty and M. Long (eds.), *The Handbook of Second Language Acquisition*. Oxford: Blackwell.

Ellis, R. 1991. *Second Language Acquisition and Second Language Pedagogy*. Avon: Multilingual Matters.

2003. *Task-based Language Teaching and Learning*. Oxford:Oxford University Press.

Johns, T. 1991. 'Should you be persuaded – two samples of data-driven learning materials'. In T. Johns and P. King (eds.), *Classroom Concordancing*, ELR Journal 4. CELS: University of Birmingham.

2002. 'Data-driven learning: the perpetual challenge'. In B. Kettemann and G. Marko (eds.), *Teaching and Learning by Doing Corpus Analysis*. Amsterdam and New York: Rodopi.

Mauranen, A. 2004. 'Spoken – general: spoken corpus for an ordinary learner'. In J. Sinclair (ed.), *How to Use Corpora in Language Teaching*. Amsterdam: John Benjamins.

O'Keeffe, A., M. McCarthy and R. Carter. 2007. *From Corpus to Classroom*. Cambridge: Cambridge University Press.

Römer, U. 2006. 'Pedagogical applications of corpora: some reflections on the current scope and a wish list for future developments'. *Zeitschrift für Anglistik und Amerikanistik*, 54(2): 121–34, available at www.uteroemer.com/ZAA 2006 Ute Roemer.pdf

Schmidt, R. 1990. 'The role of consciousness in second language learning'. *Applied Linguistics*, 11(2): 129–58.

Sinclair, J. (ed.). 2004. *How to Use Corpora in Language Teaching*. Amsterdam: John Benjamins.

Skehan, P. 1994. 'Interlanguage development and task-based learning'. In M. Bygate, A. Tonkyn and E. Williams (eds.), *Grammar and the Language Teacher*. Hemel Hempstead: Prentice Hall International.

Willis, D. 1990. *The Lexical Syllabus*. Collins Cobuild. Out of print but available free on www.cels.bham.ac.uk/resources/LexSyll.shtml

2003. *Rules, Patterns and Words: Grammar and Lexis in English Language Teaching*. Cambridge: Cambridge University Press.

Willis, D. and J. Willis. 1996. 'Consciousness-raising activities in the language classroom'. In J. Willis and D. Willis (eds.), *Challenge and Change in Language Teaching*. Oxford: Heinemann ELT. Now available on the authors' website: www.willis-elt.co.uk/books.html

2007. *Doing Task-based Teaching*. Oxford: Oxford University Press.

Appendix A: Wordlists from a general research corpus

Table 3.1 *The 150 most frequent word forms occurring in The* COBUILD *Bank of English **written** corpus of 196 million words*

#	word	count	#	word	count	#	word	count
1	the	11,110,235	51	out	398,444	101	world	170,293
2	of	5,116,374	52	about	393,279	102	get	168,694
3	to	4,871,692	53	so	378,358	103	these	168,486
4	and	4,574,340	54	can	369,280	104	how	167,461
5	a	4,264,651	55	what	359,467	105	down	166,119
6	in	3,609,229	56	no	342,846	106	being	165,168
7	that	1,942,449	57	its	333,261	107	before	165,119
8	is	1,826,742	58	new	324,639	108	much	164,217
9	for	1,716,788	59	two	308,310	109	where	161,691
10	it	1,641,524	60	mr	302,507	110	made	161,595
11	was	1,395,706	61	than	297,385	111	should	159,023
12	on	1,354,064	62	time	293,404	112	off	155,770
13	with	1,262,756	63	some	293,394	113	make	153,978
14	he	1,260,066	64	into	290,931	114	good	153,878
15	I	1,233,584	65	people	289,131	115	still	151,889
16	as	1,096,506	66	now	287,096	116	're	151,359
17	be	1,030,953	67	after	280,710	117	such	150,812
18	at	1,022,321	68	them	279,678	118	day	150,684
19	by	980,610	69	year	272,250	119	know	147,052
20	but	884,610	70	over	266,404	120	through	145,920
21	are	880,318	71	first	265,772	121	say	143,888
22	have	879,595	72	only	260,177	122	president	143,502
23	from	872,792	73	him	259,962	123	don't	142,288
24	his	849,494	74	like	258,874	124	those	142,260
25	you	819,187	75	do	256,863	125	see	141,845
26	they	779,636	76	could	255,010	126	think	140,701
27	this	771,211	77	other	254,620	127	old	140,096
28	not	704,615	78	my	253,585	128	go	137,929
29	has	693,238	79	last	238,932	129	between	137,009
30	had	648,205	80	also	236,350	130	against	136,989
31	an	629,155	81	just	232,389	131	did	135,593
32	we	552,869	82	your	227,200	132	work	131,780
33	will	542,649	83	years	217,074	133	take	131,212
34	said	534,522	84	then	214,274	134	man	130,580
35	their	527,987	85	most	208,894	135	pounds	130,095
36	or	527,919	86	me	206,475	136	too	129,804
37	one	522,291	87	may	198,700	137	long	127,660
38	which	513,286	88	because	196,595	138	own	125,299
39	there	501,951	89	says	193,730	139	life	124,047
40	been	496,696	90	very	189,285	140	going	124,018
41	were	485,024	91	well	188,445	141	today	123,869
42	who	480,651	92	our	186,013	142	right	121,995
43	all	478,695	93	government	184,618	143	home	121,052
44	she	469,709	94	back	184,105	144	week	119,115
45	her	448,175	95	us	182,796	145	here	118,177
46	would	430,566	96	any	180,222	146	another	116,325
47	up	428,457	97	even	178,657	147	while	115,963
48	more	422,111	98	many	173,938	148	under	113,114
49	when	404,674	99	three	173,093	149	London	112,310
50	if	401,086	100	way	172,787	150	million	112,138

Table 3.2   *The 150 most frequent word forms occurring in The COBUILD Bank of English* **spoken** *corpus of 196 million words*

1	the	500,843	51	are	51,775	101	okay	18,757
2	I	463,445	52	got	51,727	102	much	18,567
3	and	367,221	53	don't	51,273	103	didn't	18,521
4	you	359,144	54	oh	51,013	104	thing	18,480
5	it	313,032	55	then	44,372	105	lot	18,453
6	to	308,438	56	were	41,453	106	where	18,440
7	that	284,422	57	had	41,185	107	something	18,134
8	a	273,009	58	very	41,128	108	way	17,895
9	of	242,811	59	she	38,841	109	here	17,819
10	in	187,523	60	get	38,361	110	quite	17,470
11	er	178,464	61	my	38,194	111	come	17,089
12	yeah	155,259	62	people	37,774	112	their	16,892
13	they	135,084	63	when	37,335	113	down	16,678
14	was	133,022	64	because	37,172	114	back	16,505
15	erm	132,836	65	would	35,945	115	has	16,017
16	we	124,928	66	up	35,894	116	place	15,888
17	mm	122,674	67	them	34,766	117	bit	15,520
18	is	113,420	68	go	34,127	118	used	15,267
19	know	111,741	69	now	33,801	119	only	15,159
20	but	100,648	70	from	33,633	120	into	15,094
21	so	91,836	71	really	33,444	121	these	15,064
22	what	89,364	72	your	33,310	122	three	15,059
23	there	88,938	73	me	33,278	123	work	15,005
24	on	88,456	74	going	32,598	124	will	14,939
25	yes	87,211	75	out	32,015	125	her	14,286
26	have	84,294	76	sort	31,555	126	him	14,160
27	he	79,137	77	been	30,405	127	his	14,029
28	for	77,842	78	which	30,334	128	doing	13,921
29	do	77,207	79	see	30,325	129	first	13,273
30	well	75,287	80	did	30,175	130	than	12,998
31	think	74,543	81	say	29,720	131	went	12,842
32	right	74,191	82	two	28,817	132	put	12,692
33	be	66,492	83	an	27,485	133	why	12,653
34	this	65,424	84	who	27,220	134	our	12,610
35	like	63,948	85	how	26,837	135	years	12,437
36	've	63,160	86	some	26,172	136	off	12,393
37	at	62,654	87	name	26,029	137	those	12,248
38	with	61,289	88	time	25,990	138	us	12,245
39	no	60,885	89	'll	25,154	139	course	12,211
40	as	58,871	90	more	24,586	140	mhm	12,112
41	mean	58,825	91	said	23,143	141	isn't	12,060
42	all	58,360	92	'cos	22,345	142	over	11,874
43	're	57,131	93	things	21,982	143	look	11,297
44	or	56,857	94	actually	21,131	144	done	11,247
45	if	56,774	95	good	20,783	145	year	11,224
46	about	56,321	96	other	20,378	146	take	11,190
47	not	56,109	97	want	20,375	147	being	11,153
48	just	55,329	98	by	20,260	148	should	11,007
49	one	55,189	99	could	19,435	149	school	11,001
50	can	53,090	100	any	18,958	150	thought	10,786

Appendix B

This table shows what proportion of general English text is covered by the most frequent word forms. By word forms I mean that *have, has, had*, and so on, and singular and plural nouns, for example, each count as a separate item.

Table 3.3

The most common 25 word forms account for 29% of written text and 29% of spoken text

50	36%	36%
100	42%	46%
500	56%	66%

(Source: Cobuild Bank of English: figures based on a written corpus of 196 million words and a corpus of unscripted speech of 15 million words.)

4 Telling tails: grammar, the spoken language and materials development

Ronald Carter, Rebecca Hughes and Michael McCarthy

4.1 Introduction

Descriptions of the English language, and of English grammar in particular, have been largely based on written sources and on written examples. This is inevitable since examples of written English are easier to obtain. One consequence of this situation is, however, that 'correct grammar' has come to mean 'correct grammar as represented by the written language' and that many perfectly normal and regularly occurring utterances made by standard English speakers (of whatever variety – not just standard British English) have by omission come to be classified as 'ungrammatical'.

The situation is changing, however, and a number of corpora of spoken English have now been assembled which have allowed more precise description of the properties of spoken English, thus enabling learners of English to become more aware of a wider range of forms and structures than hitherto. With reference to one such corpus this chapter seeks to outline ongoing work in the description of spoken English and to discuss some of the implications for English language teaching, and in particular materials development.

The corpus which will be referred to, the CANCODE corpus, is part of the one-billion-word Cambridge International Corpus (CIC) developed by Cambridge University Press between 1995 and 2010. The CANCODE corpus was developed between 1995 and 2002 as part of a joint research project between the University of Nottingham and Cambridge University Press (CANCODE stands for **C**ambridge **a**nd **N**ottingham **C**orpus of **D**iscourse in **E**nglish). The CANCODE corpus totals five million words, which is, as far as spoken corpora go, a large corpus – although it is still small compared with many written corpora where 100 million words is a not uncommon size. The main aim, however, was always to construct a qualitative corpus and not simply a large quantitative corpus (for a fuller account of its structure and organisation, see McCarthy 1998). The way the CANCODE corpus is constructed allows very precise contextualised description of grammar, in particular, and its design allows a discourse-based view of language to prevail in descriptions (see Hughes and McCarthy 1998; McCarthy and Carter 1994). A contextualised description of grammar means that when a particular form is described, due account is taken of typical contexts of use: for example, differences between 'going to' and 'will' relate to strength of prediction but are also different speaker choices according to interpersonal and social-context-sensitive factors such as the formality of the situation. The Cambridge and Nottingham research teams set out to collect a corpus which shows grammar at work beyond sentence-based contexts of written language and formal spoken contexts such as broadcast talk; its emphasis on grammatical choice according to different communicative contexts was also designed from the outset to make it of potential use to language teachers and learners.

4.2 Authentic vs. scripted dialogues

When naturally occurring language is compared with language constructed for the purposes of language teaching, marked differences can be observed. Here are two examples, drawn in fact from Australian English data:

Text 1: scripted text from a textbook
Making a doctor's appointment
(telephone rings)

Patient:	*Could I make an appointment to see the doctor please?*
Receptionist:	*Certainly, who do you usually see?*
Patient:	*Dr Cullen.*
Receptionist:	*I'm sorry but Dr Cullen has got patients all day. Would Dr Maley do?*
Patient:	*Sure.*
Receptionist:	*OK then. When would you like to come?*
Patient:	*Could I come at four o'clock?*
Receptionist:	*Four o'clock? Fine. Could I have your name, please?*

(Nunan and Lockwood 1991)

Text 2: authentic text
Confirming an appointment with the doctor

Receptionist:	*Doctor's rooms, can you hold the line for a moment?*
Patient:	*Yes.*
Receptionist:	*(pause) Thanks.*
Receptionist:	*Hello.*
Patient:	*Hello.*

Receptionist: *Sorry to keep you waiting.*
Patient: *That's all right um I'm just calling to confirm an appointment with Dr X for the first of October.*
Receptionist: *Oh ...*
Patient: *Because it was so far in advance I was told to.*
Receptionist: *I see what you mean, to see if she's going to be in that day.*
Patient: *That's right.*
Receptionist: *Oh we may not know yet.*
Patient: *Oh I see.*
Receptionist: *First of October ... Edith ... yes.*
Patient: *Yes.*
Receptionist: *There she is OK you made one. What's your name?*
Patient: *At nine fift...*
Receptionist: *Got it got it.*

(Burns, Joyce and Gollin 1996)

There are a number of general observations which can be made about the second text which marks it off as naturally occurring discourse. For example, in Text 2 speakers interrupt each other and speak at the same time. There are 'unpredicted' sequences such as the opening exchange in which the patient is asked to hold the line as well as content-less words (*oh*) which serve to indicate surprise or incomprehension. There are also interactive phrases which oil the wheels of the conversation rather than contribute any specific content or propositions (*oh I see*; *I see what you mean*). A number of the utterances are incomplete or are completed by the other speaker. And the conversation is terminated without the usual ritualistically polite closing strategies found in much textbook discourse.

By contrast, the language of the coursebook represents a more 'can do' society in which interaction is generally smooth and trouble-free; the speakers cooperate with each other politely; the conversation is neat, tidy and predictable; utterances are almost as complete as sentences and no one interrupts anyone else or speaks at the same time as anyone else. The two texts therefore represent different orders of reality. The scripted text is easier to comprehend but is unlikely to be reproduced in actual contexts of use; the unscripted text is real English but more difficult to comprehend and to produce, and therefore likely to be considered less appropriate pedagogically. Pedagogical issues are clearly central and it is of course not our wish in any way to imply criticism of the coursebook material, which is in any case only an extract from a much broader pedagogically rich sequence of material sensitively keyed to learning requirements at a particular stage in language development.

Issues of pedagogy and naturalness in language will be considered towards the end of this chapter as they are clearly of major importance for English language teaching. It is first necessary to illustrate some features of language and of grammar in particular which a corpus of spoken English reveals and which therefore may be of relevance for syllabus content. The features mentioned in this chapter are selected from a much more comprehensive inventory, further examples of which are given in Carter and McCarthy (2001 and 2006) and McCarthy and Carter (1997). One grammatical feature in particular is given especial consideration as it is our view that the most challenging issues for teaching, learning and materials development can be best illustrated by putting a key feature under a descriptive and pedagogic microscope.

4.3 What is a tail? *(That's just stupid, that)*

'Tail' structures are selected here because they are a prominent feature of the CANCODE corpus and because they are generally not adequately treated in conventional descriptive grammars of English, including some of the most comprehensive grammars of the English language. Tails are almost exclusive to the spoken language, and where they do occur in written English, they are selected in order to give that written text a markedly spoken character. Such forms present, therefore, a particular challenge to the materials designer wishing to provide teachers and learners with an opportunity to encounter a key feature of spoken language in use.

4.3.1 Tails: basic examples

Tails are an important feature of a listener-sensitive, affective grammar and occur frequently in informal contexts of language use (see a range of discussions of tails: Aijmer 1989; Biber *et al.* 1999: 957; Carter and McCarthy 1995; Timmis 2010). Tails allow speakers to express attitudes, to add emphasis, to evaluate and to provide repetition for listeners; and all the examples below (the tails are in **bold**) involve some kind of emphatic recapitulation, either by means of a pronoun or a clarifying noun (plus auxiliaries) or determiner plus noun or pronoun, and can even involve verbatim repetition (examples in this section are drawn from CANCODE and personal data):

He's a real problem **Jeff**

It's too hot for me **Singapore**

She's got a nice personality **Jenny has**

I'm going to have burger and chips **I am**

It can make you feel very weak **it can flu**

It was good **that book**

It's a really good film **that one**

Tails, we repeat, are not extensively treated or explicated in traditional grammars, not least because tails only rarely occur in written examples. Quirk *et al.* (1985: 1362; 1417) refer to such features but do not offer detailed treatment; Halliday (2004) provides only a more detailed discussion of 'tags' in relation to word order.

From the examples of tails above it will be seen that tails perform an essentially recapitulatory function (often necessarily so, as tails are not infrequent in unplanned discourse) and they ensure a cohesion which in pre-planned discourse can normally be effectively constructed. Tails are listener-sensitive in so far as they provide orientation and emphasis for the listener, in particular, by means of a clarifying noun, verb phrase or anaphoric pronoun. A tail can also sometimes be especially emphatic in its clarification by combining repetition of both a noun and an accompanying main or auxiliary verb:

It can make you feel very weak **it can flu**

He's a real problem **is Jeff**

She never complains, **Sue doesn't**

Tails are one element in what might be described as an *interpersonal* grammar. The 'tails' component of such a grammar serves an interpersonal function that is listener-sensitive in so far as the listener gets a clarified and 'expanded' message. But, additionally and more importantly, the speaker attempts to involve the listener by an expression of feelings and attitude. The emphasis is personal and affective and also includes some kind of positive or negative evaluation or signalling of stance towards the main proposition contained in the utterance. And it is worth underlining here that tails are not some kind of aberrant, non-standard, regional dialect form; they occur extensively in the standard English dialect and are used, as confirmed in the CANCODE corpus, by a wide range of speakers irrespective of gender, region, age or any other social or geographical factors and can be found in other languages too (see Weinert 2007 for examples from German and Spanish). If we are to allow language learners greater choice in the expression of feelings and attitudes and to help their interlocutors relate to such expressions, then tails will need to be appropriately embedded within language coursebook dialogues and, ideally, dealt with in a broader pedagogical framework which, especially in the case of more advanced students, involves greater exposure to authentic spoken discourse (see Gilmore 2007, Mishan 2004, for a review of issues relating to authenticity in language learning, teaching and materials development).

4.4 Grammar patterns and grammar as choice: some questions

From the examples of tails assembled above, it may appear that tails are relatively straightforward to analyse and articulate as structural rules. As grammatical forms, embedded within single sentences or utterances, it is not difficult to point to patterns which are ungrammatical. For example:

Jenny's a good swimmer she is

*Jenny's a good swimmer she's

She's a good swimmer Jenny is

*She's a good swimmer, Jenny's

?Jenny's a good swimmer Jenny

from which we may deduce that tails cannot be constructed from contracted forms, and that full noun head subject repetition (without an auxiliary) is not normal.

However, moving beyond structure and towards interpersonal values what are the communicative differences and distinctions between the following, well-formed, tails? Thus:

She's a good swimmer Jenny is

She's a good swimmer is Jenny

She's a good swimmer Jenny

Are these distinct choices for learners or are the subtleties sufficiently delicate for them to be discounted in a discourse grammar operating at, say, upper-intermediate levels of proficiency?

To what extent are tails available to us as **choices** and what kinds of choices are provided by tails in grammar? Clearly, tails enable us to mark an utterance as overtly spoken and interactive but it is more problematic to understand the precise nature of the choice between the following examples. Or are such choices simply between written and spoken modes of English?

It's too hot for me, Singapore

Singapore is too hot for me.

Such considerations also move us beyond the boundaries of the single 'sentence' in so far as the precise communicative value of each utterance cannot be properly assessed without the evidence supplied by a more extended, surrounding text, for the functions of tails may depend to a considerable extent on where they occur in a conversational sequence. It may be relevant, therefore, to explore tails and, where feasible, to supply learning guidance in respect of tails in extended discourse environments; it is otherwise possible (wrongly) to conclude that tails can be used indiscriminately in every utterance in a sequence. Such a phenomenon would be unusual because it is difficult to envisage a sustained conversation in which every proposition (rather than only selected propositions) were emphatically recapitulated, evaluated or overtly flagged for stance. In the case of narratives, it is difficult to envisage that any tale in which tails were selected to emphasise every event would be judged to be especially telling. Telling tales means drawing attention to key events of the fictional or represented world, foregrounding and highlighting them for the listener within the overall narrative structure. In teaching these forms, it would be essential to begin introduction of them beyond the sentence, therefore, but for the learner also to understand the structural constraints outlined at the start of this section. As noted, these structural constraints are relatively straightforward to articulate as rules; the delicate matter of choosing when to use them is more complex. It is here that some of the key issues around proficiency level, structure and a discourse-oriented grammar syllabus lie.

4.5 Sample materials

If we accept that 'tails' are a normal rather than a deviant feature of spoken grammar (to repeat: our corpus data confirms that tails are distributed across a range of different contexts) and if we accept that learners ought to be introduced to tails as an expressive resource and be guided in their choices of whether, how and in what ways to use tails, then teaching materials will need to address such conditions.

The examples in Figure 4.1 are drawn from extracts of a unit developed in 1997–8 for a 'discourse' grammar of English (now published as Carter, Hughes and McCarthy 2000, *Exploring Grammar in Context: Upper-intermediate and Advanced*), designed in particular with reference to the principle of grammatical choice and constructed in order to introduce to learners and give them practice in the comprehension and communicative use of spoken grammar, including such forms as tails.

Figure 4.1

UNIT 21: TAILS (post-posed elements of clauses)

A Introduction

1. Look at these extracts from conversations.

    - Contractions such as *he'd*, *it's*, *I'll* make the extracts informal. Mark any other words or phrases which make the conversations informal.

    - Which of the extracts (a)–(d) is the most formal? Rewrite it to make it sound more informal.

a) A: Did Max help you?

    B: Yes, he moved all my books.

    A: He said he'd try and help out.

    B: He was very helpful, Max was.

b) A: It's not a good wine, that.

    B: I'll still try some.

    A: Where's your glass?

c) A: What are you going to have?

    B: I can't decide.

    A: I'm going to have a burger with chilli sauce, I am.

    B: It's a speciality here, chilli sauce is.

d) A: That's a very nice road.

    B: It runs right across the moors.

    A: Then it goes through all those lovely little villages.

    B: Yes, the villages are beautiful.

2. Which of these sentences is more likely to be used in formal situations and which is more likely to be used in informal situations? (Remember that in informal situations it is often difficult to plan and prepare what to say and therefore to make things clear for your listener.)

    Mark each sentence in the pair (F) formal or (I) informal.

i)   (a)   Gandhi was a great leader.

      (b)   He was a great leader, Gandhi was.

ii)   (a)   He smokes too much, David does.

      (b)   David smokes too much.

iii) (a)   It's very nice, that road.

      (b)   That road is very nice.

iv)   (a)   You're always getting it wrong, you are.

      (b)   You're always getting it wrong.

v)   (a)   I'm a bit lacking in confidence, I am.

      (b)   I am a bit lacking in confidence.

vi)   (a)   Hong Kong is an exciting place.

      (b)   It's an exciting place, Hong Kong is.

vii) (a)   They're not cheap, those clothes aren't.

      (b)   Those clothes aren't cheap.

(cont.)

Figure 4.1 (cont.)

viii) (a) That's a very nice beer, Fortuna is.

      (b) Fortuna is a very nice beer.

Answers and Commentary

1. a) **Max was** b) **that** c) **I am; chilli sauce is**

Conversation d) is the most formal. A suggested more informal version is:

A: It's a very nice road that.

B: It runs right across the moors, it does.

A: Then it goes through all those lovely little villages.

B: Yes, they're beautiful, the villages are.

2. i) (a) F (b) I;   ii) (a) I (b) F;   iii) (a) I (b) F;

    iv) (a) I (b) F;   v) (a) I (b) F;   vi) (a) F (b) I;

    vii) (a) I (b) F;   viii) (a) I (b) F

- In conversation we often want to give emphasis to statements. Tails can help us to do this. Tails are single words or phrases which occur at the end of a clause and extend what has already been said. A tail often consists of a phrase which extends a pronoun or demonstrative; it normally occurs as a complete phrase even though the subject phrase which is put at the front of the clause may be contracted, e.g. **It's** an exciting place, **Hong Kong is**).

- Notice that tails often occur in statements in which the speaker is evaluating things and saying positive or negative things. You get tails in sentences in which there are words like **exciting**, **very nice**, **great**, **too much**, or **a bit lacking**.

B Discovering Patterns of Use

1. Nouns and pronouns in tails

    Look at the following conversations.

- What do you observe about the order of words in the tails?

- How do they compare with tag questions, e.g. *She does, doesn't she?* in (d)?

a) A: Did David make it on time?

    B: No, he was late. He was very cross, David.

b) A: She's a very good tennis player, is Hiroko.

    B: I know. She always beats me easily.

c) A: Did Max help you?

    B: Yes, he was very helpful, was Max.

d) A: Have you heard her sing?

    B: Yes, she sings beautifully, Laura does.

    A: She does, doesn't she?

e) A: Have you been to Singapore?

    B: Yes, but it's far too hot for me, Singapore.

    A: It's not just hot, it's humid as well.

(cont.)

Figure 4.1 (*cont.*)

2. Position and order of tails

Now look at the following sentences. The sentences are all typical spoken sentences.

The tails here are repetitions or occur with question tags.

- What do you observe about the position and order of the tails?

a) I went there early. It would be about seven o'clock, it would. It wasn't dark yet.

ii) It's difficult to eat isn't it, spaghetti? You have to suck it into your mouth.

iii) It'll melt, won't it, the ice-cream?

iv) She's a good tennis player, Hiroko is, isn't she?

v) You hardly ever show emotion, you don't. Don't you have any feelings for her?

vi) She still hasn't finished, hasn't Maria.

C Observations about tails

- Many tails consist of a noun or pronoun and a verb. A tail often extends a pronoun or noun or demonstrative which has occurred earlier in the clause. In a tail the noun can either follow or precede the verb (e.g. *He was very helpful, Max was*; or *He was very helpful, was Max*; *She still hasn't finished, hasn't Maria*; or *She still hasn't finished, Maria hasn't*).

- When a pronoun comes first in a clause and the tail is formed with a noun then the noun normally makes the comment stronger e.g. *He was a great leader, Gandhi was*.

- The noun can also be used as a tail on its own (e.g. *He was very helpful, Max*; *It's an exciting place, Hong Kong*).

- When pronouns occur in tails the word order of the preceding phrase is repeated; otherwise the sentence may be heard as a question e.g. 'You're stupid, you are', You're stupid are you?; 'It would take about half-an-hour, it would', It would take about half-an-hour would it?.

- Tails can occur with tag questions and can be placed either before or after the tag (e.g. *She's a good player, Hiroko is, isn't she?*, *It's not easy to eat, is it, spaghetti?*).

- When the tail repeats a verb which is not a verb 'to be' or an auxiliary/modal verb then a *do* verb is used (e.g. 'She sings very well, she does'; 'They complain all the time, they do').

- Tails always agree with the phrase to which they refer (e.g. 'It's not a good wine, that isn't'; 'She'll never pass the exam, won't Toni'). Negative adverbs such as *hardly, scarcely,* etc. normally keep a negative tail (e.g. 'He scarcely speaks, he doesn't').

D Follow-up and further exercises

- Rewrite the following dialogues to make them sound a little more informal.

a) A: Here's the menu. What do you fancy?

B: It's certainly a nice menu.

A: I'm going to have steak and chips.

B: I fancy the spaghetti but I always manage to drop it down the front of my shirt.

(*cont.*)

Figure 4.1   (cont.)

b)   A: I like them. David and Jean make a nice couple.

   B: Do you reckon they'll get married eventually?

   A: David is still lacking in confidence, I suppose, and Jean is a bit too young at the moment isn't she?

c)   A: Sophie will never lose weight.

   B: She hardly ever eats cakes or chips.

   A: I should eat less. I'm far too flabby.

- Re-tell this narrative, adding tails where appropriate.

It was late at night and typically, the last bus had gone. So I decided to walk home. I was really cross with Jeff. He'd left the party early because he had to be up early for work the next day. Anyway, as I walked along our road, I heard a car behind me. It was really dark. I became very frightened and started to run. A man got out of the car and started to follow me. I ran more quickly and then he began to run more quickly too. By the time I reached our house he had caught up with me. I turned round.
It was Jeff. He'd come after me to apologise ...

- Rewrite these sentences so that the tail is the clear subject of the sentence.

a)   It never occurred to me, the danger I was in. (The danger I was in never occurred to me.)

b)   That was the book I wanted, the one with the picture on the front.

c)   It was a strange feeling, walking into that place.

d)   They're far too hot, those countries where it's all humid.

4.6 Evaluating materials for spoken grammar teaching

The above draft materials were trialled (before publication as Carter, Hughes and McCarthy 2000: see Unit 21: 147–52 for the finalised version) in different parts of the world by teachers and by upper-intermediate/advanced students of English. Amongst the questions we considered, which ranged from matters of unit design and progression to broader issues of appropriate pedagogy, were the following:

(i)   To what extent is it appropriate for students to undertake pattern practice tasks in writing of forms which are almost exclusively spoken in their contexts of use?

(ii) Should tape recordings or CD-ROM support not be integral since intonation and rhythm are essential in the appropriate communicative and interactive delivery of tails?

(iii) The expectations of students and their teachers are that grammar is a sentence-based phenomenon. To what extent should materials conform to such expectations, for both pedagogic and possibly commercial reasons, or should expectations be gradually modified? Indeed, if a genuinely discourse grammar is to be taught, then texts should displace sentences, for it is only in extended stretches of language, especially stretches of spoken language in the case of tails, that the communicative value of particular forms are realised in the language, and can be processed, understood and used in different ways by learners. How far can materials go in the introduction of more extended texts?

What are the limits of tolerance both on teacher and learner expectations, and, more materially, on page design, length and economy of presentation in a grammar textbook? (In the published material we adopted a relatively conservative approach by including a significant proportion of sentence-based examples.)

(iv) What is an appropriate pedagogy for spoken grammar? What are appropriate demands for practice and production? Should greater emphasis be placed on receptive awareness of the forms in advance of production? Should production be required of learners at all? If so, can production be claimed to be faithfully taught until we know more about the phonology, intonation and communicative meanings of the grammatical patterns? What and how much about tails do we teach and what are the most appropriate and effective ways to do it?

(v) To what extent do materials writers remain faithful to their corpus? If they seek to reproduce undilutedly authentic texts, then the following, more complex examples of tails (and their accompanying lexis) will also qualify for classroom treatment:

'It can lie dormant for years *it can* though apparently *shingles*'

'... cos otherwise they tend to go cold, don't they, *pasta*'

where tails (italicised) cluster with tags, hedging and modalising items (*though, apparently*).

Our position in 2000 was to maintain a realistic pedagogic position, introducing and exposing students to authentic language wherever possible whilst recognising that there are dangers in not balancing spoken and written English and in not selecting examples which can be processed by students without undue cognitive or cultural difficulty. Our position in 2010 is one of even stronger advocacy of corpus-informed materials for the classroom, but still one of careful selection of language data according to pedagogic judgements of learner need (see also Hughes 2010a: Chapter 3 and Hughes 2010b). For example, more advanced learners in an ESL situation are more likely to need to produce naturalistic spoken grammar; other learners in EFL contexts less so. But in the case of all learners our view remains even more firmly that not to provide opportunities for exposure to authentic language use is to take away choices from both teachers and learners.

4.7 Language awareness and consciousness-raising

Research in the field of second language acquisition and development has pointed to some advantages in procedures which **raise learners' consciousness** of particular grammatical forms. Such research takes place against a background of communicative language teaching methodology which in a concern for greater fluency has focused on the learner's use of language (rather than on the learner's conscious ability). Communicative teaching, in spite of numerous pedagogic advantages, has not encouraged in students habits of observation, noticing or conscious exploration of grammatical forms and functions, and the relevant SLA research has sought to some extent to examine the consequences of a (somewhat) rebalanced methodology.

Research so far (see Ellis *et al.* 2009 for a typical example) reaches the following tentative conclusions in respect of fostering enhanced grammatical consciousness-raising in the EFL/ESL classroom:

(i)   Rather than simply receiving direct instruction, properly sequenced, controlled, conscious attention to target structures is shown to have positive results in terms of students' eventual acquisition of the structures, especially if students are helped to discover such structures for themselves.

(ii) Learning can be more effective if learners are required to process the structure without having automatically to produce it; too precipitous an invitation to production is shown to be unhelpful.

(iii) Activities should be sequenced so that students first respond to the meaning of the structure through content-based tasks, then are sufficiently encouraged to raise their consciousness to **notice** the form and function of the target structure and then finally engage in some kind of error identification activity (preferably of identifiable learner errors) where incorrect or inappropriate versions of the key structure are presented.

(iv) There is some evidence concerning the benefits of an emphasis on encouragement to students to use their own interpretive skills during the content-based tasks so that there is some initial, personalised purchase on the target structure and its general meanings.

We have already advocated (Carter and McCarthy 1995; McCarthy and Carter 1995; see also Jones 2007), in respect of spoken grammar teaching, that traditional PPP (presentation–practice–production) methodologies should be replaced by III (illustration–interaction–induction) alternatives and it is interesting to note the correspondences between this advocacy and conclusions reached in SLA research.

There are other reasons, furthermore, why an approach to spoken grammar through language awareness/consciousness-raising activities should be seriously considered and why such an advocacy may be particularly appropriate.

Work in spoken grammar is still in the early stages both of development and of systematic formal identification and description. It is likely, too, that research into grammatical choice will present some areas of grammar, not in terms of yes/no alternatives or categorical imperatives, but rather in terms of co-occurrence probabilities (see Conrad 2010 for examples). That is, learners will acquire an understanding that particular forms belong in some spoken rather than in written contexts of use and that their selection will entail a more interactive, interpersonal and affective orientation. They will learn that certain areas of grammar are probabilistically appropriate rather than absolutely or deterministically correct; that where the selection of an utterance such as a tail may be an appropriate choice, the option will still remain to select a more formal, less interpersonally orientated alternative.

It will be seen from the presentation of the above draft discourse grammar material devoted to tails that one of our main pedagogic approaches is to encourage in learners habits of observation and to help them to use such observation in the comprehension and formulation of rules for the use of forms. We would argue that interaction with the data and the induction of rules is best fostered by the largely discovery-based procedures adopted in the unit. We continue to remain more hesitant in respect of the following:

(i) Interface with the task-based approach and student motivation: the extent to which the 'illustration' is successful and produces appropriate, motivating responses in the learner.

(ii) Interface between structural **rules** and contextual choices: the extent to which it is proper to talk in terms of rules when it is more appropriate, in the case of such areas of grammar, to introduce understanding of **tendencies, variable rules** and **choices** according to context and interpersonal relations; additionally, the extent to which such notions would be unsettling to teachers and learners alike because of their unfamiliarity.

(iii) Interface between the expectations of the classroom and commercial publication and authentic speech data: the extent to which the illustrative data can and should be modified for purposes of classroom language learning or left unmodified in the raw forms in which it is collected, transcribed and stored in the corpus.

4.8 The sting in the tail: modifying the authentic

One question raised in the previous section merits separate treatment in this chapter since it bears upon the use of authentic speech data in materials produced for the language classroom. The essential pedagogic question is faced by any materials writer with access to a corpus of naturally occurring data and with a commitment to using such data for the purposes of teaching and learning (see Conrad 2000; McCarthy 2008). The basic issue was polarised above when authentic and specifically scripted dialogues were juxtaposed. It seems from such comparison that learners can benefit from exposure to dialogues which are artificially constructed for learning purposes; however, learners should not be prevented from accessing the kinds of authentic data from real conversational discourse collected as part of the CANCODE project and other similar corpora.

As a further illustration of the issues involved, here is a sample of data from the CANCODE corpus selected to illustrate tails in use but subsequently not used in the coursebook *Exploring Grammar in Context* (Carter, Hughes and McCarthy 2000). **A** is telling **B** what route he took in his car to get to **B's** house. Both **A** and **B** engage in a kind of phatic exchange, commenting on and reinforcing each other's comments on the journey in a friendly, informal and suitably interactive, interpersonal style. Repeated tails figure prominently in the exchange:

A: *And I came over Mistham by the reservoirs, nice it was.*
B: *Oh, by Mistham, over the top, nice run.*
A: *Colours are pleasant, aren't they?*
B: *Yeah.*
A: *Nice run, that.*

On initial inspection the repetition of certain items by the speakers may well serve a pedagogically reinforcing purpose, but closer inspection reveals problems of both presentation and preparation. For example: is the final tone group in line 1 (*nice it was*) a tail or is it an example of 'fronting' of the complement *nice* within its own clause – a not uncommon strategy. If the string **nice it was** is in fact a tail, then the structure has to be read as an ellipted structure which in its more complete form would be **it was nice it was**, thus paralleling the ellipted (**it was a**) **nice run that** in the final line, where we have a less ambiguous example of a tail. Pedagogically, it could be argued that the co-presence of potential ellipses complicates pedagogic exposure to the basic tail structure. The exchange as a whole is characterised by a pervasive ellipsis. Ellipsis is, of course, a core feature of the grammar of affective interpersonal exchanges (Carter and McCarthy 2006: 177–205), but to what extent might the presence of ellipsis distract attention from the target structure of **tails**, even though it is to be expected that naturalistic data will contain **clusterings** of features endemic to spoken grammar? Real data does not neatly demarcate structures for attention; it is untidy.

Lexically, too, there is the additional problem that the speakers A and B create a discourse world of reference which is similarly undifferentiated. 'Mistham' (a place) could be a distracter; the word 'reservoir' may not be known and could need glossing; the word 'run' is used in a frequent spoken sense of 'trip' or 'journey' but may be known to learners only as a verb; and the use of the preposition 'over' in the sense of 'across high ground from one place to another' possibly needs separate explanation.

One conclusion that we have reached in the preparation of discourse grammar materials is that a middle ground between authentic and concocted data sometimes needs to be occupied which involves **modelling** some data on authentic patterns (McCarthy and Carter 1994: 197–8). (As our editor, Brian Tomlinson, notes, there is also the alternative of keeping the samples authentic but only using those instances which do not present insurmountable pedagogic problems. If such instances cannot be found in the corpus, it would suggest that the selected feature might not be particularly salient or could be postponed until later in the course.)

Here is an example of a possible remodelling of the data above:

A: *And I came over by the village of Mistham. It was nice it was.*
B: *Oh you came over the top by Mistham. That's a nice journey.*
A: *The colours are pleasant at this time of year, aren't they?*
B: *Yes.*
A: *It was a nice run that.*

In terms of materials development the attempt here is to achieve clarity, tidiness and organisation for purposes of illustration, but at the same time to ensure that the dialogue is structured more authentically and naturalistically by modelling on real corpus-based English. It remains to be seen whether this is a weak compromise or a viable strategy.

It also raises the question of how extensive such modelling should be in materials and how such practices should be balanced against the use of completely authentic materials. (Our editor, Brian Tomlinson, has also commented to us that ellipsis could easily be left in the above modelled data since it is a common feature of such phatic communication and only rarely causes learners any problems in comprehension.) The differences and distinctions between **corpus-informed** and **corpus-driven** materials are useful here, with the category of **corpus-driven** suggesting a full adherence to the evidence of the corpus and the former **corpus-informed** category suggesting that some modification, manipulation and careful choice on the part of the materials writer should be preferred.

McCarthy, McCarten and Sandiford have worked with many of these issues and have produced an extensive and highly successful coursebook based on a corpus-informed view of materials that nonetheless remains committed to a view of spoken language and spoken grammar as central to its aims (see McCarthy, McCarten and Sandiford 2005a and b; 2006a and b). See also the discussion in O'Keeffe, McCarthy and Carter (2007); and for an up-to-date account of theory and practice in the teaching of spoken discourse, see Hughes (2008; 2010a).

4.9 Heads or tails: towards an interpersonal grammar for learners

Tails occur, as we have seen, at the end of clauses. Heads occur at the beginning of clauses. Here are some representative examples drawn from the Nottingham corpus:

The women, they all shouted.

That chap over there, he said it was OK.

That house on the corner, is that where they live?

This friend of ours, her daughter, Carol, she bought one.

Robert, this friend of mine I work with, his son was involved in a car crash just like that.

Heads (or headers as we refer to them in Carter and McCarthy 2006: 192–4 to avoid possible overlap with the term phrase head) perform a basically orienting and focusing function, serving to include information which speakers consider relevant to their listeners and attempting to do so economically, even if in some heads the information is quite densely packed. Often by means of a specific reference to people and places, heads also work to establish a framework of knowledge,

knowledge which can subsequently be assumed to be shared, so that listeners can respond to questions or to statements without first having to disambiguate or to seek clarification. Heads are also, in a traditional sense, grammatically anomalous, in that they are in a very indeterminate structural relationship with the item they prefigure in the upcoming clause.

Heads orient the listener to what is to follow and function to organise and structure the message before its main content is communicated; tails are a little more directly interpersonal in function since they provide a more personal, attitudinal or evaluative stance towards the message after its main ideational content has been communicated. Heads can of course include attitudinal matter (e.g. that **awful** house on the corner, is that where they live?), but the **main** purpose remains one of providing orientation.

Learning how to select and use heads and tails is an important component in competence in the spoken language, and observing and reacting appropriately to them is an important component in active listening and an appropriate response to much spoken discourse. Learning how to form and to use tails and heads is an important part of learning how to establish and maintain interpersonal relationships in and through language.

Description of grammar in more interpersonal terms represents, therefore, a challenge for research in discourse grammar; an applied linguistic goal would be to help learners to know and to understand the choices available to them when communicating in speech and in writing, both more formally or more informally and more or less interpersonally. In spite of considerable progress in the past ten years work on spoken grammar remains, however, at formative stages and it is important to recognise that it will be some time before description can match the degree and delicacy of work based on written sources, which has an extensive and centuries-old tradition of scholarly analysis to support it. For example, further data-based explanation is needed before a more precise description of differences in communicative value can be given between the following utterances:

She's a nice girl, Jenny.

She's a nice girl is Jenny.

She's a nice girl, Jenny is.

Nice girl, Jenny.

Jenny's a nice girl.

That girl Jenny, she's nice.

Description will need to take account of evaluation, emphasis, formality and listener discourse knowledge and will additionally require some explanatory context-building which goes beyond the confines and limits of a sentence into the formation of meanings across speaking turns. For the present we simply argue for the provenance of heads and tails and that learners should learn how to observe them in context, learn how to infer rules for their use and gradually learn how to produce them with general communicative intent. (Carter, Hughes and McCarthy (2000) contains a unit – Unit 22 pp: 153–60 – devoted to 'heads'.)

4.10 Rules, probabilities, choices and the hegemony of the native speaker

It is both misleading and disturbing to learners of English to suggest that grammar is simply a matter of choices. Grammatical rules exist; they have been extensively codified and form the core in the structure of the language, both spoken and written. Rules exist, for example, that prescribe in Standard British English that a plural subject has to be followed by a plural form of the verb and it is simply and unequivocally incorrect for us to write or say, therefore, that 'the buildings is very high'. Within a central core choices are not possible.

As we have seen, however, there are areas of meaning which are selected within the grammar. The choice of a correctly formed active or a correctly formed passive allows, for example, different forms of representation to be communicated and there is an extensive literature, particularly within the tradition of systemic-functional linguistics, devoted to grammar and language as choice (e.g. Halliday 2004). Within the domain of spoken grammar we have also seen that, rather than absolute rules for certain choices, it may be more accurate to speak in terms of probabilistic or variable patterns.

It can be argued that the pedagogic provision in the EFL/ESL classroom of variable, probabilistic rules is a preoccupation rooted in native-speaker modelling of target language learning. Do non-native speaking learners want to or even need to have such options? Why should they want to acquire the expressive resources of a native speaker when most communication undertaken in English as a lingua franca (ELF) is often claimed to be primarily utilitarian in orientation, and interpersonal choices may not need to extend much beyond a range of ritualistic politeness formulae? The concern for spoken grammar on the part of native-speaker pedagogues could simply be dismissed as an extension of native-speaker hegemony in English language teaching and learning contexts which undermines the position of non-native speaker teachers who, whilst expert speakers of the language, are less likely to be familiar with all the subtle, value-laden and culture-embedded nuances of native speaker communication (see Kirkpatrick 2007 and Jenkins 2007 for fuller discussion of such questions).

A counter-argument to this position may be simply to say that teachers and learners can always choose not to learn those areas of language where rules are more probabilistic than determinate, but that they have no choice at all if such options are not made available. Learners should not be disempowered and syllabuses should not be deliberately impoverished. Learning a language should also, in part at least, involve developing something of a 'feel' for that language. The folk-linguistic term 'feel' has been around for many years in language teaching, but it has remained a largely unanalysed concept. Learners who concentrate on the more rule-bound and referential domains are unlikely to develop that kind of sensitivity, personal response and affect which probably underlie 'feel' and which go some way to helping them discover, understand and begin to internalise the expressive as well as the referential resources of a language. The case for extending work on spoken grammar in particular and spoken discourse in general as an enabling procedure necessary for what in the future of videophones and video conferencing will be an even more central feature of international communication through English has been explored in numerous recent discussions (for example, Cullen and Kuo 2007; Jones 2007; Mumford 2008; Prodromou 2008).

4.11 Conclusions

The following conclusions might be drawn from current explorations into the description for pedagogic purposes of spoken English:

(i) The development of such work is in its initial stages.
(ii) A description of features of language is not the same as the pedagogic classroom presentation of those features. Concocted, made-up language can be perfectly viable, but classroom language may also be modelled on naturalistic samples and, to differing degrees, according to judgements of learner need.
(iii) A discourse-based view of grammar underlines the importance of grammatical choices; particularly in the domain of spoken grammar it is better, therefore, to work with the notion of regularities and patterns rather than with absolute and invariable rules.

(iv) Learners need to be helped to understand the idea of variable patterns. Classroom activities should therefore encourage greater language awareness and grammatical consciousness-raising on the part of the learner and try to stimulate an investigative approach so that learners learn how to observe tendencies and probabilities for themselves.

(v) As argued by Timmis (2002), we should not lose sight of learners' own feelings, aspirations and motivations which involve, as Timmis illustrates, finding ways of making their voices heard. Timmis does not underestimate the complexities but he underlines the extent to which learners and teachers can aspire to speak like native speakers.

(vi) And, finally, ideological factors cannot and should not be left in the background. Most spoken corpora constructed so far are based on the discourse of native speakers. Do teachers want to teach and do learners want to learn native speaker English? Is the native speaker the most appropriate paradigm? Is it unrealistic to expect non-native speakers to be able to or even want to express feelings, attitudes, interpersonal sensitivity in the target language? And indeed the term 'native speaker' in itself is not without problems of definition (see some eloquent arguments by Prodromou (2003; 2008) for the use of the term SUE – successful user of English – as a preferable term). In this regard it is important that corpora become extended to include greater international representativeness and data involving interaction between non-native speakers; without such a dimension it may be difficult in future to defend exclusively British or American English native-speaker-based corpora against charges of narrow parochialism.

References

Aijmer, K. 1989. 'Themes and tails: the discourse functions of dislocated elements'. *Nordic Journal of Linguistics*, 12: 137–54.

Biber, D., S. Johansson, G. Leech, S. Conrad, E. Finegan. 1999. *Longman Grammar of Spoken and Written English*. Harlow: Pearson Education.

Burns, A., H. Joyce and S. Gollin. 1996. *'I See What You Mean'. Using Spoken Discourse in the Classroom. A Handbook for Teachers*. Sydney: National Centre for English Language Teaching and Research.

Carter, R. A. and M. J. McCarthy. 1995. 'Grammar and the spoken language'. *Applied Linguistics*, 16(2): 141–58.

2001. 'Ten criteria for a spoken grammar'. In E. Hinkel and S. Fotos (eds.), *New Perspectives on Grammar Teaching in Second Language Classrooms*. Mahwah, NJ: Lawrence Erlbaum.

2006. *Cambridge Grammar of English: A Comprehensive Guide to Spoken and Written English Grammar and Usage.* Cambridge: Cambridge University Press.

Carter, R. A., R. Hughes and M. J. McCarthy. 2000. *Exploring Grammar in Context: Upper-intermediate and Advanced.* Cambridge: Cambridge University Press.

Conrad, S. 2000. 'Will corpus linguistics revolutionize grammar teaching in the 21st Century?' *TESOL Quarterly,* 34(3): 48–60.

2010. 'What can a corpus tell us about grammar?' In A. O'Keeffe and M. J. McCarthy (eds.), *The Routledge Handbook of Corpus Linguistics.* Abingdon and New York: Routledge.

Cullen, R. and V. I-Chun Kuo. 2007. 'Spoken grammar and ELT course materials: a missing link?' *TESOL Quarterly,* 41(2): 361–86.

Ellis, R *et al.* 2009. *Implicit and Explicit Knowledge in Second Language Learning, Testing and Teaching.* Avon: Multilingual Matters.

Gilmore, A. 2007. 'Authentic materials and authenticity in foreign language learning'. *Language Teaching,* 40: 97–118.

Halliday, M. A. K. 2004. *Introduction to Functional Grammar,* 3rd edn. London: Arnold.

Hughes, R. 2010a. *Teaching and Researching Speaking,* 2nd edn. Harlow: Pearson Education.

2010b. 'What can a corpus tell us about grammar teaching materials?' In A. O'Keeffe and M. J. McCarthy (eds.), *The Routledge Handbook of Corpus Linguistics.* Abingdon and New York: Routledge.

(ed.). 2008. *Spoken English, TESOL and Applied Linguistics: Challenges for Theory and Practice.* Basingstoke: Palgrave Macmillan.

Hughes, R. and M. J. McCarthy. 1998. 'From sentence to discourse: discourse grammar and English language teaching'. *TESOL Quarterly,* 32: 263–87.

Jenkins, J. 2007. *English as a Lingua Franca: Attitude and Identity.* Oxford: Oxford University Press.

Jones, C. 2007. 'Teaching spoken grammar: is noticing the best option?' *Modern English Teacher,* 16(4): 55–60.

Kirkpatrick, A. 2007. *World Englishes: Implications for International Communication and English Language Teaching.* Cambridge: Cambridge University Press.

McCarthy, M. J. 1998. *Spoken Language and Applied Linguistics.* Cambridge: Cambridge University Press.

2008. 'Accessing and interpreting corpus information in the teacher education context'. *Language Teaching,* 41(4): 563–74.

McCarthy, M. J. and R. A. Carter. 1994. *Language as Discourse: Perspectives for Language Teaching.* London: Longman.

1995. 'Spoken grammar: what is it and how do we teach it?' *ELT Journal,* 49(3): 207–18.

1997. Grammar, tails and affect: constructing expressive choices in discourse'. *Text,* 17(3): 231–52.

McCarthy, M. J., J. McCarten and H. Sandiford. 2005a. *Touchstone. Student's Book 1*. Cambridge: Cambridge University Press.

2005b. *Touchstone. Student's Book 2*. Cambridge: Cambridge University Press.

2006a. *Touchstone. Student's Book 3*. Cambridge: Cambridge University Press.

2006b. *Touchstone. Student's Book 4*. Cambridge: Cambridge University Press.

Mishan, F. 2004. *Designing Authenticity into Language Learning Materials*. Bristol: Intellect.

Mumford, S. 2008. 'An analysis of spoken grammar: the case for production'. *ELT Journal*, 63(2): 137–44.

Nunan, D. and J. Lockwood. 1991. *The Australian English Course*. Cambridge: Cambridge University Press.

O'Keeffe, A., M. J. McCarthy and R. A. Carter. 2007. *From Corpus to Classroom: Language Use and Language Teaching*. Cambridge: Cambridge University Press.

Prodromou, L. 2003. 'In search of the successful user of English'. *Modern English Teacher*, 12(2): 5–14.

2008. *English as a Lingua Franca: A Corpus-based Analysis*. London: Continuum.

Quirk, R. *et al.* 1985. *A Comprehensive Grammar of the English Language*. Harlow: Longman.

Timmis, I. 2002. 'Native-speaker norms and international English: a classroom view'. *ELT Journal*, 56(3): 240–9.

2010. '"Tails" of Linguistic Survival'. *Applied Linguistics*, 31(3): 325–45.

Weinert, R. (ed.). 2007. *Spoken Language Pragmatics*. London: Continuum.

Comments on Part A

Brian Tomlinson

The basic message which comes across from the three chapters in Part A is that many L2 learners have been disadvantaged because, until very recently, textbooks have been typically based on idealised data about the language they are teaching. Some have taught a prescriptive model of how their authors think the learners should use the target language, many have been based on the authors' intuitions about how the target language is used, most have been informed by a model of the target language based on information from reference books rather than from actual data, and nearly all have taught learners to speak written grammar. None of this is too surprising, given that until very recently textbook writers had no access to comprehensive and representative data of authentic language use. They had to make use of reference books based on rules and constructed examples rather than on instances of language use. Or they based their books on their own abstract awareness of how they, as typical educated users of the language, expressed themselves in the target language. Such awareness was inevitably biased towards the norms of planned discourse (e.g. essays, lectures) as it is difficult to be aware of how we use language in unplanned discourse (e.g. spontaneous informal conversation) in which by definition we do not plan what to say and are not usually aware of exactly what we have said. So we had, for example, the ridiculous situation of writers insisting that learners use complete sentences in their conversations when the writers rarely did so themselves. Now we have no excuse. We have access to data which tells us how the target language is typically written and spoken and we know for a fact that language use is variable and depends on the context in which it is being used. We know that the grammar of the spoken language is distinctively different from that of the written language, that the degree of intimacy and of shared experience between the participants are crucial determinants of the lexis and the structures used in discourse, that all language use is subjective, attitudinal, purposeful and strategic, and that the purposes of a communication will exert a strong influence on the language which is actually used. In grammar books and textbook dialogues language use tends to be neutral and cooperative, and grammatical rules tend to be constant (or at best to be allowed a few exceptions). In real life language use tends to be biased and competitive and grammatical patterns are variable. This is something we have always known but have rarely acknowledged in coursebooks. Though a number of applied linguists have been advocating for a long time that learners themselves should be invited to make discoveries about how English is actually used from investigations of authentic texts (e.g. Bolitho *et al.* 2003; Bolitho and Tomlinson 2005; Tomlinson 1994, 2007, 2009, 2010).

A question frequently asked these days (and at least implied in all three chapters in this section) is how much of the reality of language use do learners really need to be faced with? It can be argued that pedagogic simplifications of real language use are necessary in order to protect the learner from the apparent chaos of reality and to provide the security of apparent order and systematicity. Learners need to start learning what is simple; learners need rules; learners need to get things right. But learners also need to be prepared for interaction in the real world. They need to be aware of the intentions as well as the meanings of the speakers and writers they interact with; and they need to be able to produce language which is not only accurate and appropriate but which is effective too. They need, therefore, materials which are designed to facilitate systematic progress but which at the same time provide them with encounters with the reality of target language use. In my experience, learners have no problem with this if they are first helped to reflect on the variability of grammatical patterns in their first language, if they are not duped at the beginner stage into thinking that the target language is consistently rule-bound and if they are helped to see how languages follow principles and develop patterns rather than obey rules.

All three chapters in this section argue persuasively for the need for language-learning materials to be informed by data from corpora of authentic language use; all three warn that it is not enough to present samples of the data to learners and hope that they learn from them; and all three consider a language awareness approach to be the most profitable way of helping learners to gain from exposure to the reality of language use. I would agree with all three points and would particularly endorse the value of helping learners to invest energy and attention in discovering patterns and tendencies for themselves from guided investigations of samples of authentic language. In my experience, learners can gain confidence and curiosity by making discoveries for themselves from the earliest stages of language learning. The awareness they gain can then make them more attentive to salient features of their input and this can facilitate language acquisition, increase confidence and self-esteem and help the learners to become more independent.

One very effective way of helping learners to make use of their language discoveries is to help them to write their own grammars of the target language. The teacher provides language awareness activities from which learners make generalised discoveries and then record them with illustrative authentic instances under pattern headings in a loose leaf folder (or better still in a computer document). The learners are encouraged to revise and develop their generalisations as they encounter further evidence during and outside the course and occasionally their developing grammars are monitored by the teacher. At the end of the course each learner has a grammar of the target language written by themselves which they can take away and develop, if they want to, from their post-course encounters with the language. Another way of getting learners to make use of their own discoveries is to get them to produce a text to achieve a particular purpose (e.g. a story to amuse children; a list of rules for players new to a game; spoken instructions for making a meal), get them to make discoveries from an equivalent authentic text and then get them to improve their own text by making use of the discoveries they have made (Tomlinson 2003).

To date, published language awareness materials have tended to use constructed examples to lead learners to discoveries about the grammatical and semantic systems of languages (e.g. Bolitho and Tomlinson 1995). Useful though these materials are in encouraging learner investment and facilitating learner discovery, there is a strong argument for the development of materials which help learners to develop pragmatic awareness (Tomlinson 1994) through critical analysis of authentic discourse, and in particular of the strategy use of the participants in the discourse. Learners need not only to know what the grammatical and lexical options are but also what strategies might be effective in what situations. Such strategic awareness activities can be devised for classroom use, but even more profitable can be activities which guide learners to make discoveries from real world exposure about how users of the target language achieve their intended effects. Such investigations for many learners would focus on how successful non-native speakers (or SUEs as Prodromou (2003) calls them) achieve intended effects.

The focus of Part A is on analysis of authentic language data, but it is very important that learners experience language in use as well as by investigating it. In other words, there should be times when their attention is on meaning and on their communicative role in an interaction rather than on the language being used. If there is no target language use in their environment, then they will need their teacher and/or materials to involve them in meaningful encounters with the target language in authentic use through extensive reading, listening and viewing, through accessing comprehensible input from the Internet and from encounters with proficient users of English. This is true for all learners but especially so for those many learners whose preferred learning style is experiential rather than analytic. Language awareness activities can be extremely valuable but they can never be sufficient.

References

Bolitho, R. and B. Tomlinson. 1995. *Discover English*, 2nd edn. Oxford: Heinemann.

2005. *Discover English*, 3rd edn. Oxford: Macmillan.

Bolitho, R., R. Carter, R. Hughes, R. Ivanic, H. Masuhara and B. Tomlinson. 2003. 'Ten questions about language awareness'. *ELT Journal*, 57(2): 251–9.

Prodromou, L. 2003. 'In search of the successful user of English', *Modern English Teacher*, 12(2): 5–14.

Tomlinson, B. 1994. 'Pragmatic awareness activities'. *Language Awareness*, 3(2 and 4): 119–29. Clevedon, Avon: Multilingual Matters.

2003. 'Developing principled frameworks for materials development'. In B. Tomlinson (ed.), *Developing Materials for Language Teaching*. London: Continuum.

2007. 'Using form focused discovery approaches'. In S. Fotos and H. Nassaji (eds.), *Form-Focused Instruction and Teacher Education: Studies in Honour of Rod Ellis*. Oxford: Oxford University Press.

2009. 'What do we actually do in English?' In J. Mukundan (ed.), *Readings on ELT Materials*. Petaling Jaya: Pearson Longman.

2010. 'Helping learners to fill the gaps in their learning'. In F. Mishan and A. Chambers (eds.), *Perspectives on Language Learning Materials Development*. Oxford: Peter Lang.

Part B   The process of materials writing

5 A framework for materials writing

David Jolly and Rod Bolitho

5.1 Introduction

In this chapter we offer the reader a practical idea of the different aspects of the process of materials writing by teachers for the classroom. This is achieved through case studies illustrating the process.

The starting point for this practical overview derives from the thoughts and feelings of those most involved with language materials: the comments below are the authentic voices of students and teachers of English as a foreign language. Each statement appears to have materials-writing implications.

5.1.1 Exercise

As you read through the remarks, you may like to cover the commentary beneath each one and make a brief note about what you feel the materials-writing implications to be, focusing both on the opinions expressed and the language used.

> I have noticed that the coursebook I use doesn't seem to deal with 'real' English.
> (Italian secondary school teacher)

> My demand is becoming a reporter of the English football and I need, so, much familiarity …
> (Danish upper-intermediate student on a full-time intensive course in a British school)

There are many sources of real English within language-learning publications but clearly our Italian teacher is working with materials, perhaps prescribed, that fail to employ authentic language or texts (see Chapter 4 by Ronald Carter, Rebecca Hughes and Michael McCarthy in this volume). She has thus identified a need for materials. Similarly, though in a different context, the second quote identified a need for new materials, particularly a variety of text-types for listening and reading, since there is no widely available book or set of materials known to the authors that caters for the precise needs of this Danish student.

> The textbook my institute has written says that you use 'please' and
> 'would' for simple requests and 'would you mind' for more polite requests.
> I have heard lots of other things such as 'could you possibly …'
> (Croatian evening institute teacher)

> I get very confused with all these noughts and zeros and nothings in
> your language …
> (Argentinian part-time student on a low intensity course in Britain)

The evening institute has identified a need for materials that practise making requests, but clearly the Croatian teacher feels that she does not know enough about the language of requests to teach it as effectively as she would like to do. Textbooks inevitably and necessarily make pedagogical selections of exponents used for specific language functions which do not suit all learners or satisfy all teachers. This teacher will have to engage in some linguistic **exploration** of the functional area of 'requests' in order to produce more informative materials for her classes. The implication of the word 'confusion' in the second quotation is that here, too, the materials-writing teacher will find it necessary to do some linguistic and semantic exploration before she attempts to respond to the Argentinian's request (see Chapter 3 in this volume by Jane Willis). Even the experienced native speaker would be hard-pressed to locate and contextualise spontaneously all the uses of 'nought', 'nil', 'nothing', 'love', 'zero', 'o', and so on.

> It's a very nice book and very lively, but in the section on 'Processes'
> for example all the exercises are about unusual things for our country.
> We are a hot country and also have many Muslims. The exercises are
> about snow, ice, cold mornings, water cisterns; writing and publishing
> EFL books and making wine. I can tell you I can't do making wine and
> smoking pot in my country!
> (Experienced school teacher from the Ivory Coast)

> Previous materials were not based on life in Brazil which is why I don't
> think they worked very well …
> (Brazilian teacher of English in school)

> Sir … what is opera?
> (Iraqi student in mixed nationality class using materials designed to
> practise reading narrative)

The implications of these three quotations are not linguistic; rather, they address the problem of appropriate **contextual realisation** for materials. For the teacher in the Ivory Coast, the materials offered on 'Processes' would be outside the cultural experience of his students (possibly even threatening) and thus effectively useless; conversely, for the Brazilian teacher, the choice of Brazilian settings and familiar mores would have clear advantages over distant foreign contexts as they are essentially more motivating. The quote from the Iraqi student suggests that complete unfamiliarity with the notion of opera is likely to reduce the efficacy of the reading exercises, but in this case the student is curious and likely to regard the material as strange and exotic rather than completely alien (see Alptekin 2002 on the desirability of localised cultural content and Widdowson 1996 on the issue of authenticity and context).

The following example is based on a unit in *Developing Strategies* by Brian Abbs and Ingrid Freebairn which deals with degrees of uncertainty. In it, the students are given an example of a man going shopping in a supermarket who, when he comes to pay, discovers he has lost his wallet. The students are asked to speculate on where he lost it.

Exercise 1 (Students in British language school classroom doing exercises in pairs as suggested; the focus here is on language *use* rather than on the *content* of the students' utterances)

PAIR 1   A: His wallet must have fallen down the trolley ...

             B: He must have forgotten it there ...

PAIR 2   C: Perhaps he left it on the shopping trolley...

             D: Perhaps he left it on the car...

             E: No, perhaps he drop it in the cleaner's ...

In the exercise illustrated above the students are asked to make statements about the relative likelihood of events given the information. However, since no basis for any one hypothesis is stronger than any other basis, students doing the exercise end up making correctly formed but random statements. In terms of recognising a need, exploring the language required to meet the need and finding a reasonable context for practice, this exercise may be said to pass muster; what has clearly failed is the **pedagogical realisation** of the materials; that is, if these materials were intended to provide meaningful practice whereby students would make statements of greater or less certainty, they clearly fail. Part of the materials writer's task must be to provide clear exercises and activities that somehow meet the need for the language-learning work that has been initially recognised. Some would say that this is the core of materials writing. Part of effective pedagogical realisation of materials is efficient and effective writing of instructions, including the proper use of metalanguage; poor instructions for use may waste a lot of valuable student time, as this example reveals:

> But Paola, I didn't intend you to copy out the whole text word for word – you should just have corrected the summary version …
> (British teacher to assiduous part-time intermediate Italian student using self-access listening materials)
>
> The layout of this book is just so crowded and it's sometimes difficult to find your way around, especially on double-page spreads; my students also find it confusing …
> (British teacher on an intensive language course in a British language school referring to a well-known and popular 'global' coursebook)
>
> This picture … is dog or is … funny animal …
> (Spanish student, using a teacher-made worksheet)

The **physical appearance and production** of materials is important both for motivation and for classroom effectiveness. Teachers engaged in writing materials need to develop the same care and attention to presentation that one would expect of good publishers, though the first quote reveals that even very good publishers also fall down on the job.

> I wish I could just write materials and not teach at all …
> (British teacher at a Technical School in the Middle East)

The implication of this remark is that materials writing, to this teacher, is regarded as an end in itself. However, we take an entirely different view, believing that materials writing as a process is pointless without constant reference to the classroom. In short, a need arises, materials are written, materials are **used** in the classroom to attempt to meet the need and subsequently they are **evaluated**. The evaluation will show whether the materials have to be rewritten, thrown away, or may be used again as they stand with a similar group. Writing the materials is only a part of the activity of teaching (see Chapter 1 by Brian Tomlinson in this volume).

Exercise

You may now like to examine the quotations that follow.

Think about the implications of each one for materials writing; you may feel that some of the quotations carry more than one implication.

If possible, discuss the implications with a colleague; no commentary is appended this time.

(a) 'The book *Welcome* 3 really works well in my experience because there are modern topics, and good tapes that go with the book.' (Swiss schoolteacher)

(b) 'These listening comprehension tapes have too much noise on them, it is difficult to understand the speaker.' (Russian secondary schoolteacher)

(c) 'My students find the speaking (fluency) drills in the lab confusing.' (Austrian schoolteacher)

(d) 'The materials that in my experience don't seem to work very well are coursebooks based on communicative methods only, with a few exercises because students find it difficult to follow the book.' (Romanian schoolteacher)

(e) 'I think, Rafid, there's been a misunderstanding about what you were supposed to have written in this task … the pictures tell you what to do in order to change a bicycle wheel and I expected you to write a set of instructions to do that … but you've written about how you changed your bicycle wheel last week … why?' (English teacher in Britain marking the work of an Armenian student of academic English)

(f) 'Schon wieder so ein dummes Übungsgespräch!' ['Another stupid practice conversation!'] (Young German learner referring to a tourist/policeman dialogue in an elementary secondary school coursebook)

(g) 'In our English textbook we only read about film stars and pop stars and famous people. I want to know how the English people live.' (Turkish university student who has never visited the UK)

5.2 The process of materials writing

It would be appropriate at this point to attempt to summarise the various steps involved in the process of materials writing in the form of a flow-diagram. Figure 5.1 reveals in a simple although undynamic way how the implications raised in the statements above may be arranged into a simple sequence of activities that a teacher may have to perform in order to produce any piece of new material.

Most materials writers move in this direction, and use some or all of these steps, if not always precisely in this order: a movement from the identification of a need for materials to their eventual use in the classroom. Some such simplified version of the materials-writing process is also clearly how most publishers are constrained to work. The one-directional simplicity of this model, however, may be what makes so many materials, whether published or found in one's own or a

Figure 5.1

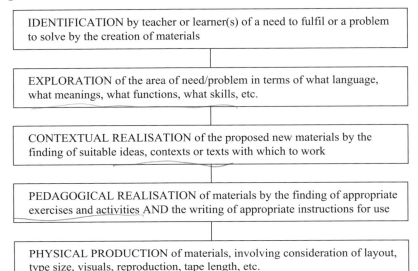

IDENTIFICATION by teacher or learner(s) of a need to fulfil or a problem to solve by the creation of materials

EXPLORATION of the area of need/problem in terms of what language, what meanings, what functions, what skills, etc.

CONTEXTUAL REALISATION of the proposed new materials by the finding of suitable ideas, contexts or texts with which to work

PEDAGOGICAL REALISATION of materials by the finding of appropriate exercises and activities AND the writing of appropriate instructions for use

PHYSICAL PRODUCTION of materials, involving consideration of layout, type size, visuals, reproduction, tape length, etc.

⤹USE in the classroom

colleague's filing cabinet, lack that final touch of excellence that many teachers and students have come to expect. In many ways, excellence in materials lies less in the products themselves than in the appropriate and unique tuning for use that teachers routinely engage in. The simple sequence in Figure 5.1 fails to illustrate the extent to which materials writing can be a dynamic and self-adjusting process.

In the first place, by ending with use in the classroom, it equates materials production and use of materials with effective meeting of identified needs. What is lacking is a stage beyond use in the classroom: evaluation of materials used. The act of evaluation (see Chapter 1 by Brian Tomlinson in this volume), at least in theory, turns the process into a dynamic one since it forces the teacher/writer to examine whether s/he has or has not met objectives: furthermore, a failure to meet objectives may be related to any or all of the intervening steps between initial identification of need and eventual use. (Failure may, of course, be attributed to poor or inadequate use of perfectly adequate materials, but that becomes a matter of classroom management rather than materials evaluation except where poor use is directly related to faulty production.)

Secondly, the human mind does not work in the linear fashion suggested above when attempting to find solutions to problems. For example, a proposal about what form a particular language exercise could

Figure 5.2 *A teacher's path through the production of new or adapted materials*

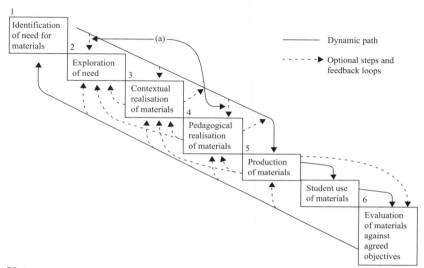

Notes

a) Even in the creation of entirely new materials, it may be the case that some of the steps envisaged have already been done for the writer.

b) Materials may be produced and evaluated without student use, e.g. by a colleague or professional. Most publishers still work this way. This does not reduce the need for evaluation after use by specific groups of students.

take may very well generate spontaneous second thoughts about the language being exercised; wondering about the physical production of a piece of material may well spark off thoughts about contextualisation and so on (see Johnson 2003). Thus, in addition to evaluation as an essential component of writing materials, we must also imagine a variety of optional pathways and feedback loops which make the whole process both dynamic and self-regulating. These, then, will allow us to deal in a concrete way with the reasons for the failure of language materials and provide us with clues to their improvement, both during the writing and after their use. See Figure 5.2.

5.3 Case studies

The case studies which follow illustrate, from different teaching contexts, how the steps in the path are taken into account in actual samples of material.

5.3.1 Case study 1

Materials produced for a class at upper-intermediate level.

IDENTIFICATION OF NEED	In reading a text, students come across the sentence: 'It's time the Prime Minister listened more carefully to his critics.' They are puzzled by the apparent clash between the past form and the actual meaning of the verb 'listened'. They ask for an explanation and further examples.
EXPLORATION OF LANGUAGE	The teacher promises to respond and consults *Practical English Usage* (Swan: 286, see Appendix) on 'it's time...', and a couple of other pedagogic grammars to get a cross section of views on hypothetical meaning.
CONTEXTUAL REALISATION	The teacher decides to produce worksheets on 'Hypothetical Meaning' to try to anchor the concept and the related language in students' minds and decides to provide simplified contexts for practice, based in students' own day-to-day experience rather than on external text sources (Figure 5.3). The worksheet is for class use, to reinforce actual teaching. The names used in **Step Three** of the worksheet are those of students in the class and of a co-teacher.
PEDAGOGICAL REALISATION	The teacher decides on a *contrastive* approach (facts vs. hypothesis) initially with an exercise focusing on the distinction, and on the verb forms involved (Step One). Enough examples are provided to establish a pattern for students to work from. Once basic **notions** are recognised, **communicative functions** of sentences involving hypothetical meaning are elicited (Steps Two and Three). The focus is on unspoken meaning and speaker's attitude. The teacher provides references for further practice/study.
PHYSICAL PRODUCTION	The worksheet is produced as a Word document, photocopied and distributed to learners.

114

USE

There is an introduction in class, followed by completion of the worksheet at home and checking in the next class.

EVALUATION

Student comments and difficulties with the worksheet, for example:

1. 'In Step One there is a fact **and** a hypothesis in the sentences. It's confusing.' (This sent the teacher back to 'Pedagogical Realisation' and led to the changed instructions and underlinings in Version 2, Figure 5.4.)
2. 'Can't the "if" sentences also be positive, do they only express regret?' (This student had noticed an important oversight which took the teacher back to the exploration stage and led to the inclusion of two further examples in Step Two of the revised version of the worksheet.)
3. Teacher noted problems with 'I wish you would finish ...' vs. 'I wish you had finished ...'. Further exploration led to production of a follow-up worksheet on 'possible vs. impossible wishes'.
4. The class liked Step Three and enjoyed making up similar sentences about other members of the group.

Figure 5.3   Version 1, Hypothetical Meaning

HYPOTHETICAL MEANING: WORKSHEET

<u>STEP ONE</u>

		FACT	HYPOTHESIS
(a)	Fact or hypothesis? Tick the right box for each statement		
1.	I'm pleased that you've finished the work.		
2.	I wish you would finish the work.		
3.	It's time you finished the work.		
4.	I wish you had finished the work.		
5.	If only you had finished the work.		
6.	I see that you've finished the work.		

(*cont.*)

Figure 5.3   (cont.)

7.   If you had more time you would soon finish
      the work.

8.   I'm surprised that you've finished the work.

(b)   Now underline the verb forms of 'finish' in each sentence. What do the <u>facts</u>
       have in common? What do the <u>hypotheses</u> have in common? What is the
       <u>paradox</u> about some of these verb forms?
       Here are some more examples, from the press, to help you with the answers to
       these questions.

       1.   It's time the Americans substituted action for words on climate
             change.

       2.   If I were in government I'd think twice before interfering in another
             country's affairs.

       3.   There are plenty of senior figures in government who wish we hadn't
             invaded Iraq.

       4.   If the UK hadn't insisted on sticking to the pound, we might not have
             been hit so hard by the recession.

       5.   If only England had a player of Ronaldo's calibre.

<u>STEP TWO</u>

There is an idea 'behind' many of these sentences with hypothetical meaning. Look at
these examples:

       It's time you had your hair cut. (It's too long)

       I wish my brother were here with me. (But he isn't)

       If only I had worked harder. (But I didn't)

(a)   Now provide the ideas behind each of these statements.

       1.   I wish you didn't smoke so heavily. (   )

       2.   It's time we went home. (   )

(cont.)

116

Figure 5.3 *(cont.)*

3.   Just suppose you had dropped the bottle. (   )

4.   If only you had listened to your mother. (   )

5.   I'd have bought the car if it hadn't been yellow. (   )

6.   It's high time you got rid of that old jacket. (   )

7.   If I were you I'd catch the early train. (   )

8.   He looked as though he'd seen a ghost. (   )

Which of the above examples expresses   (a) regret?

(b) advice?

(c) strong suggestion?

(d) a wish?

(e) reproach?

(b)   Now try to explain the difference <u>in the speakers'</u> between these pairs of statements:

I.   (a) 'It's time to leave.'

(b) 'It's time we left.'

II.   (a) 'It's time to get up.'

(b) 'It's time you got up.'

III.   (a) 'It's time for us to take a break.'

(b) 'It's high time we took a break.'

STEP THREE

Make statements to respond to or develop these situations, using the instructions in brackets in each case.

1.   It's 9.30 and René still hasn't arrived in class. (Comment reproachfully on this.)

2.   Adrian's hair is rather long. (Advise him to have it cut.)

3.   Nathalie hasn't done her homework. (Advise her to do it next time.)

4.   You haven't worked very hard during the course. (Express regret.)

5.   Pauline is still teaching at 12.45. (Reproach her.)

(cont.)

Figure 5.3   (cont.)

6.   Thomas asks to borrow your rubber for the tenth time. (Make a strong suggestion.)

7.   You went out last night and there was a James Bond film on TV. (Express regret or relief.)

8.   It's 8 pm and your landlady still hasn't put dinner on the table. In fact, she's painting her toenails. (Use a question to make a strong suggestion.)

References (for students)

Look at:

Murphy, R. 1996. *English Grammar in Use* (2nd edn.) Units 37 and 38. Cambridge: Cambridge University Press.

Swan, M. 2005. *Practical English Usage* (3rd edn.) Sections 258–264. Oxford: Oxford University Press.

Figure 5.4   Version 2, Hypothetical Meaning

HYPOTHETICAL MEANING: WORKSHEET

STEP ONE

(a)   Fact or hypothesis? Look at the verb forms underlined and then tick the right box in each case.

	FACT	HYPOTHESIS
1. I'm pleased that you've finished the work.		
2. I wish you would finish the work.		
3. It's time you finished the work.		
4. I wish you had finished the work.		
5. If only you had finished the work.		
6 I see that you've finished the work.		

(cont.)

118

Figure 5.4 *(cont.)*

7. If you had more time you <u>would</u> soon <u>finish</u> the work.

8. I'm surprised that you'<u>ve finished</u> the work.

(b) What do the <u>facts</u> have in common? What do the <u>hypotheses</u> have in common? What is the <u>paradox</u> about some of these verb forms?

Here are some more examples, from the press, to help you with the answers to these questions.

1. It's time the Americans substituted action for words on climate change.

2. If I were in government I'd think twice before interfering in another country's affairs.

3. There are plenty of senior figures in government who wish we hadn't invaded Iraq.

4. If the UK hadn't insisted on sticking to the pound, we might not have been hit so hard by the recession.

5. If only England had a player of Ronaldo's calibre.

STEP TWO

There is an idea 'behind' many of these sentences with hypothetical meaning. Look at these examples:

It's time you had your hair cut. (It's too long)

I wish my brother were here with me. (But he isn't)

If only I had worked harder. (But I didn't)

(cont.)

Figure 5.4 *(cont.)*

(a)   Now provide the ideas behind each of these statements.

1.   I wish you didn't smoke so heavily. (   )

2.   It's time we went home. (   )

3.   Just suppose you had dropped the bottle. (   )

4.   If only you had listened to your mother. (   )

5.   I'd have bought the car if it hadn't been yellow. (   )

6.   It's high time you got rid of that old jacket. (   )

7.   If I were you I'd catch the early train. (   )

8.   He looked as though he'd seen a ghost. (   )

9.   If I hadn't screamed we'd have crashed. (   )

10.   Suppose you hadn't had your chequebook with you. (   )

Which of the above examples expresses   (a) regret?

(b) advice?

(c) strong suggestion?

(d) a wish?

(e) reproach?

(f) relief?

(b)   Now try to explain the difference <u>in the speakers' minds</u> between these pairs
of statements:

I.   (a) 'It's time to leave.'

(b) 'It's time we left.'

II.   (a) 'It's time to get up.'

(b) 'It's time you got up.'

(cont.)

Figure 5.4   (cont.)

III.   (a) 'It's time for us to take a break.'

(b) 'It's high time we took a break.'

STEP THREE

Make statements to respond to or develop these situations, using the instructions in brackets in each case.

1.   It's 9.30 and René still hasn't arrived in class. (Comment reproachfully on this.)

2.   Adrian's hair is rather long. (Advise him to have it cut.)

3.   Nathalie hasn't done her homework. (Advise her to do it next time.)

4.   You haven't worked very hard during the course. (Express regret.)

5.   Pauline is still teaching at 12.45. (Reproach her.)

6.   Thomas asks to borrow your rubber for the tenth time. (Make a strong suggestion.)

7.   You went out last night and there was a James Bond film on TV. (Express regret or relief.)

8.   It's 8 pm and your landlady still hasn't put dinner on the table. In fact, she's painting her toenails. (Use a question to make a strong suggestion.)

References (for students)

Look at:

Murphy, R. 1996. *English Grammar in Use* (new edn.) Units 37 and 38. Cambridge: Cambridge University Press.

Swan, M. 2005. *Practical English Usage* (3rd edn.) Sections 258–264. Oxford: Oxford University Press.

5.3.2 Case study 2

| IDENTIFICATION OF NEED | Materials to practise the description of development and change over time (need identified by teacher with reference to the writing syllabus). |

| EXPLORATION OF LANGUAGE | Not carried out. |

| CONTEXTUAL REALISATION | Simple, universal context of an isolated island seen at four stages in its history. |

| PEDAGOGICAL REALISATION | Introduction to information. Instructions to student. Four labelled diagrams, showing development in pictorial form and notes (Figure 5.5). |

| PHYSICAL PRODUCTION | Introduction and instructions at top. Pictures hand-drawn and hand-written, photocopied. |

| USE OF MATERIALS | With European, Asian and North African students on an academic writing course. Students asked to produce drafts; no time limit. |

| EVALUATION OF MATERIALS | This revealed that: |

1. The need had been correctly **identified**.
2. That other needs remained unfulfilled because no adequate **language exploration** had been done, e.g. language of time duration.
3. The **contextual realisation** was very good and well understood, but in some ways factually inaccurate.
4. There were flaws in the **pedagogical realisation** which had led to poor practice by students: (i) writing was distorted through lack of a sense of audience; (ii) the instructions were confusing; (iii) some labelling was confusing.
5. There were flaws in the **physical production**, particularly in the visual aspects which confused students.

Figure 5.5 *Version 1, The Volcano on Heimaey*

<u>Writing</u>   DEVELOPMENTAL NARRATIVE

THE VOLCANO ON HEIMAEY

<u>Introduction</u>   Heimaey is an island near Iceland. Volcanoes which have been inactive

(dormant) for a long time may erupt violently, blowing out previously

solidified material and scattering volcanic ash.

<u>Writing</u>   Study the following pictures carefully and then write a description of the

development of the island of Heimaey during the last 1,000 years.

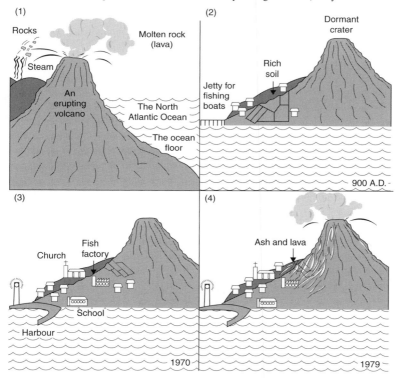

Rewriting of materials

The evaluative feedback led to a revamping of the materials and the production of Version 2 (Figure 5.6) in which changes were made on the basis of (3), (4) and (5) above.

Figure 5.6 *Version 2, The Volcano on Heimaey*

DESCRIBING DEVELOPMENT AND CHANGE IN THE PAST

Writing   THE ISLAND OF HEIMAEY

Introduction   Heimaey is an island near Iceland, in the North Atlantic Ocean. It is a

volcanic island, formed in the year 300. Volcanoes which have been

inactive for a long time may erupt violently, blowing out volcanic ash

and previously solidified material.

Writing Task Study the following pictures carefully. They show the changes on

Heimaey from its formation to 1973. Write a description of this

development, on the page opposite, using the notes given to you.

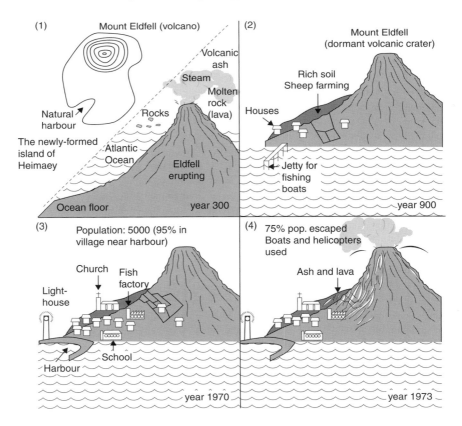

Figure 5.6   *(cont.)*

Before the year 300 AD, the island of Heimaey did not exist.
At about that time,

_____

_____

_____

_____

In approximately 900 AD, people came from Iceland and
settled on Heimaey.

_____

_____

_____

_____

In the next thousand years,

_____

_____

_____

_____

_____

A few years ago, Heimaey's peaceful development was suddenly
disrupted when

_____

_____

_____

_____

_____

_____

_____

5.3.3 Case study 3

With this case study (Figure 5.7) we intend to highlight the fact that the writing of materials is rarely a neat, self-contained, linear process, but an activity which is intimately bound up with all questions that teaching itself raises: learners' needs, syllabus, schemes of work, lesson plans, classroom management, resources, outcomes and assessment, the relation of learning/teaching to real life and so on.

Figure 5.7 *Teacher's evening reverie*

EVALUATION

IDENTIFICATION
OF NEED

LINGUISTIC
EXPLORATION

CONTEXTUAL
REALISATION

LINGUISTIC
EXPLORATION

PEDAGOGICAL
REALISATION

PHYSICAL
PRODUCTION

PEDAGOGICAL
REALISATION
AND USE

PHYSICAL
PRODUCTION

... that session on shopping with group 4 today was a bit flat ... in fact, can they shop effectively at all ... I mean, can I really say, hand on heart, that Duda or Kristina could get a small sachet of lemon shampoo from the pharmacy, ... or Miguel his cotton shirts? ... I'll have to give it another go tomorrow, but I can't have them sitting in pairs doing an A-B exercise ... what do I want? ... They must be able to ask for an item, and ask about size, colour, amounts, quantities ... The contents of the book were OK, perhaps a bit too diverse ... Shall I concentrate on food, clothes, newsagents and general personal items you can get from the pharmacy? ... But sitting in pairs was very flat, no urgency, ... they weren't really ... Now what happens when they need to go and shop for something, what is going on? Yes, you've got an idea of what you want, say bananas or apples and you also have other things in your head, like how many you want and you also want to find things out like where the apples come from, whether they are sweet or less sweet ... so ... so ... what I can produce is a set of cards, cue-cards which they can work from ... the cards should be analogous to what would be in their heads as they went into the shop. I can put a picture or draw one on each card to represent the items and on the right-hand side I can put various cue words to indicate what needs to go on in the shop. I'd better go over the cue words in a quick exercise before we start ... what sort of cues ... you need some general clues such as 'sizes' or 'colours' so that they can ask 'What colours do you have?' and so on ... and you also need specific cues, such as 'small' or 'red' so that they have to ask things like, 'Have you got a small one?' ... What I need is some card divided into two by three inch rectangles ... I could colour code it so that blue cards are newsagents items and red ones are for food shopping and so on ... should be easy enough. Perhaps

126

Figure 5.7 *(cont.)*

PEDAGOGICAL REALISATION AND USE	they can do it in groups first ... one group doing the food cards and one doing the clothes and one for the pharmacy and so on ... then I can shuffle the cards and they can practise on me as the shop assistant ... not a bad role if you work it up ... they can take random cards further ...
further EXPLORATION after IDENTIFICATION	hang on ... they were having problems with containers and things so maybe I'd better do a preliminary exercise on that ... box, packet, sachet, tube tub, car, tin ball, packet, carton, bundle ... any more ... ? I'll go and look in the cupboard downstairs ... yes bottle, mustn't forget that
PEDAGOGICAL REALISATION	one! ... yes I'll give them a simple list of items and they can give me the right containers ... or do it with each other and then have me check them ... now, I'd better make some notes on all this before I forget it ...

NOTES MADE

language exploration	FOOD:	Special questions – quantity/amount
		General questions – types? sizes?
	CLOTHES:	Special questions – colours, sizes, materials
		General questions – colours? materials?
		(Items: jeans, blouses, shirts, skirts, socks ...)
pedagogical realisation	signs on cards	! = REQUEST
		? = QUESTION

Examples of Materials Written

physical production

material?
blue?
grey?
sizes?
2!

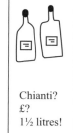

Chianti?
£?
1½ litres!

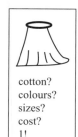

cotton?
colours?
sizes?
cost?
1!

Irish?
cost?
1½ kilos!

5.4 Conclusions

In this chapter we have outlined and illustrated a framework for materials writing. Underlying this framework are some beliefs and working principles which we would like to make explicit and comment on here.

1 Materials writing is at its most effective when it is turned to the needs of a particular group of learners.

Sooner or later, every teacher of any subject comes up against a need to write materials. How they respond to this need depends on all sorts of variables:

- the prevailing norms in a specific educational context
- the amount of time available
- the availability of reprographic facilities
- the teacher's background and training
- in some contexts, teachers are expected to adhere rigidly to a pre-scribed coursebook
- most teachers are too busy to contemplate writing their own material from scratch, though there are few who do not adapt their textbooks in some way
- photocopying and other forms of reproduction depend on the availability of technical back-up and supplies of paper
- materials evaluation, adaptation and production are often neglected or underemphasised on initial training courses.

British publishers do great business in many parts of the world with mass-market English language coursebooks. In Eastern and Central Europe, for example, in the years immediately after the collapse of Communism, the welcome given to *Discoveries*, the *Cambridge English Course*, *Headway* and similar courses was, after decades of restriction, understandably warm. Yet, in many countries in the region, the initial enthusiasm was quick to wear off, and a number of them have now produced and are using their own 'home-grown' school textbooks. The logic is inescapable. A 'home-produced' course-book, if it is well produced, stands a much greater chance of success locally simply because the authors are more aware of the needs of learners in that context, and are able to design the materials in such a way as to fit in with their own learning and teaching traditions, and with the conceptual world of the learners. Put another way, the further away the author is from the learners, the less effective the material is likely to be.

To sum up, the most effective materials are those which are based on a thorough understanding of learners' needs, that is their language difficulties, their learning objectives, their styles of learning, the stage of their conceptual development and so on. This implies a learning-centred approach to materials writing, rather than one which is driven purely by the subject through syllabus specifications, inventories of language items and so on.

2 Teachers understand their own learners best.

Teachers understand their learners' needs and their preferred learning styles. The more they become sensitive and responsive to these needs, the more they become involved in researching their own classrooms. Indeed, we believe that the teacher as materials writer belongs firmly in the (recent) tradition of the teacher as researcher (see Burns 1999).

3 All teachers need a grounding in materials writing.

It is not until teachers have attempted to produce their own materials that they finally begin to develop a set of criteria to evaluate materials produced by others. Only then does the full range of options, from blind acceptance of other materials, through adaptation and supplementation, to the production of 'purpose-built' materials, become clear. The process of materials writing raises almost every issue which is important in learning to teach: the selection and grading of language, awareness of language, knowledge of learning theories, socio-cultural appropriacy – the list could be extended. And to extend point 2 above, the current emphasis on action research in teacher education programmes needs to be backed up by the establishment of materials writing as a key component of initial training courses and a regular feature of in-service training programmes. Teachers need to be enabled to write their own materials when circumstances demand it, not only in order to reduce their dependency on published materials but also as a means of professional development (see Popovici and Bolitho 2003).

4 All teachers teach themselves.

Teachers teach specific groups of learners, as discussed above. They also, inevitably, 'teach themselves' and this has powerful implications when it comes to the materials they are to teach with. All the evidence we have gathered from teachers we have worked with suggests persuasively that 'teaching against the grain' leads to dissatisfaction, loss of confidence and learning failure. Enabling teachers to produce their own effective materials minimises this possibility and helps them to 'teach themselves'.

5 Trialling and evaluation are vital to the success of any materials.

Learners are the users of materials, and we have to heed their opinions and listen to their feedback. This is easy enough for teacher-writers, working with their own group of learners. Yet it is a message which many publishers have been slow to take on board. Even when trialling takes place, it is most often teachers' feedback, rather than learners', which is sought. In presenting our framework, we hope to have demonstrated how evaluation, by both learners and teachers, based on learning objectives, can cut down on wasted time and effort and result in clear pinpointing of the steps which require attention in the subsequent process of revision (see McGrath 2002).

Part of our purpose in writing this chapter has been to help to empower teacher-readers to write their own material within a principled framework arising from our experience. Learning to write materials is, inevitably, a matter of trial and error. We hope that the steps we have described will at least provide a generative model which will cut down on some of the risks involved and help the reader to feel more secure whilst experimenting.

References

Abbs, B. and I. Freebairn. 1980. *Developing Strategies*. Harlow: Longman.

Alptekin, C. 2002. 'Towards intercultural competence in ELT'. *English Language Teaching Journal*, 56(1): 57–64.

Burns, A. 1999. *Collaborative Action Research for English Language Teachers*. Cambridge: Cambridge University Press.

Johnson, K. 2003. *Designing Language Teaching Tasks*. Basingstoke: Palgrave Macmillan.

McGrath, I. 2002. *Materials Evaluation and Design for Language Teaching*. Edinburgh: Edinburgh University Press.

Popovici, R. and R. Bolitho. 2003. 'Professional development through writing'. In B. Tomlinson (ed.), *Developing Materials for Language Teaching*. London: Continuum.

Widdowson, H. 1996. 'Authenticity and autonomy in ELT'. *English Language Teaching Journal*, 50(1): 67–8.

Appendix

A materials writer's kitbag

The list below is neither a conventional bibliography nor a set of references. It consists of books, procedures and thinking prompts which we have found useful at each stage of the materials-writing process. Readers may wish to add to it from their own experience.

Stage	Suppport, resources and procedures
1. Identification	Questionnaires; feedback from students in class; formal or informal diagnosis of errors and shortcomings in learners' competence; analysis of existing course materials; pre-course needs analysis.
	Dubin, F. and E. Olshtain. 1986. *Course Design*. Cambridge: Cambridge University Press.
	Dudley-Evans, T. and M-J. St John. 1998. *Developments in English for Specific Purposes*. Cambridge: Cambridge University Press.
	Hutchinson, T. and A. Waters. 1987. *English for Specific Purposes*. Cambridge: Cambridge University Press.
	Nunan, D. 1988. *Syllabus Design*. Oxford: Oxford University Press.
2. Exploration	Syllabus models (e.g. in the books under 'Identification' above); a copy of your own syllabus.
	Alexander, L. G. *et al*. 1975. *English Grammatical Structure*. Harlow: Longman.
	Arndt, V. *et al*. 2000. *Alive to Language*. Cambridge: Cambridge University Press.
	Biber, D. *et al*. 1999. *Longman Grammar of Spoken and Written English*. Harlow: Longman.
	Bolitho, R. and B. Tomlinson. 1995. *Discover English*, 2nd revised edn. Oxford: Heinemann.
	Bowers, R. G. *et al*. 1987. *Talking About Grammar*. Harlow: Longman.
	Carter, R. and M. McCarthy. 2006. *Cambridge Grammar Of English*. Cambridge: Cambridge University Press.
	Hornby, A. S. 2010. *Advanced Learner's Dictionary of Current English*, 7th edn. Oxford: Oxford University Press.
	Leech, G. and J. Svartvik. 2003. *A Communicative Grammar of English*, 3rd edn. Harlow: Longman.

	Longman. 2005. *The Language Activator*, 3rd edn. Harlow: Longman.
	Longman. 2009. *Longman Dictionary of Contemporary English*, 5th edn. Harlow: Longman.
	McCarthy, M. 1991. *Discourse Analysis for Language Teachers*. Cambridge: Cambridge University Press.
	Parrott, M. 2010. *Grammar for English Language Teachers*, 2nd edn. Cambridge: Cambridge University Press.
	Swan, M. 2005. *Practical English Usage*, 3rd edn. Oxford: Oxford University Press.
	Swan, M. and B. Smith. 2001. *Learner English*, 2nd edn. Cambridge: Cambridge University Press.
	Access to as much published/unpublished material as possible.
3. Contextual realisation	Exponentially expanding, organised and assorted collection of visuals.
	Large collection of written texts, conveniently organised (e.g. by text-type, topic, degree of complexity, etc.).
	Large collection of listening material, similarly organised.
	Video material, too, if equipment is available.
	Keddie, J. 2009. *Images*. Oxford: Oxford University Press.
	Maley, A. and F. Grellet. 1981. *The Mind's Eye* (Student's Book and Teacher's Book). Cambridge: Cambridge University Press.
	Nunan, D. 1988. *The Learner-Centred Curriculum*. Cambridge: Cambridge University Press.
	Access to as much published/unpublished material as possible.
	Exercise and activity typologies.
4. Pedagogical realisation	Familiarity with as many generative frameworks as possible.
	Ideas magazines, e.g. *Modern English Teacher*, *English Teaching Professional*.

Byrd, P. (ed.). 1995. *Materials Writers' Guide.* Boston, MA: Heinle & Heinle.

Collie, J. and S. Slater. 1987. *Literature in the Language Classroom.* Cambridge: Cambridge University Press.

Ellington, H. *et al.* 1993. *A Handbook of Educational Technology.* London: Kogan Page.

Ellington, H. and P. Race. 1993. *Producing Teaching Material*, 2nd edn. London: Kogan Page.

Gairns, R. and S. Redman. 1986. *Working With Words.* Cambridge: Cambridge University Press.

Grellet, F. 1982. *Developing Reading Skills.* Cambridge: Cambridge University Press.

Lewis, M. 1997. *Implementing the Lexical Approach.* Hove: Language Teaching Publications.

Nunan, D. 1989. *Designing Tasks for the Communicative Classroom.* Cambridge: Cambridge University Press.

Ur, P. 2009. *Grammar Practice Activities*, 2nd edn. Cambridge: Cambridge University Press.

Willis, J. 1996. *A Framework for Task-Based Learning.* Harlow: Longman.

Wright, A. *et al.* 2006. *Games for Language Learning*, 3rd edn. Cambridge: Cambridge University Press.

Useful Websites
www.teflclips.com (YouTube lesson plans)
www.onestopenglish.com
www.teachingenglish.org.uk

5. Physical production

Pens / inks / pencils / rubbers / Tipp-Ex® fluid / 'luminous' text markers / scissors / ruler / gluestick / paste / stencils / Letraset / computer or word processor.

Cards / card / labels / laminating roll or laminator / polythene envelopes.

Access to a photocopier / thermal copier / scanner / print shop.

Extra copy of text, source material, etc. for first draft.

Secure systems for storing masters (either physically or electronically).

Files containing single copy of all materials in which updating and revision notes can be made.

Ellington, H. *et al.* 1993. *A Handbook of Educational Technology*. London: Kogan Page.

Ellington, H. and P. Race. 1993. *Producing Teaching Materials*, 2nd edn. London: Kogan Page.

Leach, R. 1985. *Making Materials*. London: National Extension College.

Rowntree, D. 1990. *Teaching through Self-Instruction*. London: Kogan Page (especially Chapters 8–12).

6. Evaluation

Phials containing small doses of courage and honesty enabling the writer to throw away materials that do not work or cease to enchant.

Feedback from students and colleagues on quality, effectiveness and interest value of materials.

McGrath, I. 2002. *Materials Evaluation and Design for Language Teaching*. Edinburgh: Edinburgh University Press.

Rea-Dickens, P. and K. Germaine. 1992. *Evaluation*. Oxford: Oxford University Press.

Tomlinson, B. 2003. 'Materials evaluation'. In B. Tomlinson (ed.), *Developing Materials for Language Teaching*. London: Continuum.

6 Writing course materials for the world: a great compromise

Jan Bell and Roger Gower

6.1 Introduction

Coursebook writers may set out to write materials they would want to use themselves if they were teaching in a particular situation, but their role has to be to collaborate in the publication of materials for others. They need to cater for a wide range of students, teachers and classroom contexts with which they have no personal acquaintance, even though they might be familiar with the general pedagogic situation for which the material is intended.

Writers have to try to anticipate the needs and interests of teachers and students and to modify any initial ideas they may have as a result of what they continue to learn about those needs and interests. The focus of this chapter is on that process of modification and whether the inevitability of compromise is a positive or negative force upon the writers' pedagogic principles. We will use our own experience to illustrate, and assume that readers will, despite our conclusions, make up their own minds.

6.2 Coursebooks in general: confronting the issues

For some years now there has been debate about the desirability of using coursebooks – indeed many of the issues have been raised by authors in this book. The debate has tended to be polarised between those who object to coursebooks in principle, whether they see them as instruments of institutional control supported by a range of commercial interests or as implicitly prescriptive and destroyers of teacher and learner creativity, and those who argue that coursebooks provide teachers and learners with a range of professionally developed materials within tried-and-tested syllabus structures, thereby allowing teachers to spend their valuable time more on facilitating learning than materials production. The arguments in favour of coursebooks are often made by those with vested interests – writers, publishers and distributors – and are therefore open to the accusation of special pleading. Their cause is not helped by the too-frequent adoption of coursebooks in situations for which they were not originally intended – for example, adult/young adult global coursebooks in a lower secondary school or even in junior summer schools in the UK. This is often because of misguided management, but it is too frequently encouraged by marketing teams and distributors who want to make sure their products get into as many schools as possible, no matter how suitable they are for the context.

Some also accept the need for coursebooks, but argue that the quality of many of those that are published is poor – not only because they are often produced too quickly with too little piloting, but because they do not sufficiently reflect what we know about language learning and thus fail to meet the true needs of learners. Those who have argued in favour of coursebooks include: Freebairn 2000, Harmer 2001 and O'Neill 1982; those who have argued (broadly) against include Allwright 1981, Meddings and Thornbury 2009, Roberts 2005, Thornbury 2000, Thornbury and Meddings 2001, Tice 1991.

As coursebook writers ourselves, we obviously accept that there is an important role for a coursebook in many classes. It would be impossible for us to write them if we thought otherwise. Coursebooks can provide a useful resource for teachers. Providing they are used flexibly, we think they can be adapted and supplemented to meet the needs of specific classes. But it would be foolish to ignore many of the questions raised by the debate. These are some of the more important ones.

1. If one of your pedagogic principles is that creativity is important in the classroom, then how can you make sure that your coursebook does not take away investment in and responsibility for learning from teachers and learners?
2. If coursebooks are sometimes used by schools to maintain consistency of syllabus, how can you at the same time make sure they reflect the dynamic and interactive nature of the learning process?
3. Although it is true no coursebook can cater for all the individual needs of all learners all of the time, can you provide enough material to meet most of the needs most of the time and build in enough flexibility to enable teachers to individualise it?
4. If the language presented in coursebooks includes few genuine examples of authentic or corpus-based material, how can you ensure that your samples of use are as natural as possible?
5. If coursebooks are frequently predictable in format and content, how can you bring to your material a feeling that it is not boring? (Indeed, Rinvolucri 2002 felt the need to suggest ways of 'humanising' the coursebook.)

We cannot pretend that when we started out we were fully aware of the significance of all these questions, but in different ways at different times of the process they were all asked, either by the editorial team or by ourselves.

There were other issues. In our situation we have written what is sometimes misleadingly called a 'global' coursebook – which really means a coursebook for a restricted number of teaching situations in many different countries rather than all teaching situations in all countries. And those who dislike coursebooks feel they have an even stronger case against the global coursebook: the all-singing, all-dancing, glitzy (expensive) multimedia package with a dedicated website of extras, usually produced in a native-speaker situation but destined for the world with all language in the book (including rubrics) in the target language. Indeed, as if to establish their role in commercial globalisation, publishers now regard the global coursebook as an international 'brand', and produce endless 'new editions', which makes it harder than ever to get anything different published. Words such as 'imperialist' and 'new colonialist' are sometimes used to criticise these books (see socio-political critics such as Gray 2010 and Holliday 1994). Some of those who favour this line of argument feel that many teachers without the 'benefits' of a native-speaker situation are resentful and unwilling victims of a situation manipulated by an alliance of local institution and foreign publisher. On the other hand those who argue in favour of the global coursebook – again, often those making money out of it – point out that good sales worldwide ensure a high production quality and enable publishers to finance interesting but less commercially viable publications on the backs of the big success stories.

From a pedagogic point of view we knew that one of the dangers of this kind of publication is that many of the cultural contexts in the materials and the text-topics can seem irrelevant to the learners. The material inevitably lacks the targeting to specific learning situations in a particular culture. We were also aware that many classes do not have the advantages of others. Not all of our potential users would be like the private language schools in the UK (one of our potential markets) with their small classes, courses of 19–25 hours a week and the support of the native-speaker environment. On the other hand, the UK situation has the disadvantages (as well as some advantages) of the multilingual classroom with the teacher frequently unable to speak the learners' own languages and minimally aware of their cultures.

6.2.1 The notion of compromise

With international materials it is obvious that the needs of individual students and teachers, as well as the expectations of particular schools in particular countries, can never be fully met by the materials themselves.

137

Indeed, most users seem to accept that what they choose will in many ways be a compromise and that they will have to adapt the materials to their situation.

This is a reasonable approach – indeed it prevents the illusion that situation-specific materials can do the job without the teacher having to adapt the materials to a particular group of individual students at a particular time. In other words, contrary to many current arguments about the inhibiting role of coursebooks, international course materials can actually encourage individualisation and teacher creativity rather than the opposite. It has been argued by some of the 'opponents' of coursebooks referred to above that teaching units these days are over-integrated, so that teachers get locked into one way of using them. In fact, many materials are beginning to look more like resource materials rather than traditional coursebooks and many multi-skills books help teachers to be flexible in their approach by clearly signposting where lessons can naturally finish and by making a point of not expecting users to refer back to language studied in a previous lesson. The better Teacher's Books will also suggest pathways through even well-integrated units and urge teachers to cut, adapt and supplement the material for their context, as well as introducing personalised practice where possible (for example, see Hyde *et al.* 2008; also some books on methodology such as Cunningsworth 1995 and Harmer 2007). Everything depends on the relationship that a user, in particular a teacher, has or is allowed to have with the material. Coursebooks are tools which only have life and meaning when there is a teacher present. They are never intended to be a straitjacket for a teaching programme in which the teacher makes no decisions to add, to animate or to delete. The fact that course materials are sometimes treated too narrowly – for example, because of the lack of teacher preparation time, the excesses of ministry or institution power, the demands of examinations, or the lack of professional training – should not be used as a reason to write off global coursebooks. Inevitably, in any global coursebook there will be material that will appear dated and irrelevant to the user's context, but used judiciously, published material can free up the teacher's time, not only to focus on the learning process but also to introduce into the classroom topics and material that are current and relevant.

Obviously no publisher is going to make a substantial investment unless there is a prospect of substantial sales. Material has to be usable by teachers and students alike or publishers lose their investment – hype can encourage a teacher or school to try a course once, but no amount of hype can encourage the same course to be readopted. In many cases, once a course has been adopted, financial constraints mean that the coursebooks will remain on the shelves for a long time, so it is very important that those responsible for choosing it do so for the right reasons and are sure that it is appropriate to the learners and the context, at least in the eyes of the school. In order to work, the material up to a point has to be targeted to a particular type of student, in a particular type of teaching situation, and a particular type of teacher with a particular range of teaching skills and who has assumptions about methodology which he/she shares with his/her colleagues. (See Mares 2003 on the challenge of writing for other teachers.)

There is no point in writing a course for teachers of adult students and expecting it to be used by primary teachers, although as we said above there are inappropriate adoptions. These teaching contexts are different anywhere in the world. And yet adult teaching in most countries has a lot in common – particularly these days with far greater professional integration than ever before (thanks to conferences, courses, professional magazines, ELT websites, teacher forums, the prevalence of CELTA (Certificate in English Language Training to Adults) training in some parts of the world, and so on). We felt that many of the situations around the world in which teachers would want to use our materials did have a lot in common: for example, teachers used to organising group work and aiming for improved communicative competence in the classroom and young adult students very similar to the ones we were used to in the UK.

6.2.2 The publisher's compromise

Compromise is not just something that is shared by users. Publishers also compromise – otherwise they would not get the material they want, that is material that they can not only be proud of when exhibiting against other publishers but which sells because potential users want to use it. Publishers will fail, and have failed, if they try to go for every market and produce something which is thereby only anodyne and anonymous. The Eastern, Middle Eastern, Latin American, European and UK markets may have certain things in common (they may all be prepared to commit themselves to the same grammar syllabus, for example), but their differences (for example whether or not they use the Roman script or whether or not speaking is emphasised in the secondary school system) will ensure that publishers are cautious if they aim to sell globally. And are there many examples of an overcautious coursebook succeeding commercially? Most successes (such as the adult/young adult courses *Headway* and *English File*) are usually seen to be breaking new ground at the time they are published.

Which is not to say a publisher is going to be a great innovator either – such courses, too, rarely succeed. (See Hopkins 1995 for some of the reasons why.) Indeed many of those courses that are felt to be new are in fact successful because they have something which is 'old' about them. One of *Headway*'s successes when it was first published all those years ago was that it reverted to a familiar grammatical syllabus when many other coursebooks were considered to have become too functionally oriented. The sensible balance – a compromise of principle – will surely be between innovation and conservatism, a blend of the new and different with the reassuringly familiar.

Designers may also need to compromise at times, too, since those who have too great an influence weaken materials commercially in the long-run. In our experience what is good design for a designer is not necessarily a good design for a teacher. We ourselves have heard designers severely criticise the design of successful books and praise books that are not thought by teachers to be well designed. Does it matter to a teacher whether there are one, two or three columns on a page and whether a unit is of uniform length in its number of pages? Maybe it is important to some teachers, but in our experience, what matters more is that it is absolutely clear on the page where things are and what their purpose is and that the balance (and tone) of visuals and text is right for their students. Whilst publishers would undoubtedly agree with this in principle and argue that the number of columns and pages per unit affects usability, there is sometimes a worrying gap between the aesthetic principles of a designer and the pedagogic principles of the writers.

Also there are real and necessary pedagogic constraints which designers have to accept as well as design constraints that authors have to accept. Sometimes it is necessary pedagogically to sacrifice illustration for words (texts, rubrics, etc.) in order to make a series of activities work in the classroom, just as it is sometimes necessary to cut back on, say, a practice activity to make it fit in with an adequately spaced visual. This is not to decry the role of designers. They have an essential (and integral) function in making sure that the authors' ideas are properly and attractively presented. They also need to make the students and teachers feel they are using materials with an up-to-date but usable look. Compromise has to be a benefit.

6.2.3 The authors

And what of the authors? They, too, find themselves compromising – and indeed they often feel themselves compromised by publishers, particularly authors who are experienced teachers with a strong conviction of how learners learn best. This is hardly surprising if a publisher who has done little real research of their own (with their only input coming from the hunches of marketing managers and conventional publishing wisdom) relies on the authors' own experience and then later tells them they cannot put their ideas into practice.

But teachers who are authors also have to compromise. Their teaching experience is often different from that of many intended users and their ideas might not work in a majority of classrooms. They have to beware of being too much the teacher trainer and look also at what students want, rather than concentrate on new ideas for teachers. It is very tempting to try and impose your views about what should happen in a classroom when the learning experience for different learners is so diverse. This is a common problem in coursebooks (possibly our own included) where the writers are used to working in a privileged learning environment which has such things as study centres, small motivated classes, smart boards and so on.

It is not for nothing that most global coursebooks aim to cater for a range of different strategies and learning styles. What may be successful in the context of a particular lesson for the writer or fit into a skills and supplementary book does not necessarily have a place in a coursebook where a range of syllabuses are operating, where balance of activity and skill is necessary and where there is often one eye on recycling and revision. And another major, often overlooked consideration is that the material has to fit on the page so that students can actually see it.

Authors who are not teachers also have to compromise. Whilst there are writing skills which not all teachers have – such as structuring a sequence of activities and balancing it with usable visuals – and there are skills that experienced writers have which teachers need if they are to write (see Walters 1994 for a light-hearted view), so there are teaching realities which authors long out of the classroom have to recognise if they are to produce materials that teachers want to teach with. In a lesson of 50 minutes the register still has to be taken, homework given back, announcements made and revision undertaken with students who have just come in tired from work and an irritating traffic jam. And that activity in your coursebook cannot work unless you allow an hour for it!

So all authors find themselves compromising and having compromise forced upon them.

6.3 A case study

At this point we are going to be anecdotal and talk about our own experience of when we were asked to write the first level in what was to become a 'cradle-to-grave' course series. It was an intermediate-level course for adult students both in the UK (15–21 hours a week) and in private schools overseas (2–3 hours a week). The assumption was that teachers would have experience in setting up communicative activities in the class, working with texts to develop reading and listening skills and being able to use coursebooks flexibly. By making these assumptions, we did, of course, accept that the materials might be used by less experienced teachers.

However, the brief itself indicated a need for compromise:

1. The multilingual intensive UK situation and the monolingual far less intensive situation are, as we have already seen, not the same. What is needed in the context of 25 hours a week in the native speaker environment is not necessarily needed in the 1–3 hours a week in the non-native speaker environment. For example, the latter may need (but it has to be said, not necessarily want) a lot more focus on listening and speaking than the former.

2. Monolingual situations differ. For example, can you write for both Europe and the Middle East when the shared knowledge and cultural assumptions are so different? All coursebook writers know the dangers of assuming that all students will know who the (usually Western) cultural icons are (see the introductory section of Chapter 5 by David Jolly and Rod Bolitho).

3. Despite our decisions, the material was still likely to be used by less trained, untrained or differently trained teachers. It cannot be assumed that a type of communication activity familiar to a trained teacher will be familiar to an untrained teacher. Things have to be spelled out to the inexperienced teacher without patronising the experienced teacher.

4. What is an adult? It was likely that the material would be chosen by some schools when it is inappropriate for their situation and used by learners who are too young to identify with the cultural content of the material. But could we really worry about that – no matter how keen the publishers might be on extensive sales?

5. It was likely that the materials would be used in some schools where the language syllabus and indeed the whole programme of study are framed by the coursebook, even though the aim was to try to produce materials which could be used flexibly.

6.3.1 Principles

We decided on a set of key principles:

1 Flexibility

We wanted an activity sequence that worked pedagogically. But it was important that teachers should feel they could move activities around, cut them out or supplement them according to need, all of which we made clear in the Teacher's Book. In other words we wanted to produce a coursebook with a strong resource book element. Indeed we saw the Workbook as a potential extra classroom resource for the teacher as well as a self-study book for the learner.

2 From text to language

Because of the needs of intermediate students, we wanted to provide authentic texts which contained examples of the focus language, rather than construct texts of our own. 'Language in a global context' we called it and we hoped we could draw language work out of the texts.

3 Engaging content

We wanted to provide human interest texts, which, although they came from a British or neutral context, would stimulate the students to make cultural and personal comparisons. We wanted the texts to engage the students personally. At the same time we wanted them to be used as a resource for language and as the basis for speaking and writing. We felt that some of the texts could be serious in tone, but not too many. Our experience had showed us that too many texts on such things as the environment, vegetarianism and race relations would not appeal. Whilst quite a lot of students seemed to be interested in everyday topics such as money, relationships, clothes and food, far fewer students in general language classrooms were interested in the worthier topics to be found in *The Guardian*. Of course, having said that, there are some parts of the world that would find only the 'serious topics' appropriate for their students. There needed to be a balance of serious and 'fun' articles. We realised that coursebooks are written partly to appeal to teachers; but teachers are hardly likely to accept material that bores their students. It goes without saying that, like all global coursebook writers, we were also constrained by cultural sensitivities, so that there could be no, or only very oblique and upbeat, references to sex, drugs, death, politics and religion. It was clearly more sensitive to leave the decision to use these topics to the individual teacher and their particular circumstances.

Overall we felt that the main criteria for the texts were that they should be generative in terms of language and would motivate students to want to talk or write. This meant choosing texts around old, favourite topics which make up most people's everyday experience (relationships, clothes, money, etc.), but it also meant that we had to find new angles on those topics if they were to remain fresh and interesting.

Of course, we recognise that even these decisions made cultural and situational assumptions. Some students may well prefer intellectual topics and indeed it was subsequently found by many British and American teachers working in post-Cold War 'Eastern Europe' that their students regarded 'fun' material as trivial. Many subjects which one would not consider as trivial are those which are culturally sensitive, such as non-conventional relationships, whaling and addictive behaviour; you can only really judge what is 'appropriate' within the context of the teacher, the students, the institution, the prevailing culture, the day of the week, the hour of the day and so on.

4 Natural language

We wanted spoken texts to be as natural as possible and therefore to avoid actors 'over-projecting' in the recording studio. We felt that exposure to real and unscripted language was important at this level to motivate students and help get them off the learning plateau. 'Old' language which had already been presented to them at lower levels would at intermediate level be embedded in new and natural language – from native speakers communicating naturally.

5 Analytic approaches

We wanted a variety of approaches to grammar, but decided to place great importance on students working things out for themselves – an analytic approach. After all, our target students were adults and the conscious mind has a role to play in language learning. This was particularly true for grammatical structures students were familiar with but needed more work on – the difference between the Present Perfect and Past Simple, or *will* and *going to* for example.

6 Emphasis on review

We felt the need to review rather than present a lot of grammar at this level. We assumed students already 'knew' most of the grammar and had practised it at lower levels. Yes, sometimes we felt something should be re-presented, but in general at intermediate level fluent and accurate use was what we decided to focus on rather than trying to get across the 'meaning' and use of the structure.

7 Personalised practice

We wanted to provide a lot of practice activities at this level. We felt that even oral practice of pronunciation and fixed structures should as far as possible be personalised. So for example, when practising *if* structures for imaginary situations, learners would draw on their own experience, as in the activity below.

Complete the following sentences:

(a) *I'd be very miserable if …*
(b) *I'd be terrified if …*
(c) *I'd leave the country if …*

8 Integrated skills

We believed that the 'receptive skills' of reading and listening should not be tagged on after the language work. Language use is a combined skill where everything depends on everything else – at the very least we generally listen and speak together, and whilst we read a lot more than we write, most of us also at least write short texts and email. By integrating the skills as far as possible, we were able to link speaking and writing with what the students had read or listened to, therefore providing a context and reason for communication. And we felt that, like playing tennis, communicating in language is something you only improve with practice and use (see DeKeyser 2007 on the role of practice in language learning). In our experience, knowing about the language can be helpful for adults in learning to use it, but overemphasis on the knowing about – usually the grammar – is useful for traditional exams but less useful in real life communicative situations. We believed that both language work and the productive skills should come out of work on listening and reading texts. Along with Krashen (1984), we believed in the value of texts being slightly above the level of the students and in the possibility of acquisition of language whilst focusing on content.

9 Balance of approaches

We wanted a balance in our approaches. We wanted inductive, deductive and affective approaches to grammar. We wanted fluency → accuracy work (i.e. 'process' approaches), as well as traditional accuracy → fluency work in speaking and writing, because we believed that drawing on what the students can do and improving upon it was a valid aim. And in general we would provide opportunities for both controlled practice and creative expression so that all learning styles were catered for as far as possible.

10 Learning to learn

We regarded this as very important, but we thought it best to integrate learner development work throughout rather than make it 'up-front' training. Nevertheless, we decided to have up-front work on vocabulary skills, to get students to analyse grammar for themselves and to provide a language reference for students at the end of each unit. We also wanted to encourage students to start their own personalised vocabulary and grammar books.

11 Professional respect

We wanted to produce something that gave us professional satisfaction and was academically credible to our colleagues, something we could be proud of. We also wanted a course that appeared adult and sophisticated with a clean look about it.

6.3.2 Pressures

The publishers

As inexperienced coursebook writers, we were soon confronted, not only by the harsh realities of commercial publishing but by some of the diverse needs of potential users.

The publishers were encouraging and allowed us a lot of creative freedom. They shared many of our aspirations and also wanted something that would give them academic credibility as well as healthy sales. Nevertheless, they had an eye on markets they had to sell to and did not want spiralling production costs. There was no open-ended budget for colour photographs or permissions for songs sung by famous bands. At the same time we sometimes felt – not necessarily justifiably – that they gave more attention to the 'flick-test' – the first impressions the material would make when looking though the book – than to its long-term usability. We also felt they overemphasised the need for rubrics to be intelligible to students when we were writing a classbook which would be mediated by teachers. In fact, to us teacher mediation was vital or we would end up prescribing the methodology too much (a real problem this: should you ever say 'Work in groups' when the teacher may want to do an exercise in pairs, or 'Write these sentences' when the teacher may want the students to say them?).

Schools and institutions

One of our problems was to sort out the real from the illusory in this area. A lot was made by the publishers of the fact that the main book had to be the right length, there had to be so many units, so many pages per unit – linked to so many hours of work, the syllabus had to include this and that grammatical item, there had to be tests. And yet when it came to it, our instincts told us that there was a lot more freedom in our market to do what we liked in terms of overall structure, providing our material was usable and motivating for the level of students. This was confirmed when we talked to teachers informally. Indeed many teachers seemed not to notice how many pages there were in a unit or what was in the syllabus, although administrators do, and in many contexts they are the ones who decide what coursebook to select.

Institutional needs nevertheless imposed perfectly proper constraints on our writing: the material should not be inappropriate to the context, the topics should be interesting to their students, the material should not date too much, it should be 'user-friendly', it should be usable alongside and sometimes integrated with other materials and should enable students to make rapid progress. On the production side it should be good quality but cheap and all components – coursebook, workbook, tapes, teacher's book – should be available locally on launch!

Teachers
We felt teachers wanted a book they could sympathise with in terms of its pedagogic principles. It would need to have a fresh and original feel to it and yet be reassuringly familiar. And since teachers have a lot of demands on their time, they would need it to fulfil certain criteria: not too much preparation, usable and motivating materials, fun activities that worked in terms of improving the students' communicative skills, transparent methodology, up-front grammar and a flexible approach which allowed teachers to use the materials more as a resource than a prescriptive course.

Students
Students would want material that they could enjoy and which they could identify with and learn from. Language needed to be comprehensible but there did need to be 'new' language there on the page. They needed a lot of revision, a lot of material they could use to study on their own. They needed supplementary materials such as workbooks.

6.3.3 Principles compromised

With all these factors at work, it is not surprising that the issue of compromise was central to our work. Having said that, it is surprising how many of our grand principles above more or less survived. The main areas of compromise were these.

Overall structure
It was clear that the idea of a flexible coursebook was not (at that time) fully understood by our potential users. We were aware from initial feedback that some teachers felt they had to cover everything in the book in the order presented. Our idea of using the Workbook as part of the classroom resource was not universally accepted since many students did not have access to the Workbook. In other words, the material ended up being less flexibly organised than we would have liked. However, at that time it is true that we were not sufficiently aware of the potential of the Teacher's Book to go beyond declaring intentions and suggesting ideas to providing its own resources in terms of extra photocopiable practice activities – a situation we remedied in later editions. This facility very

visibly puts into practice the principle of aiming to supply teachers with a resource to help them build up their programme.

Originally we wanted to start the book with a 'deep-end' approach and so we flagged our first four units as review units – to activate language students had already been presented with and do remedial work on it if necessary. But many markets did not like or understand this approach and wanted straightforward presentation of the main language items. Should we have compromised and provided this presentation?

Lack of space caused us great frustration at the editing stage when we saw many of our practice activities disappear or get pruned. We had to make a decision whether to cut whole activities or cut back on the number of items within an activity. The fault was probably ours for having too great an ambition for too few pages. So the compromises that were made met with some complaints from users and we have had to provide extra material in the Teacher's Book in later editions.

Methodology

We did manage to get away from a traditional PPP approach in terms of unit structure since we started each unit with a skills activity rather than a language presentation, but our original ambition to draw target language out of authentic texts failed at the intermediate level, partly because of the difficulty of finding texts which contained clear examples of the focus language together with interesting content. We got nearer to our ambition at the upper-intermediate level.

As for our approach to grammar, we found the analytic exercises were not very popular in some parts of the world – they were seen to be too serious and to expect too much from students – and perhaps we should have compromised more by having fewer such exercises. The same feeling applies to our treatment of learner training activities.

Texts

We resisted publisher pressure to make our texts more intellectual. We still think we were right – this has been supported by subsequent feedback; in fact, perhaps we should have resisted more. But it was clear there were going to be problems with unadapted authentic texts. Finding texts with a generative topic of the right length and the right level of comprehensibility for the level (i.e. comprehensible input + 1) as well as an accessible degree of cultural reference and humour was not easy. So we compromised on this ambition and wonder now whether we should have compromised more and simply gone for texts which were interesting. Here the compromise was one of logistics, publisher pressure and student expectation as well as our own greater realisation that some of our initial ambitions were unrealistic.

We also wanted our listenings to be natural and as authentic as possible – we believed you learn to listen to real English by listening to real English – but we did compromise and use some actors. On reflection, given the response of some non-UK markets to the difficulty of some of the authentic texts, we wonder now whether we should have compromised more. We put in a lot of effort to make sure the listenings were authentic, but it was not appreciated universally. Perhaps we should have made more of them semi-scripted – or at least made the authentic ones shorter and easier, and built in more 'how to listen' tasks.

Content

In terms of content we realised we could not please everyone. We did compromise and not include some texts we would have used with our own students, on the grounds that they would not go down well in such and such a country. We did not want to fight shy of the taboo subjects of sex and so on, but found ourselves doing so and being expected to do so. (At the higher level we got away with more.) There was also the great influence of political correctness at that time, particularly in the men vs. women debate, which was US/UK-teacher/publisher driven rather than student-driven. Certain texts were avoided, others were encouraged – women in important jobs, for example – and others toned down.

Piloting

There was a pilot edition of the material which proved to be good training for us as writers, but most of the material in the pilot edition did not get used except in parts of the Workbook. The process helped our thinking, but not all the feedback was as helpful as we had hoped, mainly because it was often contradictory, which meant we and the publishers had to take a view on it in the end. We also taught some of the pilot material. But for the final edition direct piloting was difficult if schedules and budgets were to be met. We relied more on our own experience and the experience of advisers.

Conclusions

This is a personal account and yet it is undoubtedly typical of most writing teams in one way or another. Compromise almost by definition is a subtle art if all sides are to be satisfied with getting less than they originally wanted, and it has not always been possible to tease out and identify all the compromises that were made when and by whom. We know we compromised our ambitions and we have no doubt our users have had to compromise theirs. We were lucky in that the publishers respected our lead in terms of the content and methodology and also compromised.

If we are to make a conclusion, it has to be that compromise is not only inevitable, it is probably beneficial. At least it was for us. Without certain compromises we would have produced less effective materials. If we had made other compromises – and been more aware of the areas where we should have compromised – we might have produced more effective materials.

References

Allwright, R. 1981. 'What do we want teaching materials for?' *ELT Journal*, 36(1): 5–18.

Cunningsworth, A. 1995. *Choosing Your Coursebook*. Oxford: Macmillan Education.

DeKeyser R. (ed.). 2007. *Practice in a Second Language*. Cambridge: Cambridge University Press.

Freebairn, I. 2000. 'The coursebook – future continuous or past?' *English Teaching Professional*, 15: 3–5.

Gray, J. 2010. *The Construction of English: Culture, Consumerism and Promotion in the ELT Global Coursebook*. Basingstoke: Palgrave Macmillan.

Harmer, J. 2001. 'Coursebooks: a human, cultural and linguistic disaster?' *Modern English Teacher*, 10(1): 5–10.

2007. *The Practice of English Language Teaching*. Harlow: Pearson Education.

Holliday, A. 1994. *Appropriate Methodology and Social Context*. Cambridge: Cambridge University Press.

Hopkins, A. 1995. 'Revolutions in ELT materials?' *Modern English Teacher*, 4(3): 7–11.

Hyde, D. *et al.* 2008. *First Certificate Expert*. Harlow: Pearson Education.

Krashen, S. 1984. *The Input Hypothesis*. Harlow: Longman.

Mares, C. 2003. 'Writing a coursebook'. *Developing Materials for Language Teaching*. London: Continuum.

Meddings, L. and Thornbury, S. 2009. *Teaching Unplugged*. Peaselake, Surrey: DELTA publishing.

O'Neill, R. 1982. 'Why use textbooks?' *ELT Journal*, 36(2): 104–11.

Rinvolucri, M. 2002. *Humanising your Coursebook*. Peaselake, Surrey: DELTA publishing.

Roberts, S. 2005. 'In defence of Dogme'. *Modern English Teacher*, 14(2), 69–72.

Thornbury, S. 2000. 'A dogma for EFL'. *IATEFL Issues* 153: 2.

Thornbury, S. and Meddings, L. 2001. 'Coursebooks: the roaring in the chimney'. *Modern English Teacher*, 10(3): 11–13.

Tice, J. 1991. 'The textbook straightjacket'. *Practical English Teaching*, 11(3).

Walters, L. 1994. 'How to be a coursebook author. A 12-point guide to becoming a publisher's paragon'. *MATSDA Folio*, 1(2): 6–7.

7 How writers write: testimony from authors

Philip Prowse

7.1 Introduction

This chapter looks at the process of materials writing from the writer's perspective. It uses two snapshots: one taken in 1994 and one taken 15 years later.

A group of ELT materials writers from all over the world met in Oxford in April 1994 for a British Council Specialist Course with UK-based writers and publishers. The personal accounts of the writing process, which make up the first and longer part of this chapter, are taken from questionnaires and correspondence with course participants and tutors, and their friends. The accounts are presented as they were written, and are grouped thematically. With technological progress some aspects of the accounts have dated, but they have been retained both out of historical interest and in order to preserve the integrity of the original. Equally references to 'new' developments are to be read in the understanding that they were new in 1994 rather than now. I owe a deep debt of gratitude to the contributors to this first section for allowing me to reproduce their responses anonymously. The contributors are: Wendy Ball (UK), Jan Bell (UK), Elisabeth Fleischmann (Austria), Judy Garton-Sprenger (UK), Ram Ashish Giri (Nepal), Simon Greenall (UK), Shamsul Hoque (Bangladesh), Marina Larionova (Russia), Tony Lynch (UK), Peter May (Belgium), Ian McGrath (UK), Olga Nikolaeva (Russia), Ruxandra Popovici (Romania), Naina Shahzadi (Bangladesh), Keith Tong Sai-tao (Hong Kong), Catherine Walter (UK).

Fifteen years later four leading ELT materials writers were asked to read the chapter and to reflect on their own practice. They were: Jeremy Harmer (author of the *Just Right* series, Marshall Cavendish), Sue Kay (co-author of the *Inside Out* series, Macmillan), Pete Sharma (author of *Blended Learning: Using Technology in and beyond the Language Classroom*, Macmillan), and Jeff Stranks (co-author of the *English in Mind* series, Cambridge University Press). Their reflections form the second part of this chapter, with three of them focusing on the writing process, and the fourth, Sharma, on the impact of technology on writing.

7.2 Writers' perspectives in 1994

7.2.1 Writing together

Most of the contributors have written at some time, or always, as a member of a team. Their accounts of collaborative writing highlight the importance of team-building, as well as divergences in working practice. Writing teams are often put together by publishers and considerable 'getting to know you' needs to take place before writing can start. A rough rule of thumb is that team-working on supplementary materials is like an affair; team-working on a coursebook is more like a marriage! 'Getting to know you' works on different levels, and the human one of shared response to experience is as important as shared methodological presuppositions. Teams who have taught together are common, and have a head start on both levels, although it can be argued that to actually start writing at once and to get to know each other as you write is equally effective.

> 'Writing together means what it says: sitting down at a table together. We meet for a whole evening at a time and are very strict with ourselves – no gossip or chatting, just work. Ideas come to you at any time, and collecting materials you can do on your own, but the actual writing process is something we have to do in the same room.'

> 'What we do is each draft a unit (we work in separate rooms), consulting with the other only if there is some knotty problem. Then each reads the other's unit and criticises: sometimes there is very little to change, sometimes a radical overhaul is necessary. We have never had any ego-problems in this area; it must be awful (and awfully time-consuming) if you do.'

> 'There's no fixed pattern. But the actual writing definitely takes place individually, at a distance. Ideally the team of writers must first meet and agree on an overall approach and methodology. Then they go away to write their own chunks, which could be thematically related or unrelated. Then they meet regularly to comment on each other's work, and go away to improve their chunks with the benefit of the feedback. Needless to say, we need good team-players – who are confident, but not arrogant, so that they can react positively to criticisms. When it comes to finalising the manuscript, it takes someone with a bit of authority to edit everything. Here I'm talking about the development of classroom materials for an institution, like the university I'm working at. When it comes to published materials, the authors can write pretty independently. I just finished writing an exam practice book with two colleagues and we hardly met over the book.'

'Our textbook team is made up of 13 members, 6 working for lower secondary level and 7 for upper secondary level. The size of the team is rather unusual and lots of people, teachers, inspectors, trainers and ourselves doubted the results of a 'mob-at-work'.

There are of course, drawbacks: mismatch between individual working styles, individual writing styles, unstandardised units, a longer than usual time for decisions as we must give credit to everyone's idea in order to reach solutions agreed, if not by all members, but by a large majority. If, however, this formula still works it is because we have found a lot more advantages than downsides: variety of ideas (both 'triggers' and 'template' type), wider range of information and methodological sources, the benefits of getting together people from different parts of the country, which means different areas of interest, conceptions, ideas, and the certainty that once an idea is accepted, it has to be a good one.

The major decisions about the content of the book, the topics to be covered, the balance of skills, the treatment of vocabulary and grammar, and the culture and civilisation input are taken from the whole team. Planning, setting up deadlines and seeing that these are met, updating all members and persons related to the project on progress of work and results, organising piloting of the materials, ensuring standardisation, avoiding overlap, reviewing the materials, workshops (organisation, management and reports), and relationships with the publishers are the project coordinator and UK consultants' job.

The mode of working we've agreed on is the following:

- During a first workshop: the group decides on topics, functions, skills focus, treatment of grammar, vocabulary, format of a unit and a lesson. Then units are allocated to each member.
- Writers go back to their hometown and devise units accordingly. They send them to the project coordinator for checking. The consultants get them for suggestions as well.
- In about three months the group meets again with the project coordinator and the consultants and common agreement for all lessons is obtained.'

'I write a first draft which I give to my co-author to comment on and adapt if necessary. If I am stuck for an appropriate activity my co-author often supplies it. Ditto for authentic materials. We work at a distance as we find that this avoids serious disagreements and both of us work better and faster when alone.

The final decision as to approach and content is with me as initiator of the work with a clear overall picture of the methodology, the progression and the 'soul' of the book. The responsibility for revising the materials is mine, partly for the reasons just outlined and partly because the materials are trialled at the institute where I work.'

'My only experience of co-authoring was when I wrote part of the Teacher's Book for an exam course and someone else did the rest. The problem was that I was up against deadlines both for the coursebook and for the Practice Tests Book, with one or two other crises going on at the same time! Living abroad also meant that communications (pre-fax) were dire: I never actually managed to discuss the book with my co-author and in the end it became the product of what editors in the UK chose from both our contributions. A real dog's breakfast, in other words.'

'My colleague and I decide on the topic to work on and we get together in the same room and try to find appropriate materials and ideas (in our library). We also bring materials from home and the bookstore, pool it and then 'disperse' to get activities prepared. Then we come together again, order our parts, decide together about order and usefulness, and after trying things out we reverse them (each looks at the other's part). Then our colleagues try the material out and give us feedback.'

'For us collaborative writing is team work. We discuss a great deal, decide what we will include in our writing in advance, make an outline and then start writing. The written materials, if they are developed separately, are discussed again. We all agree on the language, content and presentation before they are okayed. Revision is done in the same way.

Very often a member of the team becomes a scribe, and writes what others dictate to him or her after elaborate discussions.

The most senior colleague usually has the final say in case we have disagreements.'

'In general, I find it best to agree on a division of labour that reflects each person's interests and strengths and agree a deadline. Then drafts are exchanged, comments made and the draft re-worked. Perhaps I have been lucky in my co-authors, but this pattern has worked extremely well for me. It does necessitate openness (the willingness to be frank and the willingness to accept constructive criticism), of course, but the benefits are enormous.'

'I have had negative experiences in working with co-authors who are virtual strangers and who are representing the country for which the book is intended. This is often a relationship full of stresses and strains which result from approaching the project from totally different angles. Then changes made to a manuscript are often guided by motives unconnected to pedagogical considerations.'

'With EFL materials it is a matter of deciding which types of task or which unit you will take responsibility for. Each of you should produce a draft for the other to read and comment on. (Final decisions rest with whoever keys in the final version!) 'Co-writing' is ambiguous in English: 'co-writing' proper (like team-teaching) I find difficult; I suppose what I do is co-authoring.'

'We have had a few different gos at seeing which approach works best vis-à-vis working in a 'team' of two. So far we have tried:

- working together (at home, in long-hand) on the outline of a couple of units at a time. This will include basic structure, a 'pot' of ideas, suggestions for texts, but no detail. Then each of us would take a unit and write it, passing it over for comment and/or rewriting afterwards.
- dividing up the book into the first half and the second half. Having macro meetings to discuss syllabus, topics, texts, and then basically getting on with it. Obviously each draft of the unit would be commented on by the co-author.
- one person doing the 'macro' sketching out (basically the 'creative' bit) and the other one doing the filling in of exercises, detailed artbriefs, wording of Language References and other 'micros'.

We have not yet found a perfect solution!'

'Recently two of us have been working on some pilot materials for a publisher. We've both got compatible computers so the way it worked was that after lots of preparatory meetings we each started work on a different lesson. Then we would post the disks containing the rough draft to each other, and instead of commenting on it, as we used to do when it was all paper, would simply rewrite the lesson, adding or cutting, quite a lot sometimes, and send it back. In this way we ended up with a unit of lessons which weren't anyone's property. Then we sat down together at one computer and got it all in order, standardising layouts and rubrics and so on. It was a really good way to work, and would have been even quicker if we'd had e-mail.'

How to work together is clearly something which occupies materials writers. In the accounts given here we can distinguish pairs who work closely together, pairs who complement each other, and larger teams where management of the writing process becomes as important as the writing itself. As a writing team gets larger, the benefits it receives from diversity can be outweighed by the negative effects of personal and professional disagreements, but this is not necessarily the case and a larger team can draw on deeper reserves of energy and experience. There is, however, a tension between having as small a writing team as possible and coping with the demands of a large project. This tension is sometimes resolved by 'subcontracting' elements of the project, typically workbooks and test or resource packs, and also teacher's books, to other authors working under the direction of the lead authors.

7.3 The creative process

In the production process of a modern coursebook, which can take three to five years from initial idea to copies in the classroom, the actual creation of the lessons, paradoxically, can take up less time than all the other aspects of authorship. These accounts of how writing 'happens' emphasise the creative nature of the process.

> 'The only work which counts as real work for me – as opposed to meetings, presentations, revising, proof-reading, etc. – is a day spent in front of the word processor, originating the first draft of a lesson. No day involves such hard work, but no work is more rewarding. But even this day begins perhaps some months before, at the stage when the whole course design is worked out and elaborated. This stage is essential; it takes time, maybe a week or so, but it means that on the happy day of 'real' work, there's no such thing as writer's block, only bad planning.
>
> The process begins as I check the course design requirements for the lesson to be written, and then I begin a fairly lengthy process of deciding in which authentic contexts the target structures or vocabulary are likely to be heard or read. When I've thought about this, I look for input texts, which will be used as either listening or reading material in the lesson. This may involve rereading a lot of old newspapers, going to the library or just going through the bookshelves in my study.
>
> Once I have selected the main input material, I decide on the stages of the lesson, just as a teacher might draw up a lesson plan. Although the principal syllabuses will focus on the target structures or vocabulary, the secondary syllabuses of reading, writing, speaking, listening, pronunciation, socio-cultural training, among others, have to be covered as well. I like to ensure that everything occurs in activity sequences with a beginning, a middle and an end, so that a communicative context is established, and this usually involves a little ingenuity. I put on screen all kinds of possible exercises and activities, type in the input material and then just spend a lot of time thinking about the most suitable choice and order. I often do this thinking during some exercise around the middle of the day, and by the time I get back, it's miraculously clear what the activity sequence is.
>
> By the time I start to write the lesson, most of the significant decisions have been made, and everything usually goes very quickly. It will take me a couple of hours to finish a lesson – for my present series, a lesson

corresponds to a double page spread. So, in all, two pages will take me about a day to originate.

Of course there's a lot of polishing, revising and finishing to do, which is usually done in collaboration with my editor. There are also tapescripts to prepare, answers to check and the teacher's book to write, which often throws up further flaws. But all this is done later in the writing/editing process, and the certainty that these tasks remain to be done does not impinge upon the pleasure I feel at the end of this day of 'real' work.'

'Some people just sit down at the table and work. It has never been this way with me. My ideas and intentions boil inside me for a long time, even details take quite a while to mature, then at some point I feel I can start writing. Usually after this moment everything pours out in a gulp. And later on for quite a long time I may be reluctant even to look through what has been done, postpone indefinitely working over the text, editing ...

- writing is fun, because it's creative.
- writing can be frustrating, when ideas don't come.
- writing brings joy, when inspiration comes, when your hand cannot keep up with the speed of your thoughts.
- writing is absorbing – the best materials are written in 'trances'.
- writing improves with practice, but everybody needs a bit of a push to face up to their first writing assignment.
- writing is addictive – after you've completed your first job you keep asking for more.'

'When I feel inspired the writing comes easily, but when the first idea has been put on paper I tend to lose interest. I nevertheless want the work to be 'mine', and get tense when my co-author seems less committed to the storyline and the relationships between the characters than I am.'

'Writing, for me, is a tortuous activity. I think a lot, or, in a way, worry a lot, not about the mechanics of writing, but about making a bonafide beginning, and then about keeping things organised while I write.

Thinking, or what others would call 'planning', takes place everywhere – in the bus, on walks, while shopping, anything which keeps me occupied. So if I see you around Kathmandu and don't recognise you, you should not worry. I will go a little distance, remember you, and come back to say hello to you.'

'Sometimes it's hard to stop writing. Carrying on into the night – long after you're past your best and you seem to be working on auto-pilot – can bring on insomnia and reduced efficiency the day after. Meals get postponed, as does time with the family and with friends.

Why do we do it? In my case I can't offer any better reason than the 'buzz' ... I'd like to think that I write to help students learn, or even help teachers teach, but if I'm really honest with myself it's difficult to believe that I'd put in 100-hour weeks for that purpose alone.'

'In materials writing mood – engendered by peace, light, etc. – is particularly important to me and the process is also rather different from that involved in other kinds of writing. The main difference, perhaps, is that in materials writing I need to start from the germ of an idea. When I've got that, I might just let it simmer away, give it a stir from time to time, and then at a certain point have a closer look at it. I draw heavily on my own experience. I might look through what other people have done, but I basically rely on my own intuition. This suggests that I work quickly and surely. I think I do work quickly, but since I often leave gaps (for the rather tedious bits that need to be filled in later), and since I also feel the need to shape and polish, I go through endless drafts before I am more or less satisfied.'

Most of the writers quoted here appear to rely heavily on their own intuitions, viewing textbook writing in the same way as writing fiction, whilst at the same time emphasising the constraints of the syllabus. The unstated assumption is that the syllabus precedes the creation. An alternative view is to base lesson materials on topics and activities which are of interest and value in themselves, and derive the actual syllabus from the materials, using checklists where necessary to ensure sufficient 'coverage'. 'Coverage' is another unspoken assumption, as if teaching materials can encapsulate the whole of the language, rather than offer a series of snapshots of it. Whether an author starts from a pre-existing syllabus (often prescribed by a Ministry of Education) or uses a content-based starting point can depend on level – a beginner's coursebook will probably start from a language syllabus. Current interest in CLIL (Content and Language Integrated Learning) is likely to stimulate the creation of learning materials where content rather than language is the starting point.

The materials described in this section are, in the main, student materials, and where reference is made to a teacher's book it is assumed to be written afterwards. Some authors, however, prefer to create the teacher's and student's books at the same time. This approach is clearly essential with primary school materials, where the material on the student page may be entirely visual, but can be adopted at all levels. A possible practical drawback is that continuing revision and editing of the student material can necessitate the rewriting of the teacher's book a number of times. For adult learners it can be argued that student lesson material should be so clear that it could be taught 'off the page', without reference to a teacher's book, which will mainly contain extra ideas and activities.

7.4 Working with publishers

Major coursebook series these days are usually commissioned by publishers rather than suggested by authors, and the account below reflects a not untypical writing process. Missing, of course, are the endless meetings and discussions before a project is commissioned, and the post-production pressure (welcome as it is) to travel and promote the series.

Initial stage

- Research on new level – what is needed/gaps in market/weaknesses of other materials – by talking to teachers (students sometimes), looking at/teaching other materials. My co-author and I do this independently with follow-up meetings/sharing of opinions and findings.
- Meeting with co-author (at home) to discuss and draft our basic rationale. This will include book and unit structure, and a draft grammar syllabus and usually takes some time. Initially done in long-hand.
- Creation of draft unit (usually Unit 1). Planning of unit usually done together, and then divided up and worked on individually with lots of batting to and fro. Done on computer and faxed backwards and forwards for comments. Editors not involved at this stage.
- Submit rationale/draft unit/proposed grammar syllabus to publisher. This is then sent out to readers – an 'inner sanctum' of people, and a wider net to catch diverse opinions from 'the market'.

Meanwhile

- Myself and co-author continue to build up ideas for other syllabuses – vocabulary, writing, pron., etc. in terms of activity types and topic. We also build up a bank of authentic texts which we feel we can use or adapt. This is usually done separately, with follow-up meetings to discuss and decide.
- There is often a meeting with the designer and art editor at this stage to discuss the 'look' we want from the book, and how we can make it look different from other levels.
- When reports come back on draft unit and rationale there is a meeting (at a 'neutral' spot like a country hotel) with the publisher and project manager, to share views and 'take a stand' on what changes. This is where sparks usually fly!

First draft

At first draft stage we don't worry about writing to the page, detailed artbriefs, recordings, keys, etc. We send the first draft out to about 14 readers and triallers and feedback on the first draft is again followed up by a mega-meeting with publishers, when changes in content and philosophy may occur. At this point readers are encouraged to focus on the big issues rather than the 'toddlers'.

Otherwise during the first draft stage the publisher and editor keep pretty much off our back, apart from helping to find texts and researching song permissions etc. More and more, they (and we) are getting involved in 'research visits' to schools in the UK and abroad to find out 'what the market really wants' and this is fed in, where possible.

Second draft

This is usually done over a relatively intensive period and will often involve quite a lot of change – finding new texts, cutting out presentations, adding other activities, etc. At this point, we become much more critical, and start to write much more 'to the page', with an eye on design and layout.

This is also sent to readers, but by this stage (hopefully) they are commenting much more on the micros.

At this stage we also have to get involved in briefing the person writing our Workbook and Teacher's Book. This always involves more work than we remember – as the decisions for what to include rest with us.

Third draft

Usually within a very limited time, and has to involve making our own recordings, too, as well as the key. At this point the publishing team are very involved, and as we are writing, 'finished' units will be copy-edited and sent back to us, usually requesting drastic cuts. There are also meetings with designers and editors.

Finally

From the day we finish writing there is, on average, six months of non-stop follow-up production work, particularly in the area of design, cuts and rubrics. This is, perhaps, the most stressful time, perhaps because of the continual liaison with the whole team, rather than just us two.

The writer refers to the publishing team which may typically consist of a publisher in overall charge, a commissioning editor, whose project it is, one or more desk editors who work on the material in detail, and a designer (although much design work is now freelanced). Supporting this team will be a recording studio producer and actors for audio tapes, artists and photographers, picture researchers, copyright clearers and proof-readers. There will be a number of 'readers' who give feedback on the material at various stages, and 'pilot' teachers who check the material in classroom use.

Two relatively new developments are worth noting: input from marketing, and the rise of the freelance editor. For most UK publishers the influence of the marketing team over almost every aspect of materials production is now paramount, particularly as more market-specific courses are being produced. It is input from marketing which sets the parameters within which the writer operates.

Just as important as the relationships within the writing team is the relationship between writers and editors. Typically in the past materials were produced by the publisher's own staff. Cost pressures and 'downsizing' have led to the increasing use of freelance editors and designers working under the overall control of a commissioning editor. This is neither good nor bad in itself, but in a major project can lead to the authors having to relate to an increasingly large number of 'new' people, with the consequent inevitable and vital 'getting to know you' phase occupying more and more time.

7.5 Designer and illustrators

Whilst a number of the contributors complained of lack of involvement with the design of their books, the account which follows accurately reflects the current awareness of the importance of design. Frequently a design for the look of the student page is finalised before much of the writing is done, and authors write to fit the design.

'We have always been very involved in the design process. This can be highly rewarding if you have a good and congenial designer; it can be murder if you and the designer have different agendas. Of course, to some extent, you and the designer always have different agendas in the sense that she or he wants the design to be aesthetically pleasing and you want it to be pedagogically effective. We have always had a general meeting with designers before they begin working on the book, to try and communicate both ways our ideas for the book, and, for instance, to look over samples of illustrators' work to come to some kind of consensus about what we feel comfortable with. We also write a general brief covering points that are important to us, e.g. having a spread of age, race, sex, ability, social class in the people depicted in the illustrations; we request that the designer bear this in mind, and that each illustrator see it as well.

Some of the problems with designers may also come from the fact that they are operating on a tight budget and can only employ third-rate illustrators. They won't tell you this: they will try and convince you that the illustrations you are getting are actually very good.

There are sometimes problems with the artbriefs for illustrators. These come from two sources:

1. My maxim of illustrators: any one illustrator can either read or draw. So either s/he reads your artbrief carefully and takes care to observe it, in order to produce a boring pedestrian illustration that your seven-year-old could have done; or s/he produces a wonderful illustration that will really draw your learners in and make the page striking and attractive ... but the learners won't be able to do the corresponding exercise because some of the elements of the illustration are wrong or missing.
2. Suspension of Gricean maxims. You can't assume anything with an illustrator. If you say 'desert scene', it is best to specify that there should be no igloos in it. If you don't, and you complain about the igloos in the art rough, you will be told it is your fault. Learning to write a tight artbrief may be the most difficult subskill of the EFL writer's trade.'

Whilst the two 'problems' referred to above as happening 'sometimes' are not common, it is axiomatic in publishing that design and illustration can make or break a book. This has resulted in coursebooks which look more like glossy magazines than teaching materials. It would be interesting to compare the reactions of learners from different cultures to today's highly designed full-colour coursebooks. Does the expenditure of so much time and money increase the effectiveness of learning, or merely ensure that one book is purchased rather than another? To what extent is a fashionable design a barrier rather than an aid to learning?

7.6 Technology

(*Note from the Editor: The section below is reproduced from the 1998 edition of this book and describes research carried out in 1994.*)

Submission of text on disk as well as paper was the norm by 1994 rather than the exception. Ironically, publishers' desire to set text direct from disk and eliminate errors from rekeying means that the disks have to be submitted without any of the wonderful features of design and layout which modern word processing packages allow. The first of the contributions below raises the question of the extent of progress through technology.

'I write on an Apple Mac, which I enjoy, and I'm fortunate that my co-authors use the same word-processing program so it's simple to exchange disks. Sometimes we work together over cups of tea at the kitchen table, but more often we communicate by phone, post and fax. And now my editors and most of my co-authors use e-mail, so there is increasing pressure for me to follow suit. I certainly recognise the practical advantages of being able to transmit material from screen to screen when deadlines are pressing.

But the advance in electronic communication doesn't appear to have speeded up the publishing process. And there are psychological implications that worry me. If the publisher faxes me a document rather than posting it, I feel I should respond immediately. Instant transmission seems to demand instant response, constant accessibility. The medium is the message. It's easy, it's fast and it's very beguiling. Yet sometimes I don't want to be instantly accessible – I value my time and space.'

'What I write with matters a lot to me. I always start with pen and paper and my first plan (pre-draft) is usually a 'mind map', with lots of balloons and arrows and crossings out. I often use different coloured pens to help me remember to include particular exercises or quotations at particular points in what I am writing. I recently rediscovered (3,000 miles away and 15 years later) a favourite fountain pen I thought I had lost, and now I find myself using it a lot. It sounds pathetic, but I really feel more comfortable writing with it than with any other pen.'

'I write with pen and paper. Usually I use ball pens and plain A4 size paper.'

'I invariably use scrap paper (i.e. unused handouts or the blank side of previous typed drafts) – I feel less guilty about covering sheet after sheet.'

'I used to write with a pen in a thick notebook. I now have a lap-top Toshiba computer. It is an old one, but good enough for my work.'

'Most of the writing process takes place on paper. I still cannot get my mind around the typewriter/computer kind of writing.'

'I wrote my first books (early 1980s) on a typewriter, but then moved on to a personal computer. I've never written books by hand. I touch-type, so I've always been able to type faster than I can think, and get thoughts down more efficiently that way. I do remember, though, the difference it made when we moved from typewriters to word processing.'

'I usually go straight to the computer and compose at the keyboard except when I am not in my office or at home, like when I'm in a cafe when it's a very demanding writing task, say, when I have to use a lot of tact, in which case I would do a draft on paper when I need to lay out words in tabular form, e.g. when I'm designing a car hire record form, in which case I'll do a pencil sketch on paper.'

'I write straight on to the screen, no paper, no favourite pens.'

Throwing out a 15-year-old manuscript composed on a manual type-writer, covered with Tipp-Ex® blobs, and glued-on extra bits, emended in coloured pen and pencil is a salutary experience for today's author: none of us would like to go back to that time. Nevertheless, it is interesting to speculate on how different the contributions to this chapter might have been if I had asked for them on disk, rather than handwritten on a questionnaire.

7.7 A time and a place to write

Another reassuringly divergent set of views, this time on when and where to write. The final contribution may represent a dream, rather than reality!

'Usually when the kids are away. I need complete peace when I write. Distractions break my flow of ideas.'

'In my daughter's bedroom, late at night for two–three hours. The room is small, homely, and cramped, with a parrot.'

'I need solid blocks of 'private' time to do any serious writing of materials for classroom use or publication. This usually means after 10 pm after my son has gone to bed, up to 1 am or 2 am, until I start fading, or if I fade after sitting at the computer for, say, half an hour, I'll try to get up early in the morning like 5 am, to meet my own quota, or more often, publisher's deadlines.'

'When I was in the 'peaceful' position of just being a writer my best working time was evening and into the night, in my study at home, with masses of books around, and the computer in front of me and the curtains pulled.'

'I usually write in my study, at the desk, by the window. My bulldog always comes to sleep and snore near me when I work. I can never work at night; my most efficient time is morning.'

'I write mostly at night. I prefer that time as it is comparatively quieter here and I can concentrate more. I write in the family study room. When my children go to bed I come and work at my table.'

'I do my best creative writing (I think) in the morning (have to get up at 6.30 to put my young son on the school bus) and mid-afternoon. I've got a small flat about a mile away from the house where I do all my writing work. Marital harmony has followed the decision to make a total separation between family and writing.'

'I usually write at night in my sitting room-cum-study. I begin writing after supper, say between 7.30 and 8.00 and continue until 11.30 or midnight.'

'I write in a room overlooking the garden, so the only distraction out of the windows are the movements of cats and squirrels. I sometimes long for a view of the street to watch the schoolchildren, students and passers-by, but maybe I'd get less work done.'

'In a study at home, and this has its pros and cons. You don't waste time travelling, and everything is in its place. But at the beginning it took a while to train other people, neighbours, friends, that during the day I was actually working and not available for chatty phone calls or drop-in visits; with some people I would have to say on the phone 'I'm afraid I'm in a meeting just now.' And the worst aspect, I think is that it's always there: especially if you're worried about being late for a deadline, it is so easy to go and do a few more hours' work in the evening, or to get up early in the morning, and never escape from the work. This can be very stressful.'

'Somewhere quiet, comfortable, bright (ideally sunny). An armchair by the fire suits me very well for certain kinds of writing, at the drafting stage, anyway. I also like a sunny window-seat.

One particularly productive period was spent on my own on a secluded beach, just letting ideas for exercises float to the surface of my barely conscious mind. I jotted these down and worked them up into exercises later.'

7.8 Conclusion

A different set of prompts and questions would certainly have elicited different responses, and it would have been interesting to see if these had focused more on learning principles and objectives, and less on syllabus, ideas and procedures. It would also be interesting to learn more about the relationship between writers and the classroom: how many still teach regularly, visit schools and observe classes, and work with groups of teachers. Then there is the publisher's view of writers, the teacher's view of materials, and the learner's perception of the whole process. What does come through strongly in the range of views presented here is the apparent centrality of writing to the contributors' lives, and the seriousness with which they take it.

One of the delights of the course in Oxford was the sharing of experience, and the realisation that one was not alone. It is to be hoped that the above accounts will strike chords with other writers around the world, and lead to a little more understanding between writers and publishers.

7.9 Reflections 15 years later

The contributions that follow show that, whilst there has been change in the predictable area of technology, the creative and cooperative aspects of materials writing appear timeless.

7.9.1 The influence of the market

An area not often mentioned in the reflections below is the influence of the market over the writing process. The original chapter noted as a relatively new development the fact that 'For most UK publishers the influence of the marketing team over almost every aspect of materials production is now paramount' (p. 161). This view is echoed by Mares (2003: 131) who begins: 'When I first began to write commercial materials I was subconsciously writing for clones of myself' and concludes 'When writing, do not write just for yourself. Remember you are writing for a market. You need to know the market, which means getting as much information as you can about the market and writing for that market' (2003: 139). As discussed in section 7.9.5 below, Harmer also emphasises the importance of not writing for yourself. From personal experience I would emphasise the importance of market focus. Coursebook projects I have been involved in have been researched in great depth with repeated visits to the market by authors and editors whilst a project is under development and during the writing process. These visits take many forms, always including a lot of classroom observation of lessons in a range of schools and locations, discussions with students about their interests, individual and focus group discussions with teachers, meetings with educational advisers and planners, and discussions with methodologists and teacher trainers working in the market. When syllabuses and sample materials are drafted, they are discussed with and reported on by focus groups of classroom teachers, sometimes remotely but often face to face with the authors. Then as further materials are produced, the reporting and feedback meetings continue with further visits to the market. Finally, when the course is published, market visits continue for promotion but also to see the materials in action and gather feedback for further editions. This market focus effectively nails the myth that coursebook materials are essentially BANA (Britain, Australasia, America) and that they ignore the majority TESEP (Tertiary, Secondary, Primary) perspective (Holliday 1994).

7.9.2 The ELT writer and technology

Under the heading *Technology*, the original article focused on the technical aspects of writing. Interestingly these aspects are not mentioned in any of the contributions that follow. The ubiquitous computer interface has become invisible, and Pete Sharma emphasises the use of technology by writers to research the language itself and the content of materials. A direct implication of the ability of writers to use concordancers and the World Wide Web as a source for text is vastly improved access to authentic text. In reviewing the implications of SLA research for the use of authentic texts as a basis for language-learning materials, Mishan (2005: 41) concludes: 'Authentic texts provide the best source of rich and varied comprehensible input for language learners' (see also Gilmore 2007). The days of the files and boxes full of yellowing newspaper articles and magazines saved for future use are over in a world where 'google' has become an accepted verb.

The life of the ELT writer has been transformed due to advances in technology in general, and educational technology in particular. Today's author can look up thousands of words in context using a concordancer; he or she can tap into the vast source of knowledge on the World Wide Web, copy and paste text, refine and repurpose it. As a result of technology, the examples of language provided by coursebook material are more authentic, more realistic.

Before the revolution in corpus linguistics led by John Sinclair and the Collins COBUILD team, it was common for writers to invent sentences to exemplify a grammar point, or present a lexical item. The sentence: 'I usually play Bach, but today I'm playing Mozart' was clearly invented purely for language teaching purposes. Nowadays, such an artificial sentence would be ridiculed, since writers, through technology, can access real examples of how language works. The power of the computer has allowed us to see patterns which were previously invisible. ELT writers can use a concordancer to find every occurrence of a word or phrase within a corpus. A corpus is a 'collection of texts, written or spoken, stored on a computer' (O'Keeffe *et al.* 2007). To study a word in context, the writer can simply go to a free web concordance, type in a word, hit 'enter' and then look at a resulting concordance line. The search result displays the 'key word in context' (KWIC) and use of concordancers has revealed information about areas such as collocation. Coursebook writers tend to use more professional concordancing tools such as WordSmith and MonoConc or subscribe to programmes such as Sketch Engine which can provide detailed profiles of words.

ELT writers, as well as dictionary compilers, teachers and students, have gained new and vital insights into word frequency. This knowledge influences choices as to which words and expressions are worthy of inclusion in coursebooks, and at what level they could be dealt with. Many current coursebook covers include a symbol stating which corpus they are based on, such as the CIC (Cambridge International Corpus).

7.9.3 Using the Internet

'The World Wide Web is a rich source of knowledge for writers, as well as inspiration on every topic imaginable. Search engines such as Google make searches quick and painless. Sites such as Wikipedia can provide information instantly, and are largely accurate. Text from websites can be cut and pasted into a Word document. This opens up the possibility of re-purposing an original piece of writing, making it more accessible to lower levels by stripping out obscure language. Texts from different sources can be merged. Of course, it is much easier for any writer to plagiarise. On the other hand, it could be argued that it has always been possible to copy other people's ideas and words; technology has just made it easier.'

(Pete Sharma)

7.9.4 Writing together

In these two contributions Sue Kay and Jeff Stranks reflect how co-authors work together, coming to differing conclusions about being in the same room. My own experience is that working face to face is essential for the initial planning, brainstorming, creative phases as well as for discussion of material and reviewing. But new technology (and not so new, the telephone) can mean that authors can 'virtually' be in the same room whilst in different parts of the country or globe. Certainly instantaneous exchanges of text and activities and hours spent in discussion on the phone can work for some as well as physical proximity. The key point is for both to be on the same wavelength.

'Our writing partnership came about naturally, organically. We weren't manufactured by a publisher. Less Girls Aloud, more Arctic Monkeys! Some may say more Morecombe and Wise!

But it was our idea to write together, and like many good ideas, it started over a nice bottle of wine. Our starting point was finding that we both had the same ideas about what was missing in the market, and what sort of coursebook we would like to use with our students. Thanks to our open-minded publishers, our unsolicited manuscript was accepted. Since then, with the help of some highly creative people, we have managed to remain loyal to our beliefs about language learning and write a course that stands up to the 'litmus test' we wrote down over ten years ago before we'd written a word: 'Does it work in the classroom? Are the students having fun?'

When we started out, we had no idea how we were going to work together, but we quickly realised that there was no way a single word would be written with us in the same room. Possibly because through the writing partnership we've become very close friends and we love to chat, putting the world to rights, exchanging anecdotes about our children and so on.

But a way of working together emerged quite quickly – we'd brainstorm ideas together. Then I'd 'dirty the page'. In other words, I'd type lots of ideas, from the sublime to the ridiculous, into a Word document and send them over to my writing partner for his reactions. We'd choose the best topics and texts together and I'd work on the reading texts and audio content, while my writing partner would work on the language development aspect of the course, using these texts as a springboard.

Call us old-fashioned, but we can't imagine writing a course with someone who lives on a different continent. We meet a lot – and not just to gossip. Regular editorial meetings have given impetus to the writing process and fortunately for us, we've worked with the best publishers, editors and project managers in the business.'

(Sue Kay)

'I've worked with more than one co-author so things can vary a bit. However there are a couple of constants.

The primary one is that of synergy – just being in the same room helps! Writing is a creative process of course, but that also varies in degree. So when it's the really creative stuff – topics, texts, speaking activities – then there's nothing to beat thrashing it out with one or more co-authors. And that requires being in the same room – not always easy when you live continents apart, but if you have sympathetic publishers, as I always have had, then the distances can be regularly overcome.

But there are also the less creative moments – writing the grammar exercise, producing the questions for a text, checking and polishing a manuscript before delivery, etc. (This is not to diminish the importance of such undertakings – they need careful attention too, but just don't require so much creative energy or synergy, I think.) Much of this can be done alone, but it's far better if your colleague is in the room. Firstly, it's just a matter of collegiality, a sense of working together. Secondly (and here I speak only for myself), the avoidance strategies are more easily diverted – the fourth cup of coffee can wait, the game of patience doesn't get played, the swimming pool doesn't get swum in (pool in the building, I hasten to add, not a private one). This won't always mean that the phone doesn't ring or other menial daily tasks disappear, but somehow more work gets done and hence (very importantly) deadlines get met or better still, beaten.

So work together whenever feasible – this seems to be what I've learned. Email, Skype and the like are great, but, as in any relationship, eventually a poor substitute for being there. And then there's the glass of wine at the end of the day – tastes much better in company.'

(Jeff Stranks)

7.9.5 The creative process

Jeremy Harmer gives us an insight into how the creative process works for him. His account chimes with that recommended by Mishan (2005: 59): 'What is suggested here is a text-driven approach, one that is … learner-centred and works in a converse fashion [to PPP], in that it starts with (authentic) texts, and derives the language features to be studied from these'. It differs significantly from the experienced task designer quoted in Johnson (2003: 93): 'I guess I am going to try to put together ideas that I have already used in some new way or put together ideas that I have seen in books, in resources elsewhere, and combine them in my own way. That's how I usually do these sort of things. And maybe something new and revolutionary will turn up in the process.' Harmer's interesting conclusion below compares writing to teaching, a suitable way to end this comparison of how writers write now and 15 years ago.

'First of all I look for a topic or an approach that has a chance of engaging students and teachers. This is not, of course, as easy as it sounds since what interests one person may not interest another. But if teachers and students have some kind of interest in the world around them, then surely …? Well yes, but the danger is that I will fill the book with what interests me, and worse still, what interests people like me (if there are such people!) in the society and geographical reality that I inhabit – and taking into account that I, like many coursebook-writing colleagues, come from a 'humanities' background, rather than having maths and science as my benchmarks. So I immediately start to question my choice to see if it has a chance of involving other 'different' people.

Now I have fixed on a topic – a story, a theme, an extract from somewhere – and so it is time for the 'classroom-in-my-mind'. This is a kind of amalgam of classes I have taught in the UK or Mexico, or observed in countries around the world, films I have seen and endless (and fascinating) conversations about classroom incidents – successes and failures – that we teachers swap with each other (and should) whenever we meet. I'm trying, now, to think of how to bring my new topic or extract into that classroom (-in-my-mind). How will the students react? What kind of approach or activity will be most appropriate to get them going, to get them to 'buy into' what I have to offer? As I start to write I see this all playing out in my head. But who is the teacher? Me? The classroom-in-my-mind wobbles and blurs, light refracted by the many surfaces it is reflected on.

And then there's the 'language thing'! What language do I want the teacher and students to focus on? What words or grammar can I mine the text or situation for?

Writing coursebook material is like having all the resources in the world available for you but having to locate them without a map, wearing a blindfold, and having your hands tied behind your back. You know what you are looking for – kind of – but it's difficult to find, and even when you do it's difficult to 'knock it into shape'. At the back of your mind there is always the knowledge that, just as with student input and intake, there is no guarantee that other teachers and students will see things the way you do, or understand what you were hoping to achieve.

And then there's the issue of how much you can expect students and teachers to 'dialogue' with each other if and when you offer them topics to explore or conversations to create; there are issues of how to make a book live in an age when YouTube and podcasts are there for everyone to use, and when the governor of California wants to cut costs by replacing textbooks with the Internet. Is a book the right kind of teaching aid anyway, and if so, for who? These are the thoughts that lurk at the back of consciousness ready to invade us with doubt and uncertainty whenever we have a moment to stop and think!

Coursebook writing has always been like this: a genuine wish to provide material that will brighten any class; a desire to offer reliable material for the most put-upon teacher; a matter of excitement and compromises; an act of creativity that all too often seems suffocating and doomed. But when, against all the odds, and in the light of linguistic and methodological constraints, you actually manage to make something that you know will work, the feeling is fantastic. It's not actually that much different from teaching; we don't always teach great classes, but when we do we want to shout it from the rooftops. That's what it's like on the rare occasions when coursebook writers get it right.'

(Jeremy Harmer)

So, whilst much has changed in 15 years, the essential truth that coursebook writing is a creative rather than a mechanical process remains. The digital revolution may mean that in the future the 'print' coursebook as we know it vanishes, and the electronic materials which replace it are multi-authored packages assembled to meet the requirements of particular groups of students. Coursebook writers may increasingly be paid fees for sets of materials rather than sharing the risk of creating a whole book or series with the publisher by getting royalties. Nevertheless, the act of writing will remain an art which can provide satisfaction for the author as well as contributing to the learner's education. Publishing teaching materials will also remain a team effort involving people with a range of complementary skills, even if those team members may not be in the same room, or even continent. The rewards for writers will also continue to be the same: not pecuniary (except in a few lucky cases), but personal, as in watching a class use your material successfully or meeting a student who says with a big grin, 'I learned English from your book!'

Further reading

Gilmore, A. 2007. 'Authentic materials and authenticity in foreign language learning'. *Language Teaching*, 40: 97–118.

Harmer J. *et al.* 2004–2009. *Just Right*. London: Marshall Cavendish.

Hidalgo, A. C., D. Hall and G. M. Jacobs. 1995. *Getting Started: Materials Writers on Materials Writing*. Singapore: SEAMEO Regional Language Centre.

Holliday, A. R. 1994. *Appropriate Methodology and Social Context*. Cambridge: Cambridge University Press.

Johnson, K. 2003. *Designing Language Teaching Tasks*. Basingstoke: Palgrave Macmillan.

Kay, S. and V. Jones. *Inside Out*. 2001–2003. Oxford: Macmillan.

Mares, C. 2003. 'Writing a coursebook'. In B. Tomlinson (ed.), *Developing Materials for Language Teaching*. London: Continuum.

Mishan, F. 2005. *Designing Authenticity into Language Learning Materials*. Bristol: Intellect.

O'Keeffe, A., M. McCarthy, and R. Carter. 2007. *From Corpus to Classroom*. Cambridge: Cambridge University Press.

Puchta H., J. Stranks, P. Lewis-Jones and R. Carter. 2004–2008. *English in Mind*. Cambridge: Cambridge University Press.

Sharma P. and B. Barrett. 2007. *Blended Learning*. Oxford: Macmillan.

Stranks, J. 2009. 'Co-authoring coursebooks'. *Folio*, 13(2): 18–19.

Tomlinson, B. (ed.). 2003 *Developing Materials for Language Teaching*. London: Continuum.

Comments on Part B

Brian Tomlinson

The three chapters in this section offer very different perspectives on the process of creating language teaching materials, but they do share some themes and they do raise similar issues.

All three chapters stress the dynamic nature of materials development and reveal how materials, whether they be for publication or tomorrow's lesson, need to be constantly evaluated and revised. Materials should keep changing, and, in fact, I even change my own published materials every time I use them in class. Ideally materials need to be monitored by the author(s), by other 'experts' not involved in the writing team and by typical users of the material. This is the process commonly adopted on textbook projects these days and which, in my personal experience, has been very successful in increasing the learning potential of books written in the 1990s for schools in Bulgaria, Morocco and Namibia (Tomlinson 1995) and more recently for materials for teachers in Ethiopia, for young professionals in Sub-Saharan Africa, for university students in Turkey and Vietnam, and for primary students in China. The Namibian Textbook Project is a particularly interesting example of dynamic development of materials. A team of 30 writers (teachers, curriculum developers and advisers) worked together for eight days to develop a book (*On Target* 1995). During that time the team used responses to teacher and student questionnaires plus their pooled experience and expertise to determine the content and approach of the book and then to draft, revise and write it. Later it was trialled by teachers throughout the country, monitored by 'experts' and then finalised. This collaborative, interactive approach is one I would recommend whether for global coursebooks, local textbooks or even institution-specific material.

Another theme common to the three chapters is that of meeting the needs of all the interested parties (a theme also discussed by Frances Amrani when she focuses on the monitoring of materials in Chapter 11 and by Hitomi Masuhara when she considers the needs of teachers in Chapter 10). Whilst most people would agree that meeting the needs of the learners should be the primary target, it is obviously important to meet the needs of the teachers, the writers and the 'sponsors' too. If teachers are not enthused by materials, their dissatisfaction is always apparent to the learners, the materials lose credibility and the learners' motivation and investment of energy are reduced. If writers do not enjoy writing the materials and are not proud of them, this deficiency is detected by the users and the credibility of the materials is diminished. If the publishers, Ministry of Education or other sponsors are not satisfied with the materials, then they will not be active in promoting them. In my experience, the way to satisfy all the interested parties is not compromise but collaboration at all stages of the project. In the Namibian Textbook Project representatives of the Ministry of Education, the Examination Board, the publishers, the teacher trainers and the teachers were present throughout the development of the book. They gave advice, they gave feedback and they gave positive encouragement to the writers to enjoy the process of developing the book.

One of the issues touched on by all three chapters concerns the question of whether to predetermine the syllabus of the materials or to let the syllabus develop organically from the materials. In some cases the authors are writing to a specific brief and must follow an imposed syllabus absolutely. But one of the things we know about language acquisition is that most learners only learn what they need or want to learn. Providing opportunities to learn the language needed to participate in an interesting activity is much more likely to be profitable than teaching something because it is the next teaching point in the syllabus. And deriving learning points from an engaging text or activity is much easier and more valuable than finding or constructing a text which illustrates a predetermined teaching point. My own preference is for a text-driven approach to syllabus development (Tomlinson 2003a). If the written and spoken texts are selected for their richness and diversity of language as well as for their potential to achieve engagement, then a wide syllabus will evolve which will achieve natural and sufficient coverage. If the materials are constrained by an external syllabus, then a text-driven approach with constant reference to a checklist (as suggested by Philip Prowse in Chapter 7) is the most profitable approach. This is how *On Target* (see above) was written, with the writers focusing on learning points which suggested themselves from their texts, but also with me as advisor constantly checking to see if a particular point was receiving too much attention in the book so far, or not enough.

Another of the issues raised by these chapters is the question of to what extent materials should be and can be driven by learning principles. One argument is that principles are subjective and diverse and that different participants in the materials development process will follow differing principles. Compromise is therefore necessary to satisfy the different parties and also to cater for different learner styles and expectations. A counter argument is that compromised principles are no longer principles and that they can lead to an eclectic mishmash of activities which are perceived by both teachers and learners alike to lack consistency and conviction: good materials are those which are consistently informed by the same set of believed-in principles. The danger of this second argument is that closed principles can lead to inflexible procedures which cater for a minority of learners only. So a belief that listening is the primary skill in early language acquisition can lead to an edict that beginners should not see the target language written down; or a belief that practice makes perfect can lead to a plethora of mechanical drills which fail to engage the energy or attention of the majority of users of the materials. The answer is not easy; but I think it lies in the overt establishment of agreed and justifiable principles followed by procedural compromises which cater for differing preferences, providing they are driven by one or more of the established principles (Tomlinson 2003b). In other words, an approach to materials writing in which the ongoing evaluation of the materials being developed is constantly informed by a checklist of agreed principles, both universal principles applicable to any learning context anywhere and local criteria specific to the target learning context. This worked on the Namibian Project and can work on any materials project providing one of the agreed principles is that different learners learn different things and in different ways.

References

On Target. 1995. Grade 10 English Second Language Learner's Book. Windhoek: Gamsberg Macmillan.

Tomlinson, B. 1995. 'Work in progress: textbook projects'. *Folio*, 2(2), 26–31.

—— 2003a. 'Developing principled frameworks for materials development'. In B. Tomlinson (ed.), *Developing Materials for Language Teaching*. London: Continuum.

—— 2003b. 'Materials evaluation'. In B. Tomlinson (ed.), *Developing Materials for Language Teaching*. London: Continuum.

Part C   The process of materials evaluation

8   The analysis of language teaching materials: inside the Trojan Horse

Andrew Littlejohn

8.1 Introduction

One of my earliest memories as a once untrained, unqualified language teacher is of the principal of my first school proudly presenting me with my coursebook. It was, she explained, the 'best book available', with the most up-to-date method, that would guarantee excellent results. It had, what's more, a major technological innovation – a piece of green card which students should use to cover the text whilst they looked at four pictures and listened to the reel-to-reel tape recordings. She showed me how it worked. The recording would say 'It is half past nine. Deborah is having breakfast and listening to some music on the radio. The maid is carrying a tray with some more coffee on it.' Then, I was to direct the students' attention to the prompts printed next to the pictures, '(a) What time? (b) What/Deborah? (c) What/maid?', and ask them to complete questions. I was to continue like that for each of the pictures and recordings. Next, the students were to remove the card, read the texts aloud and answer more questions, before we moved on to some substitution exercises on the grammar point. Finally, there was an instalment of a story which ran through the entire book. I could make up my own questions for that, or make slashed question prompts for the students to ask each other across the classroom. The next unit would be the same, and all units after that would be the same, until, at Unit 12, the book ended. There was a teacher's book available, the principal told me, but I wouldn't need it, apparently.

She was right, of course – I didn't need the teacher's book. The book was so scripted and provided so little that it was not long before I discovered that I had to contribute a lot more if I and my students were to stay sane in the classroom. Through the process of personal involvement that this required, I actually became grateful to the book writer for allowing me such space to teach myself how to teach, whilst providing at least a backbone of something that was deemed 'a course', in contrast to the somewhat random nature of activities and texts with which I supplemented it.

It is hard to imagine beginning teachers in respectable language schools these days finding themselves in such a situation. In contrast to the slender text I was given with its 'technological innovation' of the piece of green card, teachers today, new and experienced alike, are now offered a rich palette of materials to accompany any course they choose to adopt: student's books, workbooks, detailed teacher's guides, videos, CDs, DVDs, electronic whiteboard materials, test-generating software, readers, website activities, downloadable lesson plans, teacher training packages and more. There is often so much material available that teachers could be forgiven for thinking that there is simply no need – and indeed no time – for them to supplement with anything at all.

Over the years since I entered language teaching, ELT publishing has become a fiercely competitive industry. A simple text such as the one I first used would stand no chance of surviving these days, as it would be drowned out by the abundance of materials offered by other publishers to support their main course offerings. Publishers now need to offer so much extra material, much of it free of charge, if they are to keep ahead of the competition. Whilst this plethora of material can have its advantages, one thing for sure is that it now presents a very different picture for classroom time. Whilst the reduced nature of the text I was first given meant I *had* to supplement it with my own ideas, contemporary course offerings now offer to provide for everything. The extent to which materials may now effectively structure classroom time from a distance has thus increased considerably. As Michael Apple (1985) once termed it, we now have a clear instance of the separation of the **conception** of plans for classroom work, from the **execution** of those plans. See also Aronowitz and Giroux (1987) and Canagarajah (1999: 85–8) on this point.

The issue that I wish to address in this chapter, however, is not whether this phenomenon is good or bad (and there are points for both arguments, depending on what individual materials contain), but that these developments necessitate even more than ever before a means by which we can closely analyse materials. It is by now well established that materials may have an impact beyond simply the learning of the language they present. As I have elsewhere argued at length (Littlejohn 1995, Littlejohn and Windeatt 1989) both the content and methodology of classroom work may contain a variety of 'hidden outcomes', particularly as they will always encode curriculum ideologies concerning what language use *is*, how learning is to happen, and the division of power and responsibility between teachers and learners (Canagarajah 1999: 85–8, Lesikin 2001a, Littlejohn 1997, Wallace 2006). We need, therefore, a means to examine the implications that use of a set of materials may have for classroom work and come to grounded opinions about whether or not the methodology and content of the materials is appropriate for a particular teaching/learning context.

As the claims that publishers and authors now make for their materials have extended with the increase in their provision, we additionally need to be able to test claims against what is offered: Do the materials truly help to develop autonomy? Do they actually involve problem-solving? Are they really learner-centred? Are they genuinely cross-curricular? Do they, in fact, draw on 'multiple intelligences'? Are they based on the latest 'SLA research'? We need, in short, a means of looking inside the Trojan Horse to see what lies within.

My concern in this chapter, then, is with the analysis of materials 'as they are', with the content and ways of working that they propose. This, it must be emphasised, may be quite distinct, from what actually happens in classrooms. Analysing materials, it must be recognised, is quite a different matter from analysing 'materials-in-action'. Precisely what happens in classrooms and what outcomes occur when materials are brought into use will depend upon numerous further factors, not least of which is the reinterpretation of materials and tasks by both teachers and learners (see, inter alia, Littlejohn 2008 and Littlejohn 2010, which discuss school-aged students' reinterpretation of materials for learner training, and Slimani 2001). A discussion of how effective materials may be in achieving their aims is therefore beyond my discussion here. My concern is to enable a close analysis of materials themselves, to investigate their nature, as a step distinct from evaluating their worth for specified purposes or contexts.

One of the most obvious sources for guidance in analysing materials, however, is the large number of frameworks which already exist to aid in the evaluation of course materials (e.g. Byrd 2001, CIEL 2000, Cunningsworth 1995, Garinger 2002, Harmer 2007, McGrath 2002). Whilst recognising that such frameworks frequently serve a useful purpose in guiding the selection of materials, one of the principal problems in their use is that they usually involve making general, impressionistic judgements on the materials, rather than examining in depth what the materials contain. Typically, they also contain implicit assumptions about what 'desirable' materials should look like. Thus we have evaluation questions such as 'Are the exercises balanced in their format, containing both controlled and free practice?' (Garinger 2002); and 'Do illustrations create a favourable atmosphere for practice in reading and spelling by depicting realism and action?' (Byrd 2001: 425). Each of these areas, however, will be debatable – a balance of free and controlled practice will depend on your own view of how a second language is best acquired; and the relationship between a 'favourable atmosphere' and the depiction of 'realism and action' is likely to vary depending on the reader/viewer. The principal problem is that most of these evaluative tools are presented as checklists which do not offer the teacher-analyst much assistance in how to ascertain if a particular feature is present or absent.

As a precursor to the evaluation or assessment of any set of materials, we need, then, support in arriving at an analysis of the materials, in such a way that assumptions about what is desirable are separated from a detailed description of the materials. We need, in other words, a general framework which allows materials to 'speak for themselves' and which helps teacher-analysts to look closely into materials before coming to their *own* conclusions about the desirability or otherwise of the materials. This suggests three separate questions which we need to consider carefully:

1. *What aspects* of materials should we examine?
2. *How* can we examine materials?
3. *How* can we relate the findings to our own teaching contexts?

It is to these three questions that I now turn.

8.2 A general framework for analysing materials

8.2.1 What aspects of materials should we examine?

There are very many aspects which one can examine in a set of materials. It would be possible, for example, to describe materials in terms of the quality of the paper and binding, pricing, layout, size, typeface and so on. One might also look closely at the artwork and texts in the materials to see, for example, how the sexes are represented (Ansary and Babaii 2003, Blumberg 2007, Lesikin 2001b, McGrath 2004), how cultural bias may be evident (Ndura 2004), how the materials treat 'green' issues (Haig 2006), how they promote 'consumerism' (Sokolik 2007), and so on. Each of these will be important aspects, depending on the purposes one has in looking at the materials. My focus here, however, is on materials as a *pedagogic* device, that is, as an aid to teaching and learning a foreign language. This will limit the focus to aspects of the *methodology* of the materials, and the linguistic nature of their *content*. To this end, there are a number of established analyses of language teaching which can guide us in identifying significant aspects of materials (principally Breen and Candlin 1987 and Richards and Rodgers 2001). Each of these models, however, was evolved for a specific purpose and so will not, on its own, be suitable for an analysis of *any* set of teaching materials. The framework which I propose (summarised in Figure 8.1 below), draws extensively on both the Breen and Candlin and Richards and Rodgers models in an attempt to provide the basis for a more comprehensive listing of the aspects which, from a pedagogic viewpoint, need to be taken into account when analysing materials.

Figure 8.1 *Aspects of an analysis of language teaching materials*

1. Publication
1. Place of the learner's materials in any wider set of materials
2. Published form of the learner's materials
3. Subdivision of the learner's materials into sections
4. Subdivision of sections into sub-sections
5. Continuity
6. Route
7. Access

2. Design
1. Aims
2. Principles of selection
3. Principles of sequencing
4. Subject matter and focus of subject matter
5. Types of teaching/learning activities
   • what they require the learner to do
   • manner in which they draw on the learner's process competence (knowledge, affects, abilities, skills)
6. Participation: who does what with whom
7. Learner roles
8. Teacher roles
9. Role of the materials as a whole

The framework consists of two main sections: *publication* and *design*. *Publication* relates to the "tangible" or physical aspects of the materials and how they appear as a complete set, whether on paper or electronically. Here we will be concerned with the relationship that may exist between the student's materials and any other components (e.g. whether answer keys are only available in the teacher's materials, how the student's material relates to any audio or video recordings and so on) and the actual form of the material (e.g. durable vs. consumable, worksheets vs. bound book, paper print vs. electronic), all of which may have direct implications for classroom methodology. We may also look inside the materials to determine how they are divided into sections and sub-sections, how a sense of continuity or coherence is maintained and whether the order in which the material can be used is predetermined. This final aspect suggests one further element: how access *into* the materials is supported – for example, whether there are contents lists, wordlists, indexes, search facilities, hyperlinks, and so on.

The second section in the framework *design* (following Richards and Rodgers 2001) relates to the thinking underlying the materials. This will involve consideration of areas such as the apparent aims of the materials (such as the development of 'general English', ESP, or specific skills), how the tasks, language and content in the materials are selected and sequenced (such as a particular syllabus type and use of corpora) and the nature and focus of content in the materials (such as cross-curricular content, storylines, topics). Also of central importance in this will be the nature of the teaching/learning activities which are suggested by the materials (such as 'whole tasks', comprehension tasks, learner training, etc.). An analysis of teaching/learning activities will need to focus closely on what precisely learners are asked to *do*, and how what they do relates to what Breen and Candlin (1987) call learners' 'process competence'. Process competence refers to the learners' capacity to draw on different realms of *knowledge* (concepts, social behaviour and how language is structured), their *affects* (attitudes and values), their *abilities* to express, interpret and deduce meanings, and to use the different *skills* of reading, writing, speaking and listening. Teaching/learning activities are also likely to suggest modes of classroom participation – for example, whether the learners are to work alone or in groups – and, from this, the roles that teachers and learners are to adopt. Finally, we may examine the materials to determine what role they intend for themselves. Do they, for example, aim to 'micro-manage' the classroom event by providing detailed guidance on how teachers and learners are to work together, or do they only provide ideas that teachers and learners are actively encouraged to critically select from or develop?

Taken together, the areas listed in the framework should provide comprehensive coverage of the methodological and content aspects of any set of materials. Armed with such an analytical description of a set of materials, researchers, teachers, materials designers, educational administrators and, indeed, learners, would be in a good position to take decisions about the nature, usefulness or desirability of the materials. We are, however, faced with an immediate problem: how can we arrive at this description? How can we examine the materials to find the information required? In the next section, I would like to consider these questions and propose some practical solutions to guide the detailed analysis of materials.

8.2.2 How can we examine the materials?

Levels of analysis

Looking through the framework set out in the previous section, we can see that some of the aspects will be relatively easy to identify (for example 'published form of the materials' and 'division into sections') whilst others appear more abstract and difficult to establish (for example 'aims' and 'learner/teacher roles'). It is also clear that some of the listed aspects will involve examining different parts of the materials before coming to a general conclusion. 'Principles of sequence', for example, may require looking at the language syllabus and the precise nature of the types of teaching/learning activities (materials may, for example, become methodologically more complex in later parts).

On its own, therefore, the framework listed in Figure 8.1 has very limited use since it is not able to guide the teacher-analyst in examining the materials in any depth. The principal problem is that some aspects in the framework actually entail coming to a conclusion about other aspects in the framework. This means that in building up an analysis of a set of materials, teacher-analysts will not only have to examine different sections of the materials but, more importantly, move through different 'levels' of analysis, making more and more inferences, with increasingly subjective judgements, as they move from a consideration of the more easily identifiable aspects to the more abstract and complex. Figure 8.2 outlines the levels which may be involved, from making subjective selections of objective facts about the materials (Level 1), through deductions about the demands likely to be made of teachers and learners (Level 2), to conclusions about the apparent underlying principles and 'philosophy' of the materials (Level 3).

Figure 8.2   *Levels of analysis of language teaching materials*

1. 'WHAT IS THERE'   *'objective description'*
   • statements of description
   • physical aspects of the materials
   • main steps in the instructional sections

2. 'WHAT IS REQUIRED OF USERS'   *'subjective analysis'*
   • subdivision into constituent tasks
   • an analysis of tasks: what is the learner expected to do? Who with? With what content?

3. 'WHAT IS IMPLIED'   *'subjective inference'*
   • deducing aims, principles of selection and sequence
   • deducing teacher and learner roles
   • deducing demands on learner's process competence

The process of materials evaluation

Level 1: What is there? Objective description

At the top of Figure 8.2 lies the explicit nature of the materials, where we would expect little disagreement in describing the materials. We might begin, for example, with statements found within the materials. These might cover, for example, the publication date, the intended audience, the type of materials (e.g. 'general' or 'specific purpose', 'supplementary' or 'main course'), the amount of classroom time required, and how the materials are to be used (e.g. for self-study, in any order, etc.). Beyond this, we can also look at the physical aspects of the materials such as their published form (for example, durable books or consumable worksheets, electronic or paper), number of pages, use of colour, and the total number of components in a complete set (for example, student's book, workbook, audio materials, etc.). Looking inside the materials we can see how the material is divided into sections (for example, 'units', audioscripts, answer keys and tests) and the means of access into the materials that are provided (for example, indexes, search facilities, detailed contents listing, and hyperlinks). We might also wish to see how the various sections and means of access into the materials are distributed between teacher and learners, since this may provide data for conclusions about teacher–learner roles. Looking further into the materials we can examine how 'units', 'modules', 'blocks' and so on are subdivided, their length, if there is a standard pattern in their design or any recurring features.

As a support for recording this kind of 'explicit' information about a set of materials, Figure 8.3 provides a schedule which teacher-analysts may use to guide their investigation. As an example, the schedule presents an analysis of the 'explicit' nature of a coursebook which I have co-authored, *Primary Colours Pupil's Book 5*. The precise categories of information recorded would, however, depend on the particular materials being analysed and what information is explicitly provided. Since the length of most materials would make it impractical to analyse their entire contents in any further depth, Part B in the schedule records the proportion of the material examined and the main sequence of activity within that extract. Depending on the purpose the teacher-analyst has in mind, an in-depth analysis might be made of the students' or teachers' materials. For a 'snapshot' impression of the general nature of a set of materials, I have found it useful to analyse about 10 per cent to 15 per cent of the total material, ideally chosen around the midpoint. (For example, in a work consisting of 20 'units', this might involve an analysis of Units 9, 10, and 11.)

Level 2: What is required of users? Subjective analysis

Whilst Level 1 was mainly concerned with the 'objective' nature of the materials, the next level in the framework moves the teacher-analyst on

Figure 8.3 *Level 1 – A schedule for recording the explicit nature of a set of materials*

Title: *Primary Colours Pupil's Book 5* **Author**: Littlejohn and Hicks
Publisher: Cambridge University Press **Year**: 2008

A. COURSE PACKAGE AS A WHOLE

1. *Type*: 'general', 'main course' class use for upper elementary

2. *Intended audience*:
age-range: 9–12   school: primary schools   location: worldwide

3. *Extent*:
a. *Components*: durable 'Pupil's Book' (PB), consumable 'Activity Book' (AB), class CDs, Teacher's Book (TB), Teacher Training DVD
b. *Total estimated time*: one school year

4. *Design and layout*:
four-colour PB, two-colour AB, two-colour TB

5. *Distribution*:

a. *Material*	teacher	learners
audio	[x]	[ ]
audio script	[x]	[ ]
answer keys	[x]	[ ]
guidance on use of the material	[x]	[ ]
methodology guidance	[x]	[ ]
extra practice	[x]	[ ]
tests	[x]	[ ]
b. *Access*		
syllabus overview	[x]	[x]
wordlists	[x]	[ ]

6. *Route through the material*:

specified	[x]	
user-determined	[ ]	

7. *Subdivision*:

Six 'units', each consisting of four subsections (A/B/C/D), with some standardised elements:

Section A contains the first part of an episode of a continuing story, with comprehension exercises and language practice. Section concludes with a song.

Section B named '*Language Time*' contains practice on language items.

Section C contains the second part of the story episode, with language practice exercises.

Section D named '*Know it all!*' contains cross-curricular content related to the location of the story episode (Grand Canyon, Great Wall, Venice, Brasilia, etc.) followed by ideas for a project.

B. OVERVIEW OF AN EXTRACT FROM THE PUPIL'S BOOK
1. *Length*: one unit out of six, 16.5% of the Pupil's Book.

2. *Sequence of activity*:
5A 1. read and listen to a story episode, 2. comprehension check, 3. discussion of safety in the mountains, 4. song
5B 1. listen and make sentences, 2. language practice, 3. play a game
5C 1. read and listen to a story episode, 2. comprehension check, 3. discussion and listening
5D 1. read texts and match, share ideas, 2 share ideas (on dinosaurs), 3 research at home, project writing

to a slightly deeper level of analysis to what is probably the most important aspect of materials. Here, we need to draw deductions about what exactly teachers and learners using the materials will have to *do* (assuming they use the materials in the manner indicated). In order to come to these conclusions, we will need to divide the materials into their constituent 'tasks', and then to analyse each task in turn. It is thus important to establish as precisely as possible a definition of what 'a task' is.

One commonly encountered use of the term 'task' is that found in the literature on Task-Based Language Teaching (TBLT). Here, 'task' is seen as referring to classroom work which requires the learners to engage in the negotiation of meaning, and thereby make the language input that they receive comprehensible and thus suitable for acquisition. Thus, in the TBLT sense, 'task' refers to meaning-focused work, such as projects, problem-solving and simulations, most often which bear some resemblance to natural language use outside the classroom (see, inter alia, Nunan 2004, Skehan 1996 and 1998, Willis 1996 and Chapter 9 in this volume by Rod Ellis). For a general framework to analyse *any* set of language-learning materials, however, this definition will be too narrow, since it will be inapplicable to materials which are not meaning-focused (for example, exercises following a grammar pattern, dictations, grammar rule discovery, and so on). An alternative broader meaning, and that which is probably most used by language teachers as it predates TBLT, refers generally to 'what we give students to do in the classroom' (Johnson 2003: 5) and thus encompasses a wide range of activity, including both 'task-based' work, and more traditional form-focused work. Following Breen and Candlin (1987), therefore, the definition I propose is to say that 'task' refers to any proposal contained within the materials for action to be undertaken by the learners, which has the direct aim of bringing about the learning of the foreign language.

Such a wide definition as the one above has the virtue of recognising that there may be many different routes to classroom language learning, from large-scale 'whole tasks' to short 'gap fill' exercises, whilst at the same time excluding work that is not directly related to language learning – for example, copying a chart as a preparation for a listening comprehension exercise, the latter *in itself* not directly related to language learning. In practical terms, however, it is not always easy to determine the aim of a proposed classroom action and it is for this reason that we are now at a second level of inference. Here, then, we are talking about what the teacher-analyst understands as the aim, guided perhaps by a rationale contained in the materials.

A definition of 'task' as broad as the one adopted here, however, needs further detail in order to enable us to focus on the various aspects

188

within tasks. Drawing on the ideas outlined above we can identify three key aspects of tasks:

- How: a process through which learners and teachers are to go.
- With whom: classroom participation concerning with whom (if anyone) the learners are to work.
- About what: content that the learners are to focus on.

Using a detailed definition of this kind, it will now be possible to go through an extract of a set of materials and divide it into separate tasks. In many cases a division into tasks may align with the numbering that the materials contain. For instance, this example consists of two tasks:

1. Read the following text and find answers to these questions [Questions and text follow].
2. Write about a similar experience that you have had.

In the following, however, there would be four tasks, despite the numbering, since the mode of classroom participation changes in exercise 1 (individual to pairs), and the form of the content changes in exercise 2 (oral to written):

1. Read the following text and find answers to these questions. Check your answers with your neighbour.
2. Tell your neighbour about a similar experience that you have had. Write about it.

Figure 8.4 lists three questions we can use to help identify where task boundaries occur, and to reveal their separate nature, reflecting the three aspects of process, participation and content.

Figure 8.4 *Questions for the analysis of task*

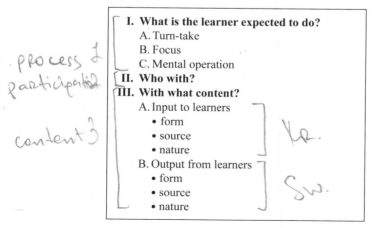

I. **What is the learner expected to do?**
   A. Turn-take
   B. Focus
   C. Mental operation
II. **Who with?**
III. **With what content?**
   A. Input to learners
      • form
      • source
      • nature
   B. Output from learners
      • form
      • source
      • nature

The first question, concerning **process**, contains three subsections which allow us to focus in detail on what precisely learners are expected to do. **Turn-take** relates to the role in classroom discourse that the learners are expected to take. Are they to produce a scripted response to direct questions, using language largely supplied by the materials (e.g. comprehension questions or drills), are they asked to 'initiate', using language not supplied (e.g. 'free writing' or asking their own questions), or are they not required to take any direct interactive role at all (for example, listening to a grammar explanation)? **Focus**, the second element, refers to whether the learners are asked to attend to the meaning of the language, its form or both. **Mental operation** refers to the mental process required – for example, repetition, deducing language rules, or broader processes such as hypothesising, negotiating and so on.

The second question asks about classroom **participation**: who are the learners to work with – alone, in pairs/groups, or with the whole class? Finally, the third question asks about the nature of **content** of the input and of the learner's expected output: is it written or spoken? Is it individual words/sentences or extended discourse? Where does it come from – the materials, the teacher or the learners themselves? And what is its nature – is it, for example, grammar explanations, personal information, fiction, general knowledge and so on?

Each of these questions can be applied to each task in an extract from the materials, and, with the aid of the teacher's materials where appropriate, help to build up a detailed picture of the classroom work that the materials propose. Working through materials in this detailed manner is likely to be very revealing of the underlying character of the materials. It is precisely in the nature of classroom tasks that materials designers' assumptions about the best route to classroom language learning become clear, and in consequence, teacher and learner roles become defined. It is also through an analysis of tasks that we can most effectively test out the various claims made for the materials. If, for example, the materials claim to be 'learner-centred', yet we find that by far most of the tasks involve the learners in 'scripted response' and in working with content supplied by the materials, there would appear to be a serious mismatch. Similarly, if the materials claim to promote cognitive work and problem-solving, but we find that this forms a very small part of the 'mental operations' required and that the rest of the tasks involve simple 'repetition', then we would have reason to doubt the accuracy of the claim. To assist in gaining an overall picture of the materials, percentages for each feature can be calculated, such that, for example, we can say that X per cent of tasks involve 'writing', Y per cent involve 'discussion and negotiation', Z per cent involve 'repetition' and so on.

To support the teacher-analyst in examining each task, Figure 8.5 provides a further schedule where features of each task can be recorded. Figure 8.6 presents two extracts from the coursebook mentioned earlier, *Primary Colours Pupils Book 5*, showing where task boundaries occur, based on the definition of 'task' given earlier. Figure 8.7, following the extracts, shows an analysis of those tasks. Since, as I noted earlier, I am a co-author of the *Primary Colours* series and since we are here at a stage of subjective analysis through reflection, the analysis here cannot be considered impartial but simply illustrative. (For definitions of the aspects of the materials set out in the analysis, see the Appendix.)

Figure 8.5   *A schedule for analysing tasks*

Task Analysis Sheet

Task number:									
I. What is the learner expected to do?									
A. TURN-TAKE									
Initiate									
Scripted response									
Not required									
B. FOCUS									
Language system (rules or form)									
Meaning									
Meaning/system/form relationship									
C. MENTAL OPERATION									
[detailed according to what									
is found in the materials]									
II. WHO WITH?									
[detailed according to what									
is found in the materials]									
III. WITH WHAT CONTENT?									
A. INPUT TO LEARNERS									
Form									
Source									
Nature									
B. OUTPUT FROM LEARNERS									
Form									
Source									
Nature									

Figure 8.6 *An extract from **Primary Colours Pupil's Book 5** (Littlejohn, A. and Hicks, D., Cambridge University Press, 2008)*

5 There's something outside ...

5A Bears!

1. 🔊 Read and listen. Why does Gary think that the bears are outside?

1. The children were flying high in the clouds. 'We'll need some food,' said James. 'You've just had a pizza!' said Alice. 'I know,' replied James, 'but we'll need some food – and a tent – for the Rocky Mountains.' 'No problem!' said Gary and in a few minutes, they landed on the ground. 'How did you do that?' asked James. Gary smiled and didn't answer.

2. 'Now we've got lots of food, a big tent and a torch' said James. 'But we have to be careful,' said Alice. 'Listen. I've just read this paper,' and she read aloud, 'There are many brown bears in the Canadian Rocky Mountains. You must be very careful. DO NOT PUT FOOD IN YOUR TENT.'

3. The carpet landed high in the mountains. 'It will be dark soon,' said Gary. 'We can't find the control card now. We can look in the morning.' They put up the tent and ate the food from the shop. It was very cold outside so they decided to go into the tent and sleep.

4. Suddenly, there was a noise. Alice woke up and she switched on the torch. 'Look!' she said. 'There's something outside. It's pushing on the tent!' 'James!' whispered Gary. 'Did you bring food into the tent?' 'I only brought some biscuits with me,' said James. 'Well, now the bears are here!' said Gary.

44

What can they do?

(cont.)

Figure 8.6 *(cont.)*

2 Read the story again. Write 'True', 'False' or 'We don't know'. Give a reason.

1 Gary is hungry.
  We don't know. Gary doesn't say, 'I'm hungry.'
2 They need to buy camping things.
3 James is surprised that Gary can control the carpet.
4 Bears can be dangerous.

5 They can see a bear.
6 They have got the control card.
7 Gary heard the noise first.
8 James did something wrong.

3a Bears are dangerous! What should you do in the Rockies? Tell the class your ideas.

Bears ... and you

What to do ...

if you want to walk   if you want to cook

if you want to camp

if you have food   if you see a bear

3b Find two pieces of advice for each topic.

If you want to walk, don't ...

do it 100 metres from your tent   don't camp near bear tracks   don't go off the path
don't move suddenly   don't put it in your tent   hang it in plastic bags in a tree
only camp in campsites   put your cooking clothes in a bag in a tree
stand still, and wait for the bear to move away   talk loudly or sing

3c What other ideas did you have in Exercise 3a?

4 Sing a song. *Please don't tell me about the big grizzly bear!*

See page 63 for the words.

45

(cont.)

Figure 8.6   (cont.)

(5D) **Know it all!** The Rocky Mountains

1a Read about the Rocky Mountains. Match two pictures with each text.

1
The Rocky Mountains go from Canada a long way down into the USA. They are almost 5,000 kilometres long. Millions of people come to enjoy the beautiful landscape every year, but they don't just climb mountains. They go camping, canoeing, walking and skiing in different parts of the Rockies.

2
There are lots of rivers in the Rockies. The mountains are very high and the rivers on each side go in opposite directions. On the east, the rivers go into the Atlantic Ocean, but on the west, they go into the Pacific Ocean.

3
Many people live and work in the Rocky Mountains. They have farms with cows and sheep, and they grow sugar, potatoes and other vegetables. There are also many mines there. These produce gold, silver and other metals. We also get a lot of wood from the forests in the Rockies because the trees there grow very quickly.

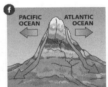

PACIFIC OCEAN   ATLANTIC OCEAN

1b Which of these questions can you answer from the texts?
Do you know the answers to the other questions?

1 Where are the Rockies?
2 What food do people produce there?
3 What fossils can you find there?
4 How old are the Rockies?

5 What is unusual about the rivers in the Rockies?
6 Where did the Rockies come from?
7 What metals come from the Rockies?
8 In what other ways do we use the Rockies?

1c Listen to Professor Know It All. Check your answers.

50

(cont.)

Figure 8.6 *(cont.)*

2a Millions of years ago, dinosaurs lived where the Rockies are now.
Look at the pictures. Tell the class what you know about dinosaurs.

2b Listen to Professor Know It All again.
Choose the correct words.

In the Rocky Mountains, you can see lots of dinosaur
footprints. Some of them are small, about
¹ 10 centimetres / **10 millimetres** across, but bigger
prints are about ² **14** / **40** centimetres across. There
are more than ³ **30** / **300** prints and we can learn a lot
from them. For example, we know that the dinosaurs
moved in ⁴ **big** / **small** groups. We also know that baby
dinosaurs walked ⁵ **next to** / **behind** their mother.
If we look at the ⁶ **shape** / **size** of the footprint, we can
tell that they were ⁷ **9** / **19** metres long. The footprints
also show us that they moved very ⁸ **fast** / **slowly**.

⭐ **YOUR PROJECT**

Find out about a place where
there are a lot of wild animals.

It can be:
- in your country
- in another country

Write about:
- the animals that lived there
  in the past
- why they disappeared
- the animals that live there
  now
- what they do

51

195

Figure 8.7 Analysis of Units 5A and 5D, **Primary Colours Pupil's Book 5** (Littlejohn, A. and Hicks, D., Cambridge University Press, 2008.)

Task Analysis Sheet	Unit 5A									Unit 5D							
Task number:	1	2	3	4	5	6	7	8	9	1	2	3	4	5	6	7	8
I. WHAT IS THE LEARNER EXPECTED TO DO?																	
A. TURN-TAKE																	
Initiate			x		x		x				x		x				x
Scripted response		x		x	x		x			x	x				x		
Not required	x											x			x		
B. FOCUS ON																	
Language system (rules or form)									x								
Meaning	x	x	x	x	x	x	x	x		x	x	x	x	x	x	x	x
Meaning/system/form relationship																	
C. MENTAL OPERATION																	
Decode semantic meaning	x	x		x	x		x			x	x		x			x	
Select information		x		x	x					x	x		x		x	x	
Hypothesize			x		x		x						x	x			
Retrieve from LTM					x		x						x	x			x
Repeat identically								x									
Apply general knowledge					x								x	x			
Research																x	
Express own ideas/information					x								x	x			x
II. WHO WITH?																	
Learners individually simultaneously	x	x		x	x		x			x	x		x		x		x
Learner to whole class			x			x		x				x	x				
Learner individually outside the class																x	
III. WITH WHAT CONTENT?																	
A. INPUT TO LEARNERS																	
a. Form																	
Extended discourse: written	x	x								x						x	
Extended discourse: aural	x	x								x			x		x	x	
Words/phrases/sentences: written			x	x	x	x	x	x	x		x	x					
Words/phrases/sentences: aural								x									
Graphic														x			
b. Source																	
Materials	x	x	x	x	x	x	x	x	x	x	x		x	x	x		
Learners											x						
Outside the course/lesson																x	
c. Nature																	
Fiction	x	x	x	x	x												
Non-fiction						x	x	x		x	x	x	x	x	x	x	
Song									x								
B. EXPECTED OUTPUT FROM LEARNERS																	
a. Form																	
Words/phrases/sentences: oral		x	x			x	x	x	x	x	x	x		x			
Words/phrases/sentences: written				x	x										x		x
b. Source																	
Materials		x		x	x		x			x	x	x			x		
Learners			x			x		x					x		x		x
c. Nature																	
Fiction		x	x	x	x												
Non-fiction						x	x	x		x	x	x		x	x		x
Song									x								

Level 3: What is implied? Subjective inference

The final level of analysis draws on findings at Levels 1 and 2 to come to some general conclusions about the apparent underlying principles of the materials, that is the **design** elements as set out in Figure 8.1. Working from a description of the explicit nature of the materials (Level 1) and an analysis of tasks (Level 2), it will now be possible to make statements about the overall **aims** of the materials and the basis for **selecting and sequencing** both tasks and content. Also at this third level of description, we should now be able to come to a conclusion about the **roles proposed for teachers and learners.** We may do this partly by examining how various sections of the material are allocated to teachers and learners (for example, who has answer keys, audioscripts, etc.) but we are likely to find greater evidence for this in the analysis of tasks, particularly under **turn-take** and the various categories under input and output **source.** Here, also, we will be able to produce a general statement about the nature of the demands placed upon learners to accomplish their learning. Finally, at this level, we will be able to come to a conclusion about what appears to be the **role of the materials as a whole** in facilitating language learning and teaching – does it appear, for example, that they endeavour to guide all classroom work or do they simply intend to stimulate teachers'/learners' creative ideas and own decision-making?

To draw this together, Figure 8.8 summarises the various aspects set out above, and how the schedule for recording the explicit nature of materials (Figure 8.3) and the schedule for an analysis of tasks (Figure 8.5) can help to find the required information. Figure 8.9 presents a complete analytical description of the two extracts of *Primary Colours Pupil's Book 5*, arrived at using the two schedules. As noted earlier, since I am a co-author of these materials, the description cannot be considered impartial, and is presented here for illustrative purposes only.

8.2.3 How can we make use of the findings from the analysis?

At the start of this chapter, I stressed that my main purpose was to develop a framework which separates an analysis of materials from assumptions about what is desirable. Many evaluation instruments, I suggested, contain within them the designer's own beliefs about how language teaching *should* be, and so prohibit a 'neutral' description of the materials and the application of the teacher-analysts' own views of what is appropriate for their context. In the closing section of this chapter, therefore, I want first to set out how I believe the analytical framework can be used to aid in materials evaluation and decision-making.

Figure 8.8 *Summary of how the analysis schedules provide information for an analytical description of materials*

Levels of inference		Corresponding source of evidence in the schedules (Explicit Nature and Task Analysis)
Aspects of the materials: Publication		
Level 1: 'What is there'	Place of learner's material in the set	EN/A3 Extent, A5 Distribution
	Published form of the materials	EN/A3 Extent, A4 Design and layout
	Subdivision of learner's materials	EN/A7 Subdivision, B2 Sequence of Activity.
	Subdivision of sections into sub-sections	EN/A7 Subdivision, B2 Sequence of Activity
	Continuity	EN/A7 Subdivision, B2 Sequence of Activity
	Route	EN/A6 Route
	Access	EN/A5b
Aspects of the materials: Design		
Level 2: 'What is required of users'	Subject matter and focus	TA/III With what content?
	Types of teaching/learning activities	TA/I What is the learner required to do?
	Participation: who does what with whom	TA/II Who with?
Level 3: 'What is implied'	Aims	Syllabus, sequence of activities (EN/B2)
	Principles of selection	Nature of the tasks (TA/I-III)
	Principles of sequencing	Sequence of tasks
	Teacher roles	Distribution (EN/A5), turn-take (TA/IA)
	Learner roles (classroom)	Source (TA/III)
	Learner roles (in learning)	Demands on process competence (TA/I-III)
	Role of the materials as a whole	Deductions from levels 1 to 3

Key
EN   schedule for recording the explicit nature of the materials
TA   schedule for analysing the tasks
A3, A4, I, II, III   item/question on the appropriate schedule

The framework is, however, also relevant for at least three other purposes: teachers' own professional development, materials designers' critical self-evaluation and researchers' study of language teaching.

Materials evaluation

As I have emphasised, my purpose in this chapter is to set out a means of **analysing** materials. This, I have argued, is a necessary and preliminary step to any desire to **evaluate** materials for use in a specific context. Taken together, the three levels of analysis and the two schedules for examining a set of materials provide a very powerful means of revealing the underlying nature of a set of materials. They provide, then, a

Figure 8.9 *An example analytical description*

A sample analytical description: *Primary Colours Pupil's Book 5*
1. Publication

1. *Place of learner's materials in the set*
   - part of a 'complete package'
   - means of access into the materials provided for teacher and learners; support facilities (answer keys, transcript etc.) provided for the teacher only
   - learner's materials may largely be used independently of the teacher's materials
   - learner's materials form focal point for classroom work

2. *Published form of the learner's materials*
   - monolingual throughout
   - durable and consumable materials for the learner
   - four-colour for learner's durable materials; two-colour for other components of set

3. *Subdivision of the learner's materials*
   - subdivided into six 'Units' with a standardised number of pages for each one
   - each unit has standardised A/B/C/D subsections
   - revision sections follow after every two units

4. *Subdivision of sections into sub sections*
   - patterning within Units: 'A' sections provide the first part of an episode in a story, which is continued in the 'C' section. Both 'A' and 'C' sections provide comprehension exercises and practice exercises related to the language point of the subsection. Section 'B' provides additional practice exercises focusing on language points. Section 'D' features non-fiction texts and exercises related to the context of the story. Revision sections provide more practice of language covered in the preceding two units.

5. *Continuity*
   - provided by a continuous storyline related to the adventures of a group of children
   - subsections within a unit exploit the context/location of the episode as a basis for content of exercises
   - an incremental syllabus of grammar and vocabulary

6. *Route*
   - one route through material proposed: to use the material in the order presented
   - Teacher's Book suggests ways route may be extended

(cont.)

Figure 8.9 *(cont.)*

7.   *Access*
     - means of access into the materials: a listing of unit/lesson names, a listing of unit/lesson objectives; listing of language items under grammatical type

2. Design

1.   *Aims and objectives*
     - to develop learner's linguistic competence in all four skills
     - to develop and draw on cross-curricular and cross-cultural knowledge
     - to encourage the learners to express their own ideas and to adopt an *initiate* role in using language

2.   *Principles of selection*
     - types of tasks: reproductive language practice, speculation and hypothesising, working with complete texts, drawing on student's knowledge/ideas
     - content: age-appropriate storylines, cross-curricular topics; learner's personal information/ideas
     - language: grammar areas, combined with vocabulary relevant to the topic

3.   *Principles of sequencing*
     - tasks: movement from language presentation/input via a story text, comprehension tasks and language practice on the language presented in the story
     - content: no clear principle for the sequence of content
     - language: simple to complex in terms of surface structure, largely following traditional grammatical sequence

4.   *Subject matter and focus of subject matter*
     - fictional story and cross-curricular content related to the context of the story
     - no metalinguistic comment on forms presented

5.   *Types of teaching/learning activities*
     - pupil's focus is directed exclusively to meaning
     - most tasks require a scripted response, with some opportunities for learners to adopt an 'initiate' position
     - materials direct classroom interaction for both teachers and learners
     - predominant operations required: decode semantic meaning and select information
     - mother tongue not called upon
     - emphasis on exposure to connected text; reading rather than listening, speaking rather than writing

6.   *Participation: who does what with whom*
     - most tasks require learners to work individually simultaneously

7.   *Classroom roles of teachers and learners*
     - 'decision-making' weighted towards the teacher by the materials (guidance on using the materials and provision of answer keys for teacher)

(cont.)

Figure 8.9   (cont.)

- both teachers and learners, however, are expected to follow directions in the materials
- teacher's role: to manage the classroom event and monitor language output
- learners' role: to follow the task directions

8.   *Learner roles in learning*
   - undertake tasks as directed by the materials
   - learning as the gradual accumulation of implicit grammatical items and vocabulary

9.   *Role of the materials as a whole*
   - to structure the teaching and learning of English, classroom time and classroom interaction
   - to provide a route for teaching and learning English
   - to provide a resource of motivating content (stories, cross-curricular topics) and engaging tasks

thorough basis for testing out how far both aims and claims in materials are met and thus will aid anyone involved in materials selection (see Sahragard *et al.* (2009) for an example, using an earlier version of this analytical framework). Whilst the framework will reveal much, a next step towards fully evaluating materials – that is, deciding their pedagogic worth relative to the proposed context of use – will in principle require an equally careful prior analysis of what teachers/students/institutions expect from materials, to see how far the two (that is materials and expectations) relate to or match each other. Figure 8.10 provides a brief outline of how this may work.

At the heart of Figure 8.10 lies a clear distinction between an analysis of the materials, an analysis of the proposed situation of use, the process of matching and evaluation, and subsequent action. By clearly dividing the various stages involved in this way, careful account can be taken of each element in materials evaluation. As we have seen in this chapter, materials may be analysed and described so as to expose their internal nature and, at the same time, make the analyst's subjective interpretations more easily visible. Similarly, the nature of the situation in which the materials would be used and the requirements which are to be placed on the materials can also be analysed and described independently. In addition to the obvious requirement of meeting the language needs of the proposed course where the materials may be used, it will also be necessary to identify cultural aspects, such as views of what learning should involve, the self-image and nature of the institution of

Figure 8.10   *A preliminary framework for materials analysis, evaluation and action*

Analysis of the target situation of use
The cultural context
The institution
The course
(proposed aims, content, methodology and means of evaluation)
The teachers
The learners

Materials analysis
From *analysis*:
1. What is their explicit nature?
2. What is required of users?
3. What is implied by their use?
To *description:*
Aspects of design
Aspects of publication

Match and evaluation
How appropriate are the *aspects of design* and the *aspects of publication* to the target situation of use?

Action
Reject the materials
Adopt the materials
Adapt the materials
Supplement the materials
Make the materials a critical object

use, the nature of the teachers (for example, prior experience, training, motivation and their beliefs about teaching) and the students (for example, language and educational level, predominate learning styles and motivation). Just as materials analysis involves increasing levels of subjective interpretation, however, so too will an analysis of the target situation of use. It is beyond the scope of this chapter to detail this, but it will certainly involve moving from describing 'objective' facts about the context, to making a subjective analysis of expectations and needs, to making subjective inferences about the appropriateness and value of particular methodologies and content.

Matching and evaluation can then follow in which an evaluator would need to set out precisely which aspects of the materials are appropriate or inappropriate and why. In practice, for example, this might involve a group of teachers (and, possibly, students) *first* identifying what they require of materials, perhaps talking through what they see as 'desirable' answers to the categories shown on the two schedules (Figures 8.3 and 8.5) as way of raising their own consciousness. The materials may then be analysed in detail so that the extent of the match between the teachers'/ students' expectations and the nature of the materials can be seen.

The final stage in Figure 8.10, 'action', involves evaluators in making decisions over what to do next in the light of matching and evaluation. A number of conventional responses are listed here, but there is also the possibility of adopting a set of materials in order to make it an object of critical focus. In this way the contents and ways of working set out in the coursebook can be viewed as **proposals** which may be open to critical examination and evaluation by teachers and learners.

The main assumption here has been that materials evaluation (via materials analysis and the analysis of the target situation of use) would be done **prospectively**, that is, prior to a decision to use a set of materials. The procedure described in Figure 8.10, however, would also offer benefits in identifying why materials already adopted are not achieving the intended goals, or why teachers and/or learners voice a desire to change. It is not unusual for materials to be abandoned and another set adopted without any detailed analysis of why the change needed to be made, apart from a general observation that (most frequently) the teachers involved wanted a change. Not surprisingly, this situation often then repeats itself within a relatively short period of time, with significant costs in terms of restocking materials, teacher training and course continuity.

Materials designers

For materials designers the process of applying the schedules for analysis to their own work under development or in piloting can be a salutary experience. An analysis of materials, followed by the simple question *Is this what I am aiming at?* can cause a writer to rethink the design of the materials. Two examples of this come to mind. Some years ago I was working with a colleague who was attempting to produce a set of materials ostensibly based on critical pedagogy – in this case, the materials were aimed at developing learners' critical engagement with the media, for example by showing them how newspaper articles could be 'deconstructed' to reveal bias, how advertising attempts to influence you emotionally, and so on. The materials, my colleague suggested, would enable the learners to become independent thinkers and thus 'more empowered'. Working with an earlier version of the model developed in this chapter, however, it soon became clear that there was a seemingly direct contradiction between the aims of the materials (independence and criticality) and the design of tasks which emphasised right/wrong answers, scripted lessons and contents entirely supplied by the materials. In this case, the materials analysis enabled a rethink of the methodology proposed.

A similar tension between the methodology proposed by materials and its espoused aims also became clear in relation to a project to develop a Self-Access Centre. Here, the planned centre intended to develop the learners' independence in learning and offer them opportunities to decide what and how they wished to learn. Careful analysis of the purpose-designed materials to be included in the centre, however, revealed that they largely reproduced the same relations that existed in the school's classrooms: closed exercises with right/wrong answers, a focus on the linguistic syllabus, and an attention to 'item level' learning. In this case, the analysis prompted a reconsideration of the materials to be offered and an attempt to design more open-ended materials with a focus on interesting content. (See also Littlejohn 1997 for a related discussion and Chapter 17 in this volume by Brian Tomlinson.)

Teachers' professional development

As probably the main 'tool of the trade' in language teaching, an analysis of teaching materials can offer considerable insights into how it is proposed that learning 'gets done'. A detailed analysis at the level of tasks (as defined here) can facilitate teachers' deep understanding of what is involved in the teaching–learning relationship, and why some tasks 'fail' whilst others 'succeed' (however defined) in the classroom. A detailed analysis of materials may also aid teachers in understanding their own teaching style, and why they feel particularly comfortable or uncomfortable with the way of working that materials propose.

Researchers in language teaching

As a detailed framework for analysing materials 'as they are', the schedules may also be of use to researchers in language teaching theory. Guilloteaux (2010) provides a good example of how this can be done. In her analysis of textbooks in Korea, Guilloteaux first sets out current recommendations for classroom work from the perspective of SLA theory (drawing mainly on Ellis 2005), which she then extrapolates into 'desirable features for learning materials' aligned to SLA theory. Using an earlier version of the model presented here, Guilloteaux then shows how the schedules can be used to 'operationalise' these SLA theory-derived features in the design of materials.

Away from the direct analysis of materials, however, the model presented here also has the potential for supporting classroom research. The three questions of *what is the learner expected to do*, *with whom* and *concerning what* go to the heart of the purposes of classroom work and therefore potentially provide a basic structure for a data collection framework, through, for example, classroom observation to capture what is happening rather than what is proposed.

8.3 Conclusion

I began this chapter by suggesting that the complex nature of modern-day materials, and the extent to which their use is now widespread, necessitates a means of closely analysing materials so that we can see 'inside' them and take more control over their design and use. As I have already remarked, materials are one of our main 'tools of the trade' so it is important that we understand their nature. One of the downsides of the professional production of contemporary materials is that, for many teachers and learners, materials appear as fait accomplis, over which they can have little control – the separation of conception from execution which I spoke of earlier. One of the aims of this chapter has been to endeavour to dispel the myth that materials are a closed box and reveal, through a process of 'reverse engineering' how they work. By guiding the deconstruction of materials, the model proposed here aids teacher-analysts to see the materials' internal character. In this way, the analytical framework may be seen as potentially empowering teachers, learners, educational administrators and others to voice their needs and to take more control over the materials with which they are involved.

References

Ansary, H. and E. Babaii. 2003. 'Subliminal sexism in current ESL/EFL textbooks'. *Asian EFL Journal*, 5(1). Retrieved 5 November 2009 from www.asian-efl-journal.com/march03.sub1.php

Apple, M. 1985. *Education and Power*. London: Ark.

Aronowitz, S. and H. Giroux. 1987. *Education Under Siege: The Conservative, Liberal and Radical Debate Over Schooling*. London: Routledge Kegan & Paul.

Blumberg, R. L. 2007. *Gender Bias in Textbooks: A Hidden Obstacle on the Road to Gender Equality in Education.* Paris: UNESCO.

Breen, M. P. and C. N. Candlin. 1987. 'Which materials?: a consumer's and designer's guide'. In L. E. Sheldon (ed.), *ELT Textbooks and Materials: Problems in Evaluation and Development.* ELT Documents 126. London: Modern English Publications and The British Council.

Byrd, P. 2001. 'Textbooks: evaluation for selection and analysis for implementation'. In M. Celce-Murcia (ed.), *Teaching English as a Second or Foreign Language*, 3rd edn. Boston, MA: Heinle & Heinle.

Canagarajah, A. S. 1999. *Resisting Linguistic Imperialism in English Teaching.* Oxford: Oxford University Press.

CIEL Language Support Network. 2000. 'Resources for independent language learning: design and use'. Retrieved 31 March 2010 from www.llas.ac.uk/resources/gpg/1405

Cunningsworth, A. 1995. *Choosing your Coursebook.* Oxford: Heinemann.

Ellis, R. 2005. 'Principles of Instructed Language Learning'. *System*, 33: 209–24.

Garinger, D. 2002. 'Textbook selection for the ESL classroom'. *Center for Applied Linguistics Digest.* Retrieved 2 November, 2009 from www.cal.org/resources/digest/digest_pdfs/0210garinger.pdf

Guilloteaux, M. J. 2010. 'Korean middle school English textbooks: do they reflect SLA-derived principles?' *Journal of Modern British & American Language & Literature.* Seoul, Korea.

Haig, E. 2006. 'How green are your textbooks? Applying an ecological critical language awareness pedagogy in the EFL classroom'. In S. Mayer and G. Wilson (eds.), *Ecodidactic Perspectives On English Language, Literatures And Cultures.* Trier: Wissenschaftlicher Verlang, pp. 23–44.

Harmer, J. 2007. *The Practice of English Language Teaching*, 4th edn. Harlow: Longman ELT.

Johnson, K. 2003. *Designing Language Teaching Tasks.* Basingstoke: Palgrave Macmillan.

Lesikin, J. 2001a. 'Potential student decision making in academic ESL grammar textbooks'. *Linguistics and Education*, 12(1): 25–49.

2001b. 'Determining social prominence: a methodology for uncovering gender bias in ESL textbooks'. In D. Hall and A. Hewings (eds.), *Innovation in English Language Teaching: A Reader.* Abingdon: Routledge & Kegan Paul.

Littlejohn, A. 1992. 'Why are English language teaching materials the way they are?' Unpublished PhD thesis. Lancaster: Lancaster University. (Also available at www.AndrewLittlejohn.net)

1995. 'Language learning in schools: what do students learn?' In D. H. Hill (ed.), *Bologna '94: English Language Teaching.* Milan: British Council. (Also available at www.AndrewLittlejohn.net)

1997. 'Self-access work and curriculum ideologies'. In P. Benson and P. Voller (eds.), *Autonomy and Independence in Language Learning.* Harlow: Longman.

2008. 'Digging deeper: learning strategies and learner disposition'. In G. Cane (ed.), S*trategies in Language Learning and Teaching*. Singapore: RELC.

2010. 'Real world language teaching'. In A. Ahmed, G. Cane and M. Hanzala (eds.), *Teaching English in Multilingual Contexts: Current Challenges, Future Directions*. Cambridge: Cambridge Scholars Publishing.

Littlejohn, A. and S. Windeatt. 1989. 'Beyond language learning: perspectives of materials design'. In R. K. Johnson (ed.), *The Second Language Curriculum*. Cambridge: Cambridge University Press.

McGrath, I. 2002. *Materials Evaluation and Design for Language Teaching*. Edinburgh: Edinburgh University Press.

2004. 'The representation of people in educational materials'. *RELC Journal*, 35(3): 351–8. Sage Publications.

Ndura, E. 2004. 'ESL and cultural bias: an analysis of elementary through high school textbooks in the western United States of America'. *Language, Culture and Curriculum*, 17(2): 143–53.

Nunan, D. 2004. *Task-Based Language Teaching*. Cambridge: Cambridge University Press.

Richards, J. and T. Rodgers. 2001. *Approaches and Methods in Language Teaching*. Cambridge: Cambridge University Press.

Sahragard, R., A. Rahimi and I. Zaremoayeddi. 2009. 'An in-depth evaluation of interchange series', 3rd edn. *Porta Linguarum*, 12: 37–54. Retrieved 31 March 2010 from www.ugr.es/~portalin/articulos/articles-index.htm

Skehan, P. 1996. 'A framework for the implementation of task-based instruction'. *Applied Linguistics*, 17(1): 38–61.

1998. *A Cognitive Approach to Language Learning*. Oxford: Oxford University Press.

Slimani, A. 2001. 'Evaluation of classroom interaction'. In C. N. Candlin and N. Mercer (eds.), *English Language Teaching in its Social Context*. London: Routledge & Kegan Paul.

Sokolik, M. E. 2007. 'Grammar Texts and Consumerist Subtexts'. *TESL-EJ*, 11(2). Retrieved 10 November 2009 from http://tesl-ej.org/ej42/a6.html

Wallace, C. 2006. 'The text, dead or alive: expanding textual repertoires in the adult ESOL classroom'. *Linguistics and Education*, 17: 74–90.

Willis, J. 1996. 'A flexible framework for task-based learning'. In J. Willis and D. Willis, *Challenge and Change in Language Teaching*. Oxford: Heinemann.

Appendix: Aspects of tasks – some definitions

The list in Figure 8.11 comprises examples of aspects of tasks found through an analysis of extracts from materials aimed at primary and secondary school learners, and adult learners. It is not an exhaustive list of all possible task aspects, but shows those which were found in sets of materials analysed (see Littlejohn 1992). Other materials may contain quite different features.

Figure 8.11

I. WHAT IS THE LEARNER EXPECTED TO DO?		
FEATURE	DEFINITION	EXAMPLE
A. TURN-TAKE	the learner's discourse role and discourse control	
1. initiate	the learner is expected to express what he/she wishes to say without a script of any kind	free discussion
2. scripted response	the learner is expected to express him/herself through language which has been narrowly defined	guided writing
3. not required	the learner is not expected to initiate or respond	listen to explanation
B. FOCUS	where the learner is to concentrate his/her attention	
4. language system	a focus on rules or patterns	substitution tables
5. meaning	a focus on the message of the language being used	comprehension questions
6. meaning/ system/form relationship	a focus on the relationship between form and meaning	tracing anaphora
C. OPERATION	what the mental process involves	
7. repeat identically	the learner is to reproduce exactly what is presented	oral repetition
8. repeat selectively	learner is to choose before repeating given language.	dialogue frames
9. repeat with substitution	the learner is to repeat the basic pattern of given language but replace certain items with other given items	substitution drills
10. repeat with transformation	the learner is to apply a (conscious or unconscious) rule to given language and to transform it accordingly	change statements into questions
11. repeat with expansion	the learner is given an outline and is to use that outline as a frame within which to produce further language	composition outlines
12. retrieve from STM/working memory	the learner is to recall items of language from short-term memory/working memory, that is, within a matter of seconds	oral repetition
13. retrieve from LTM	the learner is to recall items from a time previous to the current lesson	recall vocabulary from last lesson
14. formulate items into larger unit	the learner is to combine recalled items into, e.g., complete sentences, necessitating the application of consciously or unconsciously held language rules	discussion

(cont.)

Figure 8.11   *(cont.)*

15. decode semantic/ propositional meaning	the learner is to decode the 'surface' meaning of given language	read a text for its meaning
16. select information	the learner is to extract information from a given text	answer questions by reading a text
17. calculate	the learner is to perform mathematical operations	solve maths problem
18. categorise selected information	the learner is to analyse and classify information selected through operation 17	sort information into groups
19. hypothesise	the learner is to hypothesise an explanation, description, solution or meaning of something	deduce meanings from context
20. compare samples of language	the learner is to compare two or more sets of language data on the basis of meaning or form	compare accounts of the same event
21. analyse language form	the learner is to examine the component parts of a piece of language	find the stressed syllable in a word
22. formulate language rule	as 20, but learner is to hypothesise a language rule	devise grammar rule
23. apply stated language rule	the learner is to use a given language rule in order to transform or produce language	change direct to reported speech
24. apply general knowledge	the learner is to draw on knowledge of 'general facts' about the world	answer questions on other countries
25. negotiate	the learner is to discuss and decide with others in order to accomplish something	in groups, write a set of instructions
26. review own FL output	the learner is to check his/her own foreign language production for its intended meaning or form	check own written work
27. attend to example/ explanation	the learner is to 'take notice of' something	listen to a grammar explanation
28. research	personally find relevant information from sources not provided in the classroom	look for information relevant to a personal project
29. express own ideas/ information	using the target language, express personal opinions, knowledge or other ideas	propose a solution to a complex problem

II. WHO WITH?

30. teacher and learner(s), whole class observing	the teacher and selected learner(s) are to interact	a learner answers a question; other learners listen
31. learner(s) to the whole class	selected learner(s) are to interact with the whole class, including the teacher	learner(s) feed back on groupwork

(cont.)

Figure 8.11   *(cont.)*

32. learners with whole class simultaneously	learners are to perform an operation in concert with the whole class	choral repetition
33. learners individually simultaneously	learners are to perform an operation in the company of others but without immediate regard to the manner/pace with which others perform the same operation	learners individually do a written exercise
34. learners in pairs/groups; class observing	learners in pairs or small groups are to interact with each other whilst the rest of the class listens	a group 'acts out' a conversation
35. learners in pairs/groups, simultaneously	learners are to interact with each other in pairs/groups in the company of other pairs/groups	learners discuss in groups
36. learner individually outside the class	the learner is to work alone, using content not supplied by the materials	gathering information for a personal project

III. WITH WHAT CONTENT?
A. INPUT TO LEARNERS

a. Form	**form of content offered to learners**	
37. graphic	pictures, illustrations, photographs, diagrams, etc.	a world map
38. words/phrases/ sentences: written	individual written words/phrases/sentences	a list of vocabulary items
39. words/phrases/ sentences: aural	individual spoken words/phrases/ sentences	prompts for a drill
40. extended discourse: written	texts of more than 50 written words which cohere, containing supra-sentential features	a written story
41. extended discourse: aural	texts of more than 50 spoken words which cohere, containing supra-sentential features	a dialogue on tape
b. Source	**where the content comes from**	
42. materials	content (or narrowly specified topic) supplied by the materials	dialogue/text in the coursebook
43. teacher	content (or narrowly specified topic) supplied by the teacher	teacher recounts own experiences
44. learner(s)	content (or narrowly specified topic) supplied by the learner(s)	learner recounts own experiences
45. outside the course/lesson	content not supplied in the classroom or via the materials	encyclopedia
c. Nature	**type of content**	
46. metalinguistic comment	comments on language use, structure, form or meaning	a grammatical rule
47. linguistic items	words/phrases/sentences carrying no specific message	a vocabulary list
48. non-fiction	factual texts/information	a text about a foreign culture
49. fiction	fictional texts	dialogue between imaginary characters

(cont.)

Figure 8.11 *(cont.)*

50. personal information/ opinion	learner's own personal information or opinion	details of learner's interests
51. song	words/sentences set to music	song

B. EXPECTED OUTPUT FROM THE LEARNERS

a. Form — **form of content to be produced by learner**

52. graphic	pictures, illustrations, photographs, diagrams, etc.	a plan of one's house
53. words/phrases/ sentences	individual written words/phrases/sentences	write sentences using a specified word
54. words/phrases/ sentences: oral	individual spoken words/phrases/sentences	response to a drill
55. extended discourse: written	texts of more than 50 written words which cohere, containing supra-sentential features	a story in writing
56. extended discourse: oral	texts of more than 50 written words which cohere, containing supra-sentential features	an oral account of an event

b. Source — **where the content originally comes from**

57. materials	content (or narrowly specified topic) supplied by the materials	dialogue/text in the coursebook
58. teacher	content (or narrowly specified topic) supplied by the teacher	teacher dictates a personal text
59. learner(s)	content (or narrowly specified topic) supplied by the learner(s)	learner recounts own experiences to other learners
60. outside the course/lesson	content not supplied in the classroom or via the materials	encyclopedia

c. Nature — **type of content**

61. metalinguistic comment	comments on language use, structure, form or meaning	a grammatical rule
62. linguistic items	words/phrases/sentences carrying no specific message	naming objects
63. non-fiction	factual texts/information	knowledge from other areas
64. fiction	fictional texts	a story
65. personal information/ opinion	learner's own personal information or opinion	details of learner's interests
66. song	words/sentences set to music	song

211

9 Macro- and micro-evaluations of task-based teaching

Rod Ellis

9.1 Introduction

Task-based language teaching (TBLT) constitutes a strong form of communicative language teaching. It aims to develop learners' knowledge of a second language (L2) and their ability to use this knowledge in communication by engaging them in a series of communicative tasks. It differs from other approaches in that it does not attempt to teach learners predetermined linguistic items (i.e. vocabulary and grammar). TBLT is based on a view of language learning that claims that an L2 is best learned through learners' efforts to communicate with it. Central to an understanding of TBLT is the concept of 'task'. Therefore, I will begin by a definition of this pedagogic construct.

9.2 Defining 'task'

Various definitions of a 'task' have been provided (see Ellis 2003: 4–5) but most of these indicate that for a language-teaching activity to be a 'task', it must satisfy the following criteria:

1. The primary focus should be on 'meaning' (by which is meant that learners should be mainly concerned with processing both the semantic and pragmatic meaning of utterances).
2. There should be some kind of 'gap' (i.e. a need to convey information, to express an opinion or to infer meaning).
3. Learners should largely have to rely on their own resources – linguistic and non-linguistic – in order to complete the activity (i.e. the task materials do not dictate what linguistic forms are to be used).
4. There is a clearly defined outcome other than the use of language (i.e. the language serves as the means for achieving the outcome, not as end in its own right).

On the basis of such criteria, a distinction can be made between a 'task' and 'a situational grammar exercise'. Whereas the latter may satisfy criteria (2) and (3), it does not satisfy (1) as the learners know that the main purpose of the activity is to practise correct language rather than to process messages for meaning, nor does it satisfy (4) as the outcome is primarily the use of correct language. See Ellis (2010) for a detailed account and examples of the distinction between situational grammar exercises and tasks.

The distinction between 'task' and 'situational grammar exercise' underlies another important distinction, namely that between 'task-based' and 'task-supported language teaching'. The former requires a syllabus consisting of unfocused tasks; that is, the content of the instructional programme is specified in terms of the tasks to be completed (as in Prabhu 1987). The latter utilises a structural syllabus and typically involves 'PPP' (presentation–practice–production), with the final stage taken up with what is often referred to as a 'task' but more correctly constitutes a 'situational grammar exercise'. According to Widdowson (2003: 119), task-supported language teaching is likely to result in 'encoded usage rather than realisation as purposeful use'. However, as Widdowson goes on to argue, such teaching is not to be dismissed if it can inspire 'engagement'. Contrivance and language display may have their place in language teaching. Thus, in distinguishing between task-based and task-supported language teaching, I do not intend to present the former as desirable and the latter as undesirable. A case can be made for both.

Tasks can be distinguished in a number of ways:

1. They can be 'unfocused' or 'focused'. Unfocused tasks are tasks that are designed to provide learners with opportunities for using language communicatively in general. Focused tasks are tasks that have been designed to provide opportunities for communicating using some specific linguistic feature (typically a grammatical structure). However, focused tasks must still satisfy the four criteria stated above. For this reason the target linguistic feature of a focused task is 'hidden' (i.e. learners are not told explicitly what the feature is). Thus, a focused task can still be distinguished from a 'situational grammar exercise' as in the latter learners are made aware of what feature they are supposed to be producing. In other words, learners are expected to orient differently to a focused task than to a situational grammar exercise.
2. Tasks can also be 'input-providing' or 'output-prompting'. Input-providing tasks engage learners in listening or reading, whilst output-prompting tasks engage them in speaking or writing. Thus, a task can provide opportunities for communicating in any of the four language skills. Many tasks are integrative; they involve two or more skills.
3. Tasks can have 'closed' or 'open' outcomes. A closed task is one that has a single or, at least, a limited number of possible outcomes.

For example, a Spot the Difference Task can be considered closed if there are a finite number of differences in two pictures to be identified. An open task is a task where there are many possible outcomes and what constitutes the 'best' one is a matter of opinion – for example, a task that provides students with information about four patients all in need of a heart transplant and asks them to decide who was the most deserving of the one heart available. By and large, this distinction corresponds to another way in which tasks can be distinguished – between information-gap and opinion-gap tasks. The former commonly have closed outcomes whereas the latter have open outcomes.

9.3 Approaches to evaluating TBLT

TBLT has attracted increasing attention from researchers and teacher educators. This approach to language teaching – it cannot be said to constitute a distinct 'method' – has drawn extensively on research into L2 acquisition (i.e. SLA), as reflected in books by Crookes and Gass (1993), Ellis (2003), Samuda and Bygate (2008) and Skehan (1998). It is worthwhile noting, however, that it is not just SLA researchers who are its advocates; teacher educators such as Estaire and Zanon (1994), Nunan (1989, 2004), Prabhu (1987) and Willis (1996) have also presented a strong case for it, drawing on both their own experience of language teaching and general educational theory. There are also documented examples of actual TBLT, starting with Prabhu's (1987) account of the Communicational Language Teaching Project, and, more recently in books reporting case studies of TBLT (e.g. Edwards and Willis 2005; Leaver and Willis 2004; Van den Branden 2006; Van den Branden, Bygate and Norris 2009). TBLT has clearly progressed well beyond theory into actual practice.

However, as is often the case when a 'new' approach receives the support of theorists and researchers in academe, resistance can set in. TBLT challenges mainstream views about language teaching in that it does not constitute a systematic attempt to teach the language bit by bit (as in approaches based on a structural syllabus). Not surprisingly, therefore, TBLT has been subjected to intensive evaluation and criticism – often strident – by those teachers and educators who favour an approach that involves more direct intervention in learning (e.g. Sheen 1994; 2003; Swan 2005; Widdowson 2003). These criticisms are theoretical in nature. However, an alternative approach to evaluating TBLT – the one that I want to examine in this chapter – involves investigating TBLT empirically by examining it in action.

There are, in fact, a number of published studies reporting attempts to implement TBLT in different instructional settings. These have led to questions being raised by Butler (2005), Carless (2004), Li (1998) amongst others, as to whether TBLT is practical in countries where teachers are likely to adhere to a philosophy of teaching that is radically different to that which underlies TBLT and where they also face practical problems such as limited second-language proficiency and the washback from tests for which they need to prepare their students.

These empirical evaluations of TBLT have been 'macro' in nature. That is, they have investigated whole courses based on tasks. There is also a need for evaluations of a more 'micro' nature, where the implementation of specific tasks is studied. I will begin by discussing this distinction between 'macro' and 'micro' evaluation and then review a number of evaluation studies of both kinds.

9.4 Macro-evaluation

Macro-evaluation can be defined as evaluation that seeks to answer one or both of the following questions:

1. To what extent was the programme/project effective and efficient in meeting its goals?
2. In what ways can the programme/project be improved?

The first of these questions relates to what Weir and Roberts (1994) refer to as 'accountability evaluation' and the second to 'development evaluation'. In order to carry out a macro-evaluation of a programme/project, the evaluators need to collect various kinds of information relating to one or both of the following:

1. Administrative matters (i.e. the logistical and financial underpinnings of the programme).
2. Curriculum matters, which, in turn can be broken down into a consideration of:
   (a) materials
   (b) teachers
   (c) learners.

A macro-evaluation, then, is an evaluation carried out for accountability and/or developmental purposes by collecting information relating to various administrative and curricular aspects of the programme, including teaching materials.

Most of the work on the evaluation of language teaching has involved the macro-evaluation of whole programmes and projects. A brief look at the evaluation case studies in Alderson and Beretta (1992), Kiely and Rea-Dickens (2005), Weir and Roberts (1994), and in the special issue of *Language Teaching* (Vol. 13.1) on 'Understanding and improving language education through program evaluation', testifies to this over-arching concern with macro-evaluation. For example, in Alderson and Beretta's edited collection, Alderson and Scott (1992) report an evaluation of a national ESP project in Brazil, Lynch (1992) discusses an evaluation of the Reading English for Science and Technology Project at the University of Guadalajara and Mitchell (1992) summarises her work on a bilingual education project in Scotland. Only one of the evaluations in this book reported a study of a task-based language teaching project – Beretta (1992) reported his evaluation of the Communicational Language Teaching Project in India.

Whilst there is an undoubted need for macro-evaluations of the kind reported in Alderson and Beretta (1992), it might be argued that such an approach to evaluation does not accord with the perspective which many teachers have about what evaluation involves. Teachers are obviously concerned with whether they are accomplishing their goals and whether they need to make changes to their programme. However, their attention is likely to focus less on the programme as a whole and more on whether specific activities and techniques appear to 'work' in the context of a particular lesson. In other words, any macro-evaluations that teachers make are likely to be the result of a whole series of micro-evaluations carried out on a day-by-day and lesson-by-lesson basis. If this argument is right, a teacher-oriented approach to evaluation will emphasise micro-evaluation.

9.5 Micro-evaluation

A micro-evaluation is characterised by a narrow focus on some specific aspect of the curriculum or the administration of the programme. Each of the curricular and administrative aspects referred to above lends itself to a micro-evaluation. Thus, in the case of teachers/teaching one might focus on the kinds of questions teachers ask in a lesson (see Ellis 1994). In the case of learners one might focus on which learners participate productively in a lesson. In the case of materials, we might ask whether a particular task is effective or efficient. These questions may be informed by a desire to obtain information that will speak generally about the effectiveness and efficiency of the learners, the teachers and the materials in achieving learning goals (i.e. they may be shaped and directed in top-down fashion by an attempt to collect information for a macro-evaluation) or, as I suspect is often the case, they may be informed by more local, on-the-spot considerations.

Figure 9.1   *Macro- and micro-evaluations in language teaching*

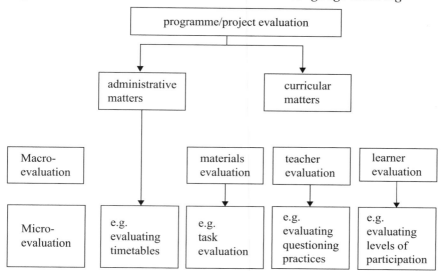

It is quite likely, of course, that a macro-evaluation may eventually emerge, bottom-up, from repeated micro-evaluations. Thus there is a relationship between macro- and micro-evaluations, as shown in Figure 9.1. Macro-evaluations address every aspect of a course/programme (i.e. both administrative and curricular matters). Micro-evaluations of tasks can help to inform macro-evaluations of curricular matters by providing information about the materials used, the teachers implementing the course and the performance (and learning) of the learners. However, I also claim that micro-evaluations are of value in themselves both because they provide a basis for deciding whether specific tasks work, and also because they serve as a source of teacher self-reflection and development.

In the sections that follow I will examine the methodology and findings of first macro- and then micro-evaluation studies of task-based teaching, focusing on the materials (i.e. the 'tasks') used.

9.6 Macro-evaluations of task-based teaching

The first published macro-evaluation of task-based teaching was of Prabhu's Communicational Language Teaching Project (see Prabhu 1987). This was a project designed to introduce task-based teaching into a number of secondary school classrooms in southern India. Beretta and Davies (1985) sought to compare the learning outcomes of learners involved in the Project (the experimental group) with those in 'traditional' classes, where the structural-oral situational method was followed (the control group). To avoid bias in testing, Beretta and Davies devised a battery of tests that included tests that 'favoured' the experimental group (i.e. a task-based test), tests that 'favoured' the control group (i.e. a structure test) and also three 'neutral' tests (i.e. contextualised grammar, dictation and listening/reading comprehension). The results lend support to the effectiveness of task-based teaching. In the neutral tests, the experimental group clearly outperformed the control group. However, on the group-biased tests, whilst the experimental group did better on the task-based test, the control group scored higher on the structural test. Beretta and Davies conclude that the results of the evaluation support the claim that task-based instruction produces significantly different learning from traditional form-focused instruction and that this is reflected in the task-based learners' superior acquisition of structures that have not been explicitly taught and also in their ability to deploy what they have learned more readily. However, Beretta and Davies also point to a number of problems with their evaluation, in particular the difficulty in planning and conducting such an evaluation post-hoc (i.e. after the project has already started).

Beretta's (1990) evaluation addressed a different aspect of the Communicational Teaching Project – whether the methodological innovations proposed by Prabhu were actually implemented by the teachers involved in the project. Beretta collected historical narratives from 15 teachers and then rated these according to three levels of implementation: (1) orientation (i.e. the teacher demonstrated a lack of understanding of task-based instruction and failed to implement it), (2) routine (i.e. the teacher understood the rationale of the project and was able to implement it effectively) and (3) renewal (i.e. the teacher had adopted a critical perspective and could demonstrate awareness of its strengths and weaknesses). Beretta found that 40 per cent of the teachers were at Level 1, 47 per cent at Level 2 and 13 per cent at Level 3. However, when he distinguished between regular and non-regular teachers involved in the project, he found that three out of four regular teachers were at Level 1. Beretta concluded that task-based instruction of the kind practised in the Project may not easily be assimilated by regular classroom teachers in southern India. He pointed to these teachers' lack of English proficiency as one reason for their failure to adopt task-based teaching.

Since then there have been a number of other evaluations. A representative set of these are summarised in Table 9.1. An inspection of the

Table 9.1 Summary of macro-evaluation studies of task-based teaching

Study	Context	Purpose	Evaluation method	Findings
Li (1998)	The introduction of communicative language teaching into secondary schools in South Korea where traditionally a grammatical syllabus had been used.	To investigate Korean teachers' perceptions of the implementation of CLT. The Korean teachers were all experienced and studying in the Korean Teacher Education Program in a Canadian University.	1. Questionnaire: A pilot survey led to the development of a questionnaire with Likert-scale items and open questions – administered to 18 secondary school EFL teachers. 2. In-depth semi-structured interviews with ten of the participants. Qualitative and quantitative (number of mentions) analysis of the data.	Teachers reported difficulties in using CLT in Korea: 1. Difficulties caused by the teacher's: - deficiency in spoken English - deficiency in strategic and sociolinguistic competence - lack of training in CLT - few opportunities for retraining in CLT - misconceptions about CLT - little time to develop materials. 2. Students: - low proficiency in English - lack of motivation to develop communicative competence - resistance to class participation. 3. Educational system: - large classes - grammatical-based examinations - insufficient funding - lack of support. 4. CLT: - inadequate account of EFL teaching - lack of appropriate assessment instruments.

(cont.)

Table 9.1 (*cont.*)

Study	Context	Purpose	Evaluation method	Findings
Mitchell and Lee (2003)	Two settings explored: 1. 11–12-year-old students in an English secondary school learning French. 2. 10–11-year-old students in a Korean primary school learning English. The teachers (Teacher E and Teacher K) of these classes were both female and experienced and they spoke the TL as an L2.	To examine how the 'communicative approach' was interpreted and how the role of the 'good language learner' was constructed in the two settings. Also, to examine how the construct of 'whole-class interactive teaching' was manifest in the pedagogy of the two classes.	Twenty recorded lessons for each classroom, teacher interviews and back-up documentation. The analysis of the recorded lessons focused on 'critical incidents'.	1. Both teachers reflected a 'weak' interpretation of CLT, i.e. they aimed to provide learners with a fixed body of predetermined expressions with little opportunity for creative language use. Both teachers eschewed explicit grammar teaching. 2. The two teachers differed in their expectations of student behaviour. Teacher E adopted an egalitarian, undifferentiated approach, whereas Teacher K privileged the more-able students to provide good models. Overall, both classroom cultures were 'teacher led, neobehaviourist in learning philosophy' (p. 58).
Carless (2004)	Primary school classrooms in Hong Kong. The three teachers in these classrooms were attempting to implement a 'target-oriented curriculum' by means of a task-based syllabus.	Two RQs: 1. What are the teachers' attitudes toward and understandings of task-based teaching?	Data collected by means of: 1. classroom observation (17 lessons per teacher) – field notes and lesson transcriptions	Overall, the tasks represented language practice activities rather than genuine communication and the teachers manifested a poor understanding of what a task was. Three key issues in implementing task-based teaching were identified:

(*cont.*)

Table 9.1 (cont.)

Study	Context	Purpose	Evaluation method	Findings
		2. How are the teachers attempting to implement task-based teaching and what issues emerge from these attempts?	2. Six semi-structured interviews 3. An attitude scale. Data analysed qualitatively with findings presented in terms of representative classroom episodes for each teacher.	1. Use of mother tongue – MT quite widely used and teachers expressed concern about its use, although two of them acknowledged that some use was legitimate (e.g. to facilitate the activity). 2. Discipline challenges – there was a tension between the need for students to talk and the desire to maintain a quiet, orderly classroom. 3. Target language production – tensions arose when the tasks did not result in the teachers' expectations about student use of English (e.g. students spent too much time on non-linguistic activities such as drawing).
Butler (2005)	The governments of Korea, Japan and Taiwan have introduced English teaching in primary schools with the expectancy that the focus will be on oral communication.	To identify and compare local elementary school teachers' concerns regarding the introduction of 'communicative activities' in Japan, Korea and Taiwan.	Multivocal ethnography involving presenting teachers with videotaped scenes from lessons in the different countries to elicit inside and outside comments.	1. Teachers in the different countries employed similar activities but with different motives (e.g. modelling language vs. authentic communication) which led to different 'activities'. 2. Teachers expressed concerns about how to develop communicative activities that were developmentally suitable for higher grade students.

(*cont.*)

Table 9.1 (*cont.*)

Study	Context	Purpose	Evaluation method	Findings
				3. Class harmonisation seen as problematic in English lessons, especially in Japan.
McDonough and Chaikitmongkol (2007)	Innovative task-based course (the first of a four-part series) for students at Chiang Mai University, Thailand. The course replaced a traditional focus-on-form course and was developed by teachers involved in the programme. The course included a learning-strategies component, and in addition to self-made materials, utilised a commercial textbook. A key focus of the course was the use of English for international communication.	Two RQs: 1. What were Thai teacher and learner reactions to a task-based EFL course? 2. If they had any concerns about the course, how were these concerns addressed?	1. Task evaluations – open-ended questions. 2. Students kept a learning notebook. 3. Observations by teacher-participants. 4. Course evaluation – open-ended questions. 5. Interviews with students and teacher-participants. 6. Field notes – kept by a researcher-participant. Analysis – six key themes identified.	A. Teacher and learner reactions: 1. Increased learner independence. 2. Course content – initially teachers and learners were concerned by lack of grammar but they became more positive as the course progressed. 3. Real world relevance – participants recognised relevance to their real world academic needs but not to needs outside the academic context. B. Addressing participants' concerns: 1. Revisions undertaken to help participants adjust to the course. 2. Providing learner support – supplementary materials developed to help students understand task assignments. 3. Managing course materials – the number of materials and activities for each lesson reduced.

'Purpose' column suggests that these evaluation studies had two general aims: (1) to identify teachers' perceptions of and attitudes to task-based teaching and (2) to examine how the teachers implemented TBLT in their different teaching contexts. Interestingly, none of the evaluations attempted to investigate the effectiveness of TBLT by obtaining data relating to learning outcomes. The methods used to collect data for the evaluations reflect the two general aims. Thus, various types of teacher self-report (using questionnaires, interviews, stimulated recall based on the replay of recorded lesson scenarios) were used to investigate aim (1), whilst observation of actual lessons was used to investigate aim (2).

Reading through these evaluations of task-based teaching, one is struck by how little attention was paid to the actual teaching materials used in the courses (i.e. the 'tasks'). However, some interesting observations emerge from the reports. Butler (2005: 435), for example, noted that even when the teachers she investigated employed the 'same' communicative activities, the 'actual activities' that the students engaged in were often very different, 'depending on the motives and goals that teachers set for such activities'. Butler's observation lends support to a sociocultural view of 'tasks' (see, for example, Coughlan and Duff 1994), according to which a clear distinction needs to be made between 'task' (i.e. the actual materials that comprise the workplan for the activity) and 'activity' (i.e. the learner behaviour that ensues when learners perform the task). Carless (2004) reported that the primary school teachers he investigated had mixed and sometimes confused notions of what a 'task' involved. For example, one of the teachers he investigated defined tasks as activities involving 'active participation, real-life relationship, learning by doing, putting language and learning to use' (2004: 647), whilst another teacher defined a task as an activity that 'mainly has objectives and it can link the pupil ability of understanding, conceptualising, that kind of communication' (2004: 648). Whilst the first definition bears a reasonably close resemblance to the one I provided above, the latter is vague and, as Carless points out, fails to distinguish 'task' from other types of activities. McDonough and Chaikitmongkol (2007) have the most to say about materials. One of the problems they identified concerned how to interlink the task-based materials specifically developed for the university level course they evaluated with the materials from a commercial textbook. Another issue that emerged was the quantity of materials, with some teachers experiencing problems in carrying out all the tasks assigned for a lesson. McDonough and Chaikitmongkol conclude that an important issue in task-based courses is 'whether teachers create their own materials or obtain commercially available textbooks' and note that 'they should take care to ensure the curriculum dictates the use of the textbook rather than allowing the textbook to dictate the content of the course' (2007: 125).

The main concern of all of the macro-evaluations was the extent to which task-based teaching was implementable in the different teaching contexts. In all of the contexts investigated, TBLT constituted an innovation and, as such, its uptake was influenced by the various factors that have been shown to affect whether or not an innovation takes root (see Ellis 1997). However, such macro-evaluations, whilst shedding light on the viability of TBLT, offer little insight into the effectiveness of specific tasks or types of tasks, even though ultimately the effectiveness of a TBLT course/programme must depend largely on the individual tasks that comprise it. It is for this reason that there is a need for micro-evaluations of individual tasks, especially those conducted by teachers themselves.

9.7 Micro-evaluations of tasks

As with macro-evaluations, micro-evaluations of tasks can be directed at 'accountability' or 'improvement'. In the case of accountability, the evaluator will need to investigate to what extent the task achieves the aims set out for it. For an 'unfocused' task this will involve examining both the product of the task (i.e. the outcome) and the process (i.e. the actual performance of the task). Here it is worth noting that even if learners are successful in achieving the outcome of the task, they will have gained little unless the processes involved in performing the task can be shown to be of value to learning. Evaluating unfocused tasks is challenging because of the difficulty of demonstrating that any learning has resulted. This is a point I will return to later. An accountability evaluation is easier in the case of 'focused tasks', as the investigation can centre on the linguistic feature that is the specific target of the task. In the case of an evaluation directed at 'improvement', the aim must be to discover how the design features or implementation of a task influenced performance processes, outcome and learning. For example, it might consider to what extent the cognitive or linguistic complexity of the input provided by the task affected the learners' performance of the task or whether allowing learners an opportunity to plan prior to performing the task had a beneficial influence on performance, outcome and learning.

A micro-evaluation can involve the collection of different types of information: (1) information regarding the learners' opinions about the task, (2) information about how the task was performed, and (3) information about what learning took place as a result of performing the task. Corresponding to these types of information are three different approaches to evaluating tasks: (1) a student-based evaluation, (2) a response-based evaluation (where the evaluator seeks to determine whether the task elicited the performance processes and outcome intended) and (3) a learning-based evaluation (where the evaluator investigates whether the task has resulted in any learning). Each of these approaches requires different types of data. A student-based evaluation can be conducted using self-report instruments such as questionnaires, interviews and focus group discussions. A response-based evaluation requires observation/recording of learners' performance of a task and also any product that results from the outcome of the task. A learning-based evaluation ideally requires some kind of pre- and post-test to determine when any changes in learners' ability to use the L2 have occurred. However, it might also be possible to demonstrate learning through the detailed analysis of learners' performance of the task.

In Ellis (1998: 227–31) I outlined a procedure for conducting a micro-evaluation of a task:

1. The starting point is a description of the task in terms of its objectives, the kind of input provided by the task (e.g. pictorial or linguistic), the task procedures (e.g. whether or not there is opportunity for students to plan before they perform the task) and the nature of the intended outcome.
2. The next step is to plan the evaluation by deciding on:
   - the objectives and purpose (i.e. accountability or development)
   - the scope of the evaluation (e.g. whether the evaluation will simply focus on whether the intended benefits were achieved or whether there were also unexpected benefits)
   - who will conduct the evaluation (i.e. the teacher or some 'outsider')
   - the timing (i.e. whether the evaluation is formative, involving collecting data during the progress of the task, or summative, where data is collected only on completion of the task) and
   - the types of information to be collected (e.g. relating to whether the evaluation is student-, response- or learning-based).
3. The data for the evaluation are collected.
4. The data are analysed.
5. Finally, conclusions and recommendations need to be made.

Such a procedure is systematic and can lead to some informative evaluations (as illustrated below), but clearly it is also time-consuming.

Micro-evaluations of tasks are rarely published. However, over the years I have asked students in my master level classes at various institutions to carry out micro-evaluations of tasks following the procedure I outlined above, and I will now provide brief summaries of a number of these. I will then comment on the methodologies they employed and point to a number of uses of such micro-evaluations.

Simons (1997) evaluated an unfocused information-gap task with a closed outcome in a partial replication of Yule and McDonald's (1990) study. The task was performed in pairs. It required student A to describe a route marked on a map so that student B could draw in the route on his/her map. The two maps were not identical; Student A's map included some information that was missing from Student B's map, thus creating a number of referential discrepancies. The students were told that they could offer or ask for information in any way they liked when they performed the task. Simons' aim was simply to establish whether the task was successful in eliciting 'meaningful communication'. To this end, he audio-recorded two students performing the task, with the lower proficiency student (Student A) having the map with the route drawn in. Their performance was transcribed and analysed by classifying the functions performed by each student's turn. Five general functional categories were identified: telling, questioning, acknowledging, responding and miscellaneous. Each of these categories was further subdivided. Overall, the task resulted in 357 turns, 180 by Student A and 177 by Student B. There were marked differences in the functions performed by the two students. For example, Student A engaged predominantly in 'telling' and 'responding' whilst Student B engaged in 'questioning'. Simons also noted that the task resulted in a high level of involvement, with the students reporting that they found the task challenging and amusing. The following extract from the task performance illustrates the type and quality of the interaction that took place:

Student A: *to the station can you find the station*
Student B: *station?*
Student A: *yeah*
Student B: *what station?*
Student A: *I don't know*
Student B: *no (laughs)*
Student A: *subway station*
Student B: *subway station I don't have that here*
Student A: *do you do you have uh um railroad?*
Student B: *no*
Student A: *no?*
Student B: *no*
Student A: *mm (laughs)*
Student B: *(laughs) I'm in the shopping center and I'm lost*

When faced with referential discrepancies, as in the example above, the students worked through an extended sequence to build a solution to the problem collaboratively. Simons concluded that this information-gap task was an effective device for inducing learners to use the L2 communicatively. He also noted that giving the key information to the less proficient student and introducing referential discrepancies led to a lively interaction marked by laughter and a willingness to grapple with the referential problems.

The second micro-evaluation is more elaborate. Freeman (2007) set out to evaluate a dicto-gloss task[1] (Wajnryb 1990). This required students to listen to a listening text nine sentences long on the subject of obesity. They listened three times. On the first occasion they were asked to answer a multiple choice question designed to establish whether they had understood the general content of the text. On the second occasion, the students were told to note down the key content words, whilst on the third occasion different students were required to focus and take notes on the use of different linguistic forms (i.e. relative clauses, passive verb forms and transition signals). The students then worked in groups of three to reconstruct the text and write it out. Freeman's evaluation was designed to establish both accountability (i.e. whether the task met its objectives) and to provide information about how to improve the task. To this end she collected a variety of data – the notes the students made during the third listening (i.e. the extent to which they noticed and noted the target forms they were directed to attend to), the reconstructed text, a questionnaire to elicit the students' opinions of the task, a transcript of the discussion that took place whilst the students were reconstructing the text, notes made by observers of the lesson and a summative reflective report by the teacher. The analyses of these data sets demonstrated that the students were successful in noticing and noting the target structures, that they attempted to use the target forms in their reconstructed text, that they engaged in a number of language-centred episodes as they discussed their reconstruction (most of which led to correct language use), and that they reported the task had enabled them to communicate freely and that the interactions they engaged in during the discussion helped them with grammar. Freeman concluded that the students were largely successful in achieving the outcome of the task (the reconstruction of the text), that the task was successful in inducing noticing of the target forms, and also encouraged attendance to other aspects of language and led to active engagement (although not equally for all students). By and large, then, she felt that the task had achieved its objectives. However, she also identified a number of ways in which it could be improved. For example, she suggested that

[1] A dicto-gloss task is a focused task. That is, the text that the learners listen to is designed to focus on specific linguistic features. It qualifies as a task because the learners work in groups to discuss how to reproduce the text together. In effect, then, language becomes a topic to talk about whilst the talk itself requires them to use their own linguistic resources.

because the students were allowed to share the notes they had taken, this reduced the amount and quality of the interaction and that a better procedure would be to have the students put away their notes before they started to reconstruct the text. Another suggestion was to assign the task of scribe of the reconstructed text to the least proficient of the students to encourage greater participation by this student.

The third task evaluation, conducted by Yuan (1997), examined two decision-making tasks (i.e. unfocused tasks with open outcomes). Yuan was interested in investigating the effect of one implementational variable – pre-task planning. She asked two advanced language learners (TOEFL (test of English as a foreign language) 600) to complete two tasks. The first was based on Foster and Skehan (1996); it required the learners to act as judges to decide what prison terms should be meted out to a list of offenders. The second was borrowed from Ur (1981); the learners were asked to decide the amount of scholarships to be awarded to four candidates. For the first task no planning time was allocated, whilst for the second the learners were given ten minutes to plan what they would say. Yuan audio recorded the learners' performances and transcribed them. Analysis focused on syntactical complexity, syntactical variety and lexical variety. Syntactical complexity was measured in terms of the ratio of finite or non-finite clauses to c-units (defined as independent units providing referential or pragmatic meaning). Syntactical variety was operationalised as the number of different verb forms used[2]. To measure lexical variety a count was made of the different content words used by each learner in the two tasks. The results are shown in Table 9.2. An interesting finding is that the opportunity to plan did not affect the learners' performance of the tasks in the same way. In the case of Learner A it had little effect. However, Learner B benefited considerably, with all three measures of complexity increasing when planning time was allowed. Yuan noted that whilst the two learners produced more or less equal amounts of talk in Task 1, Learner B talked more than Learner A in the second task. This suggests that the two learners may have oriented differently to the tasks, indicating that although they were performing the same task, they were not engaging in the same activity.

Table 9.3 summarises the main dimensions of these three micro-evaluations. It shows the range of possibilities available in this kind of evaluation. All three evaluations were concerned with establishing

[2] Verb forms include simple verb (e.g. 'eat'), past tense form (e.g. 'ate'), past participle (e.g. 'eaten'), the various auxiliary forms (e.g. 'is/was' and 'have') and modal verb forms (e.g. 'must'). The range of forms used is employed as one measure of syntactical complexity.

Table 9.2 *Effects of planning on learners' performance of two tasks*

	Task 1 (no planning)			Task 2 (planning)		
	Syntactical complexity	Syntactical variety	Lexical variety	Syntactical complexity	Syntactical variety	Lexical variety
Learner A	1.23	10	32	1.28	7	39
Learner B	1.60	8	53	1.81	15	74

Table 9.3 *Summary of the three micro-evaluations*

Type of task	Purpose	Approach	Data collected	Analysis
Study: Simons				
Information-gap (unfocused; closed)	Accountability	Response-based	Transcripts of students' performance of the task	Frequency of different language functions
Study: Freeman				
Reconstruction task (focused; closed)	Accountability and improvement	Response-based and student-based	Student responses to questionnaire; observation notes; transcriptions of audio recording; students' notes; students' final product (reformulated text)	Students' attitudes towards task; use of target features in language-related episodes; observers' comments; accuracy of final product
Study: Yuan				
Decision-making task (unfocused; open)	Accountability	Response-based	Transcripts of audio-recording of the task	Measures of linguistic complexity

whether the tasks achieved what they were designed to achieve, but only one (Freeman) also considered how the task might be improved. Arguably, from a teaching perspective micro-evaluations need to be developmental as well as demonstrate accountability. All three evaluations were response-based; that is, they examined what transpired when students performed the task with a view to determining to what extent the 'activity' generated by the task matched that intended by the task workplan. By and large, it did. However, a finding of two of the studies (Simons and Yuan) was that students' performance of a task varied quite markedly. Thus, whilst Seedhouse's (2005) claim that it is not possible to predict what activity will result from a task is not supported, it is clear that students' will vary considerably in how they cope with the demands of a task, in part because of how they orientate to it. Only Freeman's study included a student-based approach. None of the studies attempted a learning-based approach, reflecting my earlier observation that it is difficult to investigate whether a task actually results in learning. Of the three studies only Freeman's focused task really lent itself to a learning-based evaluation (i.e. it would have been possible to have included some kind of pre-test to establish the students' ability to use the target structures accurately prior to their performing the task). The three evaluations employed a variety of data collection methods, but recording and transcribing of the students' performance of the task was clearly the preferred method, reflecting the importance of examining the actual language generated by a task in order to demonstrate accountability. The methods of analysis were chosen to reflect the specific focus of each evaluation (e.g. Simons examined communicative functions as a way of investigating whether the task resulted in communicative language use, whilst Yuan used measures of complexity to establish what effect planning had on the learner's production). Freeman's study employed a variety of analytical methods in an effort to achieve triangulation.

Teachers who have undertaken micro-evaluations almost invariably comment on the time-consuming and laborious nature of such research, reflecting Allwright's (2003) critique of much teacher research. This is a valid criticism. Nevertheless, the comments made by teachers who have conducted such micro-evaluations suggest they are worthwhile. Chan's (1995) summing up of her own experience of doing a micro-evaluation is typical of the comments produced by my MA students:

> Micro-based task-evaluation is a good introspective opportunity for evaluating teaching techniques and materials. There's only one disadvantage: it takes a lot of time to carry out. Therefore, it may not fit some busy teachers' schedule. But I had a lot of fun.

A micro-evaluation forces a teacher to examine the assumptions that lie behind the design of a task and the procedures used to implement it. It requires them to go beyond impressionistic evaluation by examining empirically whether a task 'works' in the way they intended and how it can be improved for future use. Micro-evaluation of tasks, in fact, constitutes one way in which teachers can conduct action research. Teachers may find that choosing a task to submit to empirical scrutiny constitutes an easier entry into action research than the customary starting point for this kind of research – identifying a 'problem' – which, as Nunan (1990) pointed out, many teachers struggle with.

Clearly teachers will not be able to undertake micro-evaluations of tasks on a regular basis, but it ought to be feasible for them to do so occasionally. The simplest micro-evaluation might involve a student-based evaluation (i.e. asking students to complete a questionnaire after they have completed a task). A somewhat more ambitious micro-evaluation would involve audio recoding one pair or small group of students performing a task, transcribing the recording and analysing the interactions that occur. Such evaluations can provide teachers with the data they need to make a conference presentation.

Micro-evaluations of tasks also have a contribution to make to research. Much of the research that has investigated task-based language teaching has been experimental in design, seeking to show how specific design features or implementational procedures influence task performance. Such research aims for generalisability by comparing groups of learners. However, it provides little detailed information about how specific learners grapple with particular tasks. All three of the micro-evaluations reported in this section demonstrate that learners often respond to tasks in different ways depending on such factors as their proficiency and their orientation to the task. Whilst it is of obvious importance to try to identify the generalisable effect of task features, it is also important to identify the factors that influence learners' variable response to a task. Micro-evaluations are one way of investigating these factors.

Micro-evaluations can also help to combat some of the criticisms that have been levelled at task-based teaching. Seedhouse (1999), for example, claimed that the performance of tasks is characterised by indexicalised and pidginised language as a result of the learners' over-reliance on context and the limitations of their linguistic resources. The evidence from the micro-evaluations reported above, however, shows that this need not be the case. Another criticism that can be challenged using the evidence from micro-evaluations of tasks is that 'the only grammar to be dealt with (in TBLT) is that which causes a problem in communication' (Sheen 2003). Freeman's evaluation, for example, showed that learners attend to linguistic form not only when they are in communicative difficulty and that the forms are not restricted to grammatical ones. The detailed quantitative and qualitative evidence provided by micro-evaluations can go a long way to removing these kinds of misunderstandings about task-based teaching.

9.8 Conclusion

This chapter has examined the case for carrying out both macro- and micro-evaluations of task-based teaching and has reported examples of both types. A number of macro-evaluations have been published. In contrast, micro-evaluations of tasks rarely find their way into journals. Such studies are often seen as too localised and too small scale, and so theoretically uninteresting. In contrast, there is substantial body of published research that has investigated tasks. Such studies are theory-driven (e.g. the numerous studies that have investigated tasks from the perspective of the negotiation of meaning). Their primary purpose has been theory-testing or theory development rather than the improvement of pedagogy. In contrast, the evaluation of individual tasks is intended 'to elucidate a problem in action' (Norris 1990: 98); that is, it seeks to establish whether and in what ways a 'task' works.

The case for both macro- and micro-evaluations of task-based teaching is a strong one. Task-based teaching constitutes an innovation in many teaching contexts and like all innovations needs to be studied in context. The essential difference between 'research' and 'evaluation' is that whereas the former typically ignores or tries to control contextual variables, the latter aims to investigate how they impact on the effectiveness of the materials and teaching. Evaluators accept that tasks can only be studied in the context in which they are used. Only in this way is it possible to ascertain whether they 'work', and if not, what factors prevent them from doing so.

It is too easy to critique task-based language teaching from the 'outside'. It is noticeable that all the main critics of task-based teaching (Sheen, Swan and Widdowson) base their criticisms on theory or on their own experience of what works. They have not engaged themselves in evaluating tasks and they do not cite studies that have done so[3].

---

[3] Sheen has attempted to conduct experimental studies comparing task-based instruction with some other form of more traditional instruction (e.g. Sheen 2006). However, these studies suffer from the same problems experienced by earlier global method comparisons (e.g. Smith 1970) and certainly do not support the specific criticisms that Sheen has levelled against TBLT.

Ultimately, though, task-based materials, like all teaching materials, require empirical validation. Only with the evidence from actual evaluations will it be possible to determine whether task-based teaching is capable of creating the kinds of opportunities that foster language learning and what individual and contextual variables mediate its effectiveness.

References

Alderson, J. and A. Beretta (eds.). 1992. *Evaluating Second Language Education*. Cambridge: Cambridge University Press.

Alderson, J and M. Scott. 1992. 'Insiders, outsiders and participatory evaluation'. In J. Alderson and A. Beretta (eds.), *Evaluating Second Language Education*. Cambridge: Cambridge University Press.

Allwright, D. 2003. 'Exploratory practice: rethinking practitioner research in language teaching'. *Language Teaching Research*, 7: 113–41.

Beretta, A. 1990. 'Implementation of the Bangalore Project'. *Applied Linguistics*, 11: 321–37.

1992. 'Evaluation of language education: an overview'. In J. Alderson and A. Beretta (eds.), *Evaluating Second Language Education*. Cambridge: Cambridge University Press.

Beretta, A. and A. Davies. 1985. 'Evaluation of the Bangalore Project'. *ELT Journal*, 39: 121–7.

Butler, Y. 2005. 'Comparative perspectives towards communicative activities among elementary school teachers in South Korea, Japan and Taiwan'. *Language Teaching Research*, 9: 423–46.

Carless, D. 2004. 'Issues in teachers' reinterpretation of a task-based innovation in primary schools'. *TESOL Quarterly*, 38: 639–62.

Chan, S. H. 1995. 'A micro-evaluation-based task evaluation'. Unpublished MA paper, Temple University, Philadelphia.

Coughlan, P. and P. A. Duff. 1994. 'Same task, different activities: analysis of a SLA task from an activity theory perspective'. In J. Lantolf and G. Appel, *Vygotskian Approaches to Second Language Research*. Norwood, NJ: Ablex.

Crookes, G. and S. Gass (eds.). 1993. *Tasks in a Pedagogical Context: Integrating Theory and Practice*. Clevedon, Avon: Multilingual Matters.

Edwards, C. and J. Willis (eds.). 2005. *Teachers Exploring Tasks in English Language Teaching*. Basingstoke: Palgrave Macmillan.

Ellis, R. 1994. 'Second language acquisition research and teacher development: the case of teachers' questions'. In D. Li, D. Mahoney, and J. Richards (eds.), *Exploring Second Language Teacher Development*. Hong Kong: City Polytechnic.

1997. *SLA Research and Language Teaching*. Oxford: Oxford University Press.

1998. 'The evaluation of communicative tasks'. In B. Tomlinson (ed.), *Materials Development in Language Teaching*. Cambridge: Cambridge University Press, pp. 217–38.

2003. *Task-based Language Learning and Teaching*. Oxford: Oxford University Press.

2010. 'Second language acquisition research and language teaching materials'. In N. Harwood (ed.), *Materials in ELT: Theory and Practice*. Cambridge: Cambridge University Press.

Estaire, S. and J. Zanon. 1994. *Planning Classwork: A Task Based Approach*. Oxford: Heinemann.

Foster, P. and P. Skehan. 1996. 'The influence of planning and task type on second language performance'. *Studies in Second Language Acquisition*, 18: 299–323.

Freeman, J. 2007. 'A task evaluation'. Unpublished MA paper, University of Auckland, Auckland.

Kiely, R and P. Rea-Dickens. 2005. *Program Evaluation in Language Education*. Basingstoke: Palgrave Macmillan.

Leaver, B. and Willis, J. (eds.). 2004. *Task-based Instruction in Foreign Language Education*. Washington DC: Georgetown University Press.

Li, D. 1998. 'It's always more difficult than you planned. Teachers' perceived difficulties in introducing the communicative approach in South Korea'. *TESOL Quarterly*, 32: 677–703.

Lynch, B. 1992. 'Evaluating a program inside out'. In J. Alderson and A. Beretta (eds.), *Evaluating Second Language Education*. Cambridge: Cambridge University Press.

McDonough, K. and Chaikitmongkol, W. 2007. 'Teachers' and learners' reactions to a task based EFL course in Thailand'. *TESOL Quarterly*, 41: 107–32.

Mitchell, R. 1992. 'The "independent" evaluation of bilingual primary education: a narrative account'. In Alderson and A. Beretta (eds.), *Evaluating Second Language Education*. Cambridge: Cambridge University Press.

Mitchell, R and J. Lee. 2003. 'Sameness and difference in classroom learning cultures: interpretations of communicative pedagogy in the UK and Korea'. *Language Teaching Research*, 7: 35–63.

Norris, N. 1990. *Understanding Educational Evaluation*. London: Kogan Page.

Nunan, D. 1989. *Designing Tasks for the Communicative Classroom*. Cambridge: Cambridge University Press.

1990. 'The teacher as researcher'. In C. Brumfit and R. Mitchell (eds.), *Research in the Language Classroom. ELT Documents 133*. Modern English Publications.

2004. *Task-based Language Teaching*. Cambridge: Cambridge University Press.

Prabhu, N. S. 1987. *Second Language Pedagogy*. Oxford: Oxford University Press.

Samuda, V. and M. Bygate. 2008. *Tasks in Second Language Learning*. Basingstoke: Palgrave MacMillan.

Seedhouse, P. 1999. 'Task-based interaction'. *ELT Journal*, 53: 149–56.

2005. '"Task" as research construct'. *Language Learning*, 55(3): 533–70.

Sheen, R. 1994. 'A critical analysis of the advocacy of the task-based syllabus'. *TESOL Quarterly*, 28: 127–57.

2003. 'Focus-on-form – a myth in the making'. *ELT Journal*, 57: 225–33.

2006. 'Focus on forms as a means of improving accurate oral production'. In A. Housen and M. Pierrard (eds.), *Investigations in Instructed Second Language Acquisition*. Berlin: Mouton de Gruyter.

Simons, G. 1997. 'Finding your way communicatively: a micro-evaluation of a task'. Unpublished MA paper, Temple University, Philadelphia.

Skehan, P. 1998. *A Cognitive Approach to Language Learning*. Oxford: Oxford University Press.

Smith, P. 1970. 'A comparison of the audiolingual and cognitive approaches to foreign language instruction: the Pennsylvania Foreign Language Project'. Philadelphia: Center for Curriculum Development.

Swan, M. 2005. 'Legislating by hypothesis: the case of task-based instruction'. *Applied Linguistics*, 26: 376–401.

Ur, P. 1981. *Discussions that Work*. Cambridge: Cambridge University Press.

Van den Branden, K. (ed.) 2006. *Task-based Language Education: From Theory to Practice*. Cambridge: Cambridge University Press.

Van den Branden, K., M. Bygate and J. Norris. 2009. *Task-based Language Teaching: A Reader*. Amsterdam: John Benjamins.

Wajnryb, R. 1990. *Grammar Dictation*. Oxford: Oxford University Press.

Weir, C. and J. Roberts. 1994. *Evaluation in ELT*. Oxford: Blackwell.

Widdowson, H. 2003. *Defining Issues in English: Language Teaching* (Chapter 9 – Pedagogic Design). Oxford: Oxford University Press.

Willis, J. 1996. *A Framework for Task-Based Learning*. Harlow: Longman.

Yuan, F. 1997. 'Planning and complex language production: a micro-evaluation of two tasks'. Unpublished MA paper, Temple University, Philadelphia.

Yule, G. and D. McDonald. 1990. 'Resolving referential conflicts in L2 interaction: the effect of proficiency and interactive role'. *Language Learning*, 40: 539–56.

10 What do teachers really want from coursebooks?

Hitomi Masuhara

10.1 Introduction

If I had been asked what I wanted from coursebooks when I was teaching languages in Japan, England, Singapore and Oman in the last 30 years, my answer would have always been the same: 'I want coursebooks that are so engaging, inspiring, flexible and effective that I can just teach without much extra work.' In reality, I had to adapt materials every time I used them. For example, the Ministry-approved coursebooks often seemed to me so constrained by a syllabus, by rigid methods and by exams, that I found it difficult to make use of them. Global coursebooks from English-speaking countries, on the other hand, seemed impressive, with more fashionable approaches promising success, but their contents seemed too alien to be imported directly into my classrooms. The only time that adaptation was minimal was when I had tailor-made the materials myself. My language-teaching colleagues in all the institutions I worked in often grumbled how language teachers have to work harder compared with other subject teachers, whose content and approaches seemed to remain consistent and who do not have to adapt materials or produce supplements. Even after all these years, my ideal materials only exist in my dreams and my lament seems to echo amongst my colleagues from all over the world. Surely teachers' needs and wants should have been taken more seriously by now?

From the 1980s to the early 1990s learner variables attracted a lot of attention in the research (Ellis 1994; Larsen-Freeman and Long 1991). The increasing global need for English as a lingua franca also led to explorations of learner-centred curricula (Johnson 1989; Nunan 1988) and of needs analysis (Hutchinson and Waters 1987). Coursebooks reflected this change and their blurbs often emphasised that their product was designed to satisfy learners' needs and interests.

From the late 1990s to 2000s L2 learners' profiles have become far more complex and learner variables have attracted even more attention (Doughty and Long 2003; Ellis 2008). The portraits of L2 users these days show incredible diversity (Cook 2002; Graddol 1997, 2006). Some learners, for example, may be immigrants at various socioeconomic and

236

linguistic levels, others may be young learners studying content subjects in a target language in their own countries, and others might need different levels of international communication skills in their professions. Long (2005: 1) acknowledges the complexity of learner variables these days and argues: 'Just as no medical intervention would be prescribed before a thorough diagnosis of what ails the patient, so no language teaching program should be designed without a thorough needs analysis.'

What is alarming is that, in contrast to the range and number of studies on learner variables, studies of teacher variables have been and still are hard to find. Who are, for example, teaching these varieties of learners worldwide? The teachers' profiles are obscure in the background of learner studies. Much of the literature on language teaching seems to regard teachers as anonymous passive beings who are expected to adapt flexibly to the roles determined by the objectives of the method and by the learning theory on which the method is based (Larsen-Freeman 2000; Richards and Rodgers 2001).

The literature on teacher education seems to go along with such a view and to focus mainly on helping teachers to change. Even when individualistic aspects of teachers' needs and wants are brought to light through journal studies and classroom observation, they seem only to feature as evidence of teacher transformation that led to the success of learner achievements (Freeman and Richards 1996; Richards and Nunan 1990).

Richards (2008) reflects on how teacher education in the past tended to focus on transmitting 'knowledge about' (which includes knowledge about language and about language learning and teaching) and also 'knowledge how' (which involves the methodology of teaching and practical classroom management skills). He points out that traditional teacher education assumed that the teachers would become able to teach well once they learned either or both kinds of knowledge. He then describes a more recent approach in teacher education which is informed by sociocultural theory (Lantolf 2000) and by studies on teacher cognition (Borg 2006). In such an approach teachers are guided to become aware of their own beliefs and the principles behind their practice through dialogic and collaborative inquiry:

> While traditional views of teacher-learning often viewed the teachers' task as the application of theory to practice, more recent views see teacher-learning as the theorisation of practice – in other words, making visible the nature of practitioner knowledge and providing the means by which such knowledge can be elaborated, understood and reviewed.

> (Richards, 2008: 164–5)

237

I would strongly argue that we need a lot more studies on teacher needs and wants. Teachers are ultimately in a crucial position in language teaching and learning because they are the ones that realise curricula, syllabuses, methodology and materials in classrooms. Teachers play central roles in materials development – for they are the ones who select materials (or, at least, have some influence in the selection process), who actually teach the materials and who adapt and develop materials. Tomlinson and Masuhara (2004: (ii)) believe that 'all teachers have their own intuitive theories of language learning and argue that helping them to develop and articulate these theories in principled and coherent ways can help them to develop and use effective language learning materials'. The students come and go and so do materials, but a large number of teachers tend to stay.

In this revised version of Masuhara (1998), therefore, I intend to update the literature review of the studies on teacher variables since 1998 and to reappraise some potential benefits of studying teacher variables. Specifically I would like to focus on how teachers' needs and wants from coursebooks can be identified and catered for in the processes of materials development.

10.2 Needs and wants analysis?

Needs analysis has featured prominently in the literature of language teaching since the 1980s (e.g. Hutchinson and Waters 1987; Johnson 1989; Long 2005; Richards 1990; Robinson 1980 and 1990). All of the literature without exception, however, seems to focus on learners' needs. Teachers' needs, if discussed at all, are treated as a part of situation analysis in terms of general parameters of a language programme.

How are 'needs' defined in the literature? They seem to be defined in terms of: (a) ownership (whose needs are they?), (b) kinds (what kinds of needs are identified?) and (c) sources (what are the sources for the needs?). Table 10.1 summarises the needs which are identified in the literature.

Differentiating needs as in Table 10.1 seems useful in demystifying some of the unclear areas in previous survey studies in materials development. Take an example of a coursebook which claims to have been tested to satisfy the needs and interests of the students. In order for the claims to be valid, the data must be taken directly from the learners and from relevant documents by objective means (e.g. corpus studies of language use in prospective fields, documents of future job specifications, the learners' strengths and weaknesses in L2 performance observed in class or measured in diagnostic tests) as well as by subjective means (e.g. learner questionnaires, interviews, journals, etc.). Subjective data can be informative but tends to be variable and vulnerable in terms of

Table 10.1 *List of needs identified in needs analysis literature*

Ownership	Kind	Source
LEARNERS' NEEDS	personal needs	age sex cultural background interests educational background
	learning needs	learning styles previous language-learning experiences gap between the target level and the present level in terms of knowledge (e.g. target language and its culture) gap between the target level and the present level of proficiency in various competence areas (e.g. skills, strategies) learning goals and expectations for a course
	future professional needs	requirements for future undertakings in terms of: knowledge of language knowledge of language use L2 competence
TEACHERS' NEEDS	personal needs	age sex cultural background interests educational background teachers' language proficiency
	professional needs	preferred teaching styles teacher training experience teaching experience
ADMINISTRA-TORS' NEEDS	institutional needs	sociopolitical needs market forces educational policy constraints (e.g. time, budget, resources)

reliability. Therefore, the claims of satisfying learner needs deserve criticism if they are based solely or largely on questionnaires given to teachers asking if the coursebook has satisfied their learners' needs. Such surveys only measure teachers' perception of learners' needs, which does not necessarily represent the actual learners' needs (see Masuhara 1994; Tomlinson 1995 for critical discussions).

A summary of needs, as in Table 10.1, is also indispensable in describing how each different category of needs could influence the others. When teachers are asked what their needs from a coursebook are (see Masuhara and Tomlinson 2008; Tomlinson and Masuhara 2008 for such research reports), for example, their responses may be influenced by:

1. teachers' perception of administrative needs
   e.g. The school is under-resourced and a very strict syllabus is imposed, which the teachers are expected to obey.
2. measured learners' needs
   e.g. The teacher has administered a diagnostic test at the beginning of the course and is aware of the learners' communicative needs.
3. teachers' perception of learners' needs
   e.g. The teacher believes that Japanese students are quiet and shy and thus require special training in speaking.
4. teachers' wants
   e.g. Even though ELT experts recommend a learner-centred approach these days and the other colleagues at the language centre follow the trend, the teacher prefers and also secretly believes in the value of a teacher-centred approach for certain learners.

In order to avoid such confusion, it seems vital to extract, from Table 10.1, only the teachers' *own* needs and wants, and to design a more refined framework which can facilitate our investigation. Figures 10.1 and 10.2 are an attempt to provide such a framework for the studies of teachers' own needs and wants.

Teachers' needs (see Figure 10.1) would consist of two general areas: one deriving from personal traits such as their age, sex, personality, own preferred learning styles, cultural and educational background, and the other from their professional traits, such as areas and levels of expertise, length and types of teaching experience.

I have differentiated three kinds of needs according to how they are identified:

(a) Self-perceived needs – the needs which are reported by the teacher. These are what teachers themselves can articulate.
(b) Needs perceived by others – the needs of the teachers which they are not aware of and thus cannot articulate themselves and which are identified by others (e.g. colleagues, teacher trainers, researchers) in

Figure 10.1   Teachers' own needs

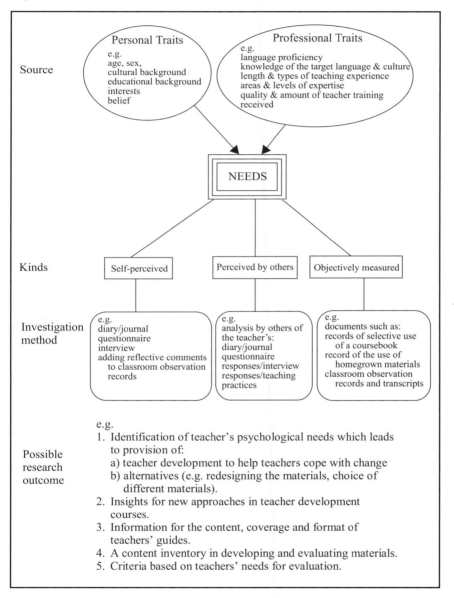

response to qualitative data (e.g. observation of the teacher's teaching, analysing tendencies in interview and questionnaire responses of the teacher).

(c) Objectively measured needs – the needs which are identified in objective studies in which quantified data is collected, analysed and interpreted by a third party who tries to be detached, unbiased and accurate (e.g. task-based needs analysis in which teachers are asked to do a certain task and the process and product is analysed by a trained researcher).

It would increase the validity and reliability of the study if subjective data of self-perceived needs was triangulated or validated by other kinds of data (i.e. needs perceived by others, objectively measured needs). For example, a teacher reported his lack of confidence in classroom management. His lack of confidence was confirmed in a series of classroom observations by others. The quantitative study of teacher–learner interactions revealed that the teacher seemed to have trouble especially when coordinating group work to facilitate open discussion. Further analysis revealed that in fact the textbook presupposes much smaller classes than the size of the classes this teacher faces every day. Therefore, the solution for this case may not be teacher training to help him to cope with the material but the provision of alternatives (e.g. a textbook which is appropriately designed for a large class situation).

The study of teachers' needs would provide useful information, for example, for the content, coverage and format for producing a teachers' guide. An inexperienced teacher might need more detailed instructions and suggestions on teaching methods in the teachers' guide compared to experienced teachers, who might prefer a teachers' guide to supply a lot of different optional activities or interesting raw materials which can be exploited.

The identification of needs could also make an interesting small action research project investigating which teachers' needs would predict the final selection of a coursebook, and which needs could be generalised, for instance, as an indicator for the popularity of a particular coursebook. Studies of teachers' needs may also provide a content coverage inventory in developing and evaluating materials.

In many cases, what may be identified by the teachers themselves and by a third party as their 'needs' could be their 'wants' as well. For example, an intermediate general English course may include an extensive reading class twice a week, based on the needs assessment of the learners and also on the pedagogical decisions by the administrator, but also because the teacher wants to promote an extensive reading approach because he/she firmly believes in the value of such an approach.

Teachers' wants (see Figure 10.2), however, can be distinguished from needs when there is preference, despite the fact it may not be necessary, obligatory, encouraged or assumed. For instance, I would call it a teachers' want if they prefer to employ a certain approach (e.g. teaching grammar with a discovery approach) even though it is not considered to be important or even suitable by their administrators and colleagues. Or teachers may want to set up some creative writing activities in their speaking classes as consolidation, even though it is not what is usually associated with oral classes. The study of teachers' wants in this sense may lead to discoveries of idiosyncratic aspects of teaching, of gaps in materials coverage, or even of innovative approaches to development or use of materials. The study of teachers' wants may reveal their preference for materials and for methods that could eventually lead to effective language learning. Figure 10.2 summarises the source and kinds of teachers' wants and possible research methods and outcomes.

The theoretical framework which Figures 10.1 and 10.2 try to illustrate should help untangle a seemingly irreconcilable and recurring debate between the supporters and sceptics of coursebooks. Teachers' needs and wants from coursebooks have often featured on both sides of the debate as evidence. Let us look at a classic case from the past. Sheldon (1988) described quite persuasively the teachers' need for more theoretically and practically sound coursebooks and their frustration in not getting them. And he welcomed, as one future option of 'published' core materials, computer programs, which teachers could modify and supplement as required according to their local and on-the-spot needs. Note here that the advancement of web authoring programs and of multimedia is gradually enabling teachers in resource-rich environments to enjoy such freedom. Hutchinson and Torres (1994), on the other hand, argued for the benefit of structured coursebooks, quoting the result of Torres's survey showing teachers' needs for security in classroom management. Reading both articles, the readers are left unsettled as to what exactly is the teachers' need for future coursebooks: a flexible coursebook which presupposes exploitation by the users or a structured and visible coursebook which is foolproof? The needs of teachers reported by Sheldon seem very different from those claimed by Torres. Solutions based solely on one claim would not solve the problems of teachers reflected by the other claim. This debate between those who regard the coursebook as a tool and those who regard it as a script seems to recur with different guises (Thornbury 2000, 2005; Tomlinson 2008a).

The theoretical framework (see Figure 10.1) is useful in putting each claim into perspective. When examined against the framework, the force of both claims starts to reduce. First, in both cases teachers' needs are assumed and not defined. Secondly, the source and methods of how

Figure 10.2   Teachers' own wants

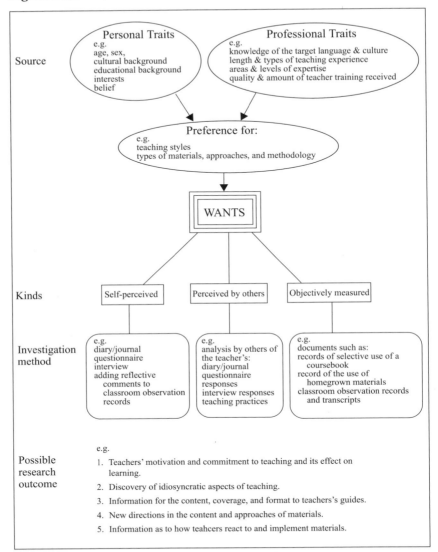

the particular teachers' needs were identified are not made explicit. For instance, Sheldon (1988) uses anecdotes to illustrate teachers' needs without specifying who the teachers are or how the sampling was done. Hutchinson and Torres (1994) do base their claims on a questionnaire survey, but the non-representativeness of the sample seems to limit the generalisability of their arguments.

The framework (see Figure 10.1) is also helpful in locating where the source of conflict lies. The apparent contradiction between Sheldon (1988) and Hutchinson and Torres (1994) seems to me to derive, in fact, from the same root. In this case, the teachers' confidence and professional expertise influenced their perception of what they need from coursebooks. Therefore, the real issue here is the necessity to explore how to cater for different needs which derive from varying degrees of teachers' professional ability and confidence.

10.3 Teachers – an endangered species

Exploring teachers' needs and wants is crucial when the role division between the materials producers (e.g. professional materials writers and publishers) and the users (e.g. teachers, educational administrators and learners) seems to be becoming more and more evident. Remarkable technical advancement has brought sophistication and a great proliferation of ESL/EFL coursebooks, but it has also created a wider role division between materials producers and materials users. The sheer scale and amount of time, energy and different expertise required in contemporary coursebook production (Donovan 1998; Amrani – Chapter 11 in this volume) seems to be alienating teachers as potential materials writers, because they often have a heavy workload in often under-resourced teaching contexts. The teachers' homegrown materials may be more finely tuned to local classroom needs with valid methodological awareness, but the colourful or glossy appearance of commercial coursebooks may be more eye-catching and may even seem to the learners to have more face validity (Zacharias 2005).

The division between the producers and users has also affected the coherent linear sequence of curriculum development/course design processes to the level that concerns are being expressed that the materials could carry the threat of deskilling teachers by reducing the teachers' role.

Traditionally the process of course design (e.g. Dubin and Olshtain 1994; Johnson 1989; Richards 1990) suggests that materials design or selection should come at a later stage of the process. The sequence of course design recommended by these experts may be summarised as the linear Model X in Figure 10.3.

Figure 10.3   *Model X – course design procedures*

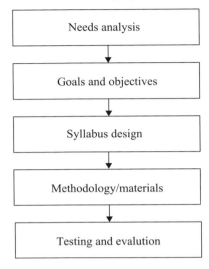

This Model X shows how the teaching contexts and the learners' needs provide a framework for the objectives and then the decisions concerning the best methods and materials are made accordingly. Ideally teachers should be involved as major members of curriculum development teams to make the whole sequence coherent (as in Carl 2009). The recent models seem more complicated and non-linear, but basic principles of profiling of learners and setting up objectives seem to appear at an early stage and the selection of materials comes toward the end (Gustafson and Branch 2002; Wiles and Bondi 2010).

Many practitioners, however, may find that this theoretical Model X does not represent the actual sequence that they experience in their ELT institutions all over the world. Instead, a more familiar sequence may be described in the following manner.

First, the teachers and administrators draw up a very general profile of a particular class and learners. In this profile the characteristics of the learners are defined in terms of the learners' preference for a course and the levels of their proficiency based on the tests administered at the beginning of the course. The goal of teaching is usually represented in the name of the course (e.g. First Certificate Preparation Course, Oral Communication I).

Materials selection holds a crucial position in the second stage of the course design sequence; the teachers and administrator select from commercially available coursebooks the one suitable for the class defined in the initial stage. The stages such as needs analysis, objectives specification, syllabus design and selection of methodology which Model X presupposes to happen prior to materials selection are assumed to have been taken care of by the producers (e.g. materials writers and publishers). In fact producers provide prospective selectors (e.g. administrators and teachers) with information as to the target learners, objectives and methodology in the blurbs or in the introductions of the books. They may also provide a syllabus map indicating how units are integrated into a coherent course. The sequence of course design introduced above may be summarised as Model Y (see Figure 10.4).

By contrasting Model Y with Model X, it becomes apparent how crucial stages of the course design have been moved from the hands of the teachers and administrators into those of materials producers.

The careful and thorough analysis of learning and teaching situations recommended by the experts (Long 2005) as a prerequisite in Model X may not seem appropriate to the teachers and administrators operating in the system represented in Model Y; loose specification of the learners' level and purpose is sufficient in selecting a coursebook from a limited number of available pre-designed materials.

The writers and publishers of a textbook may or may not have gone through the stages of needs analysis, specifications of the goals and objectives, designing the syllabus and choosing the methodology (see producers' accounts in Amrani – Chapter 11 in this volume; Bell and Gower – Chapter 6 in this volume; Donovan 1998; Prowse – Chapter 7 in this volume), but the teachers and administrators are even less able to oversee these processes than before, except through the selection of and

Figure 10.4 *Model Y – course design procedures in practice*

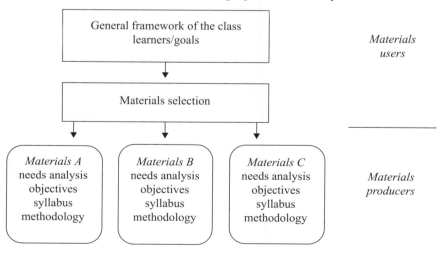

the flexible use of the materials. In such cases, the materials writer and the publisher who produced the materials can be said to have more direct control of the course design processes than the teachers. The degree of dominance depends on how much and how closely the teachers choose to follow the coursebook or how much teachers take the initiative in making flexible use of the materials. There are some recent studies which provide evidence of how teachers use coursebooks as resources (e.g. Gray 2002; Lee and Bathmaker 2007), but other studies show how teachers tend to revere the published coursebooks and rigidly use them as a script (e.g. Bacha *et al.* 2008; Ghosn 2003; Zacharias 2005).

In fact, the phenomenon of the coursebook possibly diminishing teachers features in the debate on whether the textbook could cause teachers to be overdependent on books or not. Littlejohn (1992: 84), in his PhD thesis, reported in Hutchinson and Torres (1994: 315), expressed such a concern by saying that 'the precise instructions which the materials give reduce the teacher's role to one of managing or overseeing a pre-planned classroom event'. Similar debate recurs in the Dogme argument in which Thornbury advocates the teachers' independence from course-books (Thornbury 2000, 2005; Meddings and Thornbury 2009).

These debates seem to me to testify to the negative manifestation of the conflicts inherent in the system depicted in Model Y above. With the diversification of learners and teaching contexts in recent years, catering for needs and wants of users may pose an overwhelming challenge to coursebook producers. It seems surprising that the theorisation of such widely practised procedures represented in Model Y does not seem to have been attempted in curriculum development, not to speak of the discussions on how best the procedures can be made use of without producing negative effects.

Tomlinson and Masuhara (2010) include ten case studies of in-house and localised materials development in which the users have decided to become the producers and to take back the full control of course design through materials development, assessment and evaluation. Al-Busaidi and Tindle (2010), for example, report the whole process of an institution-based materials development project and its effects on teachers and students. Those studies in Tomlinson and Masuhara (2010) seem to provide counter-evidence against the apprehensions expressed in the past that in-house materials may be poorly produced, may be theoretically and pedagogically unsound, and may lack face validity in the eyes of students (Hutchinson and Waters 1987; Sheldon 1988). The majority of teachers, however, may not have such institutional support or may be happy to remain users of ready-made coursebooks.

On a more positive note, this role division between the producers and users of materials may even be seen as sensible and realistic *provided* teachers' needs and wants are reflected in materials, that theoretical validity is pursued by the producers, and that the teachers have overall control in the teaching. The crucial question is how can teachers' needs and wants be tapped and catered for in the materials production process. If the two contemporary phenomena of role division and reversal of the course design sequence were to stay and the final responsibility for successful teaching is still attributed to teachers, then efficient and effective systems must be established in order to empower teachers.

10.4 Empowerment of teachers

10.4.1 The need for objective measurements of the quality of published coursebooks

Suggestions

Sheldon (1988) advocated several ways of achieving objective measurements. They included:

- the desirability of introducing a *Which?* magazine for ELT coursebooks (Brumfit 1980: 30).
- improvement and innovation in *ELTJ* reviews in order to enhance their validity, usefulness and availability, for example collaborative teachers' and learners' reviews.

Developments

- The *Which?* magazine for ELT coursebooks has not materialised, possibly because the increasing diversity of users and contexts does not allow simple comparisons. Far more publications, however, seem to be available these days on research-based reports of the evaluation of current materials (Bao 2006; Mukundan 2006; Tomlinson, 2008b; Tomlinson and Masuhara 2010, Truong and Phan 2009).
- Improvement and innovation in *ELT Journal* reviews have taken place and this seems to be functioning well. In addition to traditional impressionistic pre-use reviews by experts, collaborative and systematic pre-use reviews (e.g. Masuhara *et al.* 2008; Tomlinson *et al.* 2001) at regular intervals seem to provide cross-sectional and longitudinal evaluation of coursebooks.
- Online book reviews are becoming widely available these days. Some providers (e.g. Google Book) offer links to reviews published in scholarly journals.

10.4.2 Stricter and more systematic material selection procedures

Suggestions

In the 1998 version of this chapter I suggested that it would be useful to have a systematic review comparing evaluation checklists and that empirical studies of learners' and teachers' needs could facilitate data-based development of evaluation criteria.

Developments

- Even more checklists and frameworks are now available which are designed to enable systematic selection of materials (e.g. Breen and Candlin 1987; Cunningsworth 1984; Hutchinson and Waters 1987; Masuhara *et al.* 2008; McDonough and Shaw 2003; McDonough, Shaw and Masuhara 2011; Sheldon 1987; Skierso 1991; Tomlinson *et al.* 2001; Tomlinson 2003; Tomlinson and Masuhara 2004).

- In a shrinking world where English is becoming one of the basic skills, there are growing demands for accountability for ELT materials, as is evidenced by the proliferation of evaluation checklists. Mukundan and Ahour (2011) have attempted to evaluate the evaluation checklists from the 1970s to 2007.

- The increase in the reports on materials development projects all over the world in *Folio* (the journal of the international materials development association MATSDA) seem to testify that the users at institutional and national levels seem to be taking the initiative in the evaluation, selection and development of their own materials (see, for example, Al-Busaidi and Tindle 2010; Tomlinson and Masuhara 2010).

- Tomlinson (2003) developed a procedure in which teachers are helped to articulate their implicit theories in the process of developing their own evaluation criteria. He argues that writing criteria for evaluation provides opportunities to reflect upon teachers' own practice in their contexts and to critically evaluate the criteria listed by experts. What distinguishes his approach to developing checklists is that he separates universal criteria (those applicable to any learning context anywhere) from local criteria (those specific to a particular context) and that the criteria are not taken from external sources. Instead the evaluation criteria are developed by teachers themselves, thus embodying their needs and wants and reflecting their perceptions of learners' needs, wants and requirements in their teaching contexts. Tomlinson (2003) recommends teachers to refer to language-learning principles (Tomlinson 1998; Tomlinson-Chapter 1 in this volume) so teachers can critically verify their own practice against relevant theories. Tomlinson and Masuhara (2004) provide a practical account of how articulating principled evaluation criteria can help the selection, adaptation and development of materials.

10.4.3 Establishing methods and feedback routes of users' evaluation

Suggestions

Rea-Dickins (1994) summarises three kinds of evaluation:

- pre-use evaluation which can be done prior to the use of a coursebook (for the purpose of checking the construct validity and the match with the needs)
- in-use evaluation
- post-use evaluation, measured in terms of learners' performance.

Rea-Dickins and Germaine (1992) and McGrath (2002) advocate more attention being paid to in-use and post-use evaluation (see Chapter 9 by Rod Ellis in this volume for suggestions of how to do this).

For the division of producers and users to work coherently, it is vital that results of systematic whilst- and post-use evaluation of published materials are fed back to the materials producers to be reflected in future production. I also believe that more whilst- and post-use evaluation should be published. In this sense, the post-use reviews in *MET* (*Modern English Teacher*) should be recognised for their pioneering efforts.

Developments

- There seem to be more and more postgraduate students engaged in research on materials development which involves whilst-use and post-use evaluation (see Tomlinson and Masuhara 2010). The Materials Development Association (MATSDA) has continued to publish reports on overseas materials development projects in *Folio* and also offers annual conferences to provide a forum for reporting on such projects and for suggesting ways of improving materials for teachers, teacher trainers, publishers, materials writers and researchers.
- Some writers and publishers are trying to incorporate whilst- and post-use feedback in their materials through piloting (see Donovan 1998; Bell and Gower – Chapter 6 in this volume). However, more recent reports from the producers such as Amrani (Chapter 11 in this volume; McCullagh (2010) and Watkins (2010) describe how the speed and variety of publishing makes such feedback difficult to obtain and make use of.

10.4.4 Establishing systems for teachers' needs and wants to be reflected in the production processes

See Section 10.5 Opportunities for change for more discussion.

10.4.5 Wider perspectives in teacher development.

Suggestions

In the 1998 version of this chapter I suggested inclusion on teaching development courses of components of materials evaluation, adaptation and writing, and also the inclusion of research methodology training in postgraduate courses in TEFL/TESL and Applied Linguistics.

Developments

In the UK and in South Korea there are dedicated materials development MA courses and a number of universities all around the world now offer materials development modules on their postgraduate courses in TEFL or Applied Linguistics. The Higher Education Funding Council in England now requires research methodology courses to be part of postgraduate studies.

10.4.6 More acknowledgement of the teachers' non-teaching expertise and workload.

Johnson (1989), summarised in Table 10.2, stages decision-making roles and products in curriculum development.

Table 10.2

Developmental stages	Decision-making roles	Products
1. Curriculum planning	policy makers	policy document
2. Specification: ends means	needs analysts	syllabus
	methodologists	
3. Programme implementation	materials writers	teaching materials
	teacher trainers	teacher-training programme
4. Classroom implementation	teacher	teaching acts
	learner	learning acts

252

In reality, however, such group cooperation of 'experts' may rarely happen except under highly privileged circumstances. In fact, a teacher may be expected to function as a course designer, needs analyst, methodologist and materials writer. Often these non-teaching activities seem to be considered as part of teachers' duties without them being properly appreciated or acknowledged and without the teachers being trained to do these activities effectively. More systematic materials selection, for example, could really be achieved if teachers were given the time, a place and encouragement. I also feel that institutions could make more use of staff meetings to provide opportunities for teacher development (see Section 10.5 Opportunities for change for more discussion). Thus, it seems vital to encourage institutional support for all the above suggestions to be materialised.

10.5 Opportunities for change

Judging from the fact that the 'for and against coursebooks' debate recurs and persists, regular and successful communication between materials producers and users does not seem to be taking place. Therefore, I intend to go through the process of materials production and use, acknowledging current practice and suggesting some new angles in order to reflect teachers' needs and wants.

For more details as to current practice, readers may like to refer to publications by publishers on their needs analysis, market research and materials trialling. My efforts to locate such literature, however, have met with a lot of difficulty. Personal communication with those involved in past studies revealed that there is a considerable amount of study conducted by individual publishers, but the actual reports often remain confidential. More publications from the materials producers, such as Amrani (Chapter 11 in this volume), Donovan (1998) and Singapore Wala (2003a, 2003b) would be a great step forward in promoting open and effective communication between the producers and users.

It is interesting to note that, in my personal communications, a certain reservation and scepticism toward the value of questionnaire surveys was expressed by representatives of major publishers on the grounds that the teachers (a) do not seem to have many opinions, (b) do not do what they say and (c) are not cooperative in returning the questionnaires.

I think that the research methodology literature could give more detailed and user-friendly accounts of the strengths and limitations of questionnaire surveys (and of other research methods for that matter). In a survey, the questionnaire appears to be an obvious method to be employed: it is comparatively economical in terms of cost, time, personnel and the ease of the control of the scale. Also it is potentially informative if it is used well.

Table 10.3 *Opportunities for reflecting teachers' needs and wants –*
production stage

Stages of production	Agent	Kinds of investigation	Methods
1. Planning	publisher in-house investigator	needs analysis market research	questionnaires interviews
	materials writer(s) outside investigator		classroom observation
2. Drafting	materials writer(s) publisher	–	–
3. Evaluation	'reviewers' selected by publisher	reading of the materials	criterion-referenced evaluation
4. Piloting	publisher teachers learners	trialling	questionnaires interviews classroom-observation testing
5. Production	materials writer(s) publisher designer	consultation	–
6. Post-production	reviewers researcher analyst	book reviews sales record	evaluation analysing data

However, less understood is the fact that getting generalisable results
out of a questionnaire requires very careful and systematic thinking
and monitoring. Research methodology books (e.g. Dörnyei 2007)
warn that expertise is called for in each stage from the questionnaire's
construction, distribution, administration, collection and analysis to
the interpretation of its results.

In the construction stage, for instance, the designer must have clear
objectives and strive to write precise and specific questions which will
elicit informative responses. A vague question such as 'How do you

feel about the format of the teacher's book?' would only bring forth a non-informative vague answer. Or a question such as 'Would you like the coursebook to include systematic coverage of a learner training syllabus?' may puzzle some respondents who have little idea of what a 'learner training syllabus' is. Even if a respondent had general knowledge of learner training, 'systematic coverage' could mean many things.

The most difficult part of a questionnaire survey may be, in fact, obtaining a sufficient number of representative responses back. Unless the teacher has a stake in it, answering questionnaires is often perceived as a tedious extra chore which will at best bring very little reward and thus goes fairly low in the long priority lists of things to do. If the questionnaire is designed to elicit teachers' views about fundamental issues, answering such questions requires a lot of effort from the respondent to articulate and to communicate complex thoughts. This is demanding in itself, even more so if you are asked to respond straight away after glancing at a question cold. As for providing innovative ideas for future coursebooks, the task may seem too much, especially without any guarantee of the idea being attributed to those who proposed it or of it being realised in the near future. In this sense, the questionnaire may not be the best means if we want feedback on delicate issues such as teachers' needs and wants and the future directions of coursebooks.

What has been lacking, it seems to me, is our awareness that probing teachers' needs and wants should be a major undertaking in the exploration of new directions. And this requires more creative thinking and new approaches; in order for the teachers to be willing to be involved, then the procedures in themselves should be intrinsically rewarding for them. So far, the feedback and piloting seem to me to have often been done as acts of, more or less, goodwill, and therefore, I suspect, accompanied by an attitude of the less the burden, the better. I would like to put forward some other activities as possible alternatives or useful additions.

10.6 New opportunities: teachers' forums organised by publishers

10.6.1 Example A: evaluation meetings

Representative samples of teachers are invited to a half-day lunch and coffee meeting with all expenses paid plus some payment on top if possible, in which:

(a) the newest commercially available coursebooks are presented (better still, if demonstrated in a mock classroom situation)

(b) what the teachers consider to be good and useful activities are identified
(c) discussions as to why the activities identified in (b) above are useful are conducted with monitors and a facilitator (e.g. materials writer) organising the session.

Many variations of this kind are possible, depending on the objectives. For example, using one coursebook, teachers could be invited to select useful activities from the book. Then discussion could be held about why these activities are perceived as useful. Or teachers could focus on suggesting ways of improving the activities to suit their needs and wants. This would be especially suitable at an early stage of materials production to give indications to the materials writers as to what kinds of materials and approaches are needed. Online discussion may be possible, but a face-to-face meeting would be the best for sparking off ideas and for immediate negotiation. Teachers may have differing views, but through negotiation their convergent needs and wants are likely to emerge. The divergence, on the other hand, will provide interesting issues for further exploration.

10.6.2 Example B: 'take your pick' sampling meetings

The materials writer produces three kinds of prospective mini-course-books (black and white copies of a few units, for instance, would be enough) in which a controversial point of choice is embodied. For example, three mini-coursebooks are all text-based with the same text, but each one employs a different approach; one is structure-based, the second is explicit strategy training oriented and the third aims at implicit strategy training through tasks which first aim at global understanding then become language awareness activities.

10.6.3 Example C: users meet to become producers

Tomlinson (1995) reports a very interesting case in Namibia of teachers producing materials at national level in collaboration with a publisher. Representative and recommended teachers meet together for a short period of time. During this period, brainstorming about the type of coursebook they need, syllabus design, raw materials searching, writing units, being given feedback by other participants and by a facilitator, and editing are carried out under the supervision of a facilitator. The materials are then taken back by the teachers to their schools and tried out and the results inform the revision process. This option seems preferable to other suggestions in a sense that:

(a) it provides solutions to many of the problems caused by the role divisions (e.g. materials not meeting the local needs, teachers not understanding the materials writers' approach)
(b) the materials themselves address the teachers' needs and wants and the possible ways of satisfying them without actually having to go through intricate research procedures to identify them
(c) the materials can be used in classrooms and then revised.

For those who are interested in this option, I would recommend Tomlinson (1995) for a suggestion of how this system can successfully be realised. Tomlinson and Masuhara (2010) provide more recent case studies carried out by institutions and individuals.

In all three examples above of teachers meeting together, the criteria for success would be as follows:

- The teachers' work is acknowledged and a time, a place and a reward are properly supplied.
- There is a substantial prospect that in the near future the teachers' efforts could result in lessening the frustration of not having the kinds of coursebook they want.
- The meetings give teachers opportunities to meet other teachers and discuss issues which are relevant and useful to their own development.
- The discussions are never held cold; there are interesting and useful stimuli first which are directly relevant to everyday teaching or are thought-provoking for future self-development.
- When asked an opinion, there are concrete examples in front of the teachers which they can react to.
- Before being asked for choice, options are provided and demonstrated.
- There is some possibility of career advancement and of social acknowledgement.
- The discussion analysing the reasons for the choice are held *after* the teachers have made selections. This is crucial: the facilitator should be aware that she is probing both for the teachers' perceived and unarticulated needs and wants. Furthermore, provided that enough such meetings are held, the characteristics of popular principles or approaches may emerge by quantifying the teachers' choice through tallying the kinds of books or the kinds of activities chosen by the teachers – thus substantiating the study with more objective data.

What sort of opportunities, then, are there for reflecting teachers' needs and wants through the stages of materials use? Table 10.4 illustrates the stages and various possibilities for reflecting teachers' needs and wants.

*Table 10.4   Opportunities for reflecting teachers' needs and wants –
stages of use*

Stages of use	Agent	Kinds of investigation	Methods
Pre-use (materials selection)	Teachers Director of Studies	Collecting information about the books	ELT reviews reputation colleagues' opinions based on experience of use
		Impressionistic pre-use evaluation	Looking through the books for: • overall impression • syllabus • topics/subjects • illustrations
		Systematic pre-use evaluation	(a) making use of self-generated criteria (b) making use of experts' checklists
Whilst-use	Teachers Director of Studies Publishers	Analysis of subjective data by the teacher and by others	The teacher's diary/ journal/interview/ forum
		Quantitative and qualitative analysis	Classroom-observation data
		Analysis of objective data	Keeping records of:
			(a) selective use of units and parts of units
			(b) supplementary use of homegrown materials
			(c) adaptation of the coursebook

(cont.)

Table 10.4 *(cont.)*

Stages of use	Agent	Kinds of investigation	Methods
After-use	Teachers Director of Studies Publishers	Impressionistic post-use evaluation	Questionnaire Interview Diary/journal
		Systematic post-use evaluation	Evaluation using evaluation sheet Validation of pre-use evaluation record

I have tried to suggest some new approaches as well as to list those which are currently practised. Some of the new approaches will now be exemplified in more detail.

10.6.4 New opportunities: institution-based evaluation

Example A: Pre-use evaluation of materials being timetabled as a staff meeting in teaching hours

It seems to me materials selection and materials evaluation should be given far more significance and a system should be set up with institutional support. For instance, for materials selection a staff meeting could be held and teachers who will be in charge of certain courses or those who have been involved in the past could form groups. First, each group member reflects and lists criteria they think are important for the prospective course. Teachers may find it useful to take three steps in identifying the needs: first, just listing the needs and wants, secondly categorising them (e.g. administrative needs, learners' needs and teachers' needs and wants), and lastly prioritising them. Then the criteria could be gathered and compared, first in the group in order to discuss issues and problems and then each group could report to the whole group the most important issues for further discussion. Then groups could pick up candidates from the available collection of textbooks and new sample copies and start evaluating them against the criteria. The list of criteria produced can be filed as the criteria for post-use evaluation and also for similar future materials selection sessions in staff meetings.

Example B: Keeping records of use

It would make a very interesting study to keep records of which parts of a coursebook are used and which are not. Keeping records should be fairly simple if the teachers are asked to tick the parts used (with brief comments if possible). If there are online systems that allow modifications that can be traced, the records will provide interesting data from which insights could be drawn. Teachers' meetings can be held to reflect and analyse why some parts of the same book get used and others discarded. Such a study would be likely to reveal the hidden needs and wants of teachers. This exercise would offer a new angle for piloting based on objective data.

In the same way, the study of the production and use of supplementary home-grown materials may offer insights and suggest new directions for future materials. An indicator memo can be attached to the top of home-grown materials when produced. On the indicator memo the purpose, the target learners and the relationship with the main coursebook can be specified and kept in files. Such collections can then be analysed in terms of when, why and how teachers supplement the main coursebook. Another option may be a record of how teachers exploit the coursebook.

Example C: Post-use – validating the selection criteria at a staff meeting

It seems to me to be very productive to hold a post-use evaluation meeting. In such a meeting the pre-use selection criteria which are produced prior to the course can be validated. The re-evaluation of the materials can be attached to the coursebook for later use and as a basis for publication of collaboratory post-use reviews in English teaching journals.

Publishers may benefit from establishing some systems under which this kind of post-use evaluation of coursebooks can be fed back to the materials writers and editors.

In all three examples above, the criteria for success would be as follows:

- Materials selection and evaluation is acknowledged as an important aspect of teaching and teacher development. Therefore, a time and a place is properly secured within teaching hours.
- Teachers are given opportunities to discuss issues with colleagues, to share experience and expertise and to build teachers' resources in collaboration, thus reducing the amount of individual work.
- There is for teachers a substantial prospect of future benefit of:
  (a) reducing the problems from having chosen a wrong coursebook as a result of a rushed solitary decision
  (b) publication of materials evaluation and reviews, since systematic group evaluation could give more depth, and this could enhance careers as a result of publication
  (c) having a good, accessible and user-friendly collection of evaluation comments for future reference.

If institutions support and acknowledge such activities as those above, they may benefit from the positive gains of having a well-analysed bank of coursebooks and home-grown materials, from possibly more useful contacts with publishers, and from more publicity for the name of the institute to be acknowledged in international publications.

10.6.5 New opportunities: teachers' professional development through material evaluation, adaptation and development

Masuhara (2006) argues that materials development is one of the most effective approaches to teacher development and that it can help teachers become more aware, able, critical, creative and effective in their teaching. She illustrates her points through an example of the materials adaptation process. Canniveng and Martinez (2003) evaluate general teacher education courses and maintain that materials evaluation and development lead to professional development that is more situated and specific than a teacher education course. Tan (2006) describes how a group of student teachers developed themselves through a materials development project as part of a teacher education programme. As Masuhara (2006: 35) points out, 'After a teacher training course, teachers have knowledge and skills. After a materials development course, teachers not only have knowledge and skills but also materials they can use tomorrow'.

Al-Busaidi and Tindle (2010) report the process of developing in-house materials and of measuring their effects for pre-faculty students in the Language Centre at Sultan Qaboos University, Oman. After years of unsuccessful trialling of materials, their Language Centre decided to develop its own materials. It invited experts and offered materials development courses as part of professional development for its staff. It recruited writers amongst the staff and established writing, editing and publishing teams with the experts as advisors. Al-Busaidi and Tindle provide assessment results as well as survey results for whilst-use and post-use evaluation of the materials. In the case of the Namibian Textbook Project (reported in Tomlinson 1995), the Ministry of Education and a commercial publisher were involved in the production of a national level coursebook. In many teaching situations users of coursebooks are becoming more and more aware that 'one size does not fit all'. Such a trend may be evidenced in the increasing number of national or regional projects in which materials have been developed locally to replace commercial coursebooks. I have been involved in such projects in China, Bulgaria, Ethiopia, Morocco, Namibia and the sub-Sahara, and know of other such projects in Georgia, Russia, Romania and Venezuela (see, for example, Bolitho 2008; Popovici and Bolitho 2003). This kind of collaborative materials development with professional development seems very promising.

10.7 Conclusion

So what do teachers really want from coursebooks? Teachers may or may not be able to articulate their answers. They may contradict themselves. Their views and opinions are likely to be different from each other. This chapter has tried to examine why this may be so and has explored ways of tapping valuable resources which teachers could provide.

This chapter has also drawn attention to the fact that the majority of steps identified in traditional curriculum development models seem to be undertaken by the materials producers (i.e. materials writers and publishers) these days and that the users (i.e. administrators, teachers and learners) have little control over how their needs and wants are realised in the materials they use. In this sense, the emerging trend of collaboratory materials development between the producers and users seems promising (see various reports in Tomlinson and Masuhara, 2011).

Various suggestions have been proposed that may lead to improving communication between the users and the materials producers. It is a pleasure to note that some of the suggestions made in the previous version of this chapter (Masuhara 1998) seem to be gradually happening (see, for example, Chapter 11 in this book by Frances Amrani). There is, however, also a worrying trend. The reviews of current coursebooks (Masuhara *et al.* 2008; Tomlinson 2008b) reveal that publishers seem to tackle the diversity of user needs through 'pick and mix' or 'take what you want' approaches. The trend of multi-components, such as interactive tests, web-based materials and DVD materials sounds fascinating; however, it may mean more production cost reflected in the price and the loss of focus and coherence as a course. As Masuhara *et al.* (2008: 311) plead, 'what teachers want are not prescriptions but engaging texts, activities, advice, and suggestions so that they can personalize, localize and adapt the global coursebooks to suit their specific learners in their classrooms in diverse contexts.'

References

Al-Busaidi, S. and K. Tindle. 2010. 'Evaluating the impact of in-house materials on language learning'. In B. Tomlinson and H. Masuhara (eds.), *Research for Materials Development in Language Learning – Evidence for Best Practice*. London: Continuum.

Bacha, N., I-K. Ghosn and N. McBeath. 2008. 'The textbook, the teacher and the learner: a Middle East perspective'. In B. Tomlinson (ed.), *English Language Learning Materials – A Critical Review*. London: Continuum.

Bao, D. 2006. 'Breaking stereotypes in coursebooks'. In J. Mukundan (ed.), *Readings on ELT Materials II*. Petaling Jaya: Pearson Malaysia.

Bolitho, R. 2008. 'Materials used in Central and Eastern Europe and the former Soviet Union'. In B. Tomlinson (ed.), *English Language Learning Materials – A Critical Review*. London: Continuum.

Borg, S. 2006. *Teacher Cognition and Language Education*. London: Continuum.

Breen, M. P. and C. N. Candlin. 1987. 'Which materials?: a consumer's and designer's guide'. In L. E. Sheldon (ed.), 1987. *ELT Textbooks and Materials: Problems in Evaluation and Development*. ELT Documents 126. London: Modern English Publications and The British Council.

Brumfit, C. J. 1980. 'Seven last slogans'. *Modern English Teacher*, 7(1): 30–1.

Canniveng, C. and M. Martinez. 2003. 'Materials development and teacher training'. In B. Tomlinson (ed.), *Developing Materials for Language Teaching*. London: Continuum.

Carl, A. E. 2009. *Teacher Empowerment through Curriculum Development: Theory into Practice*, 3rd edn. Cape Town: Juta and Company Ltd.

Cook, V. (ed.). 2002. *Portraits of the L2 User*. Clevedon: Multilingual Matters.

Cunningsworth, A. 1984. *Evaluating and Selecting ELT Materials*. London: Heinemann.

Dörnyei, Z. 2007. *Research Methods in Applied Linguistics*. Oxford: Oxford University Press.

Donovan, P. 1998. 'Piloting – a publisher's view'. In B. Tomlinson (ed.), *Materials Development in Language Teaching*. Cambridge: Cambridge University Press.

Doughty, C. J. and M. H. Long. (eds.). 2003. *The Handbook of Second Language Acquisition*. Oxford: Blackwell Publishing.

Dubin, F. and E. Olshtain. 1994. *Course Design*, 7th edn. Cambridge: Cambridge University Press.

Ellis, R. 1994. *The Study of Second Language Acquisition*. Oxford: Oxford University Press.

2008. *The Study of Second Language Acquisition*, 2nd edn. Oxford: Oxford University Press.

Freeman, D. and J. C. Richards (eds.). 1996. *Teacher Learning in Language Teaching*. Cambridge: Cambridge University Press.

Ghosn, I-K. 2003. 'Talking like texts and talking about texts: how some primary school coursebook tasks are realized in the classroom'. In B. Tomlinson (ed.), *Developing Materials for Language Teaching*. London: Continuum Press.

Graddol, D. 1997. *The Future of English? A Guide to Forecasting the Popularity of the English Language in the 21st Century*. London: British Council.

2006. *English Next*. London: British Council.

Gray, F. 2002. 'The global coursebook in English language teaching'. In D. Block and D. Cameron (eds.), *Globalization and Language Teaching*. London: Routledge.

Gustafson, K. L. and R. M. Branch. 2002. *Survey of Instructional Development Models*, 4th edn. Syracuse, NY: ERIC Clearinghouse on Information & Technology.

Hutchinson, T. and E. Torres. 1994. 'The textbook as agent of change'. *ELT Journal*, 48(4): 315–28. Oxford: Oxford University Press.

Hutchinson, T. and A. Waters. 1987. *English for Specific Purposes*. Cambridge: Cambridge University Press.

Johnson, R. K. (ed.). 1989. *The Second Language Curriculum*. Cambridge: Cambridge University Press.

Lantolf, J. (ed.). 2000. *Sociocultural Theory and Second Language Learning*. Oxford: Oxford University Press.

Larsen-Freeman, D. 2000. *Techniques and Principles in Language Teaching*, 2nd edn. Oxford: Oxford University Press.

Larsen-Freeman, D. and M. Long. 1991. *An Introduction to Second Language Acquisition Research*. London: Longman.

Lee, R., and A. Bathmaker. 2007. 'The use of English textbooks for teaching English to "vocational" students in Singapore secondary schools: a survey of teachers' beliefs'. *RELC Journal*, 38(3): 350–74.

Littlejohn, A. P. 1992. 'Why are ELT materials the way they are?' Unpublished PhD thesis. Lancaster: Lancaster University.

Long, M. (ed.). 2005. *Second Language Needs Analysis*. Cambridge: Cambridge University Press.

Masuhara, H. 1994. 'But that's what the teachers want!' *Folio*, 1(1): 12–13.

1998. 'What do teachers really want from coursebooks?' In B. Tomlinson (ed.), *Materials Development in Language Teaching*. Cambridge: Cambridge University Press.

2006. 'Materials as a teacher development tool'. In J. Mukundan (ed.), *Readings on ELT Materials II*. Petaling Jaya: Pearson Malaysia.

Masuhara, H. and B. Tomlinson. 2008. 'Materials for general English'. In B. Tomlinson (ed.), *English Language Teaching Materials – A Critical Review*. London: Continuum.

Masuhara, H., N. Hann, Y. Yi and B. Tomlinson. 2008. 'Adult EFL courses'. *ELT Journal*, 62(3) 294–312.

McCullagh, M. 2011. 'An initial evaluation of the effectiveness of a set of published materials for Medical English'. In B. Tomlinson and H. Masuhara (eds.), *Research for Materials Development for Language Learning – Evidence for Best Practice*. London: Continuum.

McDonough, J. and C. Shaw. 2003. *Materials and Methods in ELT*, 2nd edn. Oxford: Blackwell Publishing.

McDonough, J., C. Shaw, and H. Masuhara. In press. *Materials and Methods in ELT*, 3rd edn. Oxford: Blackwell Publishing.

McGrath, I. 2002. *Materials Evaluation and Design for Language Teaching*. Edinburgh: Edinburgh University Press.

Meddings, L. and S. Thornbury. 2009. *Teaching Unplugged: Dogme in English Language Teaching*, 8–10. Peaslake, Surrey: Delta.

Mukundan, J. 2006. 'Are there new ways of evaluating ELT coursebooks?' In J. Mukundan (ed.), *Readings on ELT Materials II*. Petaling Jaya: Pearson Malaysia.

Mukundan, J. and T. Ahour. 2011. 'A review of textbook evaluation checklists across four decades (1970–2007)'. In B. Tomlinson and

H. Masuhara (eds.), *Research for Materials Development in Language Learning – Evidence for Best Practice*. London: Continuum.

Nunan, D. 1988. *The Learner-Centred Curriculum*. Cambridge: Cambridge University Press.

Popovici, R. and R. Bolitho. 2003. 'Personal and professional development through writing: The Romanian Textbook Project'. In B. Tomlinson (ed.), *Developing Materials for Language Teaching*. London: Continuum.

Rea-Dickins, P. 1994. 'Evaluation and English language teaching'. *Language Teaching*, 27: 71–91. Cambridge: Cambridge University Press.

Rea-Dickens, P. and K. Germaine. 1992. *Evaluation*. Oxford: Oxford University Press.

Richards, J. C. 1990. *The Language Teaching Matrix*. Cambridge: Cambridge University Press.

2008. 'Second language teacher education today'. *RELC Journal*, 39(2): 158–77.

Richards, J. C. and D. Nunan. 1990. *Second Language Teacher Education*. Cambridge: Cambridge University Press.

Richards, J. C. and T. Rodgers, 2001. *Approaches and Methods in Language Teaching*, 2nd edn. Cambridge: Cambridge University Press.

Robinson, P. 1980. *English for Specific Purposes*. Oxford: Pergamon.

1990. *ESP Today*. Hemel Hempstead: Prentice Hall.

Sheldon, L. E. (ed.). 1987. 'ELT textbooks and materials: problems in evaluation and development'. *ELT Documents* 126. London: Modern English Publications and The British Council.

Sheldon, L. 1988. 'Evaluating ELT textbooks and materials'. *ELT Journal*, 42(4): 237–46.

Singapore Wala, D. A. 2003a. 'A coursebook is what it is because of what it has to do: an editor's perspective'. In B. Tomlinson (ed.), *Developing Materials for Language Teaching*. London: Continuum.

2003b. 'Publishing a coursebook: completing the materials development circle'. In B. Tomlinson (ed.), *Developing Materials for Language Teaching*. London: Continuum.

Skierso, A. 1991. 'Textbook selection and evaluation'. In M. Celce-Murcia (ed.), *Teaching English as a Second or Foreign Language*. Boston: Heinle and Heinle.

Tan, B. T. 2006. 'Student-teacher-made language teaching materials: a developmental approach to materials development'. In J. Mukundan (ed.), *Focus on ELT Materials*. Petaling Jaya: Pearson Malaysia.

Thornbury, S. 2000. 'A Dogma for EFL'. *IATEFL Issues*, 153: 2.

2005. 'Dogme: dancing in the dark?' *Folio*, 9(2): 3–5.

Tomlinson, B. 1995. 'Work in progress: textbook projects'. *Folio*, 2(2): 26–31.

1998. 'Introduction'. In B. Tomlinson (ed.), *Materials Development in Language Teaching*. Cambridge: Cambridge University Press.

2003. 'Materials evaluation'. In B. Tomlinson (ed.), *Developing Materials for Language Teaching*. London: Continuum.

2008a. 'Humanising an EAP Textbook'. *Humanising Language Teaching Magazine*, April 2008, short article.

Tomlinson, B. (ed.) 2008b. *English Language Learning Materials – A Critical Review*. London: Continuum.

Tomlinson, B. and H. Masuhara. 2004. *Developing Language Course Materials*. Singapore: RELC.

2008. 'Materials used in the U.K.' In B. Tomlinson (ed.), *English Language Teaching Materials – A Critical Review*. London: Continuum.

2010. *Research for Materials Development in Language Learning – Evidence for Best Practice*. London: Continuum.

Tomlinson, B., B. Dat, H. Masuhara and R. Rubdy. 2001. 'ELT courses for adults'. *ELT Journal*, 55(1): 80–101.

Truong, B. L. and L. H. Phan. 2009. 'Examining the foreignness of EFL global textbooks: issues and proposals from the Vietnamese classroom'. In J. Mukundan (ed.), *Readings on ELT Materials III*. Petaling Jaya: Pearson Malaysia.

Watkins, P. 2010. 'Evaluating the effectiveness of *Learning to Teach English* as an introduction to ELT'. In B. Tomlinson and H. Masuhara (eds.), *Research for Materials Development – Evidence for Best Practice*. London: Continuum.

Wiles, J. W. and J. C. Bondi. 2010. *Curriculum Development: A Guide to Practice*. Upper Saddle River, NJ: Merrill/Prentice Hall.

Zacharias, N. 2005. 'Teachers' beliefs about internationally-published materials: a survey of tertiary English teachers in Indonesia'. *RELC Journal*, 36(1): 23–37.

11 The process of evaluation: a publisher's view

Frances Amrani

11.1 Introduction

In the original edition of this book Peter Donovan (Donovan 1998) looked exclusively at piloting as a way in which publishers evaluate material. Whilst this remains one of the ways in which materials are evaluated, it is no longer the main way that publishers do this. In this chapter I have tried to reflect more broadly what the current practice is for evaluating materials and influencing their design for most ELT publishers. The comments contained within this chapter should be considered as my personal comments based on over 20 years in the world of ELT and ELT publishing. Whilst my recent experience is largely with Cambridge University Press, the comments may apply equally to other ELT publishers.

When the first edition of this book was published in 1998, the world of ELT and specifically ELT publishing was a very different place. We were just discovering the joys of task-based learning and using the relatively new teaching procedures offered by the communicative approach. To a certain extent the ELT panorama is more of a known landscape now, where teachers have had more exposure to different ideas, with the Internet providing access to more information and resources than ever before. Many teachers now know which method is effective in producing the desired outcomes for their teaching environment; this could be that a student can produce accurate or fluent language in an appropriate register from a certain type of task, or internalises a grammatical rule better using language presented in a meaningful context. Teachers also know what sounds like a good idea but is actually unlikely to produce the desired outcomes with their class. Whilst it may well be true that there are still many inexperienced teachers who need basic guidance and more experienced teachers who need their convictions to be challenged, there is more information available to teachers than ever before; specialist magazines in ELT, professional conferences such as local IATEFL (International Association of Teachers of English as a Foreign Language), TESOL (Teachers of English to Speakers of Other Languages) and British Council conferences and ELT websites. These all offer information and an opportunity for teachers to discuss different ideas and approaches. This new landscape means that teachers often have different, informed opinions about approaches, methodologies and materials and it is a much greater challenge for publishers to cater to all of these.

The 'hot topics' in ELT at the time of writing are CLIL (Content and Language Integrated Learning) which involves teaching a curricular subject, topic or skill learners are interested in through the medium of a language other than that normally used, ELF (English as a lingua franca) and blended learning with integrated digital components. By this I mean where the digital components are a core feature of the course and may actually replace the printed materials, and are embedded within the whole syllabus rather than just a few add-on optional practice activities. The challenges facing the ELT publisher today are less to do with modifying fundamental materials design for main course development and more to do with how to blend and marry topics or formats into existing well-established core course content.

Course content, approach and task design is often already established by exam syllabuses guidelines or standards such as the Common European Framework. This means that publishers have less of a free hand than previously as there are clearly defined international market expectations which they now need to work within to secure course adoptions. In addition to having tighter parameters, a striking difference in much of this new course material development is that the timeframes are much shorter than previously, for example often two years where previously there might have been four years. Also, in order to test digital materials, publishers now have to be at a nearly final stage because, since many of them are interactive, they cannot be tested properly unless they are in a final digital format. This means by the time they are ready to test, it may already be too late and expensive to implement any major changes.

11.2 Choices and challenges

In the first edition of this book Peter Donovan also alluded to the fact that development cycles were getting shorter. This has proved to be increasingly true. Most ELT publishers now develop new materials every year. Whereas in the early 1990s a development time of seven years for a course from concept to launch was not unheard of, most publishers are now working to development cycles of only two or three years. This leaves little if no time for full piloting, which by its very nature requires almost a year to test sequencing and a full range of units across the same school year in order to ensure standardised results. So it is not surprising that hardly any publishers rely on piloting alone to provide the market research they require to adapt and modify materials in development.

Publishers want and need feedback from potential end-users, and not just to get a product right for the marketplace so that they secure a sale. Publishers are also aware that they have a responsibility to deliver high-quality materials which will teach language students effectively, so that their reputations as professional experts in materials development are maintained. In order to achieve this, the market research of materials has evolved and dialogue with teachers has increased in importance.

In the 1980s it was not uncommon to trial a whole course from start to finish in multiple schools. Simple pilot editions of courses were prepared, often with little or very rough artwork which was there purely to ensure the materials could be used and evaluated by teachers. By the late 1990s pilots became shorter, so that the whole course was not trialled with the same school, but units were split between schools in different sets. This enabled more material to be assessed in a shorter time frame. When shorter sets were being prepared for piloting, it became more practical to ask reviewers also to review materials based on their expertise either as an academic or experienced teacher. They were asked to assess how the materials lived up to SLA theory or how they could imagine using the materials with their familiar class in a setting where they regularly taught. The shorter grouping of materials also lent itself to focus group scrutiny where aspects such as design could be explored more thoroughly.

In the early 1990s publishers would send out materials as hard copy, often bound to resemble a finished book, for piloters to assess. Nowadays publishers rarely send out materials in any format other than PDF or Word digital files as email attachments. This is normally how feedback is returned to the publisher too, often using track changes. This helps speed the whole process along, particularly when piloting from the UK in markets which are far away, such as Brazil. A package which would have taken two or three weeks to arrive and then another two or three weeks to be sent back can be sent in a matter of seconds, shaving off about six weeks from the piloting/reviewing process.

As publishers became aware of the way piloting was instrumental to external pre-launch promotion and high-quality desktop publishing became more commonplace, they realised that the pilots had to be closer to finished products, in colour with reasonable artwork. Otherwise the materials would be judged in their raw state, and rather than creating a positive impression on the market as being a publisher who tried and tested their materials thoroughly, the publisher risked being judged prematurely on the basis of draft materials, and adoptions could be lost. This means that there is now less piloting of material than previously and straightforward reviewing has become more commonplace.

Publishers also look at post-publication feedback and online reviews from existing courses on their backlist (see Chapter 10 by Hitomi Masuhara in this volume). This can be from anecdotal comments from important markets or from customer comments and complaints – publishers love getting comments both positive and negative about published products. It can also take the form of more structured analysis in the form of questionnaires and focus groups. From this data publishers make decisions on what to do differently next time.

Other important sources of evaluation are ongoing criterion-referenced evaluation by the authors themselves and ongoing criterion-referenced evaluation by the editorial team. This is normally based on the brief which will have been given to authors before any writing takes place. The brief for a project is always based on a needs analysis or what publishers normally call 'the must haves list'. This reflects the universal and local criteria prior to the drafting of the materials. The 'must haves lists' used by commissioning editors for courses are normally generated from a generic list which is continually evolving. The 'must have list' is tailored to each individual project, rather than a new one being started from scratch each time.

11.3 Differences between the teacher perspective and the publisher perspective

Materials evaluation is nothing new to teachers. They do it all the time from wandering casually around a bookshop choosing a new book or borrowing a new idea gleaned from a conference presentation or colleague to surfing the internet discussion and resource sites to gather together new materials. Their evaluation can range from choosing a course to last a whole school age range of perhaps five consecutive years to sourcing a quick warm-up activity to tack onto a particularly dry lesson. Whilst this type of impressionistic evaluation may not be totally valid or pedagogically reliable, it is a common behaviour which many teachers adopt. There are also teachers who carry out extensive error analysis with their students and look in depth at how their current materials perform in order to identify what additional materials and strategies are required to improve their students' linguistic performance and learning.

Teachers evaluate material before they teach in terms of imagining how it will work with students they normally know very well and are used to working with in a familiar setting with agreed expectations. In short, the teacher is already in possession of lots of known information, even including personal knowledge of their students' likes and dislikes and previous educational experience. Every time they teach a lesson,

270

they have an opportunity to review and refine the material for the next time, modifying their lesson plans whether they are fully written out or simply something carried in their heads. They can reflect on what worked well, what was a disaster, what took too long, what was too easy or too difficult and anything which was missing. Teachers are normally in a position where they can implement these changes in the next lesson, be it with a parallel class or in the following academic year. If the materials do not work, a teacher risks an unhappy class of a handful of students for a day or so and can normally rectify the situation by the next lesson.

A publisher is normally preparing materials for unknown classes of students (see Chapter 15 by Alan Maley in this volume). In fact, in many cases these will be lots of different types of classes with different expectations and different previous knowledge of language, culture and technology. The materials will be used in different educational contexts, from those where the teacher always leads from the front to those where the approach is student-centred and student autonomy is encouraged. Publishers have access to information about the learning context, class sizes, the syllabus and other hard facts from education ministries, exam boards, local teacher training colleges and local sales offices, who have built up market profiles over many years. However, publishers do not have the same level of information about the students as individuals. Even when materials are evaluated for a specific narrow market, such as the state sector version in a small country, the students still represent an anonymous end-user. The publisher can only make educated guesses as to student likes and dislikes. Particularly with schoolbook materials developed for specific ages, this can be a highly complex area. What works with a 14-year-old in one country may well not work in another; not because the linguistic aim and task are intrinsically wrong, but simply because the local cultural approaches to literacy or skills development may be valued differently; or the artwork proposed is considered too adult or childish. This can impact on student motivation and their engagement with the materials.

There is no real opportunity to gradually review and refine materials already in use. (The main exception to this is that with the growth of digital online activities, these can be corrected or changed very quickly.) Once printed, the materials are fixed for years and any major changes can only realistically be made when a new edition is published. This is time-consuming and expensive. Once published, if any shortcomings are apparent, the materials are in circulation to an audience of literally hundreds of thousands of students and teachers. More serious problems can result in the loss of adoptions and consequently money. An error for a teacher can result in a temporary loss of face, but for a publisher it is more likely to be a significant loss of revenue and, potentially, jobs.

11.4 Why do publishers evaluate materials?

Publishers evaluate materials for much the same reasons as other people such as teachers, directors of studies and ministries. They want to ensure that the materials are effective, that the level is consistently appropriate (e.g. at an agreed standard such as Common European Framework A1), that the instructions are easy to understand, that the staging of any tasks is easy to set up, that the time taken for the execution of a set of materials is realistic and that the materials deliver the desired outcomes.

Most ELT publishers and editors have a teaching background with at least a CELTA qualification and will have worked in at least two or three countries for a minimum of three years. Many have substantially more classroom experience and editors with a Masters in Education or ELT are fairly common. This means that publishers are used to looking at materials as teachers. But in their role as a publisher they also have other considerations. In addition to pedagogical effectiveness, they need to assess the commercial attractiveness of a product and the cost of developing it. Instead of deciding what to choose to buy from a list of possibilities as a customer would, the publisher is deciding what to offer for sale with their name on. For a customer the most important thing is that these particular materials work with their students, but the publisher has to think how the materials reflect on their reputation and also sit beside their existing publications in the market.

Material is typically selected for review in three main ways for different purposes:

- First, as a random set of materials to help the publisher evaluate generic questions regarding international market requirements for structure, layout, type of artwork and timing. This normally does not require specific materials as long as it is a typical unit or module of a given course or publication. The objective here is to identify customer expectations or attitudes to material types; for example some markets react negatively to any mention of grammar whilst others require a grammar-translation approach. Throughout the world these attitudes fluctuate due to influences such as ministry recommendations, keynote speakers at local professional conferences, internal political changes and a new generation of teachers coming through who are open to new unorthodox ideas. This is particularly evident in the rapid change in attitudes to digital products as younger teachers who are digital natives begin to advance in the teaching profession. Publishers need to remain aware of general changes in market trends so they can develop all their materials with these in mind.

- Secondly, materials can be reviewed for a very specific reason, for example to assess to what extent the material matches an exam's syllabus or if a specific section fulfils a genuine purpose, such as the tests on a course.
- Thirdly, materials can be selected for evaluation to see how the scope and sequencing[1] work in terms of a fuller syllabus. This requires a longer selection of material of at least three or four units and a full list of proposed contents. Reviewers would be expected to comment not just on the effectiveness of a single task or unit, but rather the syllabus structure itself and whether units are presented in a logical order.

A publisher also has to consider how commercial a product will be. Some materials may be ideal for a very small niche market, but very few publishers would consider publishing for such a narrow market unless there was another business reason to do so, because they are unlikely to recover their investment. In short, materials for publishers need to be able to satisfy a wide range of end-users. This means that instead of evaluating whether materials are ideal for a very specific audience, the publisher is often evaluating whether materials are suitable for the widest range of possible users, or at the very least versatile enough to be adapted easily. It is about developing materials which offer the highest possible return on investment without compromising essential minimum customer expectations. Because of their teaching backgrounds ELT publishers also have high expectations when it comes to quality; but they need to assess the financial potential of a product as well. This aspect of assessing general flexibility in materials together with shorter development cycles means that full piloting is no longer the main research method of choice for publishers. However, piloting is still used on a smaller scale for specific research, for example when commissioning a local version of a popular coursebook.

In Chapter 10 in this volume Hitomi Masuhara mentions three different kinds of needs: self-perceived needs, needs perceived by others and objectively measured needs. Publishers are interested in all three of these since sales of materials are often dependent on:

1. self-perceived needs – for example, I need some extra work on my pronunciation so I'll buy a self-study pronunciation book;
2. needs perceived by others – for example, ministry recommendations; we need all our students to be able to use American English on

---

[1] **Scope and sequencing** is a term used in ELT publishing to mean the plan for a course syllabus and in what order items are presented. It normally includes grammatical aspects, lexical items and subskills, but will also indicate where review and test material are situated.

the telephone to support our tourist industry or to support our call centres so we need more focus on American listening and speaking skills; and
3. objective research which tries to address needs which neither the learner or teacher may be aware of.

11.5 Which different research methods are used?

Publishers rely on a number of different methods for their market research requirements. The magic word is 'triangulation'; that is, at least three different methods are used to assess the same material or feature and the results are cross-referenced to establish key points or issues. If only one method is used, this can result in an over-reliance on the results from just one perspective, for example that of the individual teacher. If just two methods are used, there is a possibility of two contrasting sets of results and the publisher being unclear which is the more important. Using at least three methods in market research helps the publisher establish which are the recurrent issues that at least two out of the three methods highlight. It means the publisher has access to weighted results and can determine the priority of issues raised by market research.

11.5.1 Piloting

There are four main reasons why publishers evaluate material through piloting:

1. The most obvious is to test material out genuinely in real classrooms with a view to adapting it based on the findings. ELT publishers have reputations which have taken years to establish and which they need to protect by ensuring that their products are suitable for the intended customers.
2. Other reasons are to raise the profile of a product in development with sales teams and to make sure that all relevant in-house staff are aware of it. Basically it is an opportunity to send a subtle message to your sales team – *Warning – this new product is in development. You might want to start thinking about who in your market would be interested in buying it – why not take part in this pilot to test the water to see if you're targeting the right customers?* This also has an important additional benefit of allowing the editorial team to identify more precisely who the end-users are likely to be before publication and consequently to develop and adapt the material with their requirements in mind.

3. Another reason for evaluating material out in the markets is to raise the profile of a product externally and to begin to build up a client base through key piloters/reviewers who are often selected because they are seen to be trendsetters in the marketplace. If someone has been involved in testing a product, they are more likely to have an interest in its launch and support the powerful marketing tool word-of-mouth within the ELT community.

4. Most courses have a list of piloters on the acknowledgements page and it often includes market-specific names – for example obvious Polish piloters or Spanish piloters. This can help to add to the trust customers have in a new, unknown product, as it sends the message this has been tried and tested by teachers like you and so should be just what you need.

Piloters are normally sent a short selection of material which can easily be integrated into their normal teaching programme. They are usually asked to complete a separate teaching diary and to annotate the unit pages. They are asked to comment on what went well (e.g. by the end of the task students had learned to pronounce 'th' correctly), what went wrong (e.g. the task took twice as long as the suggested time), and to comment on other features such as the clarity of rubrics, the ordering of activities, whether the learning objectives have been achieved, whether anything is missing, students' questions, whether the timing is appropriate, and so on.

Once feedback is received, this is normally collated into a single pilot report which can be searched by unit with generic issues listed separately. The editor analysing the data from the pilot will look to see if more than one piloting centre has mentioned the same point. If a point is mentioned by just one centre, the editor will then decide whether to include the comments in a feedback report for the authors concerned. The report will incorporate comments from the editorial team, as it is unlikely that raw data from a pilot would be particularly helpful in guiding an author team in a particular direction. Pilot feedback needs interpreting and cross-referencing against other forms of evaluation before being translated into real information or instruction.

In order to be effective, piloting needs to be extensive and specific. Materials which are intended for use in private language schools (PLS) are going to be different to those for most state schools because there are different parameters, expectations and requirements, be they class size, language focus, exam profile or student and parental expectations. In many markets materials for state schools are required to follow local ministry requirements and often have to prepare students for local exams and focus more on accuracy, whereas PLS classes are in addition to the regular school classes and tend to be seen as providing extra opportunities to extend exposure to English and to improve fluency.

Pilots need to reflect the real end-users, but they are expensive and they are complex and time-consuming to set up. It tends to be the very motivated, experienced teachers who volunteer to participate in piloting, and this can mean that they bring that experience to bear on the results of the pilot, which a less experienced teacher might not. If the materials are being developed just for very experienced teachers, this might be fine, but increasingly publishers are looking to develop materials which will support teachers with different backgrounds, many of whom actually require a high level of support and direction. These kinds of teachers are unlikely to be willing or able to participate in piloting – perhaps because they are holding down two jobs and are too busy, or are just getting by delivering their existing materials without the added complication of participating in a pilot (see Chapter 10 by Hitomi Masuhara).

11.5.2 Reviewing

With shorter lead times driven by factors such as technology and, increasingly, by high market expectations, most publishers rely on extensive reviewing of materials by experienced teachers who, like the teachers mentioned above, can relate the materials to their familiar real situations and students – imagining how something will work in their own situation. Reviewers also include academics or other experts who understand the latest pedagogical theory and research and can look at materials in a more objective light.

One of the inherent problems with having reviewers set up by sales offices is that although a wide geographical spread is achieved, they are normally existing customers, which means any information from these reviews is from those people who have already decided to adopt the publisher's product and are already fairly satisfied with it. It is much harder to find reviewers who are unfamiliar with those products. This is particularly important if a publisher is seeking to extend its current customer base or move into a new territory.

Reviewers are normally sent a small selection of materials from a course; typically a couple of units, list of contents, course rationale and some end matter – for example tests or workbook exercises. They are then sent a list of specific questions to answer in the form of a review sheet.

Here are examples of review material from *Messages* Student's Book Level 1, Unit 1 (Goodey and Goodey 2005).

Figure 11.1 _Review sheet for Unit 1 (**Messages** Student's Book, Level 1) (Goodey and Goodey 2005)_

Unit 1 What can you remember?

Please look through the exercises in this unit. Then, assess each exercise using the following tick system:

✓ ✓ ✓ _Excellent_
✓ ✓   _Good_
✓   _Satisfactory_

Put the appropriate number of ticks immediately after the exercise heading. Then write your comments after the ticks.

You might like to consider the following checklist when writing your responses:
Level: Is the exercise at the appropriate level, not too easy or difficult for the intended students?
Clarity: Are the instructions clear? Do you understand what to do?
Interest: Is the exercise interesting, relevant, enjoyable for students of this age?

Please feel free to write as much as you like about each activity.

Step 1
Practise what you know

What can you say

Use what you know

Song

Punctuation

Greetings and goodbyes

Step 2
Learning English

Reading

Meet Joe, Sadie, Sam and Jack!

Use what you know

Step 3
Letters and sounds

Test a friend

Numbers

Test a friend

Dates

On the telephone

Role play

Ask and answer

Use what you know

Overall comments on the unit:

Would this approach be suitable for your students and the way you teach?

Do you have any comments specifically on the way the author treats grammar, vocabulary and pronunciation?

How do you feel about the balance of skills?

How interesting do you think the content will be for your students?

What do you think about the balance of real world content and invented/imaginary content?

Unit aims and headings – how helpful are they? Is it clear what is being taught and where?

Thank you

Figure 11.2 *Unit script for Unit 1 (**Messages** Student's Book, Level 1) (Goodey and Goodey 2005)*

Unit 1 What can you remember?

STEP 1

In Step 1 you revise
• words that you know in English
• greetings and goodbyes
  so that you can
• make sentences in English
• tell the class about yourself
• begin and end your lessons in English.

music	like	I'm
a	computer	animals
bike	fine	computers
Live in	twelve	pizza
I	camera	sport
thirteen	I've got	

Practise what you know
⊕ **1   Write the alphabet** (A, B, C ...) **in your notebook. Try to find an English word for each letter. You've got 3 minutes!**

Animal
Bag
Cat
Desk

What can you say?
3 Look at the words in the balloons. How many sentences can you make?

I've got a bike.

Now write at least two sentences. Are the sentences true for you? Write T (true) or F (false).

Work with a friend and compare your lists.

2   Work with your teacher. Use words from your list and make groups of words on the board.

Use what you know
4 Introduce yourself!

Hi! My name's Roberto.
I like sport and computers.

Animals	Days	Food	Things in the classroom
elephant	Monday	pizza	bag
cat	Tuesday	apple	desk

Hello! I'm Maria.
I'm twelve

(cont.)

Figure 11.2 *(cont.)*

Punctuation

. full stop   , comma   ? question mark
! exclamation mark   **B** capital letter

We use a ... at the beginning of a sentence. We use a ..., a ... or an ... at the end. We use a ... in the middle of a sentence.

**6 Complete the sentences in the box.
Then check your sentences in Activity 5. Is your punctuation correct?**

Greetings and Goodbyes
7 At the end of the lesson, tell your teacher:

**5 Before you listen, look at the letters in the sea and make three words from the song.
What do you think the song is about?**

Goodbye. See you tomorrow / on Monday / on Tuesday, etc.

Now listen to the song. Then put the words in the right order and make four sentences from the song.

At the beginning of the next lesson, greet your friends in English:

1 it / what / is
2 sea / a / in / it's / the / bottle / in /message / a
3 in / it's / English
4 you / do / understand
Listen again and check.

Hi! How are you? I'm O.K., thanks.

Fine, thank you.

Think of a title for the song.

(cont.)

The process of materials evaluation

Figure 11.2 *(cont.)*

Step 2

In Step 2 you revise
• classroom language: *I don't understand.*
What does it mean? Ask the teacher.
so that you can
• ask for help
• understand a letter in English, and answer
the questions in the letter.

Reading
2 Read the message and use the ideas in the Key
Skills box. Some of the words aren't clear, for
example: XXland

Can you guess what they are?

---

                                            25 Maple Road
                                            Exeter EX11 4NP
                                                       U.K.

                                            30th August

Hi!
This is a letter from a XX in the U.XX. I live in
Exeter, in the south-west of Xxland. I'm twXX. I
like mXX and I'm interested in cXXters.
I've got a brXXer and a sXXer. We've got XX dXX
called Sam and a tortoise XX Lightning.
What about you? Where do you live? What
natXXlity are you? How old are you? WXXt's your
Xxme? Please write to me.
With best wishes from XX.

Learning English
1   What can you do when you don't
understand? Here are some suggestions.

Guess!   Say 'I don't   Don't
             understand'.   panic!

Have you got any other ideas? Tell the class, then
check in the Key Skills box.

3   Find something in the letter that you don't
understand and ask for help.

A *What does 'best wishes' mean?*
B *I don't know. Ask C.*
C *I think it means … , but I'm not sure. Ask the*
teacher.

Key skills

When you don't understand?
• Ask the teacher
• Ask a friend
• Use a dictionary
• Try to guess
• Look at the word list
• Say: I don't understand
  Pardon? Can you say that again?
  What does ? mean?
  Can you help me?
• Don't panic!

(cont.)

280

Figure 11.2 *(cont.)*

Meet Joe, Sadie, Sam and Jack!

4 **The message is from one of these three people. Can you guess who it is?**
🔊 **Close your book and listen to Joe, Sadie and Jack.**

Hello! I'm Joe. I live in
Exeter, at number twenty-five
Maple Road. I like music and
I'm in a band. This is my
sister. Her name's Sadie.

Hi! I'm Sadie, and this is our
dog Sam. I'm twelve. My brother's
fifteen and my sister Kate's eighteen.
She's at university.

Hi! My name's Jack. I live
next door to Sadie, at number
twenty-seven. I'm interested
in computers and I like animals.

Listen again and read the three descriptions.
Who's the message from?

5 Complete the information:
The message is from ... because he/she is ... *(age).*
He/She has got ... His/Her address is ...

🔊 **Close your books and listen to the message in a bottle.**

Use what you know
What about you ?

6 Look at the four questions at the end of the letter.
Work in pairs and ask and answer the questions.

What nationality are you? *I'm ...*

Write your answers.

(cont.)

Figure 11.2   (cont.)

Step 3

In Step 3 you revise
• the alphabet and numbers
• classroom language: *How do you spell ...?   How do you say ...?*
  so that you can
• spell words in English
• understand and use numbers
• ask how to say things in English.

Kate - a h k

Mike - I

Joe - o

Lee - b c e p t v

Mel - f l m n x

Sue - q w

Mark - r

Letters and sounds

1 Say the letters on the T-shirts.

What are the 7 missing letters? Put them in the right group: *J rhymes with Kate.*
🔊 **Listen and check.**

Say the alphabet in English.

2 Dictation
Listen to your teacher.   Write the letters, then say the words.

Test a friend
Think of a word. Dictate the letters to a friend. Check his/her answer. Is it right or wrong?

Numbers

3 Say the numbers, then say the next number in the series.
a. 1 3 5 7 ...   b. 2 4 6 8 ...
c. 11 12 13 ...   d. 20 30 ...
e. 65 70 75 ...   f. 21 28 35 ...
🔊 **Listen and check.**

Test a friend
Write another series of numbers. Read the numbers to a friend. Can he/she say the next number?

Dates

*My birthday's on the twenty-fifth
  of September. What about you?*

4 When's your birthday? (It's on the ... of ...)
What's the date today? (It's the ... of ...)

> We write: 25th September
> We say: the twenty-fifth of September

(cont.)

282

Figure 11.2 *(cont.)*

On the telephone
5 What can you say about the photos?

🔊 Close your book and listen. What homework
has Jack got?

WOMAN Hello.

JACK Hi! It's Jack.

WOMAN Pardon?

JACK Is that 802465?

WOMAN No, it's 802467.

JACK Sorry! I've got the wrong number.

....

SADIE Hello. 802465.

JACK Hi, Sadie. It's Jack. How are you?

SADIE All right, thanks.

JACK Sadie, can you help me with my homework?

SADIE Sure.

JACK How do you say 'It's great' in French?

SADIE C'est chouette.

JACK How do you spell it?

SADIE I think it's C - apostrophe - E - S - T

C - H - O - U - E - double T - E.

JACK Thanks, Sadie.

SADIE You're welcome. See you tomorrow, Jack.

Bye!

🔊 Listen again and follow in your book.

6
1 Say the right telephone number.
2 Write the wrong number. *(Eight 0 ....)*
3 How do you say 'It's great' in your language?
4 How do you spell 'apostrophe'?

Role play
7 a) Act the conversation between Jack and the
woman. Change the name and telephone numbers.
OR
b) Make another dialogue like the one between
Jack and Sadie.

Ask and answer

Name	Telephone number
RIVERA Maria	01782 365924

8 Talk to your friends and write their
names and telephone numbers.

A *Maria, how do you spell your surname?*
B *R- I - V - E - R - A.*
A *What's your telephone number?*
B *It's 01782 365924.*
A *Thanks very much.*
B *You're welcome.*

Use what you know
  Write a letter to Sadie

9 Look at the letter on page 00, then write a reply.
Use words from Steps 1 and 2.

> Your address
> The date.
>
> Dear Sadie,
> I've got your message! My name's... . I live in ....
> I ....
>
> With best wishes from ...

If you aren't sure, ask your teacher:
How do you spell ... ?
How do you say ... in English?

The process of materials evaluation

Figure 11.3 Unit 1: Published pages (**Messages** Student's Book, Level 1) (Goodey and Goodey 2005)

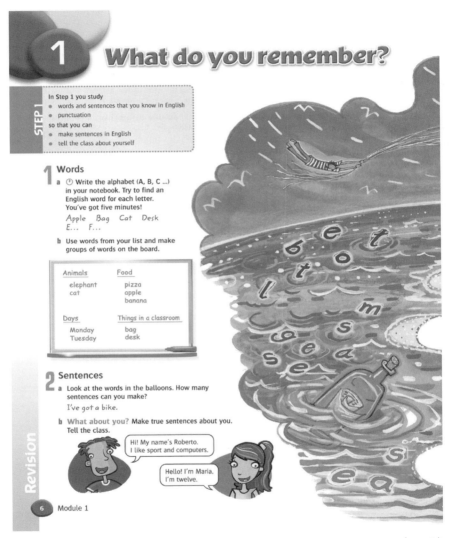

(cont.)

Figure 11.3 *(cont.)*

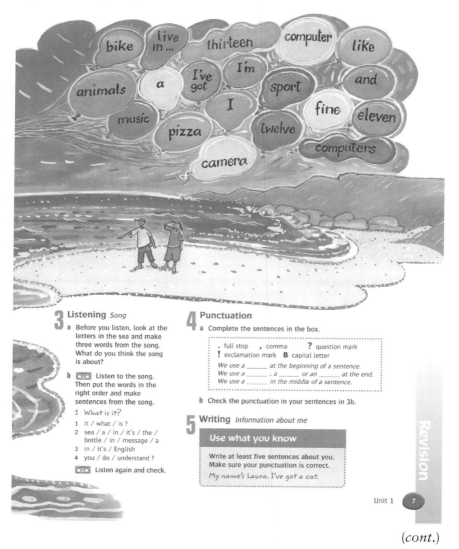

3 Listening *Song*

a Before you listen, look at the letters in the sea and make three words from the song. What do you think the song is about?

b [cassette] Listen to the song. Then put the words in the right order and make sentences from the song.

1 *What is it?*

1 it / what / is ?
2 sea / a / in / it's / the / bottle / in / message / a
3 in / it's / English
4 you / do / understand ?

[cassette] Listen again and check.

4 Punctuation

a Complete the sentences in the box.

> . full stop , comma ? question mark
> ! exclamation mark **B** capital letter
>
> We use a _____ at the beginning of a sentence.
> We use a _____ , a _____ or an _____ at the end.
> We use a _____ in the middle of a sentence.

b Check the punctuation in your sentences in 3b.

5 Writing *Information about me*

> **Use what you know**
>
> Write at least five sentences about you. Make sure your punctuation is correct.
> *My name's Laura. I've got a cat.*

Unit 1 **7**

Revision

(cont.)

285

Figure 11.3   (cont.)

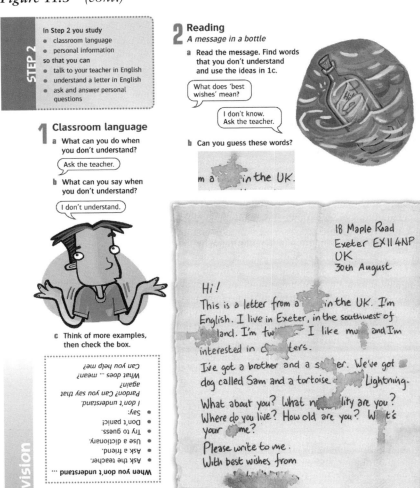

In Step 2 you study
- classroom language
- personal information

so that you can
- talk to your teacher in English
- understand a letter in English
- ask and answer personal questions

STEP 2

1 Classroom language

a   What can you do when you don't understand?

Ask the teacher.

b   What can you say when you don't understand?

I don't understand.

c   Think of more examples, then check the box.

When you don't understand ....
- Ask the teacher.
- Ask a friend.
- Use a dictionary.
- Try to guess.
- Don't panic!
- Say:
  I don't understand.
  Pardon? Can you say that again?
  What does ... mean?
  Can you help me?

Revision

2 Reading
A message in a bottle

a   Read the message. Find words that you don't understand and use the ideas in 1c.

What does 'best wishes' mean?

I don't know. Ask the teacher.

b   Can you guess these words?

m a   in the UK.

18 Maple Road
Exeter EX11 4NP
UK
30th August

Hi !

This is a letter from a   in the UK. I'm English. I live in Exeter, in the southwest of   land. I'm tw   I like mu   and I'm interested in c   ters.

I've got a brother and a s   er. We've got   dog called Sam and a tortoise   Lightning.

What about you? What n   lity are you? Where do you live? How old are you? W   t's your   me?

Please write to me.
With best wishes from

8   Module 1

(cont.)

286

Figure 11.3 *(cont.)*

3 Meet Joe, Sadie, Sam and Jack!

a 🔊 Close your book and listen to Joe, Sadie and Jack. Who is the message in the bottle from?

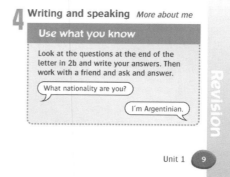

> Hello! I'm Joe. I live in Exeter, at number eighteen Maple Road. I like music and I'm in a band. This is my sister. Her name's Sadie.

> Hi! I'm Sadie, and this is our dog Sam. I'm twelve. My brother's fourteen and my sister Kate's eighteen. She's at university.

> Hi! My name's Jack. I live next door to Sadie, at number twenty. I'm interested in computers and I like animals.

b 🔊 Listen again and follow in your book. Then complete the information.

The message is from .... because he/she is .... years old.
He/She has got ....
His/Her address is ....

c 🔊 Close your book and listen to the message in the bottle.

Remember!

Her name's Sadie. **She's** twelve.
His name's Joe. **He's** fourteen.

4 Writing and speaking *More about me*

Use what you know

Look at the questions at the end of the letter in 2b and write your answers. Then work with a friend and ask and answer.

> What nationality are you?

> I'm Argentinian.

Revision

Unit 1 **9**

(cont.)

Figure 11.3   *(cont.)*

1 Numbers

a Say the numbers, then say the next number in the series.

1 1   3   5   7   ...9...
2 2   4   6   8   ....
3 11 12 13   ....
4 20 30   ....
5 65 70 75   ....
6 21 28 35   ....

🔊 Listen and check.

b Test a friend
Write another series of numbers. Read the numbers to a friend. Can your friend say the next number?

4, 8, 12 ...

2 Dates

Answer the questions.

SEPTEMBER

25

⟨ It's the twenty-fifth of September. ⟩

1 What's the date today?
2 When's your national day?

Remember!

We write: 25th September
We say: the twenty-fifth **of** September

See page 143 for dates and months.

⑩ Module 1

Revision

3 The alphabet

a Say the letters in each group.

Kate /eɪ/	Lee /iː/	Mel /e/	Mike /aɪ/
A H K	B C E P T V	F L M X Z	I

Joe /əʊ/	Sue /uː/	Mark /ɑː/
O	Q W	R

b Now put these letters in the right group. *D — Lee*
D   G   J   N   S   U   Y

🔊 Listen and check.

4 Things in the classroom

a Say the names of at least two things in the classroom.

⟨ Window, dictionary. ⟩

b 🔊 Listen and write the letters. 1 R–U–L–E–R
Now say the words.

⟨ Ruler ... ⟩

(cont.)

288

Figure 11.3   (cont.)

5 Asking for permission

a Match the questions with the pictures.

1 Can I use your ruler, please?
2 Can I look at your dictionary, please?
3 Can I close the window, please?

b Ask and answer the questions in 5a.

> Can I look at your dictionary, please?

> Yes, of course. / No, sorry.

c If you have time, make more questions:

Can I use your rubber, please?

6 Asking for help

a What can you say about the photos?

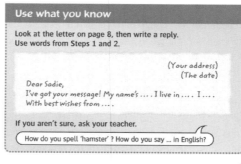

b 📼 Close your book and listen. What homework has Jack got?

SADIE: Hello. 802465.
JACK: Hi, Sadie. It's Jack. How are you?
SADIE: All right, thanks.
JACK: Sadie, can you help me with my homework?
SADIE: Sure.
JACK: How do you say 'It's great' in French?
SADIE: *C'est chouette.*
JACK: How do you spell it?
SADIE: I think it's C - apostrophe - E - S - T, C - H - O - U - E - double T - E.
JACK: Thanks, Sadie.
SADIE: That's OK. See you tomorrow, Jack. Bye!

c 📼 Listen again and follow in your book. Then put the words in the right order. Ask and answer the questions.

1 say / language / do / how / in / you / 'It's great' / your ?
2 you / 'great' / how / do / spell ?

d Role play If you have time, act the conversation between Jack and Sadie. Change some details if you like.

7 Writing *A letter to Sadie*

Use what you know

Look at the letter on page 8, then write a reply.
Use words from Steps 1 and 2.

> *(Your address)*
> *(The date)*
>
> *Dear Sadie,*
> *I've got your message! My name's .... I live in .... I ....*
> *With best wishes from ....*

If you aren't sure, ask your teacher.

> How do you spell 'hamster' ? How do you say ... in English?

Revision

Unit 1   **11**

289

11.5.3 Focus groups

Focus groups are another way in which publishers can gauge how materials will be received in the real world. A focus group is essentially a small group of selected people who match a specific profile and who are brought together in a face-to-face meeting with a facilitator. In ELT publishing focus groups the facilitator can typically be a market research professional or an experienced editor. The techniques the facilitator uses are prompt questions to initiate discussion and probe questions to explore deeper-held beliefs and reactions. A common situation would be a general prompt question such as: *'Do you like any of these units?' 'Unit 3.'* This would then be followed by wh- type questions such as: *'What specifically do you like about it?' 'It's the way it is structured' 'Why do you like the structure' 'Because it has a clear warm-up activity, presentation activity, grammar activity, vocabulary section, skills activity and review and nice workbook activities.' 'When would you use the workbook activities?' 'As homework.' 'Why don't you like the other two units?'...* This process keeps going until the group runs out of things to say. Each new bit of information is explored fully to ensure that as many aspects are considered as possible, even ones which the researcher has never considered before. There is also a further benefit with focus groups in that they allow task-based observation where the researcher can observe what actually happens rather than what the participants say happens.

An example of this is a recent focus group for the Cambridge Handbooks for Language Teachers series which gave a group of teachers a selection of handbooks with activities and told the teachers in the focus group to imagine the situation where they had been asked to cover a class for a colleague the following day. They had half an hour to plan a lesson for the class. They were given information about the level, size, age and nationalities in the class. Observers made notes about how the teachers used the Index and the Contents page, and generally how they navigated the book, and the session was also recorded. Notes were also made on comments as to whether they looked at the activity summary descriptions, if they referred to the activity titles or any other aspect which seemed to influence the activities considered, selected and rejected. The teachers were then asked to present their lesson plans and explain why they had chosen the activities they did, how they had navigated the book and what aspects had influenced their decisions. The most striking thing about this was that many of the teachers could not remember how they had used the index or if they had selected based on class profile or grammatical function. It was an illustration of how what people say they do and what they actually do is often different and why, in addition to asking teachers how they navigate resource books, publishers also need to observe how teachers actually do it and not just rely on one source of information.

The advantages of using a focus group are that it allows two-way immediate interaction and allows the publisher the opportunity to ask follow-on probe questions to explore any particular issue which comes up in more detail. It also allows discussion between the participants. This often means that one person's simple comment can open up a rich discussion on an important issue between all the participants. If the research had only been done as a pilot or review, these discussion comments would have remained dormant. The limitations of focus groups are that they can only be done with a small number of people, typically in one country. This means they are ideal for a publisher researching local editions, but have to be repeated in several different markets to be of more general use.

There are other inherent issues attached to working in a group like this. Sometimes teachers do not say what they really think but, rather, what they want the rest of the group to hear. Is anyone really going to admit, for example, that they find teaching pronunciation hard and do not understand phonemic symbols if they are in a group of strangers or (sometimes worse) a group of colleagues? Or would they ask for advice on how to set up an information gap activity which is not clear from the instructions if they have been teaching for years and do not want to be seen as being inexperienced?

Another problem is that of 'group think'. In other words, as soon as one dominant member of the group expresses an opinion, it is taken up by the other members of the group. Conversely, in some groups there may be participants who want to make an impression and will disagree with every point raised by other group members. The facilitator needs to control the dynamics of the group and sometimes set up a counter-argument to test the group's real views. Although there are obvious benefits from the dynamics a group offers, the results need to be analysed carefully. No publisher would make a change on the basis of one focus group. It is the layering of information from holding several focus groups where the same point comes up again and again, and is also backed up by another source such as expert opinion or questionnaire data, that informs publisher decisions.

11.5.4 Questionnaires

This is probably the easiest method used by publishers. It enables them to cover a lot of ground with limited time and expenditure. To be effective, questionnaires need to be short and specific. They are normally completed online using systems such as SurveyMonkey.com. The drawback with these is that in order for them to be useful, the questions need to ask exactly what the publisher needs to know – this is typically things which relate to the teaching environment and available technology. This information would help a publisher assess, for example, if teachers can actually use a DVD in their classroom or not. It also helps to establish what other commercially produced teaching materials are available and how they are used.

11.5.5 Expert panels

Some publishers appoint a specially selected panel of experts to review materials and advise on current trends. They may meet regularly face-to-face for mini-conferences, perhaps annually or twice a year. Panel experts would normally be selected not just for their prominence and experience in a certain list area,[2] but also so that a wide range of geographical areas were represented. The number of people on a panel can range from four or five to a much larger number. Having a panel means that a publisher can develop very specific briefs for potential authors before any materials are actually commissioned. Increasingly publishers are proactive in their approach to publishing rather than reactive to materials being submitted in an unsolicited manner by potential authors. Most publishers now know well in advance exactly what they are looking for and will normally invite potential author teams to join a competitive tender process where the brief for the materials design is already well defined. Whereas 20 years ago it was common to have ideas, proposals and even whole manuscripts submitted by prospective authors to publishers, ELT publishing is now a much more tightly controlled and planned environment and this is another reason why piloting is on the decline.

11.5.6 Cooperation with academics and materials developers on research projects

In addition to the expert panels mentioned above, publishers sometimes work in cooperation with academics or materials developers on research projects. For example, Cambridge University Press was involved in a recent research project on the use of technology with ELT materials in adult classes with Manchester University Department of Education. The English Profile Project is a good example of a long-term

---

[2] **List areas** are the way publishers divide their publishing into specialist areas, so typically an ELT publisher would have a grammar list area, an exams list area, an adult list area and a primary list area, etc.

collaborative research project between academics, teachers, publishers, materials developers and language testers with the aim of providing reference level descriptions for English linked to the Common European Framework of Reference for Languages (www.english profile.org/).

11.5.7 Editorial visits and classroom observation

Publishers send editors around the world to observe students in a cross-section of different classrooms using both their own and competitor materials (see Chapter 10 by Hitomi Masuhara in this volume). During piloting, classroom observation is also sometimes carried out. The presence of an observer can affect the way the teacher uses the materials, so this needs to be taken into account and minimised if possible by the observer being as unobtrusive as possible. Whilst many of the methods used are similar to those used in teacher training such as those found in *Classroom Observation Tasks* by Ruth Wajnryb (1993), the focus is much more on the way in which materials are used and whether the design of the materials is executed as planned. If teachers are using them in alternative ways, what are the reasons behind this? Publishers are interested in why teachers adapt material and in what ways. They need to know whether it is to do with the published materials needing fundamental changes, which is potentially serious if it indicates deficiency, or if it is just the teacher wanting to own the activity by stamping it with their identity and personal teaching style.

11.5.8 Desk research and competitor analysis

Publishers regularly visit the Internet to see what is new. In particular they will look at other publishers' websites and analyse the strengths and weaknesses of the competition. Publishers also like to access specialist sites to monitor what is new in terms of training and materials developments, such as:

The British Council: www.britishcouncil.org/learning-learn-english.htm

JALT: http://jalt.org

IATEFL: www.iatefl.org

TESOL: www.tesol.org/s_tesol/index.asp

MATSDA: www.matsda.org.uk

ELT Journal: http://eltj.oxfordjournals.org

11.6 Benefits: who gets what from evaluating materials for publishers?

To piloters and schools there are financial benefits from fees associated with piloting and reviewing and there is also the kudos associated with a relationship with a major publisher. Free books can help furnish better-equipped libraries for participating schools and some piloting schools benefit from payment in kind such as projectors for interactive whiteboards. However, perhaps more importantly teachers and schools help ensure their needs are taken into consideration and that commercially produced materials are available for their teaching requirements.

For publishers materials evaluation not only supplies the obvious benefits of market credibility and an assurance that a major financial investment is based on sound research, but it also has the added benefit of supplying future authors. Many teachers and academics who start out by answering a questionnaire or working on a pilot go on to become regular reviewers. Proven reviewers who have shown they have a good writing style and a comprehensive understanding of ELT and a particular aspect or market in it are often approached to write web materials or teacher's books or supplementary materials. If they do that successfully, they can find themselves being asked to tender as an author for bigger projects. It should be pointed out that it is more likely to be those reviewers who show an objective critical analysis of the materials and are prepared to point out the things which could be improved, backed up with informed argument, who are more likely to be approached. Materials evaluation is one of the main sources for publishers finding new prospective authors and being alerted to new ideas.

11.7 What can go wrong?

There are obviously lots of things which can go wrong when evaluating materials:

1. Some reviewers or piloters do the minimum and do not provide any useful information or do not answer the questions posed.
2. Some reviewers or piloters tell the publisher what they think the publisher wants to hear; for example, 'your materials are wonderful as they are and need no changes or additions'. This can be particularly frustrating as it does not help the publisher keep ahead of the curve with any new trends in real classrooms.
3. Some piloters criticise materials without really identifying what the problems are or how they can be addressed. This means it is difficult

for the publisher to assess what needs to be done to improve the materials.

4. There are risks attached to putting unpublished ideas out for trial – the more people who are involved, the more likely your competitor may find out about what you are developing. Normally reviewers and piloters are asked to sign confidentiality clauses.

5. Obtaining a range of representative trialling centres can often be difficult; in spite of careful planning, some centres can find that they have to withdraw from a trial, which can lead to an imbalance in the representation of certain countries or sectors.

11.8 The future of evaluation

Material is evaluated throughout the development of a product at various stages. Historically it was just pre-publication, but now it is equally common to have post-publication reviews, particularly if a new edition or similar product is being considered for future development. As courses are delivered online, there will also be more opportunity to gather data by the same means. This may also be extended into virtual focus groups and lesson observations using webcams.

Increasingly, post-publication review will inform future materials development. Unless there is enough market evidence that a certain approach or type of product is required well before the author even sets pen to paper, it is unlikely authors will even have an opportunity to tender for a project. This is equally true of digital materials which need to be fully specified prior to development. In all likelihood evaluation will become less of a clear-cut stage prior to publication and be more of an ongoing process where materials are refined and even changed throughout the life of a product.

References

Donovan, P. 1998. 'Piloting – a publisher's view'. In B. Tomlinson (ed.), *Materials Development in Language Teaching*, 1st edn. Cambridge: Cambridge University Press.

Goodey, D. and N. Goodey. 2005. *Messages*. Cambridge: Cambridge University Press.

Wajnryb, R. 1993. *Classroom Observation Tasks*. Cambridge: Cambridge University Press.

Comments on Part C

Brian Tomlinson

The obvious link between the different chapters in Section 3 is their insistence on the need for more feedback (and for more systematic feedback) from materials users to materials producers. All too often major decisions are made about the content, approach, procedures and design of learning materials based on assumptions of user needs and wants and on impressions of what 'works' in the classroom. Often these assumptions and impressions are illusory, misinformed or unrepresentative and mistakes are made which contribute to dissatisfaction and failure. One of the things that always amazes me is that, as I travel around the world meeting teachers at conferences and workshops, the impression I am given is that most teachers are dissatisfied with the materials available to them. Yet publishers and ministries tell me that their impression is that the teachers are basically satisfied with these same materials. I suspect that both impressions are wrong because they are based on unrepresentative samples of teachers and because of the ways in which the impressions were gained. Many teachers who come to conferences and workshops are untypically knowledgeable, enthusiastic and discerning. If given a chance to express their views to somebody like me, who does not represent a publisher or authority and who is keen on the development of innovative materials, they are more likely to tell me what they do not like about their materials than what they do like. On the other hand, teachers, when being interviewed by publishers or officials (or even when responding to their questionnaires), are more likely to be polite and/or cautious and to incline more towards the positive in their responses (see Chapter 11 in this volume by Frances Amrani and Singapore Wala 2003a, 2003b). Both my impressions and those of the 'authorities' are often not only misleading, but they are also too crude to be informative. What we need is fine-tuned information about the outcome of materials use in terms of what the teachers and learners actually did, what they felt about what they did and what the consequences were of what they did. As all the chapters in this section have pointed out, whilst-use and post-use evaluations can be extremely valuable, but they are difficult to carry out as they require not only expertise but great investment of teacher energy and time. We can observe materials being used, we can test learners before and after their use of materials and we can administer questionnaires to the users of materials. But it is the teachers who could tell us the most. They use materials every working day and they could participate in intensive and longitudinal studies of materials in use. But they would need to be trained and rewarded and to be supported by valid and reliable instruments of evaluation if they were to be valuably informative. This could be achieved if publishers, ministries of education and university departments of applied linguistics formed consortia to fund and develop research projects which aimed to record the actual outcomes of particular sets of learning materials. MATSDA would be more than willing to help set up such consortia and we intend to make a small start in this direction by holding a materials evaluation workshop at which the participants will be helped to develop instruments for whilst-use and post-use evaluation and then to use these instruments in longitudinal studies of the materials they are using. The results of these studies will be reported in the MATSDA journal, *Folio*, and could form a basis for further, more extended studies and even for use by such consortia as suggested above.

One of the major problems of getting user feedback is that normally the users are not given choices to consider. They are asked to give their responses to a particular set of materials and therefore their feedback can only give information about the effectiveness and not the efficiency of the materials (see Chapter 9 by Rod Ellis in this volume). It can only tell us about their evaluation of that set of materials in relation to their objectives and experience; it does not tell us about the relative value of the materials compared to other sets or types of materials. Also teachers can only express their needs and wants in relation to what they have experienced; they cannot be expected to be aware of all the materials options which could cater for their needs and wants. What I would like to see is a development of what Hitomi Masuhara suggests in Chapter 10 when she proposes meetings of teachers in which they give their responses to alternative versions of the same base materials. I would like to see teachers presented with a number of alternative versions of materials for pre-use evaluation. Each teacher would select two of the versions and then teach them to two equivalent classes so as to be able to carry out whilst- and post-use evaluations of the materials. The teachers could then produce an efficiency evaluation comparing their two versions of the materials. Such a project could only be feasible if the teachers were rewarded or if the evaluations were carried out as part of the research component of a postgraduate degree. How about a number of universities cooperating in research which involves a group of PhD candidates developing such a project? Or how about universities including a teaching practice component on their MA in Applied Linguistics/TEFL courses (as Leeds Metropolitan University is doing) so as to facilitate such research? In MATSDA we intend to make a contribution by including comparative evaluation as a component of the MATSDA materials evaluation workshop mentioned above. Maybe we can then follow this up by helping some of the participants to carry out and write up whilst-use and post-use efficiency evaluations of comparable materials after the conference. For suggestions for how to carry out evaluations of materials see McDonough, Shaw and Masuhara (2011), McGrath (2002), Rubdy (2003) and Tomlinson (2003), and for an evaluation of evaluation checklists see Mukundan and Ahour (2010).

Another link between the chapters in this section is a plea for evaluation to focus on what actually happens as outcomes of material use rather than on the reactions of the teachers and the learners to the materials. Too often judgements about materials are based on considerations of interest and enjoyment. These are important factors in achieving learner engagement, but it is possible for learners to enjoy using materials without learning very much from them and it is also possible to learn a lot from materials which are not particularly interesting or enjoyable to use. What we need to know is, did the teacher and the learners do what the materials intended, were the learning objectives achieved and did unintentional learning also take place? It is easy enough to produce a narrative of observable behavioural outcomes (by, for example, videoing lessons as a matter of routine); it is possible to work out a narrative of mental activity during the lesson (through, for example, speak-aloud protocols, reflection tasks, questionnaires and interviews); it is possible to gain information about short-term learning gains (through administering pre- and post-use tests), but it is very difficult to find out what we really want to know about the long-term learning gains which are attributable to the materials. This could be done on a macro-scale by finding (or better still assembling) two classes which are equivalent in level and motivation, which are taught by the same teacher and which have no contact with the target language outside the classroom. The two classes could be administered a series of pre-tests which focus on the performance objectives which two equivalent but different sets of materials have in common. The two classes could then be taught with each class using a different set of comparable but crucially differentiated materials. At the end (or preferably after the end) of the course the two classes could be administered post-use tests and the differences in progress between the two classes could be measured. Such an experiment involving a number of classes of young adult learners of Bahasa Indonesia is reported by Barnard (2007), who designed two sets of materials which taught the same language teaching points but differed in that one set adopted a language production approach and the other adopted a language comprehension approach.

Another, more manageable, procedure would be for the research to focus on the comparative progress towards a very specific and measurable objective made by two comparable classes using different materials. This could be done with learners living in the target language culture if both classes had equal access to relevant experience outside the classroom; or if no relevant experience was available to any of the learners. Examples of such areas of focus could be increase in the mean length of utterance in conversation, increase in the range of vocabulary in written storytelling, increase in the range and appropriacy of exponents of a particular function, increase in the range and appropriacy of tense use in unplanned discourse. Tomlinson and Masuhara recently carried out such research in two Malaysian institutions for a British publisher when they compared success in the learning of specific lexical items between a control class which had no treatment, a class which read stories extensively in which the items had been embedded and recycled, and a class which were taught the items explicitly.

Another procedure would be for a novel element to be added to the learning experience of students and for attempts to be made to measure the consequences of that addition. Dat (2003) reports doing this with students in Vietnam and focuses in particular on the effect which a change in the treatment impacted on the students' reluctance to talk in English. Barker (2010) reports on the effects which offering opportunities for unstructured and unmonitored student interaction had on the fluency and accuracy of university students learning English in Japan. And Al-Busaidi and Tindle (2010) report on the effects of adding an experiential, process-writing approach to the course for first year students of English at Sultan Qaboos University in Oman.

In short, we need much more research into the effects of types of materials if we are to contribute to the development of materials which not only attract and impress but which actually facilitate learning too. Such research is not easy and cannot really be conclusive because it is difficult to control variables with real classes being taught in real time in real contexts. But it is definitely worth attempting and in Tomlinson and Masuhara (2010) there are chapters reporting such evaluations in countries all over the world.

References

Al-Busaidi, S. and K. Tindle. 2010. 'Evaluating the impact of in-house materials on language learning'. In B. Tomlinson and H. Masuhara (eds.), *Research in Materials Development for Language Learning: Evidence for Best Practice*. London: Continuum.

Barker, D. 2010. 'The potential role of unstructured learner interaction'. In 'Acquiring a foreign language'. Unpublished PhD thesis. Leeds Metropolitan University.

Barnard, E. S. 2007. 'The value of comprehension in the early stages of the acquisition and development of Bahasa Indonesia by non-native speakers'. In B. Tomlinson (ed.), *Language Acquisition and Development: Studies of Learners of First and Other Languages*. London: Continuum.

Dat, B. 2003. 'Materials for developing speaking skills'. In B. Tomlinson (ed.), *Developing Materials for Language Teaching*. London: Continuum.

McDonough, J., C. Shaw. and H. Masuhara. 2011. *Materials and Methods in ELT: A Teachers' Guide*, 3rd edn. Oxford: Blackwell.

McGrath, I. 2002. *Materials Evaluation and Design for Language Teaching*. Edinburgh: University of Edinburgh Press.

Mukundan, J. and T. Ahour. 2010. 'A review of textbook evaluation checklists across four decades (1970–2007)'. In B. Tomlinson and H. Masuhara (eds.), *Research in Materials Development for Language Learning: Evidence for Best Practice*. London: Continuum.

Rubdy, R. 2003. 'Selection of materials'. In B. Tomlinson (ed.), *Developing Materials for Language Teaching*. London: Continuum.

Singapore Wala, D. A. 2003a. 'A coursebook is what it is because of what it has to do: an editor's perspective'. In B. Tomlinson (ed.), *Developing Materials for Language Teaching*. London: Continuum.

2003b. 'Publishing a coursebook: completing the materials development circle'. In B. Tomlinson (ed.), *Developing Materials for Language Teaching*. London: Continuum.

Tomlinson, B. 2003. 'Materials evaluation'. In B. Tomlinson (ed.), *Developing Materials for Language Teaching*. London: Continuum.

Tomlinson, B. and H. Masuhara. 2010. *Research in Materials Development for Language Learning: Evidence for Best Practice*. London: Continuum.

Part D   The electronic delivery of materials

12 Developing language-learning materials with technology

Gary Motteram

12.1 Introduction

In this chapter I am going to explore ways of creating materials for language learning that make full use of the advantages of digital technologies. I will also take due account of our responsibilities as language teachers to develop multi-literacies, as argued by Warschauer and Healey as early as 1998, and a common theme now both in the field of language learning and technology and of general education (Pegrum 2009). I will show how teachers can blend resources they would typically have in their classroom with the increasing range of technologies that are made available by publishers, and also with the large number of Web 2.0 technologies that can be found on the Internet. I will focus on discussing ideas that are achievable by many teachers. Towards the end, however, I will push the boundaries a little and present one or two technologies that may currently be available only to a very few of us.

12.2 Technology and language learning

In most classrooms the drivers of activity are the examination and a centralised curriculum, and as a result textbooks and teaching often reflect this. In many parts of the world, for example, spoken language is not examined and so, although it might appear in the curriculum, it does not get taught. Teachers need, then, to be creative, if they want to give their learners a greater chance of being able to communicate. Teachers try to use technology to supplement language classes, because they believe there is very little time for real language use in typical language classes. Teachers are also conscious that learners do not always see why they are expected to study languages and they try their best to make the learning meaningful and real, to encourage their learners to engage. Many younger learners fail to understand why they are learning a language that appears to have little relevance to their daily lives; it is simply a part of the curriculum; it is on the timetable. This is something that a teacher can address by trying to help the learners make connections to the outside world where the language is being used for real tasks.

12.2.1 What are the opportunities presented by new technology?

At the time of writing, we are in a period of transition. The underlying shift that has been going on for some time is the move from analogue to digital, but there is also the change on the Internet from what is now called Web 1.0 to Web 2.0. Web 2.0 allows many more people to be creative with digital technologies. For example, I can sit at my computer and record a video clip using the camera that is embedded in the laptop's lid. I could also record this directly on to the Internet and then link that directly to a blog, or a wiki, or to my institution's virtual learning environment (VLE). This puts the possibilities of the adaptation and creation of a broad range of language-learning materials directly into the hands of the teacher, but also into the hands of the learners. Web 2.0 has made the production of pictures and text even easier and the localisation or production of audio and video is now possible for teachers and their learners.

Many of the early books about using technology in language education were written in a period that would be described now as Web 1.0. This was a time when materials only really flowed from organisations such as publishers or individual small-scale developers and could often only be used as they were created. Teachers like to be able to adapt materials, what these days would be described as 're-mixing' (Pegrum 2009), as do learners. Teachers need to do this to meet localised learning needs. Materials do need mediation and with Web 2.0 this is increasingly possible. See, for example, the use of video described in the examples below. We can find attractive and appropriate input material and build classroom activities around it.

All that has been said so far has implied access to the Internet, and although teachers and learners may have access outside the classroom, Internet access cannot be relied on within many classrooms. This, then, is where materials such as CDs or DVDs that accompany textbooks come into their own, or where teachers and learners can bring materials to class that they have downloaded elsewhere for use in the lesson. These materials can work wherever there is an appropriate player and do not require a direct internet connection. Teachers can supplement what comes with the textbook in a number of different ways to make the material more relevant to modern learners. Textbook materials go out of date very quickly, but references to aspects of culture can be quickly updated by adding more recent material from the Internet. If learners can access this material themselves, then all to the good, but if not, the teacher can find something more relevant and bring this to the class.

12.2.2 Tasks and exercises

I am going to make use of the distinction made by Ellis (2003: 3, Chapter 9 in this volume) between task and exercise to help me delineate the differences in how different technologies are deployed and the roles that they play: '"Tasks" are activities that call for primarily meaning-focused language use. In contrast "exercises" are activities that call for primarily form-focused language use.' Examples of exercises are gap fill, multiple choice and word games. Such exercise types have been produced from the earliest attempts to use computers in language education, with Higgins and Johns (1984) being two early producers of such software. A very commonly and freely available piece of software in this continuing tradition is the Hot Potatoes suite, which is available for download from the Web (http://hotpot.uvic.ca/). This enables teachers to create small exercises to practise discrete aspects of grammar or vocabulary development. With a little additional effort, the completed exercise can be linked to a listening or reading text to make a complete comprehension exercise. Feedback can also be added and learners can work on these exercises independently of the teacher, or together in class. This gives the teacher more space to work on parts of the curriculum that need more direct teacher intervention. Exercise types of this nature are part of many examination systems and they can be created quite quickly and easily, either by individuals or groups. They can also be quickly adapted and changed to keep them up to date. Increasingly learners are being asked to sit web-based exams, and web practice of examination task types can provide the necessary digital literacy skills for learners to do well in these new testing modes. Perhaps these exercise types do not stretch our digital learners, but they can be seen as providing useful practice, at least for the exam, and may persuade the learners that using computers can be effective in supporting their language development. We can also find exercise types like these on CD MultiROMs as well as online with a variety of different publishers. Macmillan, for example, offers a range of games and activities (Figure 12.1) that reflect the general principles of Hot Potatoes files, but might look more attractive to the learners and have the advantage of being readily available. However, with Hot Potatoes the teacher needs to author the materials herself.

With Hot Potatoes the material needs to be created using authoring tools such as Flash and requires access to good graphics, and is therefore not easy for the average teacher to be able to achieve. In addition, some of the materials on some of the publishers' sites require payment.

Figure 12.1 *An example of an exercise made available online by a publisher (Source: www.digitaltaj.com/sample/mlg005082/ mlg005082.htm)*

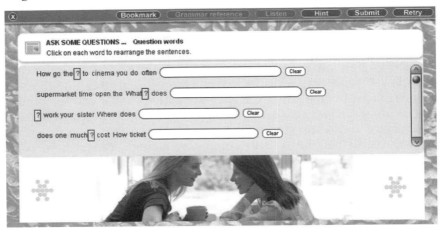

Other publishers such as Oxford University Press offer similar materials (Figure 12.2), but these are freely available. Some of them can also be printed, if multiple computers and an internet connection are not available.

The example in Figure 12.2 is a grammar exercise, based on the textbook *English Result*. As can be seen in the menu on the left, there are exercises in a range of different language areas. These materials can provide focused and useful practice in the early stages of language learning and can provide experience of the formats learners will find in examinations.

Materials of this nature can be found all over the Internet, often produced by individuals who start by trying to address the needs of their own classes, but end up addressing the needs of many more.

12.2.3 Authentic texts

As well as providing a way of accessing exercises either created by publishers or by other teachers, the Internet provides a useful resource for all kinds of authentic texts, by which I mean texts not produced specifically for learning languages, most of which are free at the point of delivery. The most obvious examples of this are sites such as Wikipedia and YouTube. Wikipedia is like an online reference book with accompanying pictures on many, many subjects. The text can be used as the

Figure 12.2 *An exercise from the Oxford University Press website (Source: www.oup.com/elt/global/products/result/ engpreint/a_grammar/unit01/1c_1/)*

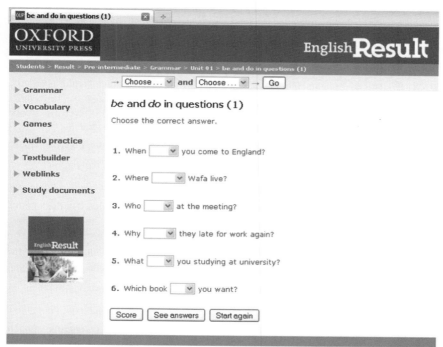

basis for lessons. YouTube is an online video site where you can find short video clips (no longer than ten minutes) on a very broad range of topics. If you do not have internet access in your classroom, videos can be downloaded and used on a stand-alone computer. Authentic materials can be useful on their own, particularly with higher-level classes looking for stimulating topics to explore, but can also be combined with either exercises or tasks, depending on the needs of the classes you are teaching. See the example on pink dolphins in 12.4.1.

12.2.4 Authentic tasks

Other real world tasks can also be set up with authentic material; for example, learners can be asked to engage in the types of activity that would be performed in the target language, such as finding how to get somewhere, choosing a holiday destination, selecting presents for family and friends, doing research on a topic of interest and so on. These activities can be set up offline by using printouts, or downloading parts of websites for local storage and delivery.

We have recognised for a long time now that using language is central to developing the ability to communicate effectively. Time is usually very limited in language classes and the productive skills are the ones that often suffer. However, the range of technological tools that enable us to be social in all sorts of ways can do a lot to extend what is done in class. The collaborative and interactive side that is so prominent in Web 2.0 has the potential to help teachers a great deal to develop their learners' output. The production of text has grown exponentially on the Web in the recent past. We have seen the use of blogs and wikis in language learning grow considerably (Ducate and Lomicka 2005; Godwin-Jones 2003), but also collaborative writing software such as Google Docs, as well as the more traditional text chat tools, for example Microsoft's Messenger software (MSN), or Google Talk, contributing to the output of language. All of these tools allow learners to produce language in various forms; blogs and wikis favour traditional written text whereas chat tools allow the practice of conversation, albeit written down. Learners work with each other to create language and then can display it for others to see. There is the opportunity to get feedback from the teacher, but others may also see and comment on what has been written.

12.2.5 Spoken English

Spoken language practice has also become much easier to organise with individuals or groups of learners being encouraged to communicate with other individuals or groups of learners around the world. The number of tools through which you can talk online has also seen a considerable growth. The use of Voice Over Internet Protocol (VOIP) tools such as Skype, for example, has made significant impact on our ability to communicate easily with other people, but we also find synchronous communication tools being included within Virtual Learning Environments (VLE), or in Virtual Classroom (VC) software. A typical VLE, which in the past might have only included text for communication either in asynchronous forums, or via text chat, now usually includes voice tools, or video conferencing. Virtual Classrooms are an online version of a face-to-face class usually built around an electronic whiteboard and other associated tools such as the ability to show webpages. These tools come into their own if learners and teachers are geographically distributed, but in contexts where these tools are not central to the delivery of learning, for example in what is now referred to as blended courses, tools of this type can be used outside of the classroom to enable learners to do pair and group work as homework, or in preparation for a class.

Tools such as Skype (www.skype.com), Wimba Voice Tools (www.wimba.com/) or WizIQ (www.wiziq.com/) also allow for the recording of the interactions, so such evidence of use can be added to a learning portfolio. VLEs can be used to develop a resource for language learning, with groups of teachers working to provide a growing collection of exercises and tasks, and also as the basis for language learning at a distance (White 2003). Tools that allow for spoken communication increasingly make it possible to see who we are communicating with via a video connection. Many online virtual classroom tools have audio and video built in as a standard. The addition of video can help people feel more connected and engaged with the lessons, thus increasing their motivation.

In addition to the tools that make it possible to communicate in real time, we have seen the increasing use of recorded and live audio and video available on the Web. Online audio material is called a podcast and video materials called vodcasts or vidcasts. I have already referred to YouTube, but there are many places where audio and video can be found. With the advent of Web 2.0, it is relatively easy for learners and their teachers to add material to the Web; for example, schools can engage their learners in doing projects that can be added to the Web for all to see and comment on.

12.2.6 Digital literacies

Online tools such as Wikipedia can be the basis for lessons on digital literacy. There has been a recent debate about the accuracy of open source tools such as Wikipedia, for example Chesney (2006), and a task that you could ask more advanced learners to do is to compare the information provided by different websites. The learners are asked to consider why they might trust one site rather than another. If they are subject specialists, for example economists or engineers, they might compare their own understanding of a subject area with what they find about it on the Internet. When we use the Internet or other resources, we must always be aware of copyright (Cha *et al.* 2007), and whilst it is acceptable to make use of such material as a part of a class, it is important to seek permission if the material is going to appear in a publication.

12.3 How can we design materials using new technology?

When designing materials using technology, it is useful to have a framework from which to judge the potential value of an activity before devoting time and effort to its implementation. Although not in the field of language teaching, Bates has been a strong advocate of the uses of technology to support learning both in his long career at the Open University and subsequently. His ACTIONS model (1995) is a very useful tool to help teachers analyse whether they should try out a particular technology. It can also be helpful at the management level for deciding on whether to take a school or college down a particular technological path:

Access: how accessible is a particular technology for learners? How flexible is it for a particular target group?

Costs: what is the cost structure of each technology? What is the unit cost per student?

Teaching and learning: what kinds of learning are needed? What instructional approaches will best meet these needs? What are the best technologies for supporting this teaching and learning?

Interactivity and user-friendliness: what kind of interaction does this technology enable? How easy is it to use?

Organisational issues: what are the organisational requirements, and the barriers to be removed, before this technology can be used successfully? What changes in organisation need to be made?

Novelty: how new is this technology?

Speed: how quickly can courses be mounted with this technology? How quickly can materials be changed?

I will make use of this model to analyse the different examples of materials development discussed below.

12.4 Worked examples: starting with simple materials

Starting with simple materials means that costs will not be high, providing that some technological infrastructure is already in place, and allows us to focus on the learners and the teachers, and their educational realities. I am going to start by assuming that the teacher has access to his/her own computer, or can perhaps use one in a staff room, or a teacher's resource centre.

12.4.1 An example from Hong Kong

This example from Hong Kong takes the topic of the environment, one used in many syllabuses, and relates it to the local context. In a training session with teachers from Hong Kong we looked together at websites reporting on the activities of conservationists interested in pink dolphins. A quick search using Google found a website that showed that this was still a live issue in that region: www.hkdolphinwatch.com/. On that website were texts and pictures, as well as information about excursions, merchandise and links to other websites. The website made it clear that this material could be used, but permission needed to be sought.

12.4.2 Some options

Teachers can print out some pictures of the dolphins and take them to the class as a stimulus. A text from this site could also be printed out and used along with texts from other sites to build up a description of the features of this local dolphin. A text on the dolphin from Wikipedia, for example, says that the pink dolphin was 'discovered' in 1637 by Peter Mundy. A higher level class could be asked to comment on this notion of discovery, thus building their digital literacy skills.

If the teacher has access to a computer in their class, or a digital projector, but not a live internet connection, then pages can be downloaded on to a storage device, such as a USB drive and taken into the school or college. In Figure 12.3 we see a text taken from Wikipedia.

Figure 12.3 *A text about the Chinese white/pink dolphin (Source: http://en.wikipedia.org/wiki/Chinese_White_Dolphin)*

Chinese White Dolphin

From Wikipedia, the free encyclopedia

Not to be confused with the Baiji (Chinese River Dolphin).

 This article **does not cite any references or sources.**
Please help improve this article by adding citations to reliable sources. Unsourced material may be challenged and removed.
(August 2007)

The **Chinese White Dolphin** (*Sousa chinensis chinensis*; traditional Chinese: 中華白海豚; pinyin: Zhōnghuá bái hǎitún), also called **Indo-Pacific Humpback Dolphin**, is a species of the Humpback dolphin and is one of eighty cetacean species. The adult dolphin is usually white or grey in colour. The population along the Chinese coast is unique in that they exhibit a pink-coloured skin.[2] This colour of the skin is not a result of colour pigmentation, but is actually from blood vessels used for thermoregulation to prevent overheating during exertion. The adult's body length is about 200 - 350 centimetres and the infant's body length is about 1 metre. The average weight of an adult is around 150 to 230 kilograms.

The Indo-Pacific dolphins can be found throughout Southeast Asia, and they breed from South Africa to Australia. There are two subspecies, with Sumatra, one of the Indonesian islands, as the dividing line between the Chinese and the Western subspecies, *Sousa chinensis plumbea*.

The two subspecies differ in color and size of their dorsal fin. There is also a pink dolphin.

The subspecies found in Southeast Asia has pinkish white skin and a larger dorsal fin but lacks the fatty hump of its South African and Australian counterparts.

Chinese White Dolphin

Conservation status

Extinct   Threatened   Least Concern

EX EW CR EN VU NT LC

Portable USB storage devices (also referred to as pen or flash drives) are now cheap and can be used to store sound or video files, as well as webpages and text.

It was easy enough to find a short YouTube video in English about pink dolphins and this could be downloaded and saved on to a portable device. In the video (www.youtube.com/watch?v=CL_xK2c5Zqg) we hear an English interviewer talking about what he calls the 'white dolphin', which he later describes as being 'bubble-gum pink'. He also talks to one of the tour guides, interviewing her in English, showing the learners the values of English for their future life. We see children enjoying their experience of dolphin-watching and in Figure 12.4 we see their reactions to the day. Children in a class you teach can be encouraged to react in the same way and create texts of various types around their experience. Children's reactions to technology do not have to be high-tech if they do not have access to computers.

Figure 12.4   Thank you letters from people who have been watching pink dolphins (Source: www.hkdolphinwatch.com/)

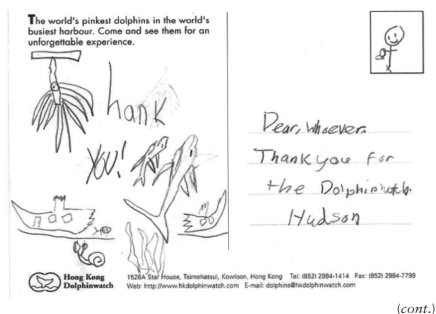

(cont.)

Figure 12.4 *(cont.)*

The world's pinkest dolphins in the world's busiest harbour. Come and see them for an unforgettable experience.

Dear Dolphin watch people,

    I'm Clarice! Thankyou for replying to my e-mail! Since then, I've written a report, gathered some petitions and collected some information on the pink dolphins! which we're sending to the Chief Executive! Bye!\!!/

Dolphin Watch   Hong Kong

1528A Starhouse,

Tsimshatsui,

Kowloon, Hong Kong SAR

Hong Kong Dolphinwatch   1528A Star House, Tsimshatsui, Kowloon, Hong Kong Tel: (852) 2984-1414 Fax: (852) 2984-7799
Web: http://www.hkdolphinwatch.com E-mail: dolphins@hkdolphinwatch.com

12.4.3 An example from Sri Lanka

If technology is available locally for the children to use, then we can take these ideas further. In my own practice working for the British Council and Save the Children Fund, I supported a small group of children from various communities in Sri Lanka, teaching them to create digital materials. This was part of a broader initiative to bring communities together. The children met in Colombo with adult helpers who worked with them in after-school clubs in their regions. The final output was a website, the home page of which you can see in Figure 12.5.

In preparing to produce this website, children spent time in their local communities collecting resources and then worked together in Colombo to learn how to produce a website using web authoring tools. As a part of the lessons, they visited the local zoo where they conducted interviews with the visitors and workers (Figure 12.6).

Figure 12.5   *Kids in Touch homepage (no longer available online)*

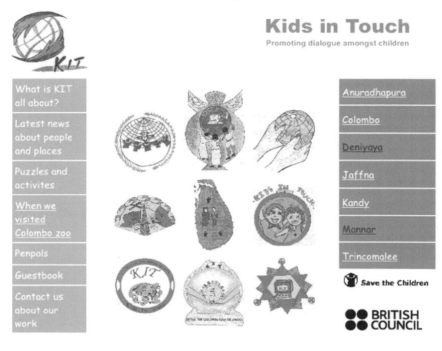

Figure 12.6   *Children interviewing a zoo keeper (photograph courtesy of Gary Motteram)*

Children worked in teams to produce a mock-up of the website structure before we put it all together. Figure 12.7 gives an example of this presented as a wallchart. As can be seen from the front page of the website (Figure 12.5), the logos from the different teams were drawn and then scanned in. As a part of the activity, we had a competition for the best logo.

It is possible to start quite simply by finding different kinds of information on the Internet and taking it into class. This can progress quite quickly into developing significant digital skills for the learners, as well as making use of language to carry out the activities. The interviews with the zoo workers were not conducted in English, but the output from the learners was. The context encouraged them to produce language. Whilst I lay no real claim for developing these children's digital skills, I am still in touch with some of them through Facebook, which suggests that they continue to use these skills and to use English very effectively to communicate with others.

Figure 12.7   A wallchart showing how the website would look

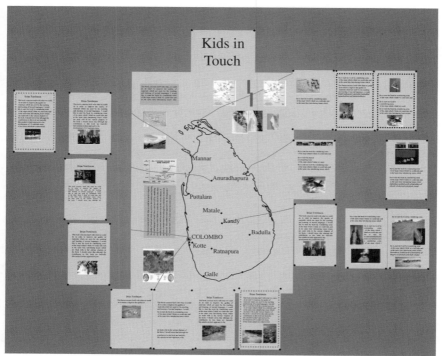

12.4.4 Evaluating the activities

Bates's ACTIONS model can help us to see why these activities work:

Access: how accessible is a particular technology for learners? How flexible is it for a particular target group?

In the Sri Lankan example we started not by asking the learners to access technology but simply got the teachers and learners to bring whatever materials they had into the class. In the Hong Kong example materials needed to be found on the Web.

Both of the activities that have been described are flexible enough to suit different contexts and I have shown how you can vary a similar activity to suit the availability of different levels of technology.

Costs: what is the cost structure of each technology? What is the unit cost per student?

Costs for this can be kept very low. Of course, in a situation in which every student is accessing his or her own computer, then the cost per learner is quite high. In the Hong Kong example there was a teacher with a computer (shared with a number of others in a staff room), printer, internet connection and USB stick. If a teacher is working in a similar way with a number of classes, costs can be kept low.

Teaching and learning: what kinds of learning are needed? What instructional approaches will best meet these needs? What are the best technologies for supporting this teaching and learning?

These activities can be adjusted to suit the needs of the context, as previously shown. The instructional approaches here are quite active and encourage engagement of the learners in real world tasks from quite a low level. As has been illustrated, a variety of technologies can be brought into play.

Interactivity and user-friendliness: what kind of interaction does this technology enable? How easy is it to use?

The technologies are quite easy to use and allow for considerable interactivity. As an extension of the work we did in Colombo, I used chat to connect the children to my daughter in Manchester. During my first visit to Sri Lanka, I bought a toy elephant, which I took home to my daughter. As part of the second visit, the children contacted 'the elephant' to ask questions about life in school in the UK. This is an extension of the idea of travelling teddy bears, which has been widely used to motivate young language learners.

Organisational issues: what are the organisational requirements, and the barriers to be removed, before this technology can be used successfully? What changes in organisation need to be made?

If there are no computers in the school or college then it is still possible to do these activities if the teacher has access to them at home, or in a resource centre. It may well be that by taking such initiatives, the organisation will take notice and start to think that perhaps technology will be a useful asset in the institution.

Novelty: how new is this technology?

These are not new technologies and so ought to be easily available and replicable in many classrooms around the world.

Speed: how quickly can courses be mounted with this technology? How quickly can materials be changed?

Developing such materials takes no time at all and, once created, they can be used with a variety of different classes.

12.5 Developing your skills

Once the initial step in using digital technologies to support language learning has been made, there are many ways in which teachers can further develop their skills. Many teachers look for ways that they can supplement or support their learners with additional skills development beyond the classroom, and many institutions are making use of Virtual Learning Environments (VLEs) for all aspects of curricular support. Interactive whiteboards (IWBs) are being used in a variety of ways to deliver curricular materials in classrooms. They are often used to help with the management of activities as well as to display and work with interactive exercises. Mobile phones have not featured significantly in classes as yet (and, in fact, are often banned) but their use for educational purposes is becoming more common. They are in effect small portable computers which can be used to present and interact with materials of various types, including text, audio and video. For more on VLEs, IWBs and mobile phones see sections 12.7, 12.8 and 12.9 in this chapter, as well as Chapter 13 by Lisa Kervin and Beverly Derewianka in this volume and Reinders and White (2010).

12.6 Building a blog

Language teachers have been using blogs for some time now (Ward 2004), but they have developed from being text-based web diaries to be being full-blown multimedia tools. So, as well as text, pictures, sound, video and interactive games can also be added, as with so many modern internet tools.

A blog is a good starting place for many teachers and can be used for a variety of purposes. At the University of Manchester in the UK on our MA in Educational Technology and TESOL course we are now teaching our students how to use a blog as an alternative to a webpage, treating the blog as a content management system (CMS). On this course we cover traditional webpage design, but a blog allows us to develop more sophisticated materials more quickly. You can find the materials that we use with this course at this address: http://blogs.humanities. manchester.ac.uk/mewssgjm/.

I am going to illustrate how we can create effective classroom support materials through one of our MA student's blogs, continuing with the theme of the environment. Diana, at the time of creating this blog space, was working with secondary-age learners (English Form 5) in a Malaysian School following the standard textbook for the year. The topic is deforestation. On the first page of the blog the task is described and the learning outcomes are established. On the second page there is a video to watch with an accompanying task (Figure 12.8). This is used as part of a regular class in the first instance and then the learners can revisit the materials at home, if they wish. The learners are asked to view the video and offer some opinions about its content.

Notice that this is not so different from the earlier example, but it is created to be a permanent resource, which can be used in or out of the classroom. This could be put on to a VLE, but a blog might offer the teacher more control. The tasks are carefully crafted to reflect the reality of the teaching context, that is, four learners to a machine. In large groups, there may still be problems with the 40 or 50 learners all viewing the clip at the same time, though one learner can be assigned the headset and then the others can ask questions, or they can take it in turns to listen and ask each other questions to clarify what is happening in the video. The language of the questions on the screen may be a little sophisticated, but these are interesting tasks and link well to the reading text task that follows. Note that the students are guided to keep a record of their answers to the questions on a task sheet that has been handed out by the teacher. All of these elements encourage the learners to engage with the language in meaningful ways, so even if they discuss the ideas in the local language, they have to write something down in

Figure 12.8 *Blog-based pre-reading exercise (Source: http://blogs. humanities.manchester.ac.uk/mewxhda2/)*

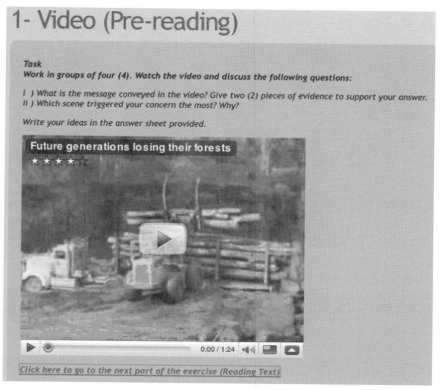

English. Within the blog structure, you can take a number of routes through this task, but at the end of each page there is a link to the next one, to make sure the learners do not get lost in cyberspace (Cousin 2005). On the next page in the materials (Figure 12.9) there is a reading text with links and pictures that support understanding of the text (Clark and Mayer 2007).

The links are also there to aid understanding. Clicking on the green underlined words provides a situated definition. The purple words highlight what the grammar focus is within this lesson and there are links in the blog to guidance on this particular grammar item. Further down the page there are some carefully constructed exercises to help the learners think about what they have been reading (Figure 12.10).

The electronic delivery of materials

Figure 12.9 *Blog-based while-reading exercise (Source: http://blogs. humanities.manchester.ac.uk/mewxhda2/)*

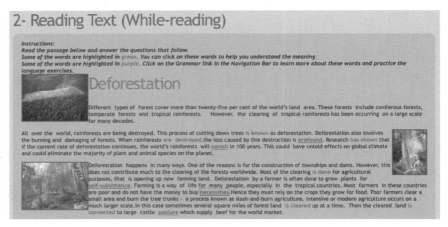

Figure 12.10 *Exercises to aid the reading process (Source: http:// blogs.humanities.manchester.ac.uk/mewxhda2/)*

This is well thought through from a pedagogical perspective, but at the same time makes an interesting use of the technology to support the learners in thinking about their answers. The buttons reveal information about the topics under discussion in pop-up windows.

Throughout the lesson the students are adding to the printed text supplied by the teacher. This acts as a permanent record for the learners, but can also be checked over by the teacher to make sure that there are no issues that need to be dealt with. As well as this reading exercise to get them engaging with the text, there is also a multiple choice question and a gap fill exercise produced in Hot Potatoes. These materials can be used in class and for extension and follow-up. Using a blog like this is motivating for students because it is recognised as being part of their digital reality beyond the classroom. It is not difficult for the teacher to add to this content, or for other teachers in the school or college to be given space so that they can produce further lessons, and in this way a bank of materials can grow.

This blog material contains the fundamental elements that are described in the introduction to this chapter: it relates to a textbook but to this has been added an authentic video and other support and activities to enable the learners to work through with greater autonomy. The teacher's role becomes one of supporting the learner and making sure that everyone in the class is able to progress effectively.

12.7 Virtual Learning Environments

Virtual Learning Environments (VLEs) bring together a number of different tools in one place and can be seen as a further development in terms of building a teacher's digital skills. VLEs are often bought by institutions at great cost and are sometimes used as a way of ensuring that teachers use digital technologies with their learners. However, if they are introduced sensitively and with consultation, they can be used effectively to deliver a useful institutional resource.

I am going to look here at the Open Source VLE: Moodle (http://moodle.org) and this time I will pick an example that is built around a particular examination offered by Cambridge ESOL: BEC (Business English Certificate) Higher.

Whilst a blog can enable discussion outside the class via the comments function and additional tools can be embedded for providing feedback of various types, a VLE has specific tools for communication built in. In the top-left hand corner of the screen shot (Figure 12.11), under the heading Activities, you can see that this particular Moodle course is making use of quizzes (Choices), discussion forums, a glossary, various files that have been created and uploaded, and a wiki. In addition, in the right-hand column there is an embedded link to the Cambridge dictionaries online and at the bottom a news feed of Business English from the BBC. In the central column is the course itself. The first part of this course focuses on developing an understanding of how the examination develops listening skills. The course itself includes a number of different resources including digital audio and downloadable texts. These are mixed in with reflective forums on the process of participating in the course.

Teachers might need a few additional skills to develop and teach this course, as well as the ability to create or source the different digital resources. They also need the skills of managing task creation for work in forums, and then, in addition, the skills of getting the most out of the

Figure 12.11 A Moodle course at the University of Manchester to support the BEC exam

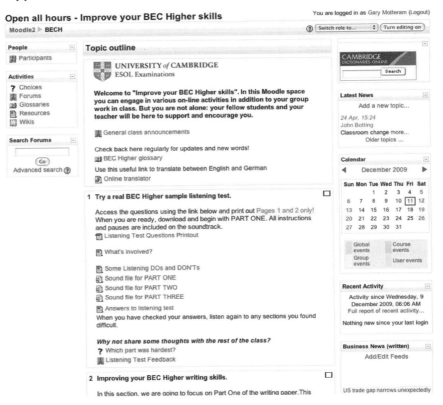

learners as they post comments on the forum. If teachers want to, they can set up and run a version of Moodle on their own server space; this may sound complex, but is really a matter of following the onscreen instructions, and a quick glance at the wealth of Moodle spaces online shows how many people are already doing this.

12.8 Interactive whiteboards (IWBs)

In some parts of the world IWBs have made a significant impact. UK schools, for example, have invested in them quite heavily, particularly in the primary sector, and many large private language schools around the world have also introduced them.

A number of the publishing companies have invested in producing versions of their coursebooks that work with IWBs. Cambridge University Press is one such company and they have produced a very good set of video tutorials explaining the basic function of IWBs which can be found on the Cambridge University Press website (www. cambridge.org) by searching for: 'How to use an interactive whiteboard'.

An IWB, as its name suggests, allows you to manipulate material directly on the board, usually making use of an electronic pen or your finger. All the boards come with software that allows you to create your own lessons, referred to as 'flipchart software', but you can utilise any piece of software on the computer that is attached to the IWB. You can easily create lessons using the flipchart software or show and demonstrate other materials. You can extend the IWB by using voting systems (Cutrim 2008) or portable tablets that the learners have on their desks. Whilst some teachers like these tools, there has also been criticism, mainly focusing around the fact that IWBs are said to encourage teacher-centred teaching (Orr 2008).

I am now going to analyse the use of the blog and the VLE using Bates's model.

12.8.1 Access: how accessible is a particular technology for learners? How flexible is it for a particular target group?

Both the use of the blog and the VLE imply that either the school or college has access to computers in a lab, or that the learners have access from home or via internet cafes. Both tools allow flexibility of access, either in class or outside of it, almost anytime, anywhere. Blogs and the Moodle VLE can also be used on mobile devices.

Interactive whiteboards are usually fixed within a class; however, they can be moved and in fact one type is designed to adhere to any shiny surface. If you move the IWB, you have to recalibrate it before each teaching session.

12.8.2 Costs: what is the cost structure of each technology? What is the unit cost per student?

Setting up and running a blog or Moodle on an existing server is not expensive, certainly not for an institution, but their use by learners does imply access to multiple computers.

IWBs are expensive; you need the board itself and a computer and projector. To equip a whole school is a considerable investment.

12.8.3 Teaching and learning: what kinds of learning are needed? What instructional approaches will best meet these needs? What are the best technologies for supporting this teaching and learning?

I have focused here on materials that are more related to regular teaching, showing how technologies can both expand the lesson but also stay within the needs of the curriculum. Many teachers find it difficult to do what they would like to do with their learners because there simply is not time, or they are constrained by exams. Using these technologies can provide the space to add to the learners' experiences of language and perhaps excite them at the same time.

There is a good deal of discussion about whether IWBs promote teacher-fronted classrooms and many teachers see them as having a negative impact on attempts to promote learner communication. This is because they are seen to place the teacher centre-stage, managing and orchestrating the class.

12.8.4 Interactivity and user-friendliness: what kind of interaction does this technology enable? How easy is it to use?

The tools are easy to use and the level of interactivity depends on what the teacher wants to include in their materials.

If set up correctly and calibrated, IWBs can be used very effectively to display and demonstrate language material.

12.8.5 Organisational issues: what are the organisational requirements, and the barriers to be removed, before this technology can be used successfully? What changes in organisation need to be made?

Both blogs and Moodle can be set up in an organisation, or they can be mounted on an external server. Most teachers can learn how to do this without any problem. Access to computer rooms in schools is often difficult for language teachers, but perhaps by doing this kind of activity, the guardians of the computer room key can be persuaded that the teacher is trusted to use their shiny new boxes.

It is clear that equipping every classroom with an IWB is a big investment. The teachers will also need to be trained to use them. If only a few classrooms are fitted with IWBs, then there is the need to have a booking system and to move classes around.

12.8.6 Novelty: how new is this technology?

All of these technologies have been around for some time, and have a large user base of people doing similar things.

12.8.7 Speed: how quickly can courses be mounted with this technology? How quickly can materials be changed?

This material takes longer to produce than that described in the first section, but the skills are an extension of the earlier developments. The materials can be changed and updated very quickly.

This section has shown how teachers using blogs and VLEs can build and develop their materials development skills in small stages, so that they move from consumers of the digital world to contributors along with their learners. IWBs also enable teachers to extend their basic skills in materials development and they can either use the ready-made software that accompanies coursebooks or, using the flipchart software, can extend what they were doing at the basic level.

12.9 Pushing the boundaries further

There are many tools available to help teachers enhance what they do in classrooms. All the materials that I described earlier could be produced in software tools such as Flash; this is a programming environment that allows for the development of animated materials. In a larger organisation there may well be staff who are able to use Flash and can be called upon to help develop specific materials. Many of the interactive exercises that are produced and sold on CD-ROMs or found on the Internet are produced using this software. A teacher can go further with blogs, or learn how to create a website with more traditional tools. If they want to develop more social interaction with their learners, they can explore other types of social networking software, or perhaps venture into a virtual world. The basic materials development techniques that have been discussed here can be built on and extended. For example a virtual world such as Second Life can either be used as a place to go and meet, or a school or college can rent its own island (in fact the British Council does so) and begin to create virtual spaces that can be used for a variety of activities (see Chapter 13, section 13.2.2 for more on the British Council island on Second Life). Teachers can learn how to build and script the objects that make the virtual world what it is.

Another area for development is that of mobile technologies. Many of us carry a powerful teaching tool in our pockets and whilst mobile phones have not been used extensively yet in language teaching, they are a technology that our learners are familiar with and we will clearly be seeing more of them alongside other mobile devices.

I have made the case that teachers should engage with digital technologies. They are now an important part of people's everyday lives and should be seen in educational contexts. To avoid them is to impoverish education, and in this chapter I hope I have shown how to get started with materials development using new technologies, and how to build on that initial step to create ever more interesting and worthwhile materials.

References

Bates, A. 1995. *Technology, Open Learning and Distance Education*. London: Routledge.

Cha, M., H. Kwak, P. Rodriguez, Y. Y. Ahn, and S. Moon. 2007. 'I tube, you tube, everybody tubes: analyzing the world's largest user generated content video system'. *Proceedings of the 7th ACM SIGCOMM Conference on Internet Measurement*. San Diego, California, USA.

Chesney, T. 2006. 'An empirical examination of Wikipedia's credibility'. *First Monday*, 11(11). Online: http://firstmonday.org

Clark, R. C and R. E. Mayer. 2007. *e-Learning and the Science of Instruction: Proven Guidelines for Consumers and Designers of Multimedia Learning*. San Francisco: Josey Bass.

Cousin, G. 2005. 'Learning from cyberspace'. In R. Land, R. Bayne and S. Bayne (eds.), *Education in Cyberspace*. Abingdon: RoutledgeFalmer.

Cutrim, E. S. 2008. 'Using a voting system in conjunction with interactive whiteboard technology to enhance learning in the English language classroom'. *Computers and Education*, 50(1): 338–56.

Ducate, L. C. and L. L. Lomicka. 2005. 'Exploring the Blogosphere: Use of Web Logs in the Foreign Language Classroom'. *Foreign Language Annals*, 38(3): 410–21.

Ellis, R. 2003. *Task-Based Language Learning and Teaching*. Oxford: Oxford University Press.

Godwin-Jones, R. 2003. 'Emerging technologies: blogs and wikis: environments for on-line collaboration'. *Language Learning & Technology*, 7(2).

Higgins, J. and T. Johns. 1984. *Computers in Language Learning*. Collins ELT.

Orr, M. 2008. 'Learner perceptions of interactive whiteboards in EFL classrooms'. *CALL-EJ Online*, 9(2). Online: www.tell.is.ritsumei.ac.jp/callejonline/journal/9–2/orr.html

Pegrum, M. 2009. *From Blogs to Bombs*. Crawley, Western Australia: University of Western Australia Press.

Reinders, H. and C. White. 2010. 'The theory and practice of technology in materials development and task design'. In N. Harwood (ed.), *English Language Teaching Materials; Theory and Practice*. Cambridge: Cambridge University Press.

Ward, J. M. 2004. 'Blog assisted language learning: push button publishing for pupils'. Online: www.teflweb-j.org/v3n1/blog_ward.pdf

Warschauer, M. and D. Healey. 1998. 'Computers and language learning: an overview'. *Language Teaching*, 31: 57–71.

White, C. 2003. *Language Learning in Distance Education*. Cambridge: Cambridge University Press.

13 New technologies to support language learning

Lisa Kervin and Beverly Derewianka

13.1 Introduction

Language classrooms have always used technologies of various kinds, from the blackboard through to the language laboratory. In recent decades, however, there has been an explosion in the resources available to teachers, to the point where many feel overwhelmed. This chapter, therefore, does not attempt to provide a comprehensive review of 'state of the art' technologies – primarily because the ground is shifting so rapidly that any such endeavour would soon be out of date. Rather, we have kept in mind an audience who are not necessarily interested in the finer points of technological innovations but who are seeking some practical input on those advances that are productive in fostering their students' learning.

When it comes to electronic learning materials, we need to take into account the hardware, the software and the actual content such resources make available and the methodologies they promote. Ultimately, however, we are concerned with the quality of learning that these resources facilitate and the extent to which their use reflects sound learning theory:

- is the input relevant, accurate, accessible and yet rich?
- what kinds of interaction are encouraged?
- what degree of support is provided and how are learners encouraged towards greater autonomy?
- how is useful feedback provided?
- is motivation stimulated?

Blake (2008) describes the successful technology-enhanced FL curriculum as student-centred, carefully planned, technically well supported and, most importantly, pedagogically well constructed.

In this chapter we will look at how teaching the macroskills (listening, speaking, reading and writing) might be enhanced through the incorporation of various digital materials. At each point we provide concrete examples of resources to illustrate the use of new technologies in language learning which classroom teachers have found to be useful in supporting their students' language development. In concluding, we consider various pedagogical implications and speculate about future developments.

In exploring the role of the various technologies in learning, we have found it useful to think of language use along a continuum from 'most spoken' (oral interaction where language accompanies some activity in a shared physical environment) through to 'most written' (where texts need to be able to be understood by others who might be distant in time and space, independent of any shared experience). Moving along the mode continuum also involves a shift from more spontaneous, unplanned discourse where meanings are collaboratively constructed towards more heavily crafted, sustained, planned monologues. Learning at the more 'spoken' end of the continuum tends to involve interactive, 'first draft', exploratory language, where there is an assumption of shared knowledge. The value of such activity lies in the support provided by the immediate context and in the joint construction of meaning, with interactants supporting each other by elaborating, repeating, adjusting input, providing feedback, supplying relevant vocabulary, and so on. Towards the 'more written' end of the continuum, the learning potential changes. With the shift to a slower pace comes the opportunity to reflect on language use. There is now time to think, to consolidate, to research unfamiliar territory, to develop sustained arguments, to consider the audience's needs, and to manage the organisation of extended texts. And as a reader, there is the time to read and re-read, to make connections, to work out obscure meanings, and, in the case of multimodal texts, to study the composition of the visual elements and to examine the relationship between the images and the accompanying text.

Figure 13.1 maps the use of various technologies along the mode continuum. There is, of course, no strict correlation between medium and mode. Emails, for example, can be quite 'spoken-like'. However, it

Figure 13.1   The mode continuum

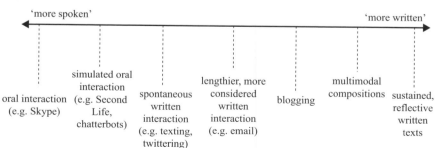

329

enables us to see how various technologies can contribute to different kinds of learning depending on where their use falls on the continuum.

13.2 Enabling interaction

At the 'most spoken' end of the continuum we find oral interaction. Current language-learning theory stresses the role of collaborative dialogue in language learning (Gass 1997; Swain 2000). Traditionally, this has meant face-to-face oral exchanges. This has posed dilemmas for many classrooms in terms of time constraints and the availability of proficient speakers as interactants. Recent advances in technology, however, have forced a rethink. We now have the capability of interacting in a variety of modes and media at the spoken end of the continuum, even though they might not always involve the physical act of speaking. Here we will note a few of these opportunities for interaction.

13.2.1 Oral interaction

The design of many digital activities invites face-to-face interactivity around problem-solving tasks in the classroom. Learners typically become so engrossed in achieving the objectives that they put aside their inhibitions around producing accurate sentences and instead push their boundaries in their attempts to make themselves understood.

Modern technology, however, also allows for oral interaction without being physically face-to-face, as in the use of Voice over Internet Protocol (VoIP) applications such as Skype, Tokbox videochat, ooVoo and Polycom systems. Each of these technologies enables voice communications to be transmitted via the Internet through use of a broadband connection and a computer with a microphone and a webcam. Whereas previously telephone conversations and videoconferences were prohibitively expensive and impractical, VoIP and Skype allow for cheap (or free) local and international interactions between individuals or groups. With a whole class it is possible to project images onto a full screen and pass the microphone around to allow individuals to talk with a guest speaker. Despite certain security issues such as susceptibility to hackers and the fact that the technology is still relatively primitive in terms of its visual quality, teachers are using these technologies to promote interaction in a variety of innovative ways:

- for online tutoring and peer tutoring
- for project work with students from other institutions

- for homework hotlines
- for conferencing with e-pals
- for connecting students from different schools who are preparing for a combined arts festival or vacation camp or immersion visit
- for groups of students participating in cultural exchange activities, talking about, for example, what they eat for lunch or their artwork or dramatisations they have prepared
- for linking students with experts in their field (e.g. medical students being interviewed by secondary students; authors being interviewed by students who are reading their novels).

The following anecdote provides an idea of how Skype is being used in classrooms:

I was walking down the corridor, when I passed a year nine boy carrying a box with straw in. When I looked to see what he had, it was a blue tongued lizard. So, I suggested he see if he could be dismissed from his usual class for 10 mins or so, as we were about to skype with Korea Uijeongbu Science HS again.

As we logged on, Nat came in with the lizard. So we were able to show our friends in Korea the lizard, which is an Australian animal, by placing him up to our small web cam. The Korean students could actually see the little blue tongue poking in and out.

Next, our students asked what the weather was today, and the reply was that it was snowing. To our amazement, they took their camera to the window and we could see a school yard of beautiful snow falls complete with a Korean sweeping the snow with his stick type broom. It was simply amazing!!! We do not get snow at Hawkesdale.

Another question posed to us was 'do we play cricket'. Cricket!!!! What a question! Of course we play cricket. One of the girls tried to describe the game but it was difficult, so she went off, collected a cricket ball, stumps and bat and demonstrated a game of cricket in the library. The questions soon came about the ball – was it soft or heavy? etc. Students lost their nervousness with each other and the self activated education flowed. Of course, we then had to get a meat pie – one of our favourite foods and show it to the camera. It is also difficult to describe verbally but is reasonably obvious visually (at least looks, shape etc, is). 'Is it sweet?', one student asked? Korean students then were able to show us their mobile phones. Next they lined up with their uniforms, which were beautifully tailored and we showed then our summer uniforms via the camera.

(http://murch.globalteacher.org.au/2007/12/07/blue-tongue-lizard-vegemite-and-cricket-what-the/)

Another example of a Skype project is *Around the World with 80 Schools*, initiated by an elementary school in Jacksonville, Florida that took on the challenge to circle the globe, connecting with at least 80 schools in different countries and continents: http://aroundtheworld with80schools.wikispaces.com/
Other useful sites[1] include:

http://skypeinschools.pbworks.com/

http://theedublogger.edublogs.org/want-to-connect-with-other-classrooms/

13.2.2 Interacting in simulated environments

Virtual worlds such as Second Life (a parallel 'society' accessed through the Internet) provide opportunities for interaction in a three-dimensional space populated by a wide variety of residents who take on new identities and create an alternative existence. Whilst not specifically designed as a language-learning resource, it does nevertheless provide the potential for interaction within a realistic, social, immersive setting that has the capacity to support learners in their attempts to construct meaning.

The British Council, for example, has created an island within Teen Second Life which is a self-access centre geared towards the learning of English in an environment that appeals to tech-savvy young people. It simulates a visit to the UK and includes interactive learning activities, games, treasure hunts and quests based on UK culture. In this environment students can explore, meet others and participate in individual and group activities.

An online language school, Avatar English (www.avatarlanguages. com/home.php?lang=en), combines Second Life with Skype and other online teaching tools which allow learners and the teacher to work together on the same activity. Classes take place in custom-built virtual classrooms that reflect the theme of the classes, such as airports, markets, banks and cinemas. Similarly, sites such as Languagelab simulate a city where language learners can engage in activities such as checking in at the airport, visiting an art museum or visiting a business centre to give a presentation.

---

[1] Throughout the chapter the URLs of various sites have been included to provide examples. We recognise, however, that there is rapid change on the Internet and the sites can become dated or even disappear. In this case, a search engine such as Google can be used to locate similar sites on the topic of interest.

Figure 13.2 *Visual from the British Council 'island' on Teen Second Life (http://teen.secondlife.com)*

Figure 13.3 *Simulated conversation on the Languagelab site (Source: www.Languagelab.com/en/)*

13.2.3 Interacting through writing

Moving along the mode continuum we find interactions which mimic oral conversations but which employ the written mode, using instant messaging applications such as Short Message Service (SMS), ICQ (a homophone for the phrase 'I seek you'), Twitter and Google Talk.

Each of these enable the transmission of short typed messages: SMS enables messages to be shared between mobile devices (such as mobile telephones), the Internet enables instant messaging through applications such as ICQ and Google Talk, and Twitter is a social networking service that enables users to send and receive messages referred to as 'tweets'. Although the interactions are now written, they nevertheless have the characteristics of language at the more spoken end of the continuum. They are typically spontaneous, jointly constructed and located in the 'here and now'. They differ, however, in the fact that the interactants don't share the same physical space and that oral cues such as intonation and facial expressions are not available. This puts extra demands on second language learners as they do not have support from the immediate context – though on the other hand they are able to relax and reflect in the protection of greater anonymity.

Whereas texting generally involves short private messages between individuals often in real time, twittering is a microblogging service where messages of less than 140 characters ('tweets') are shared publicly. Language teachers have been quick on the uptake of this resource, such as projects involving e-twinning, where tweets are exchanged in multiple languages between sister institutions in a 'twinned' relationship, as in the exchanges between students of English and Italian in the USA and Italy in Figure 13.4.

The value of instant messaging for language learning lies in the rapidity, volume and authenticity of the interactions. The repetitious nature of the messages and their use of rather elementary structures and vocabulary, however, present a limitation for the more advanced learner.

Chat rooms often enable somewhat fuller conversations. These are social spaces where a number of participants interact socially around common interests or engage in playing games. Many language teachers have embraced the use of chat as an effective communication tool. The

Figure 13.4 *Example of students using Twitter to interact (Source: http://martini.wetpaint.com/page/E-twinning)*

speed of chat presents opportunity for short, spontaneous exchanges. Systems such as AOL Instant Messenger or MSN Messenger allow the creation of 'buddy lists' – groupings of participants from different countries or social contexts who interact on a frequent basis generally in real time. Opportunities for the addition of voice and video options for communication increase the possibilities for instant messaging to support language learners.

Compared with the more nimble twittering, texting and chatting, tools such as email and listservs can appear somewhat ponderous and clumsy. Whilst the interaction is generally less immediate, they do lend themselves to more extended, considered responses of the type we would find towards the middle of the mode continuum, where there is still a degree of interactivity but the texts are often (though not always) longer and more reflective. In language learning, there is still a place for these more leisurely interactions which allow time for more careful structuring of responses, more elaborated sentences, the extension of vocabulary through the use of dictionaries and thesauri, and the more careful attention to interpersonal choices.

13.2.4 Interacting with non-human partners

Whilst natural interaction in authentic contexts represents the preferred option for language learning, it is often the case that this does not provide the kind of intensive, sustained practice needed to consolidate learning. To this end, extensive work in artificial intelligence has been undertaken in developing adaptive and responsive iCALL (intelligent CALL) programs using automatic speech recognition (ASR). Whilst some programs simply give feedback on pronunciation and syntax, others enable interaction with a 'patient tutor' as part of a self-directed learning program such as Jabberwacky. One such resource is a 'chatterbot' ('bot' being short for 'robot'), designed to simulate an intelligent conversation with a human user through both typed input and synthesised speech.

The advantages include that they can be used anywhere at any time, they are generally free or cheap, they engender confidence, they can 'converse' on a wide range of topics and engage in lengthy interactions, and they can take on 'personalities' and learn as they interact, ensuring novelty. Jabberwacky, for example, learns from every interaction and adjusts to its interactants. A transcript of conversations can be produced so that learners can return to their chat sessions and self-assess. In their current state, however, such tools are more of a novelty and most useful for advanced learners. The technology is very much in its infancy and chatterbots are incapable of providing the kind of contingent microscaffolding that teachers provide to learners.

Figure 13.5   *Example of a conversation with a Jabberwacky*
chatterbot (www.jabberwacky.com)

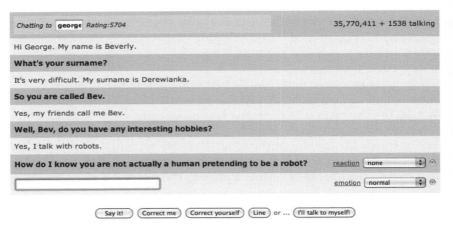

13.3 Speaking and pronunciation

For those learners who want to improve their speaking skills there are numerous software applications and programs available that encourage multiple revisitings of specific sounds and intonation patterns.

Software applications such as GarageBand provide opportunities for voice to be recorded, listened to and waveforms analysed. For example, a teacher (or other proficient language user) can record their voice on one of the available tracks. Students can then record their own voice on another track as they repeat and emulate the spoken language model provided on the first track. Comparing these tracks through the 'audio region' function enables the learner to analyse the two samples through the visual representation provided as they investigate similarities and differences between the two samples (see Figure 13.6).

A useful website from Cambridge University Press (Figure 13.7) presents entertaining animations to reinforce individual phonemes and sound patterns. If you click on the Word Stress button, for example, the word is pronounced whilst the stressed syllable of the written word becomes emboldened and expands. When a sentence is read aloud, the written text rises and falls to indicate the intonation contours. And animated cartoons illustrate particular sounds.

For detailed work on phonemes, a website designed by the University of Iowa allows you to select sounds according to their manner of articulation, their place of articulation or their voice quality. Once you have

Figure 13.6 Comparison of master track with student recording using GarageBand

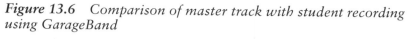

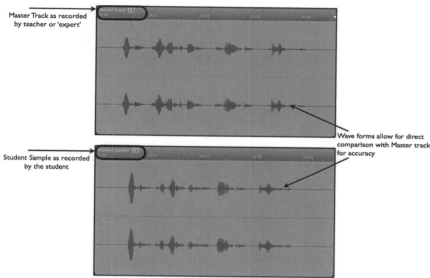

chosen a specific sound, you are provided with an animated diagram of the mouth demonstrating exactly how the sound is made along with a video of someone actually saying the sound (see Figure 13.8).

Whilst recognising the role of listening as part of an interactive exchange, it is sometimes useful to be able to treat listening as a discrete skill, providing our students with practice in purposeful attention to oral input. Attentive listening is an area that often has been relatively neglected. With the current abundance of online listening materials, however, it has started to gain increased prominence. Resources available electronically include both oral input and multimodal input (involving audio and visual material).

A major source of listening materials is made available through podcasting – the process of delivering content to an individual's computer or mobile device via an automated download through the Internet. Podcasts can take one of three forms:

1. Audio-based content (a sound file)
2. Enhanced content (inclusive of audio, visuals and text)
3. Video (often referred to as a vodcast)

The phenomenon of podcasting has quickly become a powerful tool in contemporary society. Language-focused podcasts are the most popular

Figure 13.7   *Animated sound cartoon providing pronunciation of diphthongs (Source: www.cambridge.org/elt/resources/skills/ interactive/pron_animations/index.htm)*

form of educational podcast (Apple.com/iTunes, July 2009). These free podcasts present a range of opportunities for learners to engage with listening experiences. Once a podcast library has been sourced and initially subscribed to, RSS (Really Simple Syndication) feeds update the computer or mobile device as new content is added to the library.

Oral input presented as audio files focuses the language learner on attending to the sound stream. The inclusion of both audio and visual elements (for example through still images or video clips) enables the learner to use contextual cues to support comprehension. Opportunities to both access and create these texts present potentially rich learning experiences for language learners.

The accessibility of video clips has increased enormously with the advent of Web 2.0 applications used on such sites as YouTube, MySpace and Google Video, and due to the ease of uploading video material recorded using digital cameras, PDA (Personal Digital Assistant, also referred to as a palmtop computer) webcams or even cell phones.

Figure 13.8 *Animations illustrating production of English sounds (Source: www.uiowa.edu/~acadtech/phonetics/english/frameset.html)*

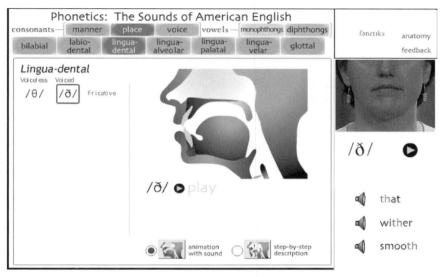

Figure 13.9 *Examples of podcast resources*

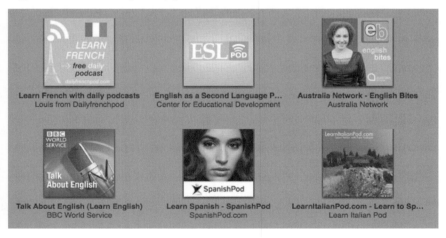

Without any prompting from teachers, learners are spending hours immersing themselves in videos covering a huge range of authentic subject matter. Many of them engage in interactions around the videos, posting their brief responses in the comment box. Apart from the video clips available on YouTube and similar sites, streaming video of many television programs is now freely available – a source of much more predictable and professional video material. The SCOLA website, for example, provides access to over 100 edited television programs in 95 different languages along with transcripts and English translations.

Apart from readily available audio and video material that learners access primarily from the Internet in their 'raw' state, there are listening materials that are structured specifically for language learners, using audiovisual content that is either authentic, semi-authentic (i.e. modified or simplified) or custom-made.

Some instructors, for example, create their own video activities on specific topics to share with their students, using video editing tools such as Jumpcut or Videoegg (Windows) or iMovie (Macintosh). To assist students to deal with listening to native speakers interacting at normal speaking rates and using authentic language, support can be provided through captions, vocabulary activities, annotations and transcripts. Victory Author, for example, from Purdue University provides templates for creating video-based lessons that include interactive exercises. Also, students can be encouraged to create their own videos for sharing with others. These might include projects they have completed, musical items or dramatisations.

For those who feel daunted by the time-consuming process of preparing video materials, there are language immersion sites such as Yabla, which provide authentic television, music videos, drama, interviews, and travel videos which can be used in slow play with integrated dictionaries, listening games and dual language subtitles.

The Virtex project (www.worldenough.net/virtex/) uses digital video clips depicting real-life scenarios to prepare foreign language students for work placements in hotels and catering. The students watch repeated replays of a conversational exchange or an on-the-job interaction. After watching the video, the students can access background information, transcripts, learning tips, isolated audio playback, cultural notes or lists of idiomatic expressions. Students are then asked to answer questions relating to the specific information in the video.

The BBC website also provides an abundance of video material both from its own archives and created specifically for language learners and teachers. The series called Six Minute English takes a current news item and reworks it for learners of English, including comprehension activities and audio podcasts that can be downloaded for listening at leisure. There is also a series on Academic Listening that introduces students to the skills involved in listening to lectures for specific information.

Figure 13.10 *Example of a video clip from Yabla with supporting activities (www.yabla.com)*

Robin (2007) makes a distinction between the kinds of 'pre-packaged' resources mentioned above (where students are reliant on audiovisual materials developed by instructors or companies) and the wealth of 'unpackaged' resources readily available through sites such as YouTube. Rather than restricting students to the pre-packaged resources, Robin argues that students should be taught to exploit the potential of the unpackaged material by learning to deploy those user-controlled technological devices that currently support mainstream listening and viewing, such as repeated audio/video delivery, slowed speed, links to related texts and images, chunking, textual and pictorial glossing aides, captioning, scripts and translation bots ('web robots' that perform specific tasks on the Internet).

13.4 Reading

One of the most obvious benefits of the Internet for language teachers is the unprecedented access to a copious supply of authentic reading material such as newspaper reports, stories, recipes, craft activities, geographic information and journal articles. Whilst these can be engaging and motivating, they can also pose comprehension problems for the language learner, particularly the more dense and abstract texts at the written end of the mode continuum.

A major obstacle to reading comprehension is encountering unknown vocabulary items. New technologies, however, provide a number of supports for the reader that were not previously so readily available during the reading process. Using the online program WordChamp, for example, you can insert a reading passage (or a URL) into a text box and then roll the cursor over any word, activating a pop-up with a definition of that word in any selected language and an audio clip pronouncing the word. Using a search facility, examples of the word from literary texts are provided to illustrate the item in use. Similarly, the Academic Word List Highlighter allows you to enter a text which is then analysed, displaying in bold all the common academic words, enabling the reader to focus on frequently encountered words from academic contexts.

Visual elements in multimodal texts provide considerable support for the reader in comprehending the verbal text. Photos, illustrations, maps and diagrams of various kinds offer visual cues, allowing the reader to make informed guesses about the meaning of unknown words. They also make available rich sources of information on culturally embedded concepts and practices.

Various software programs provide support by the inclusion of aural cues. The reader can select a sound track to accompany the written text. This can be stopped, repeated or slowed down at any point. As the sound clip plays, it is often possible to have the text highlighted in time with the spoken words.

It is often the case that readers need assistance in reading complex images and diagrams. Here animations can be used to access the visual information. A dense diagram, for example, can be built up incrementally, so that the reader can understand how the various parts of the diagram relate to each other. Magnifications can zoom in and out, highlighting particular features. Timelines can unfold to represent a series of events. Animated processes can explain how something works.

Apart from making texts more accessible, technology can be used to teach students strategies for comprehension, enabling them to become more independent readers and to engage in deep processing. Rollover prompts can be inserted into the text at key points, for example, encouraging the reader to predict, or to guess from context, or to use skimming and scanning skills, or to attend to topic sentences, or to refer to a relevant image. Use of such tools, in connection with strong pedagogical practices, can support students in achieving the deep processing of information. Similarly, questions can be inserted in the text to raise students' critical awareness: 'how does the use of this word affect your perception of the issue?'; 'why did the writer choose to use *perhaps* here?'; 'whose perspective is being privileged at this point?'; 'who is excluded from this image?' The value of such roll-overs lies in their immediacy and their embeddedness in the context, modelling for the learners the kinds of questions they themselves could be asking.

13.5 Writing and composing

Moving along the mode continuum towards the more 'written' end, beyond the spoken-like texting and twittering, we find writing of a more sustained, reflective nature, where greater attention is paid to the composing process.

Sitting around the mid-point of the continuum, we might locate discussion forums, which provide an avenue for learners to communicate meaningfully with peers and teachers. Discussion forums enable asynchronous group exchanges, and they maintain automatically a log of all messages in a threaded, hierarchical structure. Discussion forums are often seen as an equalising tool, which encourage universal participation in discussion compared to face-to-face dialogue. There is a range of software applications available to facilitate online discussion forums (such as WWWBoard, WebCT, Blackboard and WebCrossing).

In a similar vein, we have the more recent phenomenon of blogging. Blogs (or web logs) are essentially online journals. Webpages are authored with writers able to use hypertext to connect their own text to what others have written or to resources on the Web. A comment button typically follows a blog entry. This enables readers to compose a response, which is then logged and linked, along with all other comments, into the original text. Whilst most blogs are created and managed by individuals, group blogs are also possible as blogs are linked and cross-linked to create larger online communities. Although not necessarily the case, blogs tend to offer more considered views, dealing with an issue at some length. Writers tend to spend some time thinking about how to present their viewpoint and how to engage with prospective respondents. The development of the blog becomes a collaborative process, with authorship distributed amongst several interactants, in ways that writing in hard copy could never achieve. For the language learner, blogging provides an opportunity to participate in the composing process without the pressure to produce a whole text independently. Language learners could utilise a personal blog, linked to a course, as an electronic portfolio to demonstrate development over time. Sun (2009) found that students perceived blogging as a means of learning, self-presentation, information exchange and social networking and that they foster extensive practice, learning motivation, authorship and development of learning strategies. The following sites provide useful examples of blogs:

www.blogs.com/topten/top-10-language-learning-blogs/

www.transparent.com/arabic/

http://chinesequest.blogspot.com/index.html

www.transparent.com/irish/

Likewise, wikis (a website with interlinked pages that can be easily edited) allow for multiple writers to contribute towards the development of a text. In this case it is not a matter of responding to issues raised, as in blogging, but of jointly working on the construction of a text, generally providing information on a particular area of interest. Writing within a wiki enables authors to create, share and edit text on a series of interconnected webpages. Wikis feature loosely structured sets of pages, which are linked in multiple ways to each other and to internet resources. They contain an open-editing system in which anyone can edit any page using simple formatting commands (similar to word processing software). The goal of wiki sites is to become a shared repository of knowledge, with the knowledge base expanding but becoming more refined over time. In Wikipedia, for example, anyone can initiate a text on any topic. Others can then amend the details of the text or add further information. Again, the individual writer is relieved of taking responsibility for the whole text but can still experience what is involved in the writing process: researching the information, considering how best to communicate that information, selecting appropriate vocabulary, thinking about the audience and purpose, and so on.

Some useful wiki resources include:

Wikispaces – www.wikispaces.com

PB wiki – http://pbwiki.com

WetPaint – www.wetpaint.com

Stikipad – http://stikipad.com

OttoWiki – www.ottowiki.com

A common environment for telecollaboration is webquests or enquiry-oriented study, where learners undertake online research tasks involving advanced word processing skills, desktop publishing, authoring webpages, the creation and use of templates and the production of video, resulting in a multimedia composition which can be shared online with peers, parents, assessors and the general public (http://webquest.org/index.php provides an introduction to webquests). One such initiative is the Flat Classrooms Project, where students from the USA, Qatar, Oman, Spain and Australia participated in a range of projects including such topics as The New Age of Connectivity, The Changing Shape of Information, Google Takes Over the World, and Social Networking, culminating in a virtual global student summit (http://flatclassroom project2008.wikispaces.com/Topics). Using wikis and videos, students from the different schools collaborated in responding to questions such as: where will this trend take us? How do you envision the future? Do you think this trend will be replaced with another? What inventions are needed because of this trend? Collaborative projects can be stimulating contexts for deep learning of substantial content; however, they require a great deal of organisation and management. And there is the danger that the time spent on learning to use the tools and constructing the multimodal elements could outweigh the language-learning outcomes.

Whilst new technologies encourage the joint authoring of texts and interactivity between the modes ('reading to write and writing to read'), one of the greatest challenges for language learners is to independently write the kinds of extended, individually authored texts valued in academic contexts which are located firmly at the reflective, 'highly written' end of the mode continuum. Even though the composing of sustained written texts is typically a solitary, private activity, digital technologies can assist in various ways. Spelling and grammar checks and the availability of an online thesaurus have made the writing process much more efficient. Such tools, however, do not address issues concerned with the construction of meaning, the overall organisation of the text and appropriate register choices. This is where tools such as 'track changes' and 'insert comments' can allow instructors and peers to give relevant, timely feedback on such matters in electronic form. As an alternative, learners can be provided with repositories of model texts, with animations demonstrating how such texts are organised to achieve their purpose and with language features highlighted that are characteristic of such genres. A similar approach was adopted by the Bridges to China project (Brown 2005) where self-assessment was facilitated by annotated samples of learner-produced texts, elucidating both the criteria for judging performance and the standards expected. Writefix (www.writefix.com/) also models text organisation, paragraphing and transition words.

13.6 Grammar and vocabulary

Whilst there is a place for grammar and vocabulary exercises, it has to be said that there is a great deal of poorly designed material on the Internet and teachers and students are well advised to exercise care.

In the selection of web resources we would encourage consideration of the following:

• Who has created the resource?
• Who is the resource intended for?
• What is the underpinning grammatical theory?
• How accurate are any supporting notes that are provided?

Much of the material is simply textbook drills transposed online. Chapelle and Jamieson (2008: 41) caution that grammar activities presented on many websites 'are rather limited, as context is often at sentence level and practice is often in the form of recognition [instead of meaningful production]'.

There are some activities, however, which do exploit the potential of digital technology to a certain extent. Scootle (www.scootle.edu.au/ec/p/home, accessible in Australia only), for example, hosts some 8,000 digital learning resources, many of which have been created for language learning. In one learning object learners watch an animated story and then have to recreate the text by rearranging scrambled sentences, concurrently learning to recognise the grammatical categories involved (e.g., Who? Did what? Where?). The student then uses a simple 'drag and drop' technique to select and insert vocabulary items from a word bank to enhance the otherwise bland text (see Figure 13.11).

The BBC news website has a number of vocabulary activities based on current news stories (see Figure 13.12).

One area in which digital technology has been used to achieve previously impossible outcomes in relation to vocabulary and syntax is the development of language corpora – huge collections of texts assembled in a database that can be searched in a variety of ways. The Collins WordbanksOnline English corpus sampler (www.collins.co.uk/Corpus/CorpusSearch.aspx), for example, is composed of 56 million words of contemporary written and spoken text from British and American books, radio broadcasts, newspapers, magazines and transcribed speech. By using a concordancing tool, it is possible to retrieve innumerable examples of any particular word together with its immediate context. If, for example, you want to see what *anxious* is typically preceded or followed by, you might be provided with the examples in Figure 13.13.

The learner can thus see that you can *become, get,* or *be anxious,* that the degree of anxiety can be indicated by *really, fairly, a bit, very, too, quite, sort of* and *absolutely,* and that *anxious* can be followed by *about, to* and *that* constructions. Concordancers can provide instructors with a wealth of examples of authentic vocabulary used in context along with the words or structures with which they are typically

Figure 13.11   *Grammar activity from Scootle (www.scootle.edu.au/ ec/p/home)*

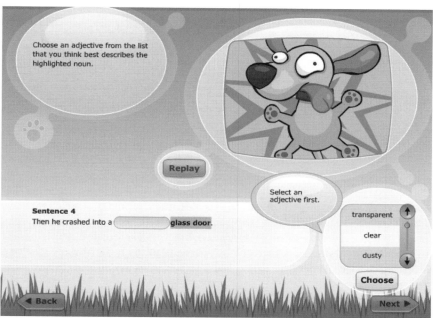

Figure 13.12   *Vocabulary activities on BBC news site*

Figure 13.13   Results from concordancing program for the word 'anxious'

```
in the city have [ZFO] in the city has become anxious about are very seriously thinking of the
family and is very good if for example you get anxious about talking like on the way here I [ZGY]
lot this weekend [MO1] Yeah. [MO6] and I'll be anxious to see what they're like. Erm beautiful
written material with the spoken [ZGY] really anxious to get [ZF1] the [ZFO] the new corpus on the
MX is now at one of the colleges there and is anxious to continue his association with us. I think
Certainly when I was in Italy I had a fairly anxious B B C man erm [MOX] Oh aye. [FOX] talking to
appendicitis you see. The mother's still a bit anxious because he also has this sore throat so she
Angry. [MOX] [ZF1] Sh [ZFO] She is really anxious to know what where we were on the roof and
her first language etcetera and she was very anxious and angry. [ZF1] You can't [ZFO] you can't
were a lot of young married women only too anxious really not to er you know she didn't feel
on that but they weren't act they were quite anxious to work in the Birmingham factories who were
Yeah. [MO2] really apart from the sort of anxious to avoid the war. [MO1] Mm. [FO1] And of
er anxious to return to this side. [MO1] Er anxious good wishes of my mother and so on 'cos you
that I told the secretary that I was very anxious to? [MO2] Return to this side. [MO1] She
people in the Conservative Party who were very anxious to have a word with er er MX [tc text=pause]
t remember w At about this time the government anxious to tell us that erm universities dealt with
The Ministry the then Ministry of Health was anxious about the shortage of houses er er in the
to write letters. And I used to be absolutely anxious to put money into [tc text=pause] er the
[FO2] And many people when they feel a bit anxious and humiliated if I had to take a letter to
I was at great pains not to be I was very anxious about talking about something painful want
er [ZF1] I was er [ZFO] I was sort of really anxious not to be erm regarded as somebody who
                                              anxious that I hope there are some girls on the
```

associated, providing the basis for exploratory, constructivist learning activities investigating how language is actually used by native speakers. Lextutor (www.lextutor.ca/concordancers/concord_e.html) offers similar concordancing resources but also includes a dictionary, a cloze building device, hypertext links and a database with an interactive self-quizzing feature.

Further information on concordancing can be found in Chapter 2 of this volume by Randi Reppen, in Chapter 3 by Jane Willis and at:

www.ecml.at/projects/voll/our_resources/graz_2002/ddrivenlrning/concordancing/concordancing.htm

13.7 Integrated learning environments

So far we have dealt with the macroskills independently of each other and with the various digital resources as relatively discrete phenomena. It is important to note, however, the ways in which these are brought together in a single online context.

Social networking sites such as Facebook and MySpace, for example, provide opportunities for motivated, authentic interaction and allow input through a variety of media (video, photos, audio). Such sites, however, are generally relatively limited in terms of providing substantial content, so sites designed specifically for language learning have been developed. These use integrative learning management systems (or personal learning environments) where students are provided with a range of tools, applications and activities in a single context which they can utilise with varying degrees of flexibility and independence, making for a richer language-learning experience, particularly when the various media support each other. Examples of such sites include Moodle (a virtual learning environment that provides access to highly collaborative communities of learning, forums, wikis, databases, quizzes and so on) and Livemocha (a social network service with three million members, which seeks to build an engaged global language community, where learners support each other through peer tutoring, along with more structured reading, listening, writing and speaking exercises). For teachers who prefer their students to interact within a closed social network site, they can use an application such as Ning – a site that allows you to create your own customised social network on which members can post discussion items, blogs, photos and videos. Rather than being limited to the categories on any 'pre-packaged' social networking site, teachers and students can create their own sites based on the interests of their specific learning community.

13.8 Pedagogical considerations

In considering the use of electronic materials and learning environments, teachers should bear in mind:

- how the electronic material fits with the aims, outcomes and objectives of the proposed learning experience:
  - Why am I using this material?
  - What connections can I make between the electronic material and curriculum expectations?
- connections between the electronic material and learning theory:
  - How does the resource match my beliefs about language learning?
- connections between the electronic materials and student learning needs:
  - How will my students engage with the resource?
  - How does it support identified learning needs?
- specific pedagogical practices needed to support the use of the electronic material during the language teaching and learning experience:
  - What information, skills and strategies do the students need to engage with the material?
  - What explicit modelling and scaffolding of the necessary knowledge, skills and strategies do I need to offer?

- How will they be able to analyse, interpret, synthesise and evaluate the input provided by the electronic material?

The electronic materials available to support language teaching will continue to change and expand. What is critical, though, is that teachers have a clear rationale for the use of any materials within teaching and learning experiences.

13.9 The potential of electronic materials to transform teaching and learning

We have seen that there is a plethora of digital resources available to language teachers and learners. In this chapter we have sampled but a few of these in terms of how they might be incorporated into language programs as we currently know them. The challenge, however, is not to see digital resources as 'add-ons' but to understand how profoundly they are changing the very nature of teaching and learning, bringing about new ways of knowing and, indeed, new ways of being. Kress (2003: 16) sees these new modes as 'governed by distinct logics [which] change not only the deeper meanings of textual forms but also the structures of ideas, of conceptual arrangements, and of the structures of our knowledge'. Not so long ago, for example, language teachers would have needed a room to accommodate their language laboratory, desktop computer, digital camera, camcorder, CD library, radio, television, tape recorder, microphones, sound system, telephone, textbooks, dictionaries and game activities. These – and more – are now converged into a single mobile device from which our students are inseparable, promoting nomadic or 'anytime, anywhere' language learning (see Chinnery 2006 and Godwin-Jones 2008). The boundaries between life activities and school continue to blur, as do the boundaries between mediated and unmediated learning. Literacy practices have undergone rapid changes with the advent of digital technologies, disrupting notions of authorship, authority, audience and text genres (Warschauer 2004). Jewitt (2003) argues that, with every new technology, new kinds of texts emerge that call into question what it means to be literate, whilst Lankshear and Knobel (2006) foresee the emergence of radically different social and cultural relations brought about by new technologies. Such developments demand that we remain open to the potential of such technologies whilst critically evaluating their pedagogical benefits.

References

Blake, R. 2008. *Brave New Digital Classroom: Technology and Foreign Language Learning*. Washington, DC: Georgetown University Press.

Brown, A. 2005. 'Self-assessment of writing in independent language learning programs: the value of annotated samples'. *Assessing Writing*, 10(3): 174–91.

Chapelle, C. and J. Jamieson. 2008. *Tips for Teaching with CALL: Practical Approaches to Computer-Assisted Language Learning*. White Plains, NY: Pearson-Longman.

Chinnery, G. 2006. 'Going to the MALL: Mobile Assisted Language Learning'. *Language Learning & Technology*, 10(1): 9–16.

Gass, S. M. 1997. *Input, Interaction, and the Second Language Learner*. Mahwah, NJ: Lawrence Erlbaum Associates.

Godwin-Jones, R. 2008. 'Mobile-computing trends: lighter, faster, smarter'. *Language Learning & Technology*, 12(3): 3–9.

Jewitt, C. 2003. 'Multimodality, literacy and computer-mediated learning'. *Assessment in Education*, 10(1): 83–102.

Kress, G. 2003. *Literacy in the New Media Age*. New York: Routledge.

Lankshear, C. and M. Knobel. 2006. *New Literacies: Everyday Practices and Classroom Learning*, 2nd edn. Maidenhead and New York: Open University Press.

Robin, R. 2007. 'Learner-based listening and technological authenticity'. *Language Learning and Technology*, 11(1): 109–15.

Sun, Y. 2009. 'Voice blog: an exploratory study of language learning'. *Language Learning and Technology*, 13(2): 88–103. http://llt.msu.edu/vol13num2/sun.pdf

Swain, M. 2000. 'Mediating acquisition through collaborative dialogue'. In J. Lantolf (ed.), *Sociocultural Theory and Second Language Learning*. Oxford: Oxford University Press.

Warschauer, M. 2004. 'Technology and writing'. In C. Davidson and J. Cummins (eds.), *Handbook of English Language Teaching*. Dordrecht: Kluwer.

Comments on Part D

Brian Tomlinson

The chapters in this section focus on the new possibilities offered to materials developers and teachers by such new technologies as blogs, chats, interactive whiteboards, Facebook, mobile phones, YouTube and wikis. I have seen these new technologies in impressive action in well-resourced institutions in Europe and in such places as Hong Kong, Malaysia and Singapore. In many cases the use of such technologies was enhancing the learning experience of the students by offering increased exposure to language in use, increased engagement and increased inter-activity between teacher and student, between student and student and between students and text. Perhaps the most productive feature of the use made of new technologies which I saw was the facility to provide a variety of relevant samples of English in face-to-face action and, in some cases, to involve the learners in such action themselves. However, in some cases the new technologies were just being used as expensive but fashionable ways of delivering old exercise types such as fill in the blank, listen and repeat and multiple choice. In such cases the new tech-nologies can not only take away funds from potentially more useful resources, such as extensive readers, but they can also demotivate learn-ers by promising much whilst delivering little and they can antagonise teachers who would prefer not to use new technologies.

I have also recently visited institutions where most of the new tech-nologies are just not available because there are no available computers, or there is no access to the Internet or there just isn't any electricity. In such places, however, most of the students do have mobile phones but are prevented from using them in class because of the understandable fear that they will distract the students. However, it seems obvious that, with a little training and stimulus, teachers and materials developers in these places could make very productive use of their own and their stu-dents' mobile phones. Some possible mobile phone activities could be:

- Students in a class form pairs/groups in which there is at least one mobile phone. They carry out a task together in relation to a text, photo or video posted by the teacher and then phone another pair/ group (possibly in another class or even school) to compare their task completions. Maybe they then phone a teacher or other profi-cient speaker of English and listen to them doing the same task. Or they listen to a recording of proficient speakers carrying out the task together.

352

- Self-access learners subscribe to a mobile 'school' and receive lessons from a 'teacher' every day. Having completed the activities set by the 'teacher', they phone a monitor and discuss their responses to the activities. The monitor gives advice and then sends a recorded remedial lesson relating to a problem which emerged when the learner was carrying out the activities.
- Self-access learners form a virtual study group by using the conference facility on their mobile phones. They receive the same text and/or task simultaneously and then cooperate with each other in carrying out the task. Whilst they are doing this a monitor listens in, and then provides feedback and responsive teaching when they have completed the task.
- Self-access learners form a virtual study group by using the conference facility on their mobile phones. They start a conversation, and if they are having problems expressing themselves in English, they ask a bilingual 'knower' to suggest what they should say. The conversation (but not the advice) is recorded and played back to the learners by the 'knower', who can then offer feedback and advice. This is an adaptation of the approach suggested long ago by Community Language Learning (Curran 1976).

The possibilities are endless for taking advantage of the features of the mobile phone to achieve a monitored interactivity which would be very difficult to achieve in the classroom and almost impossible to achieve by the self-access learner without a mobile phone. All that is needed is a little enterprise and investment and soon learners could be communicating with each other and with proficient speakers of English in rural India, in the forests of Kalimantan and in the mountains of Peru.

What is needed is for materials writers to sit down together and brainstorm what new technologies can offer pedagogically and then for consultations to take place with technologists to discuss how this can be effectively and economically achieved. For some more suggestions about the pedagogic potential of new technologies see McDonough, Shaw and Masuhara (2011) and Reinders and White (2010).

References

Curran, C. A. 1976. *Counseling Learning in Second Languages*. Apple River, IL.: Apple River Press.

McDonough, J., C. Shaw and H. Masuhara. 2011. *Materials and Methods in ELT: A Teachers' Guide*. London: Blackwell.

Reinders, H. and C. White. 2010. 'The theory and practice of technology in materials development and task design'. In N. Harwood (ed.), *English Language Teaching Materials*. Cambridge: Cambridge University Press.

Part E   Ideas for materials development

14 Seeing what they mean: helping L2 readers to visualise

Brian Tomlinson

14.1 Introduction

There is currently much concern about the apparent mismatch between what learners are asked to do in published textbooks and the reality of language use; see, for example, Masuhara *et al.* (2008), Tomlinson (2008) and (2009), and Tomlinson *et al.* (2001), as well as the chapters in Part A of this book by Jane Willis and by Ronald Carter, Rebecca Hughes and Michael McCarthy. Many think that there is also a mismatch between some of the pedagogic procedures of current textbooks and what second language acquisition researchers have discovered about the process of learning a second or foreign language (see, for example, Chapter 1 of this book by Brian Tomlinson and Chapter 8 by Andrew Littlejohn). One type of textbook which seems to be largely exempt from such criticisms of mismatch is that which focuses on helping learners to develop reading skills in an L2.

It seems to be accepted that current textbook activities designed to develop reading skills do to a large extent mirror the actual process of reading authentic texts. These activities are based on generally accepted models of the reading process which stress the active role of the reader in relating world knowledge to information in the text, the parallel interaction between low-level decoding of words and high-level processing of concepts and the way in which effective readers vary their reading techniques according to their purposes for reading. However, it is arguable that there is one significant reading strategy which has been almost entirely neglected by both general EFL coursebooks and by EFL reading skills books too. That is the strategy of visualisation, the converting of words on the page into pictures in the mind. In an analysis of EFL textbooks published in the 1990s I found no evidence at all of any systematic attempt to help L2 learners to develop visualisation skills except in *Openings* (Tomlinson 1994) and *Use Your English* (Tomlinson and Masuhara 1994). And when reviewing EFL textbooks in the last ten years (e.g. Masuhara *et al.* 2008; Tomlinson *et al.* 2001) I still have not found any attempt to help L2 readers to achieve visual imaging of reading texts.

The following chapter focuses on the neglected reading strategy of visualisation (i.e. deliberate visual imaging) as an example of how a combination of classroom experience, of informed intuition and of research can lead to the development of innovative materials which can help learners to learn more. It reports on how I have followed up intuitions about the salience of visual imaging in L1 reading and its neglect in L2 reading by studying research on imaging, by conducting a series of experiments and by writing materials aiming to promote visualisation in L2 reading.

14.2 Do L1 readers typically use visual imaging?

In experiments I conducted to investigate visual imaging in reading, a total of over a hundred proficient readers were asked to read a descriptive or narrative text. Some were asked to read a poem (*River Station Plaza* by Sheldon Flory (1990)), some read an extract from *Closing Time* by Joseph Heller (1994) and some read the opening page and a half of *Brazil* by John Updike (1994). Ninety-six per cent of these readers reported that they visually imaged the content of the texts as they read them and all 23 proficient readers in an experiment at the University of Luton claimed that they saw pictures in their minds as they read the opening of *Brazil*. Stevick reports a proportion of 95 per cent of visual imagers from his experiments with L1 listeners and readers and he states that: 'Words that have come into our heads from reading or listening commonly leave us with pictures, sounds and feelings in our minds' (1986). Other researchers have come to similar conclusions about the phenomenon of visualisation whilst reading in the L1. For example, Brewer (1988) showed that readers have 'phenomenal experience pre-, whilst-, and post-reading' and also that 'descriptive texts and narrative texts ... tend to produce imagery during reading'. Similar claims about the use of visualisation as an L1 reading strategy have been made by Arnold (1999), Avila (2005), Bugelski (1969), Esrock (1994), Mowrer (1977), Paivio (1979), Pylyshyn (1973), Stevick (1989), Thompson (1987), Tomlinson (1996), and Tomlinson and Avila (2007a).

Although it seems that most people use visual imaging when they read in their L1, not all visualisers use visual imagery with the same vividness, frequency and effect; they can be placed on a cline from very low imagers to very high (or eidetic) imagers. For example, 95 per cent of L1 respondents to a questionnaire I gave to readers of an extract from *Brazzaville Beach* (Boyd 1990) reported visual imaging whilst reading and 100 per cent of proficient readers who were asked to read the first one and a half pages of *Brazil* reported visual imaging. But in both experiments some of the respondents reported only partial, rather vague visual imaging whilst others reported differing degrees of detail and vividness. For example, some of those who read the extract from *Brazzaville Beach* saw the narrator (who was not described in the text) in clear detail, some saw her vaguely, and some did not see her at all. In another experiment 100 per cent of respondents to my questionnaire on the reading of an extract from *Closing Time* reported visual imaging, but about 25 per cent of them only reported imaging occasionally. It also seems that visualisers vary in the way they respond to different texts in different circumstances, and that some of the factors which determine vividness of visualisation are motivation, topic familiarity, topic interest, relevance to previous experience and familiarity with the language of the text. For example, some of those respondents who reported only occasional visualisation of the extract from *Closing Time* also reported lack of interest in the text, and many of the respondents visualised most vividly those parts of the extract which coincided with their own interests and experiences. Another important factor is the perceived relevance of visualisation as a strategy for reading a particular text at a particular time; texts and tasks do not always require the use of visual imaging, and when it is used, it is normally because it is 'perceived' as potentially rewarding.

The surprising thing is that despite the mass of data affirming the prevalence of visual imaging in L1 reading (and especially in the reading of narrative and descriptive texts), most books on the reading process make little or no mention of the fact that L1 readers typically visualise before, whilst and after reading. Barnett (1989), Carr and Levy (1990), Grellet (1982) and Nuttall (1995) are examples of popular books on the reading process which do not deal at all with the reading strategy of visualisation. However, Tomlinson (2000c) and Masuhara (2003) describe visual imaging as one of the important instruments of experiential reading.

It would seem that most L1 readers typically use visual imaging when reading descriptive or narrative texts, but do so with differing degrees of vividness. It would also seem that this phenomenon is not considered to be significant in books on the reading process.

14.3 Is visual imaging functional in L1 reading?

Eysenk and Keane (1990) ask whether visual imagery has 'functional significance' or whether it is a 'mere epithenomenon'. Intuitions, introspections and research lead me to agree with Esrock when she asserts that 'the reader's visual imagery can have unique cognitive and affective consequences that heighten the readers' experience' (1994). They also suggest to me that for many L1 readers visual imaging plays a major role in helping them to achieve involvement, comprehension, retention and recall.

Many claims have been made for the functional significance of visual imaging in L1 reading. It is claimed, for example, that for L1 readers visual imaging can help:

- whilst-reading retention of concepts and propositions originally represented by words which can remain in the memory for no more than ten seconds (Swaffer 1988);
- post-reading retention of the content of a text (Kulhavy and Swenson 1975);
- 'recall by furnishing the learner with a meaningful representation of the material being studied' (Kulhavy and Swenson 1975; see also Thompson 1987 who states that 'there is evidence that persons with high imagery ability are able to recall ... more ... from texts than low imagers');
- to increase comprehension of a text (Anderson and Kulhavy 1972; Knight, Padron and Waxman 1985);
- to achieve interaction between old information (represented by images activated by the reader's schemata or knowledge of the world) and new information (instantiated from data in the text) (Enkvist 1981);
- to achieve the default inferencing needed to complete the gaps created by what Eysenk and Keane (1990) call 'the writer's logical implications and pragmatic implications';
- 'to achieve an aesthetic experience of the literary work' through 'concretisation', that is through 'fleshing out the text' to complete the fictional representation' (Ingarden 1973);
- to achieve tolerance of ambiguity by enabling the reader to make hypotheses which can be retained visually until they are confirmed or revised as new information becomes available from the text (Tomlinson 1993);
- 'to create images endowed with a descriptive power capable of representing more upper levels of discourse, such as a paragraph, or a chapter, or a general theme' (Esrock 1994);
- to achieve affective impact (Esrock 1994);
- to personalise a text and make it relevant to the reader (Tomlinson 1993; and Sadoski 1985, who concludes that image elaborations are 'a means of personalising literary texts whilst also maintaining a core of shared meaning');
- to achieve a ludic, hedonistic, reading experience which gives the reader access to what Tierney and Cunningham (1984) call the 'wonder' of reading (see also Denis 1982);

- to achieve 'the "experiencing" of the text and not just the comprehension of information' (Esrock 1994);
- to contribute to the 'deep processing' of salient parts of the text and thus to achieve 'more elaborate, longer lasting and stronger traces' (Craik and Lockhart 1972) in the long-term memory.

For other functions of visual imaging see Tomlinson and Avila (2007a).

There is little doubt that visual imaging is functionally significant in L1 reading and there is a strong possibility that it could therefore play a beneficial role in L2 reading too.

14.4 What else do L1 readers do when they use visual imaging?

'In first language learning and use the meaning of utterances listened to or read is typically represented multi-dimensionally in the mind (Masuhara 2005; Tomlinson 2000b, 2001a), with visual imaging being one of the main means of achieving understanding, interpretation, representation, retention and recall of the language experience' (Tomlinson and Avila 2007a: 61). At the same time first language users are typically connecting what they 'see' to their own lives, they are evaluating its significance and they are predicting its consequences. To help them to do all this, they are often also using inner speech to talk to themselves about the experience. For example, whilst reading the line 'I saw a tram' from the poem *Amsterdam* by John Hegley (Hegley 1997: 12), I saw a tram outside a station in Amsterdam and then a tram on the promenade in Blackpool, where I grew up. I also recited the line mentally and talked to myself about the poem (e.g. 'What a silly poem ... could use it though ... get learners to write similar poems'). Later when I recalled the poem, the tram outside the station image was dominant and then the words came back to mind.

There is a substantial literature on the use of the inner voice (i.e. the mental voice inside our heads) by L1 readers and listeners. Many researchers have detailed its characteristics. For example, Korba (1986, 1990) has focused on how fast it is (at least ten times faster than outer speech), Chautauga (1992) has shown how it can be reflexive or intentional, Tomlinson (2000a) has stressed its elliptical nature, de Guerro (1994), Centeno-Cortes and Jimenez (2004) and Tomlinson (2000a) have drawn attention to how narrow, economical and yet semantically rich it is, Sokolov (1972) has demonstrated how egocentric and relevant it is and Lantolf and Pavlenko (1995) have illustrated how coherent it is. For further details of the characteristics of inner speech see Centeno-Cortes and

Jimenez (2004) and Tomlinson and Avila (2007a), where information can also be found about such functions of inner speech as reiteration (Klein 1981), mental representation (Jenkin *et al.* 1993), connection, retention (Sadoski and Paivio 1994; Paivio 2007), recall (Tomlinson 2000a), planning, reassurance and self-evaluation. See Archer (2003) for a review of the literature of L1 inner speech.

Most of the literature on visual imaging and the literature on the use of inner speech focus on reading and listening, but some researchers have considered the use of the two phenomena in speaking and writing. For example, Tomlinson and Avila (2007a: 61) say that 'during the activities of speaking and writing native speakers typically see images representing partially what they want to say, they talk to themselves about what they are going to say, they sometimes try out various options in their minds and they frequently rehearse utterances mentally before producing them'. Korba (1986) emphasises how all verbal interaction requires the use of inner speech both in preparing to talk yourself and in understanding other people talking, Steels (2003) refers to neurophysiological evidence that inner speech self-monitoring not only facilitates effective outer speech but plays a vital role in language acquisition too, and De Bleser and Marshall (2005) reveal that inner speech impairment causes outer speech communication to become unsuccessful too. Yi (in press) focuses on the use of visual imaging in narrative writing and reveals its importance for L1 writers.

Most of the literature on visual imaging and the literature on the use of inner speech is specific to one phenomenon only, but there are some researchers who have combined the two phenomena. For example, Leontiev and Ryabova (1981) discuss the roles of both phenomena in the transition from vague thought to expanded utterance, Sadoski and Paivio (1994) and Paivio (2007) focus on dual coding theory and the interaction between visual imaging and inner speech, both Herrmann (1998) and von Oech (1998) articulate theories of the roles of visual imaging and inner speech in the creative process in the brain, and Tomlinson and Avila (2007a) comment on how the two phenomena are often used together (either simultaneously or sequentially) to achieve mental representation.

14.5 Do L2 readers visualise?

In 1985 Knight, Padron and Waxman investigated the reading strategies reported by ESL and by monolingual students. They found that 'imaging was significant' for L1 readers but was not mentioned at all by the L2 readers, whose 'primary concern was with low level decoding skills'. In 1989 Barnett devised a questionnaire entitled, 'What do you do when you read?' She administered it to L2 readers and in her report she makes no reference at all to visualisation as a strategy used by anybody in her sample. This indication that L2 speakers do not typically use visual imaging is also supported by Stevick who, for example, refers to a woman who 'claimed to get pictures from words in her own native language, but not in a foreign language which she spoke very effectively' (Stevick 1986). My own experiments also suggest that most L2 readers do not seem to use visual imaging very much whilst reading. Most of the lower-intermediate to upper-intermediate Japanese students who took part in 19 experiments conducted at Kobe University and at Nagoya Women's University made no reference to visual imaging or to mental imaging of any kind when asked to reflect on how they had read a text. For example, in one experiment only 7 out of 41 students reported any visualisation when they were asked to say what they had done in order to try to understand the poem *River Station Plaza*. The main strategies reported by the others were looking up difficult words, trying to translate the poem, reading the poem over and over again, trying to memorise the poem, and 'giving up'. In another experiment only 3 out of 16 students who had been asked to read an extract from *The Bonfire of the Vanities* (Wolfe 1988) and then predict the next scene reported using visualisation to help them to understand the passage and only two said they had used visualisation to predict the next scene. Likewise in another group of 19 students who were asked to read the poem *River Station Plaza* and then to reflect on the process of reading it, only four reported visualising and only the same four reported using visualisation as a strategy to help them to overcome the difficulties they encountered in trying to understand the poem. The interesting thing is that these four students performed better than the others when asked after an interval to recall words from the poem and to write a summary of it. A similar tendency not to use visual imaging when reading in the L2 was indicated by questionnaires given to EFL students at the University of Luton, asking them to report on how they had read the first page of *A Pale View of Hills* (Ishiguro 1982), of *No Other Life* (Moore 1993) and of *Remembering Babylon* (Malouf 1993). Avila (2005) found that L2 students did not typically use visual imaging when reading and that the ability to generate mental imagery seemed to be inhibited by the cognitive exhaustion of decoding each word in the text.

In all my experiments the few students who reported using visual imaging tended to achieve greater comprehension and recall than those who did not. This was also the case when Padron and Waxman administered a reading strategy questionnaire to 82 Hispanic ESL students and found that one of the most frequently cited strategies by the successful students was 'imaging or picturing the story in your mind' (Padron and Waxman 1988). Of course this equation between visualisation and successful L2 comprehension and recall raises the question of whether imagery is 'an outgrowth/consequence of ... reading skill, rather than a contributor to it' (Esrock: personal correspondence). My view (developed in Tomlinson 1993) is that increasing an L2 reader's ability to visualise can facilitate positive engagement with the text and can increase the reader's ability to comprehend and retain what is read. This in turn can further increase the ability to visualise in the L2. In an experiment I did with myself, I read a page of an advanced French reader and found I was decoding it word by word, translating it mentally as I went along and very rarely generating any visual imagery. At the end of the page I was exhausted and could not remember what I had read. I then read another page from the reader and made myself stop translating. This time I read in chunks and visualised each one as best as I could. I also did mental visual summaries at the end of each paragraph and at the end of the page. I found that I felt positive about my reading and that I could remember what I had read, both immediately and many years later.

There is considerable evidence that L2 learners can remember vocabulary better if they are encouraged to visualise the referents of the new lexical items they encounter. For example, Dual Coding Theory (Paivio 1971, 2007; Sadoski and Paivio 1994) uses experimental evidence to claim that two independent memory codes are involved in word processing: imagery codes and verbal codes. The imagery codes create visual images to represent a word, and the verbal codes represent it linguistically. Using both imagery and verbal codes to encode new words leads to a better chance of remembering that item than relying on a single code. Further evidence of the advantages of using imagery codes in word learning is provided by, for example, Boers, Eyckmans and Stengers (2007), Levy-Drori and Henik (2006) and Mazoyer *et al.* (2002).

It seems that L2 learners do not typically visualise when reading in the L2. The indication that those who do so tend to achieve greater comprehension and recall than those who do not would suggest that we should be trying to help L2 readers to visualise more. Similar conclusions can also be drawn with regards to the use of inner speech by L2 learners. It seems to be inhibited by the focus on encoding and decoding, by the lack of thinking time given to learners in the classroom and by the premature insistence on production in most L2 beginners' courses. However, those L2 learners who have been helped to use their inner voice have gained advantages over those who have not. For details of the role of the inner voice in L2 learning see Appel and Lantolf (1994), de Guerro (1994, 2004, 2005), Masuhara (1998), McCafferty (1994a, 1994b, 1998), Tomlinson (2000a, 2001b, 2003a) and Tomlinson and Avila (2007a, 2007b).

14.6 What are the characteristics of L2 visualisation?

Anderson and Pearson (1984) point out that younger children are not predisposed to draw inferences spontaneously and they give the example of five-year-olds being less able to infer the instrument than eight-year-olds when reading the sentence, 'The man dug a hole'. My experience of L2 learners is that when they do visualise, they are less likely to make default inferences than L1 readers are and that, like the young L1 child, they are reliant on the writer providing most of the information to be visualised. For example, when asked to visualise the poem *River Station Plaza*, most of a group of Japanese students saw a yellow light described as shining on the plaza but, unlike L1 readers given the same task, they did not visualise its undescribed source. However, this child-like state seems to be typical rather than inevitable, as groups of L2 readers who have become used to doing visualisation activities in reading classes have become easily capable of seeing what is not actually described. Thus a multinational EFL class at the University of Luton saw the sun, a car headlight and a shop window as the source of light in *River Station Plaza*. In all my experiments in which L2 learners have been encouraged to visualise there have invariably been gaps in the mental pictures they have created. Thus, when drawing what they had seen whilst reading the first two pages of *Brazzaville Beach*, a group of Japanese students did not draw the topless sunbathers nor the working fishermen (sights not common on Japanese beaches), nor did they draw the itinerants and scavengers (words they did not know); but most of them did draw the volleyball players (beach volleyball is popular on Japanese television). Some of the students just left gaps in their pictures where they knew other activities should go, others compensated by seeing the volleyball game in vivid detail and many others compensated by imaging details not described in the text at all (e.g. birds in the sky and boats at sea). The L2 readers who are content to leave many gaps in their mental images of what a text represents seem to be those who achieve the least understanding of the text, whereas those who try to fill in the picture by, for example, compensating from their visual schemata, seem to understand more. Another typical characteristic of L2 visualisers in this sample was the tendency to see only prototypical or stereotypical images suggested by key words and not to develop them into instantiated images on the strength of further evidence in the text. The 'debilitating effect of' this 'premature commitment to a particular schema' (Rumelhart 1980) was most in evidence in an activity in which a class of students at Kobe University were asked to draw the party which was about to happen in an extract they were reading from Harold Pinter's *The Birthday Party* (1976). All the students drew young boys drinking soft drinks (the stereotypical image of a birthday party in a country where adults do not normally have birthday parties), even though the text made it clear that the characters were adults and the party was going to be a 'booze-up'. In the same way another class at Kobe University, when asked to read an extract from *Brazzaville Beach* and then 'draw Clovis', all drew a small boy because he is described as 'stupid'. When asked to read on and draw Clovis again, they all drew a boy again because he is described as having a finger up his nose. When asked to read on and draw Clovis again they all drew a boy again even though by now the text had made it clear that Clovis was a monkey of some sort who swings away through the trees. A multinational class at the University of Luton (who had been given some prior experience of visualisation activities) all drew boys the first two times, but some of them drew dogs and cats the third time and one of them drew a monkey. Native speakers drew boys and men for the first two extracts, but all of them changed Clovis to a monkey after reading the third extract.

It seems that many L2 readers who do visualise tend to achieve only partial visualisation and to stick to their original images despite contradictory evidence from the text.

14.7 Can L2 readers be helped to visualise more often and more effectively?

There seem to be many reasons why L2 readers typically underuse or misuse visualisation. The main reason seems to be that many of them are conditioned from an elementary level to read using primarily bottom-up strategies which focus on the low-level decoding of words. Given their inevitable lack of vocabulary, such a focus is initially unavoidable. But it is reinforced by the language-teaching focus and the comprehension-testing orientation of many of their textbooks and teachers. This insistence on understanding every word leaves little processing capacity for such high-level skills as inferencing, connecting, using the inner voice and visual imaging. So the pattern is set for many learners of relying on low-level skills for reading in the L2 and there is little encouragement for global or interactive visual imaging. Delaying the teaching of reading until learners have achieved a linguistic threshold level could help the learners to transfer their visualisation skills from their L1, especially if the initial focus is on using high-level strategies to achieve global understanding of extensive texts rather than on achieving total understanding of each word in a short intensive text (see Tomlinson 1998, 2000c for details of such an approach to teaching L2 reading).

Stanovich (1980) in outlining an 'interactive compensatory model' claims that the strong use of one strategy can compensate for weakness in another. I have found this to be true in relation to encouraging L2 learners to use visualisation as a compensation for weakness in linguistic knowledge, as well as an aid to connection, inferencing, retention and recall. Like most other reading strategies, though, it only works well if it replaces cognitive activities rather than overloading the reader's processing capacity by adding to them, and if the learners are made aware that 'accepting appropriate tolerance of uncertainty is an essential part of being a good reader' (Brumfit 1986). In my experience L2 readers can be helped to visualise effectively by encouraging a 'tolerance for inexactness, a willingness to take chances and make mistakes, formulation of hypotheses before reading, then reading to confirm, refine, reject' (Clarke 1980). They can also be helped to visualise by materials which combine visualisation strategy instruction with visualisation strategy activities.

In 19 experiments conducted with over 600 L2 students, those students who visualised (mainly as a result of being instructed or induced to do so) were able to understand and recall slightly more of the text than those who did not visualise. Thus, for example, in experiments in which half the class were induced to visualise a text whilst the other half studied it, the visualisers always outscored the studiers on recall and comprehension tests. For example, in a sophomore class at Kobe University the visualisers scored an average of 44 per cent whereas the studiers scored an average of 38 per cent. In these experiments also on average seven out of ten of the top ten scorers were visualisers and seven out of ten of the bottom ten scorers were non-visualisers (see Tomlinson 1997 for details of these experiments). In some of the experiments the initial visualisers were then asked to study a short story whilst the initial studiers were induced to visualise the story. Comprehension and recall scores for both groups on the second activity were very similar in all these experiments (possibly indicating that the initial visualisers continued to visualise when asked to study). In none of the experiments was there a statistically significant difference between the scores of the visualisers and the non-visualisers, but there were indications that visualisation instruction and visualisation induction helped students to improve slightly their reading performance in a single task. Some of the classes which participated in these experiments then followed a reading course in which the emphasis was on developing their ability to achieve effective visualisation when reading texts from a variety of genres. It seemed that most students in these classes considerably improved both their reading confidence and their reading competence, and that by the end of the semester they were able to read in English in ways much closer to the ways in which they read in Japanese. Of course, these classes were not conducted under experimental conditions, there were no control classes to compare improvements with and there were many uncontrolled variables which could have improved reading performance (e.g. rapport with the teacher, increased quantity of reading, increased acquisition of language). However, the indications of increased use of visualisation as a causal factor in improved reading performance were strong enough to support the inclusion of visualisation activities in reading skills materials and were responsible for the emphasis given to the objective of developing visualisation skills in *Use Your English* (Tomlinson and Masuhara 1994). They were also strong enough to justify the idea of a controlled longitudinal experiment with a large sample of EFL learners in which experimental classes use materials designed to develop visualisation skills whilst control classes use conventional reading skills materials in which there is no systematic attempt to promote visualisation as a reading skill at all. Such an experiment was conducted at the University of Seville by Avila (2005). He found significant evidence that helping learners to visualise resulted in increased visual imaging, greater interest and involvement in reading activities and improved reading ability. In similar experiments with experimental and control classes of writing students at a Chinese university, Yi (in press) found that those students who had been helped to visualise before, whilst and after writing narratives gained in comparison with their peers in the control classes.

The reading courses which my students at Kobe University and at the University of Luton followed included materials designed to help them to use visualisation effectively as follows.

14.7.1 Visualisation instruction

1. Students were told before reading a text not to study it or to translate it but to imagine pictures as they read it and then to change these pictures as they found further information in the text.
2. They were also sometimes told to focus their images initially on what was familiar in the text and then to use these images to help them work out what was unfamiliar in the text.

3. Another frequently given instruction was to picture a summary of each section of the text immediately after reading it and also to attempt a pictorial summary immediately after finishing the text.
4. Students were also sometimes given reading texts which contained explicit visualisation instructions either just before the text or in the margins within the text. Often these were instructions designed to help them achieve interactive imaging which would facilitate inter-pretative connections between different parts of the text (e.g. 'Try to see Nanga's face in your mind. Compare your picture to the image of Nanga's face which you "saw" when you were reading page 17').
5. Sometimes visualisation instructions were inserted into compre-hension questions to help students to make connections (e.g. 'What does the narrator's description of Hannah tell you about his atti-tude towards her? Try to see a picture of Hannah and the narrator's father in the foyer of the cinema before answering this question').

14.7.2 Visualisation activities

I found overt visualisation instruction to have beneficial effects in aid-ing comprehension of demanding narrative and descriptive texts, but agreed with Van Dijk and Kintsch that:

> a comprehension strategy which must be applied consciously is of limited usefulness, because in many actual comprehension situations insufficient resources would be available for the application of such a strategy. (1983)

I therefore also devised materials which featured activities designed to induce visual imaging subconsciously, with the intention of establish-ing visual imaging as something the students do habitually when read-ing narrative and descriptive texts in experiential ways. These activities included the following.

Drawing

I have found that pre-reading drawing activities help to make sure that the students have relevant images in their minds when they start to read the text. These images are activations of their schemata, or knowl-edge of the world. They enable them to read interactively straight away rather than being initially reliant on text data and running the risk of word dependence. These activities often involve drawing predictions of the characters, the setting or the narrative from a rapid sampling of the book or from the title, the blurb, the front cover or the introduction to the book. Or they might involve drawing scenes from the students' own lives connected to the title or front cover of a book. One such activity involved the students drawing a strange teacher they had known before reading a scene from Chinua Achebe's *Girls at War* (1972), which focused on an eccentric teacher; another asked them to draw their first day at school before reading Roger McGough's poem 'First day at school' (1979).

I have also frequently used whilst-reading drawing activities to facilitate interactive reading and thus help the students to relate data from the text to their knowledge of the world. Being asked to draw a picture of Chief Nanga whilst reading the first chapter of Achebe's *A Man of the People* (1988) helped students not only to visualise Nanga and to bring him to life, but also to begin to develop and retain an understanding of his personality. Likewise, asking students to draw the two people in Wole Soyinka's poem 'Telephone conversation' (1963) as they read it helped them to 'see' the landlady for what she was and to appreciate the dilemma of the black student trying to find accommodation in London.

Post-reading drawings have also helped students to read visually and interactively, provided that they were told what they were going to be asked to draw prior to reading the text. Thus, being told they were going to be asked to draw a picture to show what they understood of 'First day at school' helped students to gain access to the poem through focusing on what they could understand and see. It also helped them to use pictures in their mind to help them to reread the poem with greater understanding. Thus, for example, none of the students initially understood the word 'railings' in the following lines:

> And the railings.
> All around, the railings.
> Are they to keep out wolves and monsters?

But when they were encouraged to visualise what could be all around a school, they all began to draw railings without knowing the meaning of the word. In a similar way students who were asked to draw the scene in which the son discovers his father with a woman at the beginning of Nadine Gordimer's *My Son's Story* (1991) reread the extract with much greater understanding when they asked themselves what the characters looked like and what they were wearing.

In addition to writing visualisation materials which feature drawing activities, I have also added drawing activities when using published coursebooks with classes. For example, I asked students to draw their prediction of what Paul McCartney's house looks like before reading the passage in Unit 1 of *Headway Intermediate* (Soars and Soars

1986) which describes the McCartney house, and then I asked them to describe the house that the family actually did live in. Also when using *Intermediate Matters* (Bell and Gower 1991) I asked students to draw the metal boxes (i.e. cars) which the whale family in *The Great Whale's Mistake* could see people throwing rubbish from on the beach (Unit 20) and to draw what the whales thought that the people did at night (i.e. continue their activities on the beach). I also used such drawing activities with first-year students at Sultan Qaboos University in 2007 to try to make their commercial coursebook more relevant to their lives. For example, when studying a unit which featured a text on horse racing in Siena, I first of all got the students to draw pictures of local camel races, I then got them to imagine they were in the crowd in Siena and taking photos of the horse race there and then, when they had read the text, I got them to draw one of their photos of the race in Siena to show their family back in Oman. Such activities appeared to facilitate a better understanding of the texts than just using the exercises in the books, as they helped students to make connections and inferences that similar students did not make when not encouraged to visualise by drawing activities.

Connection activities

I have found that by asking learners to connect a text to an incident in their own lives or to one in another text, they automatically use visual imaging in order to achieve the connection. So if I ask a group of students to read the opening chapter of *A Man of the People* and to compare Chief Nanga to a politician they know as they read, most of them will develop images of both politicians in their minds. Likewise, if I tell students to read the opening chapter of *Brazil* and as they read to compare the beach which is described to the beach they can remember from the opening chapter of *Brazzaville Beach*, they are likely to develop images of Copacabana Beach as they read the text.

Illustrations

Illustration of texts often inhibits active visualisation because it imposes a visual interpretation of the texts. However, I have found that involving the students in relating given illustrations to their own visualisation of the text they are reading can facilitate interactive reading. For example, before reading Brian Patten's poem *Little Johnny's Letter Home* (1967) the students were asked to predict the story of the poem from four pictures and then to draw their own pictures, first of all as they listened and then as they read the poem. Also students who were asked to draw a picture of the scene in the foyer of the cinema at the beginning of *My Son's Story* were then asked to compare their drawings to two illustrations depicting slightly different interpretations of the scene.

Other types of visualisation activities exploiting illustrations include the students:

- selecting from a number of possible illustrations of a text
- completing partial illustrations by relating them to a text
- redrawing an illustration to fit their own interpretation of a text
- solving a jigsaw puzzle so that it provides a valid interpretation of a text
- reading a story in which the drawings continue the story told by the text rather than illustrating what the text says.

Miming

I have also found miming to be an effective way of inducing visual imaging. I have often mimed extracts from texts before asking students to read them, so that they start reading with pictures in their minds to relate the text to. I have also asked students to read a story in order to be able to mime it to another group, I have asked students to mime a story or poem as it is read aloud to them and then to read it silently, and I have asked students to mime a text as they are reading it. These activities seem to help to achieve a visual and kinaesthetic impact which aids involvement, understanding and retention.

Through these and other types of visualisation activities (e.g. making a video version of a poem) I believe I have helped many students to understand and enjoy texts which many teachers would consider to be beyond their linguistic level. This has been achieved by encouraging an appropriate balance between concept-driven and data-driven processing which has enabled the students to personalise, interpret and retain what they have read. For many students this has not only helped to develop their reading confidence and skills but has also seemed to result in a positive enrichment of language input and in the development of positive attitudes towards English and the educational opportunities it can open for them.

Tomlinson and Avila (2007b) give further examples of L2 activities for promoting both visual imaging and the use of the inner voice and they report a survey they did of current EFL materials, which revealed the almost complete neglect of visual imaging and the inner voice in global coursebooks. They also provide details of their suggested programme for helping learners to develop the ability to use visual imaging and their inner voice in the early stages of L2 learning.

14.8 Conclusion

In first language reading the norm is experiential reading in which high-level skills such as visual imaging, inferencing and connecting are employed automatically to deepen the reading process. In second language coursebooks the norm is studial reading in which processing energy is often devoted to low-level decoding and to cognitive strategies of comprehension. If learners do not see pictures in their minds of the texts they are reading, then they will have great difficulty in achieving global understanding and their experience of the texts will be fragmentary and shallow. Not only will they not enjoy reading, but they will not transfer reading skills which they have already developed in their L1 and their encounter with the language of the texts is unlikely to be deep and meaningful enough to facilitate language acquisition.

It is possible and desirable for materials to be developed which can help L2 learners to use visual imaging to increase their understanding of the texts they are reading, to deepen their engagement with the texts, to improve their comprehension and retention skills and to facilitate language acquisition.

References

Achebe, C. 1972. *Girls at War*. Oxford: Heinemann.
  1988. *A Man of the People*. Oxford: Heinemann.
Anderson, R. C. and R. W. Kulhavy. 1972. 'Imagery and prose learning'. *Journal of Educational Psychology*, 62: 526–30.
Anderson, R. C. and P. D. Pearson. 1984. 'A schema-theoretic view of basic processes in reading comprehension'. In P. D. Pearson (ed.), *A Handbook of Reading Research*. White Plains, NY: Longman.
Appel, G. and J. P. Lantolf. 1994. 'Speaking as mediation: a study of L1 and L2 text recall tasks'. *The Modern Language Journal*, 78(4): 437–52.
Archer, M. S. 2003. *Structure, Agency and the Internal Conversation*. Cambridge: Cambridge University Press.
Arnold, J. 1999. 'Visualization: language learning with the mind's eye'. In J. Arnold (ed.), *Affect in Language Learning*. Cambridge: Cambridge University Press.
Avila, F. J. 2005. 'El uso de la imegen mental en la lectura en el processo de adquisicion de una segunda lengua'. Unpublished PhD. University of Seville.
Barnett, M. 1989. *More than Meets the Eye: Foreign Language Reading*. Englewood Cliffs, NJ: Prentice Hall Regents.
Bell, J. and R. Gower. 1991. *Intermediate Matters*. Harlow: Longman.

De Bleser, R. and J. C. Marshall. 2005. 'Egon Weigl and the concept of inner speech'. *Cortex*, 41(2): 249–57.

Boers, F., J. Eyckmans and H. Stengers. 2007. 'Presenting figurative idioms with a touch of etymology: more than mere mnemonics?' *Language Teaching Research*, 11: 43–62.

Boyd, W. 1990. *Brazzaville Beach*. London: Penguin.

Brewer, W. F. 1988. 'Postscript: imagery and text genre'. *Text*, 8: 431–8.

Brumfit, C. 1986. 'Reading skills and the study of literature'. In C. Brumfit and R. Carter (eds.), *Literature and Language Teaching*. Oxford: Oxford University Press.

Bugelski, B. R. 1969. 'Learning theory and the reading process'. In *The 23rd Annual Reading Conference*. Pittsburgh: Pittsburgh University Press.

Carr, T. and B. Levy (eds.), 1990. *Reading and its Development: Component Skills Approaches*. San Diego: Academic Press.

Centeno-Cortes, B. and A. F. Jimenez. 2004. 'Problem solving tasks in a foreign language: the importance of the L1 in private verbal thinking'. *International Journal of Applied Linguistics*, 14(1): 7–35.

Chautauga, 1992. 'Mindfulness, mindlessness and communication'. *Communication Monographs*, 59(3): 299–327.

Clarke, M. 1980. 'The short circuit hypothesis of ESL reading – or when language performance interferes with reading performance'. *Modern Language Journal*, 64: 203–9.

Craik, F. I. M. and R. S. Lockhart. 1972. 'Levels of processing: a framework for memory research'. *Journal of Verbal Learning and Verbal Behaviour*, 11: 671–84.

Denis, M. 1982. 'Imaging whilst reading text: a study of individual differences'. *Memory and Cognition*, 10(6): 540–5.

Enkvist, N. E. 1981. 'Experiential iconism in text strategy'. *Text*, 1(1): 77–111.

Esrock, E. 1994. *The Reader's Eye*. Baltimore: The Johns Hopkins University Press.

Eysenk, N. W. and M. T. Keane. 1990. *Cognitive Psychology. A Student's Handbook*. Hillsdale, NJ: Lawrence Erlbaum Associates.

Flory, S. 1990. *River Station Plaza*. London: *The Observer*.

Gordimer, N. 1991. *My Son's Story*. London: Penguin Books.

Grellet, F. 1982. *Developing Reading Skills*. Cambridge: Cambridge University Press.

de Guerro, M. C. M. 1994. 'Form and functions of inner speech in adult second language learning'. In J. P. Lantolf and G. Appel (eds.), *Vygotskian Approaches to Second Language Research*. Norwood, NJ: Ablex.

2004. 'Early stages of L2 inner speech development: what verbal reports suggest'. *International Journal of Applied Linguistics*, 14(1).

(ed.) 2005. *Inner Speech – Thinking Words in a Second Language*. New York: Springer-Verlag.

Hegley, J. 1997. 'Amsterdam'. In *The Family Pack*. London: Methuen.

Heller, J. 1994. *Closing Time*. London: Simon and Schuster.

Herrmann, N. 1998. *The Creative Brain*. New York: Brain Books.

Ingarden, R. 1973. *The Cognition of the Literary Work of Art* (trans. R. A. Crowley, and K. R. Olsen). Evanston: Northwestern University Press.

Ishiguro, K. 1982. *A Pale View of Hills*. London: Faber and Faber.

Jenkin, H., S. Prior, R. Rinaldo, A. Wainwright-Sharp and E. Bialystok. 1993. 'Understanding text in a second language: a psychological approach to an SLA problem'. *Second Language Research*, 9(2): 118–39.

Klein, E. S. 1981. *Inner Speech Cue Preference in Reading Disabled and Normal Children*. Ann Arbor: University Microfilms International.

Knight, S. L., Y. N. Padron and H. C. Waxman. 1985. 'The cognitive reading strategies of ESL students'. *TESOL Quarterly*, 19: 789–92.

Korba, R. J. 1986. *The Rate of Inner Speech*. Unpublished PhD thesis. University of Denver.

—— 1990. 'The rate of inner speech'. *Perceptual and Motor Skills*, 71: 1043–52.

Kulhavy, R. W. and I. Swenson. 1975. 'Imagery instructions and the comprehension of texts'. *British Journal of Educational Psychology*, 45: 47–51.

Lantolf, J. P. and A. Pavlenko. 1995. 'Sociocultural theory and second language acquisition'. *Annual Review of Applied Linguistics*, 15: 108–24.

Leontiev, A. A. and T. V. Ryabova. 1981. *Psychology and the Language Learning Process*. Oxford: Pergamon Press.

Levy-Drori, S. and A. Henik. 2006. 'Concreteness and context availability in lexical decision tasks'. *American Journal of Psychology*, 119: 45–65.

Malouf, D. 1993. *Remembering Babylon*. London: Chatto and Windus.

Masuhara, H. 1998. 'Factors influencing the reading difficulties of advanced learners of English when reading authentic texts'. Unpublished PhD Thesis. University of Luton.

—— 2003. 'Materials for developing reading skills'. In B. Tomlinson (ed.), *Developing Materials for Language Teaching*. London: Continuum.

—— 2005. 'Helping learners to achieve multi-dimensional mental representation in L2 reading'. *Folio*, 9(2): 6–9.

Masuhara, H., M. Haan, Y. Yi and B. Tomlinson. 2008. 'Adult EFL courses'. *ELT Journal*, 62(3): 294–312.

Mazoyer, B., N. Tzourio-Mazoyer, A. Mazard, M. Denis and E. Mellet. 2002. 'Neural bases of image and language interactions'. *International Journal of Psychology*, 37: 204–8.

McCafferty, S. G. 1994a. 'The use of private speech by adult ESL learners at different levels of proficiency'. In J. P. Lantolf and G. Appel (eds.), *Vygotskian Approaches to Second Language Research*. Norwood, NJ: Ablex.

—— 1994b. 'Adult second language learners' use of private speech: a review of studies'. *The Modern Language Journal*, 78(4): 421–36.

—— 1998. 'Nonverbal expression and L2 private speech'. *Applied Linguistics*, 19(1): 73–96.

McGough, R. 1979. 'First day at school'. In R. McGough and M. Rosen (eds.), *You Tell Me*. London: Kestrel.

Moore, B. 1993. *No Other Life*. London: Bloomsbury.

Mowrer, O. H. 1977. 'Mental imagery: an indispensable psychological concept'. *Journal of Mental Imagery*, 2: 303–26.

Nuttall, C. 1995. *Teaching Reading Skills in a Foreign Language*. Oxford: Heinemann.

von Oech, R. 1998. *A Whack on the Side of the Head: How You Can Be More Creative*. Farmingdale, NY: Baywood.

Padron, Y. N. and H. C. Waxman. 1988. 'The effect of EFL students' perceptions of their cognitive strategies on reading achievement'. *TESOL Quarterly*, 22: 146–50.

Paivio, A. 1971. *Imagery and Verbal Processes*. New York: Holt, Rinehart, & Winston.

1979. *Imagery and Verbal Processes*. Hillsdale, NJ: Lawrence Erlbaum Associates Inc.

2007. *Mind and its Evolution: A Dual Coding Theoretical Approach*. Mahwah, NJ: Lawrence Erlbaum Associates, Inc.

Patten, B. 1967. *Little Johnny's Letter Home*. London: George Allen and Unwin.

Pinter, H. 1976. *The Birthday Party*. London: Eyre Methuen.

Pylyshyn, Z. W. 1973. 'What the mind's eye tells the mind's brain: a critique of mental imagery'. *Psychological Bulletin*, 80: 1–24.

Rumelhart, D. E. 1980. 'Schemata: the building blocks of cognition'. In R. J. Spiro, B. C. Bruce and W. F. Brewes (eds.), *Theoretical Issues in Reading Comprehension*. Hillsdale, NJ: Lawrence Erlbaum Associates.

Sadoski, M. 1985. 'The natural use of imagery in story comprehension and recall: replication and extension'. *Reading Research Quarterly*, 20: 658–67.

Sadoski, M. and A. Paivio. 1994. 'A dual coding view of imagery and verbal processes in reading comprehension'. In R. B. Ruddell, M. R. Ruddell and H. Singer (eds.), *Theoretical Models and Processes of Reading*, 4th edn. Newark, DE: International Reading Association.

Soars, L. and J. Soars. 1986. *Headway Intermediate*. Oxford: Oxford University Press.

Sokolov, A. N. 1972. *Inner Speech and Thought*. New York: Plenum Press.

Soyinka, W. 1963. 'Telephone conversation'. In G. Moore and U. Beier (eds.), *Modern Poetry from Africa*. London: Penguin.

Stanovich, K. E. 1980. 'Towards an interactive-compensatory model of individual differences in the development of reading fluency'. *Reading Research Quarterly*, 16: 32–71.

Steels, L. 2003. 'Language re-entrance and the "inner voice"'. *Journal of Consciousness Studies*, 10(4/5): 173–85.

Stevick, E. 1986. *Images and Options in the Language Classroom*. Cambridge: Cambridge University Press.

1989. *Success With Foreign Languages*. Hemel Hempstead: Prentice-Hall International.

Swaffer, J. 1988. 'Readers, texts and second language: the interactive processes'. *Modern Language Journal*, 72: 123–49.

Thompson, I. 1987. 'Memory in language learning'. In A. Wenden and J. Ruben (eds.), *Learning Strategies in Language Learning*. Englewood Cliffs, NJ: Prentice Hall.

Tierney, R. and J. W. Cunningham. 1984. 'Research on teaching reading comprehension'. In P. D. Pearson (ed.), *Handbook of Reading Research*. White Plains, NY: Longman.

Tomlinson, B. 1993. 'Do we see what they mean?' Unpublished PhD paper. University of Nottingham.

1994. *Openings*. London: Penguin.

1996. 'Helping L2 readers to see'. In T. Hickey and J. Williams, *Language, Education and Society in a Changing World*. Clevedon, Avon: Multilingual Matters.

1997. 'The role of visualisation in the reading of literature by learners of a foreign language'. Unpublished PhD thesis. University of Nottingham.

1998. 'And now for something not completely different: an approach to language through literature'. *Reading in a Foreign Language*, 11(2): 177–89.

2000a. 'Talking to yourself: the role of the inner voice in language learning'. *Applied Language Learning*, 11(1): 123–54.

2000b. 'A multi-dimensional approach'. *The Language Teacher*, 24(7): 1–6.

2000c. 'Beginning to read forever: a position paper'. *Reading in a Foreign Language*, 13(1): 523–38.

2001a. 'Connecting the mind: a multi-dimensional approach to teaching language through literature'. *The English Teacher*, 4(2): 104–15.

2001b. 'The inner voice: a critical factor in language learning'. *Journal of the Imagination in L2 Learning*, VI: 26–33.

2003a. 'Helping learners to develop an effective L2 inner voice'. *RELC Journal*, 34(2): 178–94.

2008. 'Language acquisition and language learning materials'. In B. Tomlinson (ed.), *English Language Teaching Materials*. London: Continuum.

2009. 'What we actually do in English'. In J. Mukundan (ed.), *Readings on ELT Materials III*. Petaling Jaya: Pearson Malaysia.

Tomlinson, B. and H. Masuhara. 1994. *Use Your English*. Tokyo: Asahi Press.

Tomlinson, B., B. Dat, H. Masuhara and R. Rubdy. 2001. 'EFL courses for adults'. *ELT Journal*, 55(1): 80–101.

Tomlinson, B. and J. Avila. 2007a. 'Seeing and saying for yourself: the roles of audio-visual mental aids in language learning and use'. In B. Tomlinson (ed.), *Language Acquisition and Development: Studies of First and Other Language Learners*. London: Continuum.

2007b. 'Applications of the research into the roles of audio-visual mental aids for language teaching pedagogy'. In B. Tomlinson (ed.), *Language*

Acquisition and Development: Studies of First and Other Language Learners. London: Continuum.

Updike, J. 1994. *Brazil.* London: Hamish Hamilton.

Van Dijk, T. and W. Kintsch, 1983. *Strategies of Discourse Comprehension.* New York: Academic Press.

Wolfe, T. 1988. *Bonfire of the Vanities.* London: Jonathan Cape.

Yi, Y. In press. 'The effects of visual imaging training on Chinese EFL learners' narrative writing'. PhD Thesis. Leeds Metropolitan University.

15 Squaring the circle – reconciling materials as constraint with materials as empowerment

Alan Maley

15.1 Introduction

A major dilemma faced by all writers of materials, even those writing for small groups of learners with well-defined needs, is that all learners, all teachers and all teaching situations are uniquely different, yet published materials have to treat them as if they were, in some senses at least, the same. A further problem for materials writers is that, although they are well aware that the course, the direction and the pace of learning are largely unpredictable, they have to predetermine all these things.

Prabhu (2001), among others, has pointed out the constraining effects of materials on the freedom of action of teachers (see Andrew Littlejohn and Hitomi Masuhara's chapters in this volume). In the interests of efficiency and quality (in one of its definitions at least), the writing of materials is generally delegated to a group of specialists, who produce centrally the materials to be used locally by another group: the teachers in their individual classrooms. (In a very few projects, local teachers at least contribute to the writing team, but this is very much the exception.) In this way, the materials can pre-empt all the important decisions which teachers themselves might otherwise be expected to make. The content is predetermined. The order of the content is predetermined. The rate of progression through the materials is predetermined. The procedures for using the content are also predetermined.

Clearly, what actually happens in classrooms using published materials is that there is a complex trade-off between the three major elements in the equation: the materials, the teacher and the learners.

In some cases there may be a relatively close fit between the three. This may occur when the materials have been designed for a relatively specific learning group. Even then, owing to individual differences amongst the learners and to teacher factors, there will never be a perfect fit. Such teacher factors include the teacher's:

- degree of language proficiency and confidence
- previous personal learning experiences as learners rather than as teachers

Figure 15.1

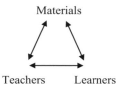

Materials

Teachers   Learners

- own personality (introvert/extrovert, open/closed, etc.)
- preferred teaching style (directive/consultative, etc.)
- cultural background.

However, in most cases, for reasons to do with the economics of publishing amongst other things, the materials are intended to be used by the largest possible number of learners. An obvious consequence is that:

> The wider the area to be served by a given set of materials, the more varied the learners' states are likely to be … (Prabhu 2001)

> In other words, the more extensive the user population, the more variety it will exhibit. All learners are different; the more of them there are, the more scope there is for difference. (Maley 1995b)

In cases like this, the materials can be conceived of as constituting a constraint upon the individual teacher's sense of what may be appropriate at a given pedagogical moment. The materials may also be far from the learners' capacity or sense of relevance at a given point:

> What typically happens in these circumstances is that the teacher has to bridge the gap between the materials and his/her sense of the learners' needs at that particular moment. So, the more widely used the materials, and consequently the more different and varied the learner need from the prescribed, pre-empted materials, the harder the teacher has to work to adapt the one to the other. (Maley 1995b)

The solution which is sometimes applied is to design materials with relatively specific groups in mind, with respect to cultural and cognitive content, local learning conditions, and so on. But this still fails to address the central problem. What is needed is 'not just a decentralisation of materials production, but a fundamental change in the design of materials' (Prabhu 2001) in the direction of providing greater flexibility in decisions about content, order, pace and procedures (see Hitomi Masuhara's chapter in this volume).

The remainder of this chapter will look at four possible responses to this problem. The first of these is no more than a set of coping strategies which teachers adopt with the materials currently available. The second is in line with Prabhu's view that we need 'a fundamental change in the design of materials'. The third concerns the exploitation of the burgeoning resources of Information Technology. The fourth has to do with the notion of content-based language learning, and in particular with CLIL (Content and Language Integrated Learning.)

15.2 Making the best of it – what teachers can do

Many teachers use some or all of the following strategies to make the published course bearable, or more effective.

15.2.1 Give it a rest

From time to time teachers will introduce additional material not in the coursebook to restore interest when it is flagging or to provide light relief (the 'wet Friday afternoon effect'). Such material typically includes songs, rhymes, games, cartoons, off-air recordings, video clips, and so on. Although such activities involve setting the coursebook aside, they are generally no more than cosmetic entertainment. However, many teachers do manage to build such activities into their teaching in a principled way, for example by using them as 'warmers' for the more extended activities which follow, or as 'coolers' to promote reflection on a previous activity.

15.2.2 Change it

For the teacher who wishes to adapt the materials, a number of options are available:

- omission: the teacher leaves out things deemed inappropriate, offensive or unproductive for the particular group.
- addition: where there seems to be inadequate coverage, teachers may decide to add material, either in the form of texts or exercise material.
- reduction: where the teacher shortens an activity to give it less weight or emphasis.
- extension: where an activity is lengthened in order to give it an additional dimension. For example, a vocabulary activity is extended to draw attention to some lexico-syntactic patterning.
- rewriting/modification: teachers may occasionally decide to rewrite material, especially exercise material, to make it more appropriate, more

'communicative', more demanding, more culturally accessible to their students, and so on.

- replacement: texts or exercise material which is considered inadequate, for whatever reason, may be replaced by more suitable material. This is often culled from published 'resource materials' (see below).
- reordering: teachers may decide that the order in which the materials are presented is not suitable for their students. They can then decide to plot a different course through the materials from the one the writer has laid down.
- branching: teachers may decide to add options to the existing activity or to suggest alternative pathways through the activities, for example, an experiential route or an analytical route or a narrative route.

For further discussion of such materials adaptation see Cunningsworth (1995), Islam and Mares (2003), McDonough and Shaw (2003), McGrath (2002), and Tomlinson and Masuhara (2004).

15.2.3 Do-it-yourself

Scissors and Paste

Skills modules

Teachers may decide to abandon the idea of a single coursebook altogether and instead to erect their own course based on one or other of the several skills series now on the market. This gives teachers the freedom to choose material at different levels for different skills, according to the needs and level of the learners. This looks easier to do than it is in practice. One of the main problems is the relative lack of coherence between skill modules. For example, if students are judged to be at level X in reading and at level Z in writing, it may be difficult to harmonise the modules in these two skill areas. It also requires an experienced teacher who can keep tabs on the overall shape of the course as it develops, and can make good any obvious omissions. This option is also subject to the problems of mixed-ability classes where students may be at different levels even within a single skill.

Resource option

This is a more radical option, in that teachers draw upon the whole range of available resource materials to put together a course they feel is in accordance with their students' needs. The materials available are now considerable and some publishers' lists include resource book series with banks of texts/activities, materials culled from existing coursebooks and skills collections. Many schools also maintain collections of 'authentic' texts (printed, audio, video, Internet, etc.) and materials tailor-made by the teachers themselves.

Again, it takes a very skilled teacher to operate this option. It requires an encyclopedic knowledge of existing resources, a sure grasp of the overview of the learning pathway for the group, and enormous energy. It is, for the present at least, most likely to be operated in the context of well-resourced private language teaching institutions working with relatively small groups on intensive courses. Most secondary school teachers would find it a daunting prospect, even were they to be permitted to cast away the coursebook in the first place. However, it can be done if teams of teachers from the same institution, city or area get together regularly to share ideas, techniques, materials and resources.

The process option

This is an even more radical alternative: teachers may decide to dispense with pre-developed materials altogether. Instead, they set the scene for a process to take place. It is the process which will generate its own content and learning activities. Examples of process approaches include the following.

Project work

In project work, the teacher simply sets up, or helps the learners decide on, a project they will work upon for an agreed period of time. For instance, they might decide to produce a booklet describing the facilities available to disabled people in the local community. To do this, they will need to discuss and plan their activities, read documents, interview people outside the school (possibly having designed a questionnaire), discuss their findings, draft and redraft their booklet until it is in final format. The teacher's role is then to monitor and support the process as required. For further information about project work, see Fried-Booth (2002), Legutke and Thomas (1991) and Philips *et al.* (1999).

Other possible projects include those based on global issues, where students research a particular area of global concern, for example waste disposal, either in its international aspects or in its local manifestations (Sampedro and Hillyard 2004).

Community Language Learning (CLL)

In this approach (Richards and Rodgers 2001) it is the learners who decide what they want to say. The teacher's role, initially at least, is to provide the foreign language equivalent of what a learner wants to say. Content is wholly in the hands of the learners, who gradually build their own 'syllabus'. The process is therefore unpredictable and precludes the use of preformatted materials. It is also highly demanding in energy and commitment, both from teachers and learners!

Drama techniques

Here, too, it is only the 'empty' shell of the technique which is provided by the teacher. Learners 'fill' the technique with their own spontaneously produced, unpredictable language (Maley and Duff 2005, Phillips 1999, Wessels 1987, Wilson 2009).

Extensive reading

All the evidence points to the fact that reading extensively (where learners read a lot, read fast, choose what to read, when to read and how to read, and where there are no tests or exercises) is overwhelmingly the most effective way to acquire, maintain and extend proficiency in the language (Day and Bamford 1998, Krashen 2004). Teachers who follow this process option essentially have three main roles: to motivate learners to participate, to set up systems for making books available and clearly signposted, and to monitor and advise (Duber 1999, Schmidt n.d., Waring 2007).

Creative writing

In the last few years, interest in promoting the creation of imaginative, representational texts by learners has gained momentum. A number of helpful books have appeared offering techniques to develop both poetry and story-writing. (Spiro 2004, 2006, Wright 2009, Wright and Hill 2009). There are also instances of teacher creative writing groups creating stories and poems for use by learners. (Maley and Mukundan 2005). Apart from the motivational impact of seeing their own work 'published' in English, and the boost this process gives to language learning, the texts which are produced are then available for use by learners in subsequent classes. The most radical experiments in creative writing have made the writing of a novel the central principle of the language course over a complete semester or year. This extreme version of the creative writing option will rarely be feasible, but a proportion of time spent on creative writing has proved effective.

Clearly, process options require great competence and skill, energy and self-confidence on the part of the teacher. They are also likely to conflict with the institutional requirements of many educational settings. They are therefore only ever likely to appeal to a minority of teachers, although elements of process approaches can and often are incorporated into more traditional, course-based teaching.

15.3 Incorporating choice – what materials writers can do

The previous section reviewed the options open to teachers for dealing with materials as they are or for incorporating various process options.

In this section I shall pick up Prabhu's proposal, referred to earlier, for a radically different way of approaching materials design.

One of the main objectives of the proposal is to pass to teachers at least some of the control over four major factors in the classroom: content (what), order (when), pace (how fast), procedure (how).

15.3.1 Prabhu's proposals

The approach to materials production which Prabhu proposes would:

> provide a range of possible inputs, without envisaging that they will be used in any one classroom or that all classrooms will use the same inputs. They may suggest different teaching agendas and lesson formats but are not themselves organised into lesson units. They may provide inputs at different levels of difficulty and in different quantities, leaving it to the teacher to select from the range in both respects. ... the expectation is ... that teachers will find it useful to draw on them in implementing the decisions they themselves make as teachers, being as faithful as possible to their own perceptions of learner states and learning processes. (Prabhu 2001).

Prabhu suggests two possible ways of categorising such resource options:

(a) Semi-materials. These can be of two kinds:

- single-type activities such as listening comprehension, writing activities, reading skills exercises, vocabulary development work, role play, and so on. Such materials would still be 'centrally' produced, that is published, but it would be left to the teacher to decide on the order of presentation, the pace and the way in which they were combined with other materials.
- collections of 'raw' input, that is, collections/selections of written, spoken or visual texts which are presented without specifying how they are to be used (Maley and Duff 1976). It is left to the teacher to decide which procedures (grammar awareness-raising activities, vocabulary in context, role play, comprehension questions, diagram completion, etc.) it is appropriate to use with a particular class at a particular moment.

(b) Meta-materials. Essentially, meta-materials are 'empty' pedagogical procedures. For example, dictation is a meta-material. Other examples would include role play, gap-filling, summary writing, jigsaw listening, drama techniques, creative writing, and so on.

The teacher decides on the nature of the input (the 'text') and applies the procedure to it. In this way, the teacher is in control of the content side of the teaching event.

15.3.2 Flexi-materials

It is possible to take these ideas of Prabhu a stage further. In fact, flexi-materials combine the notion of semi-materials with that of meta-materials.

In flexi-materials teachers are provided with a set of 'raw' texts. (They are then encouraged to add further texts they find for themselves.) They are also provided with a set of generalisable pedagogical procedures (see Appendix 1) which may be applied to any/all of the texts in any combination (Maley 1994, 1995a, 2003b, 2006). Teachers are then free to decide on which texts to use, in which order, and with which procedures. This gives them control over content, order, pace and procedure.

The flexibility of such materials lies not only in the fact that teachers can decide on the factors listed above but also in the possibility of returning to texts for a second or third time; each time using a different procedure. Figure 15.2 gives an example of this.

Any of the text-types in the left-hand column of Figure 15.2 may be used with any of the procedures in the right-hand column.

The detailed description of the application of flexi-materials is set out in Appendix 1. Worked examples of different combinations of text plus procedure are to be found in Appendix 2.

Clearly the key idea of permutating text with procedure can be applied to pictorial material, audio recordings and video as well as to printed text. It is certainly a powerfully generative idea which has been further developed (Maley 2003b, 2006). In the Inputs – Processes – Outcomes model shown in Table 15.1, raw inputs from the left-hand column can be combined with processes from the middle column (including the generative procedures described above) to produce a set of outcomes of different kinds.

Figure 15.2

Text-type	Procedure
One-line texts (proverbs, headlines, etc.)	Expansion
Haiku	Reduction
Mini-texts	Media-transfer
Epitaphs	Matching
Diary entries	Selection/ranking
Short poems	Comparison/contrast
Prayers	Reconstruction
Programme notes	Reformulation
Mini-sagas	Interpretation
Short newspaper articles	Creating text
Nasruddin stories	Analysis
Short essays	Project work

Table 15.1 *Inputs – Processes – Outcomes model*

INPUTS	PROCESSES	OUTCOMES
People (experiences, feelings, memories, opinions, appearance, etc.)	*Generic:* Time (long/short) Intensity (high/low)	Material outcomes (student texts, visual displays, performance, etc.)
Topics/themes	Type (active/reflective, interactive)	Pedagogical outcomes (evidence of learning, test results, fluency, reading speed/comprehension, learning to learn, handling feedback, meta-competence, etc.)
Texts (literary/non-literary, published/student-generated, etc. extensive readers)	Mode (individual work, pairs, groups, whole class)	
Reference materials (dictionaries, thesauruses, encyclopedias, reference grammars)	Medium (spoken/written, receptive/productive, electronic/hard copy, etc.) *Management:* routines	(NB. Material and Pedagogical outcomes are linked to 'objectives'.)
Realia (objects, texts, pictures, etc.)	instructions question types	Educational outcomes (increased social/intercultural awareness, critical thinking, creative problem-solving, autonomous learning, etc.)
Visuals (photos, videos, film, 'art' …)	*Techniques:* questioning	
Audio (spoken text, music, sounds …)	info-gap, opinion gap, etc.	
Internet (email, text messages, My Space, blogs, etc.)	jigsaw reading/listening process writing reading skills	Psycho-social outcomes (increased self-esteem, self-awareness, confidence, group solidarity, cooperation, responsibility, attitudinal change, etc.)
Games, simulations, role play, language play	visualising inner speech/rehearsal	
Oral accounts (stories, jokes, anecdotes, presentations, etc.)	*Task types:* brainstorming	
Problems (puzzles, moral dilemmas, logical problems …)	predicting classifying evaluating	(NB. Educational and psycho-social outcomes are linked to 'Aims'.)
Projects	summarising	
Techniques (dictation, translation, improvisation, etc.)	revising/editing researching problem-solving performing constructing objects *Generative procedures:* (see above and Appendix 1.)	

15.4 Using IT as a resource

Global communication has been transformed by the cyber-revolution of recent years. This has included the emergence of the Internet along with email as a major mode of communication; the expansion of computer corpora as tools for language investigation and for developing dictionaries/reference grammars; the growth in sophistication of mobile phones with multiple applications including text-messaging (Crystal 2008); the development of social networking platforms such as blogs, Facebook, MySpace, Second Life, and so on. All these resources, which can be rapidly and flexibly accessed, offer enormous potential for the freeing of learners and teachers alike from the constraints of the coursebook. So far, however, there has been only modest development and exploitation of such materials, which are attended by a new set of problems (Eastment 1994, Kramsch 1997, Kramsch, A' Ness and Lam 2000, Tenner 1996, Wolf 2008). These problems can be summarised as issues to do with More (Naish 2009), Faster (Gleick 1999), Quality and Learning Yield. Space does not allow a detailed discussion of these issues, but it is clear that the headlong rush into exponential growth has potentially negative consequences, if only because constantly evolving superchoice makes meaningful choice difficult, and infoglut makes selection of useful material a time-consuming business. Equally, there is no necessary relationship between the surface attraction of electronic communication and the quality and quantity of learning which results.

It is certain, however, that we now stand on the threshold of a new generation of materials based on these technologies and their rapidly evolving successors (see the chapters by Gary Motteram and by Lisa Kervin and Beverly Derewianka in this volume).

It is symptomatic of the difficulty of implementing such resources that they change so fast that almost any application is bound to be ephemeral. Hence the difficulty in citing current websites or programmes here, some of which are almost certain to be out of date by the time of publication. However, there are sources of up-to-date information in the regular articles in *ELT Journal* and in *Voices* (the Newsletter of IATEFL). What can be done is to indicate broad modes of application. These technology resources can be exploited for teaching/learning in four main ways:

(i) Through the development of teaching sites which offer a variety of fairly traditional activities and exercises in electronic form. A good example of this would be the Macmillan website http://onestopenglish. com, the British Council/BBC website www.teachingenglish.org. uk or Dave Sperling's Internet Activities Workbook (1999). One advantage of such materials is that they can be worked on by learners at their own pace outside class (see below) but methodologically; they are no more than familiar material delivered in a novel mode.

(ii) The Internet provides virtually unlimited access to a full range of texts, which can be quarried by the teacher or learner to meet the needs of the moment. For example, if a teacher/learner wishes to find examples of English proverbs, or Minisagas, or love poems, or jokes or even complete novels, all they need do is to call up the pages on Google or one of the other providers. These are, of course, still 'raw texts' in the sense that they come without pedagogical applications, but they are available in vast numbers at the click of a button.

(iii) The Internet also gives access to an almost unlimited number of reference sources: online dictionaries, thesauruses, grammars, corpora, encyclopedias, and so on. These can be made the base for all manner of individual research activities, independent of any coursebook, and conducted out of class (Maley 2009). Learners can also create their own, personalised online dictionaries, grammars, thesauruses, which they can share with other learners.

(iv) The use of email, texting, social networking sites such as Facebook and MySpace, and self-regulated virtual environments such as Second Life, clearly open up whole new areas for exploring communication between learners. Apart from potential ethical questions, such types of communication also raise organisational issues. How does the teacher set up systems and structures to maximise the potential benefits of these resources? There would seem to be three main ways of harnessing the attractions of these systems to language learning.

One is to incorporate training in the non-linear reading skills needed to process electronic text on screen (Tseng 2008). Learners tend to be slick at operating their computers but not necessarily very efficient at locating, selecting and processing relevant information. This kind of computer literacy training would have significant language-learning pay-offs in addition to its general educational value.

Secondly, such systems could be used for projects of various kinds involving students from different locations. Perhaps the simplest activity would be group online discussions between classes in different countries using Yahoo Groups or any other such facility. Such discussions might be linked to specific themes, such as global warming, seen from different perspectives in different countries.

Thirdly, teachers could assist learners to develop direct friendships with other learners of English to exchange personal information and opinions. This clearly carries certain moral and ethical risks, and also involves the teacher in additional logistical and monitoring activity.

Using IT has some massive advantages. It allows rapid and flexible access to unlimited information resources. It can free teachers and students alike from the constraints of the textbook. For most students motivation is already there to use these systems: it does not need to be created. Most importantly, most of the work can be done outside the classroom in the students' own time. As Barker (2009) has pointed out, the vast majority of classroom-based language learning comes nowhere near offering enough hours of exposure to the language. It is only by finding ways to engage students outside the classroom, through IT activities, extensive reading, project work, and so on, that they will get sufficient exposure.

There are, however, serious potentially negative consequences arising from an overenthusiastic adoption of IT. Already in *Technopoly* (1995) Neil Postman was sounding the alarm concerning a total capitulation to technology. More recently, Maryanne Wolf (2008) has raised the question as to whether the multitasking, rapidly switching, superficial processing of information might not impair more reflective modes of thinking.

15.5 Using content-based learning

Another radical alternative to the English language textbook is to base all work on the content of another discipline – history, geography, physical education, chemistry, mathematics, or of a topic/skill that the learners are really interested in (e.g. football, drama, rock music). The idea is not new, of course. Bernard Mohan (1986) has been advocating such an approach for many years now (Richards and Rodgers 2001). Such an approach has the great advantage of providing a subject matter to an otherwise content-empty discipline. It can also enhance motivation, as learners more easily perceive the relevance of what they are doing.

The teaching of other subjects through English has been a feature of international schools worldwide for many years too, and the explosion of such institutions, along with the IB (International Baccalaureate) in the past two decades gives some credence to the efficacy of the approach. Elite English-medium pilot schools were also an established feature of education in the then-Communist countries of the Soviet bloc, and in China. And in 2003 the Malaysian government decreed the reintroduction of English for the teaching of maths and science subjects in the Malaysian school system (though the policy has since been reversed). Most recently, the content-based approach has been given new life through the CLIL (Content and Language Integrated Learning) movement. Proponents of CLIL make a distinction between earlier versions where English was learned through the subject content of another discipline, and CLIL, which advocates the learning of other subjects through English. The difference may appear so subtle as to be insignificant, but there is a clear difference of focus, from English as primary aim, to the subject as primary aim. There is already a sizeable literature on CLIL, which has tended to enhance its near-cult status (Coyle *et al.* 2010; Deller and Price 2007; Mehisto *et al.* 2008).

The advantages of a content-based approach are plain to see. Students learn or acquire language which is of immediate relevance and use. The subject matter is generally more interesting than what they might find in a language textbook. They are motivated because the subjects they learn through English are part of their core curriculum, where failure would have real and damaging consequences for their future lives.

There are some problematic issues too, however. Teaching a subject through English (or English through a subject) does away with the need for an English language textbook, but usually a subject textbook replaces the language textbook. In many cases, too, some supplementary English materials are needed to support the content instruction. Content-based learning, and CLIL in particular, also runs up against the problem of the teacher. Most teachers competent to teach English are not proficient in the subject matter and teaching techniques for other disciplines. And subject teachers required to teach their subject through English may also lack proficiency in the English language (a major issue in Malaysia, for example) and in language teaching routines and practices. In well-resourced environments, with teachers highly proficient in English, such as international schools or some high schools in Europe, these problems are minimal. Elsewhere they are a major obstacle to the adoption of CLIL. One possible solution is team-teaching, where a subject teacher and English teacher work together with the same class. This is, however, an expensive option. It also requires the sharing of pedagogical space and an attitude of openness which cannot be taken for granted.

15.6 Some further possibilities

(a) Develop a set of texts roughly graded for length/difficulty. Alongside it, develop a set of varied activities at different levels of task difficulty (Ellis 2003, Nunan 1989, Skehan 1993, Van den Branden 2006). Teachers would then be able to choose texts at a suitable level of difficulty and match them with tasks at a corresponding level of cognitive/linguistic demand. This is a possible refinement of the flexi-materials concept (see Tomlinson's *Openings* (1994) for one way in which this can be done).

(b) Develop a course with a central core component which it would be essential for all teachers/learners to follow. This would be accompanied by a cluster of optional modules at a number of levels, focused on different aspects of the language. For example, any of the following options could be chosen: skills modules (to develop writing, listening, reading, speaking skills); vocabulary development modules; grammar awareness-raising modules; cultural awareness-raising modules; testing modules; project-based modules; thematic modules; games/fluency activities modules; and so on. Teachers/learners would then be able to select modules appropriate to their interests, learning needs and level at any particular point.

15.7 Conclusion

Materials will always be constraining in one way or another, so that teachers will always need to exercise their professional judgement (or 'sense of plausibility') about when and how a particular piece of material is best implemented in any particular case. However, it must also be clear that there are alternatives to the relatively inflexible design of most currently available published materials.

Choice is important, not only for ideological reasons but also for the opportunities it offers teachers to exercise responsibility, and in the process to continue their own professional development.

Genuine choice is also increasingly important in a consumer-driven world offering seemingly endless choice, which is in fact illusory. The high investment cost of publishing makes risk-taking unattractive; hence the near-clones offered in publishers' lists. I hope to have shown that there are realistic alternatives to teachers with the will to exercise them.

References

Barker, D. 2009. 'The role of unstructured learner interaction in the study of a foreign language'. In S. Menon and J. Lourdunathan (eds.), *Readings on ELT Materials IV*. Petaling Jaya: Pearson Malaysia.

Coyle, D., P. Hood and D. Marsh 2010. *CLIL: Content and Language Integrated Learning*. Cambridge: Cambridge University Press.

Crystal, D. 2008. *txtng: the Gr8 Db8*. Oxford: Oxford University Press.

Cunningsworth, A. 1995. *Choosing Your Coursebook*. Oxford: Heinemann.

Day, R., R. and J. Bamford. 1998. *Extensive Reading in the Second Language Classroom*. Cambridge: Cambridge University Press.

Deller, S. and C. Price. 2007. *The Teaching of Other Subjects Through English*. Oxford: Oxford University Press.

Duber, J. (ed.). 1999. *TESL-EJ*. http://tesl-ej.org/ej13/int.html, accessed 12 July 2009.

Eastment, D. 1994. 'CD-ROM-An overview of materials'. *Modern English Teacher*, 3(4) March 1994.

Ellis, R. 2003. *Task-based Learning and Teaching*. Oxford: Oxford University Press.

Fried-Booth, D. 2002 *Project Work*, 2nd edn. Oxford: Oxford University Press.

Gleick, J. 1999. *Faster: The Acceleration of just about Everything*. New York: Vintage Books.

Islam, C. and C. Mares 2003. 'Adapting classroom materials'. In B. Tomlinson (ed.), *Developing Materials for Language Teaching*. London: Continuum.

Kramsch, C. 1997. 'Language teaching in an electronic age'. In G. M. Jacobs (ed.), *Language Classrooms of Tomorrow: Issues and Responses*. Singapore: SEAMEO Regional Language Centre.

Kramsch, C., F. A' Ness and E. Wan Shun Lam. 2000. 'Authenticity and ownership in the computer-mediated acquisition of L2 literacy'. *Language Learning and Technology*, 4(2) September. 2000: 78–104.

Krashen, S. 2004. *The Power of Reading: Insights from the Research*, 2nd edn. Portsmouth NH: Heinemann.

Legutke, M. and H. Thomas. 1991. *Process and Experience*. Harlow: Longman.

McDonough, J. and C. Shaw. 2003. *Materials and Methods in ELT*, 2nd edn. Oxford: Blackwell.

McGrath, I. 2002. *Materials Evaluation and Design for Language Teaching*. Edinburgh: Edinburgh University Press.

Maley, A. 1994. *Short and Sweet I*. London: Penguin Books.

1995a. *Short and Sweet II*. London: Penguin Books.

1995b. 'Materials writing and tacit knowledge'. In A. Hidalgo *et al.* (eds.), *Getting Started: Materials Writers on Materials Writing*. Singapore: SEAMEO Language Centre.

2003a. 'Chapter 11. Creative approaches to materials writing'. In Brian Tomlinson (ed.), *Developing Materials for Language Teaching*. London/ New York: Continuum.

2003b. 'Chapter 2. Inputs, processes and outcomes in materials development: extending the range'. In J. Mukundan (ed.), *Readings on ELT Material*. Serdang: Universiti Putra Malaysia Press, pp. 21–31.

2006. 'Doing things with texts'. In J. Mukundan (ed.), *Focus on ELT Materials*. Petaling Jaya: Pearson Malaysia.

2009. *Advanced Learners*. Oxford: Oxford University Press.

(ed.) 2006a. *Asian Short Stories for Young Readers*. Vol. 4. Petaling Jaya: Pearson/Longman Malaysia.

(ed.) 2006b. *Asian Poems for Young Readers*. Vol. 5. Petaling Jaya: Pearson/Longman Malaysia.

Maley, A. and A. Duff. 1976. *Words*. Cambridge: Cambridge University Press.
   2005. *Drama Techniques*. 3rd edn. Cambridge: Cambridge University Press.
Maley, A. and J. Mukundan (eds.). 2005 *Asian Stories for Young Readers,
   Vols. 1 and 2*. Petaling Jaya: Pearson/Longman Malaysia.
   (eds.). 2005. *Asian Poems for Young Readers, Vol. 3*. Petaling Jaya: Pearson/
   Longman Malaysia.
Mehisto, P. *et al*. 2008. *Uncovering CLIL: Content and Language Integrated
   Learning and Multilingual Education*. Oxford: Macmillan.
Mohan, B. 1986. *Language and Content*. Reading, MA: Addison-Wesley.
Mukundan, J. (ed.). 2006 *Creative Writing in EFL/ESL Classrooms II*.
   Petaling Jaya: Pearson Malaysia.
Naish, J. 2009. *Enough: Breaking Free from the World of Excess*. London:
   Hodder and Stoughton.
Nunan, D. 1989. *Designing Tasks for the Communicative Classroom*.
   Cambridge: Cambridge University Press.
Philips, D. *et al*. 1999. *Projects with Young Learners*. Oxford: Oxford
   University Press.
Phillips, S. 1999. *Drama with Children*. Oxford: Oxford University Press.
Postman, N. 1995. *Technopoly: The Surrender of Culture to Technology*.
   New York: Vintage Books.
Prabhu, N. S. 2001. *A Sense of Plausibility* (unpublished manuscript).
Richards, J. C. and T. Rodgers. 2001. *Approaches and Methods in Language
   Teaching*, 2nd edn. Cambridge: Cambridge University Press.
Sampedro, R. and S. Hillyard. 2004. *Global Issues*. Oxford: Oxford University
   Press.
Schmidt, K. *Multiplying the Effects of In-class Instruction in Extensive
   Reading and Listening*. www.sendaiedu.com/06myc_keynotelecture_
   kschmidt.pdf (accessed 12 July 2009).
Skehan, P. 1993. 'A framework for the implementation of task-based learning'.
   IATEFL 1993 Conference Report.
Sperling, D. 1999. *Dave Sperling's Internet Activities Workbook*. New York:
   Prentice Hall.
Spiro, J. 2004. *Creative Poetry Writing*. Oxford: Oxford University Press.
   2006. *Storybuilding*. Oxford: Oxford University Press.
Tenner, E. 1996. *Why Things Bite Back: Technology and the Revenge of
   Unintended Consequences*. New York: Vintage Books.
Tseng, Min-chen. 2008. 'The difficulties that EFL learners have with reading
   text on the Web'. *The Internet TESL Journal*. Vol. XIV, no. 2, February
   2008. http://iteslj.org/ (accessed 12 July 2009).
Tomlinson, B. 1994. *Openings*. London: Penguin
Tomlinson, B. and H. Masuhara. 2004. *Developing Language Course
   Materials*. Singapore: SEAMEO RELC.
Van den Branden, K. 2006. *Task-based Education: from Theory to Practice*.
   Cambridge: Cambridge University Press.
Waring, R. 2007 (ed.), Special Issue of *The Language Teacher*: *Extensive
   Reading in Japan*. May 2007, 31(5).
Wessels, C. 1987. *Drama*. Oxford: Oxford University Press.

Wilson, K. 2009. *Drama and Improvisation*. Oxford: Oxford University Press.

Wolf, M. 2008. *Proust and the Squid*. London: Icon Books.

Wright, A. 2009. *Story-telling with Children*, 2nd edn. Oxford: Oxford University Press.

Wright, A. and D. A. Hill. 2009. *Writing Stories*. Innsbruck: Helbling.

Appendix 1 Twelve generalisable procedures

Each major category will be described. Examples of possible activities will then be given.

Although most of the procedures can be applied to most of the texts, they *need not all be used*. There is no point in wringing the text dry just for the sake of completeness. It is also often the case that a given text works better with certain procedures than with others. The detailed permutation of procedures and texts is in any case a decision only the teacher can properly make.

1. Expansion

   Key criterion – the text must be lengthened in some way.

   Examples:

   - Add one or more sentences/paragraphs to the beginning and end of the text.
   - Add specified items within the text (e.g. adjectives).
   - Add sentences within the text.
   - Add subordinate clauses within the text.
   - Add comment within the text.

2. Reduction

   Key criterion – the text must be shortened in some way.

   Examples:

   - Remove specified items (e.g. adjectives).
   - Turn it into telegraphese.
   - Combine sentences.
   - Remove clauses/sentences.
   - Rewrite in a different format (see also 3. Media transfer and 8. Reformulation, below).

3. Media transfer

   Key criterion – the text must be transferred into a different medium or format.

Examples:

- Transfer it into visual form (e.g. pictures, graphs, maps, tables, etc.).
- Turn prose into poem (or vice versa).
- Turn a letter into a newspaper article (or vice versa).
- Turn a headline into a proverb (or vice versa).
- Turn a poem into an advertising slogan (or vice versa).
- Turn a prose narrative into a screenplay.

4. Matching

   Key criterion – a correspondence must be found between the text and something else.

   Examples:

   - Match text with a visual representation.
   - Match text with a title.
   - Match text with another text.
   - Match text with a voice/music.

5. Selection/ranking

   Key criterion – the text must be chosen according to some given criterion. (In the case of ranking, several texts must be placed in order of suitability for a given criterion.)

   Examples:

   - Choose the best text for a given purpose (e.g. inclusion in a teenage magazine).
   - Choose the most/least (difficult, formal, personal, complex, etc.) text.
   - Choose the text most/least like the original version.
   - Choose words from a text to act as an appropriate title.

6. Comparison/contrast

   Key criterion – points of similarity/difference must be identified between two or more texts.

   Examples:

   - Identify words/expressions common to both texts.
   - Identify words/phrases in one text which are paraphrased in the other.
   - Identify ideas common to both texts.
   - Identify facts present in one text and not in the other.
   - Compare grammatical/lexical complexity. (See also 11. Analysis.)

7. Reconstruction

   Key criterion – coherence/completeness must be restored to an incomplete or defective text.

Examples:

- Insert appropriate words/phrases into gapped texts.
- Reorder jumbled words, lines, sentences, paragraphs and so on.
- Reconstruct sentences/texts from a word array.
- Reconstitute a written text from an oral presentation (various types of dictation).
- Remove sentences/lines which do not 'belong' in the text.

8. Reformulation

   Key criterion – the text must be expressed in a form different from the original without loss of essential meanings.

   Examples:

   - Retell a story from notes/memory.
   - Use key words to rewrite a text.
   - Rewrite in a different format (e.g. prose as poem). (See also 3. Media transfer, above.)
   - Rewrite in a different style/mood.

9. Interpretation

   Key criterion – personal knowledge/experience must be used to clarify and extend the meaning(s) of the text.

   Examples:

   - What does this recall from your own experience?
   - What does this remind you of?
   - What images does this throw up?
   - What associations does it have?
   - What questions would you wish to ask the author?
   - Formulate questions on the text beginning: what?, who?, where?, when?, why?, how?
   - What does the text not say that it might have said?

10. Creating text

    Key criterion – the text is to be used as a springboard for the creation of new texts.

    Examples:

    - Write a parallel text on a different theme.
    - Use the same story outline/model to write a new text.
    - Quarry words from text A to create a new text B.
    - Use the same title but write a new text.
    - Add lines/sentences to the text to reshape it. (See also 1. Expansion and 8. Reformulation, above.)
    - Combine these texts to create a new text.

11. Analysis

Key criterion – the text is to be submitted to some form of language-focused scrutiny.

Examples:

- Work out the ratio of one-word verbs to two-word verbs.
- How many different tenses are used? Which are most/least frequent?
- How many content (or function) words does the text contain?
- List the different ways in which the word X is referred to in the text (anaphoric reference).
- List all the words to do with (the sea, movement, ecology, etc.) in this text.

12. Project work

Key criterion – the text is used as a springboard for some related practical work with a concrete outcome.

Examples:

- Use the text as a centrepiece of an advertising campaign. First decide on the product. Then design the campaign posters, advertising jingles and so on. Finally present the product as a TV commercial (which must incorporate the text). If possible video it.
- This text is about the problem of X. Design a questionnaire on this problem for other groups to complete. Tabulate the results and present them to the rest of the class.
- This text presents a particular point of view. With a partner, prepare a brief magazine article which either supports or disagrees with this point of view. In both cases you will need to collect ideas and examples to support your own point of view.
- Display the articles on the class noticeboard.

Classroom procedures

Unless otherwise indicated, the normal procedure to adopt with all the suggested activities is:

1. *Individual work* – Each student first does the activity for her/himself. This ensures that everyone makes an initial personal effort.
2. *Pair work* (or work in threes) – Students work together to compare and discuss what they have produced individually.
3. *Class work* – The pair work then feeds back into whole-class discussion as appropriate.

There are a few cases when *group work* is preferable to pair work, especially in 12. Project work.

Appendix 2 Examples of text + procedures

Space does not permit me to give a complete set of activities to demonstrate how any given text might be combined with any one or more of the procedures. I hope, however, that the following will be sufficient to set teachers going if this idea appeals to them.

Text 1 Haiku

Strange to think of you

Thirty thousand feet below

And five years away.

(a) Expansion (NB. instructions are written as if direct to students.)
   (i) Rewrite the haiku 'in full'; that is, making clear what this is all about, e.g. I'm sitting in this aeroplane. We are flying over the city where I used to live five years ago and where we used to know each other. I suddenly think of you again ...
   (ii) Write a 'haiku paragraph' which might have come before this one, and one that could have come after it, e.g. When I got on the plane in Sydney, I fell asleep almost immediately. When I woke up, I realised we were over X ... As soon as I get back home, I shall call you. Old friends are precious.

(b) Media transfer
   (i) Write out the incident from the haiku as a postcard to the person who was 'Thirty thousand feet below'.
   (ii) Write an entry to the passenger's diary, recording this incident.

Here are some other haikus which could be worked on in similar ways:

Bark-skinned crocodile
One eyelid flickers open –
Sharp sliver of flint.

This sudden Spring squall
Shags the daffodils with snow –
Am I young or old?

Sounds across the valley,
In the early twilight:
Eyes dim – ears sharpen.

Alan Maley

Text 2 Short poem

The adversary
A mother's hardest to forgive.

Life is the fruit she longs to hand you,
Ripe on a plate. And while you live,
Relentlessly she understands you.

Phyllis McGinley

(a) Media transfer

Rewrite the poem as a haiku (line 1 = 5 syllables; line 2 = 7 syllables; line 3 = 5 syllables). Use words taken from the original as far as possible. For example:

Hardest to forgive
Is a mother. She so longs
To understand you.

(b) Comparison/contrast

Compare this poem with the original. Make a list of things the poems share and a list of the differences between them. Then compare your lists with another student. (E.g. Do they have any words in common? or ideas? Are the attitudes of the two 'speakers' the same? etc.)

Sorry
Dear parents,
I forgive you my life,
Begotten in a drab town,
The intention was good;
Passing the streets now,
I see the remains of sunlight.
It was not the bone buckled;
You gave me enough food
To renew myself.
It was the mind's weight
Kept me bent, as I grew tall.
It was not your fault.
What should have gone on,
Arrow aimed from a tried bow
At a tried target, has turned back,
Wounding itself
With questions you had not asked.

R. S. Thomas

(c) Selection

- Which is the most important word in the poem? Compare your answers in groups of four.

- Decide on an order from most to least suitable for the purposes to which this poem might be put. Compare your answer with a partner:
  - (i) as part of an advertisement for family counselling/advisory services.
  - (ii) as part of a letter from a daughter to her mother, with whom she is on bad terms.
  - (iii) as a poem for inclusion in an anthology for teenagers.
  - (iv) as the dedication on the first page of a book on the psychology of the family.

(d) Interpretation

- In pairs write out three questions you would like to ask the author of the poem.
- Does this remind you of any feelings you have had? Or that friends of yours may have sometimes had? Discuss this with a partner.
- The poet takes a rather negative view of mothers. Write a note to Phyllis McGinley in which you disagree with her views. Try to find at least three points in favour of your argument.

Text 3 Mini-text

He never sent me flowers. He never wrote me letters. He never took me to restaurants. He never spoke of love. We met in parks. I don't remember what he said, but I remember how he said it. Most of it was silence anyway.

Lescek Szkutnik

(a) Reconstruction

Word Array

silence	was	he
never	love	of
I	sent	anyway
took	met	letters
me	don't	spoke
most	restaurants	flowers
wrote	parks	said
to	what	how
remember	we	it
in		

Make as many sentences as you can, using only the words from the word array. (You can use the words as many times as you like and you do not have to use them all.) Then work with a partner. Use some of your sentences to write out a short story. Then compare it with the text your teacher will give you.

(b) Creating text

Imagine the couple in the text are meeting for the last time before they break up. With a partner, write the dialogue of what they say to each other.

(c) Analysis

What is the grammatical subject of each sentence? Can you see a pattern from the beginning through to the end of the text? (NB. For teachers – it moves from HE to WE to I to IT. Food for speculation!)

16 Lozanov and the teaching text

Grethe Hooper Hansen

16.1 Introduction

This chapter focuses on text writing and grammatical presentation in the Lozanov method. Rewriting it for this new edition has been a rewarding experience because in the intervening years, quantum science has become more familiar, making it easier to perceive the world as Lozanov did: multidimensional, indeterminate and participative, a reality that we influence by the way in which we live it. This has profound implications for change in education.

Suggestopedia (SP) is a controversial method of language teaching from Bulgaria that was received with incomprehension when it surfaced in the 1960s because its claims of prodigious learning could not be explained in a way consistent with the science of the time. Nor could it be explained by its founder, psychiatrist Dr Georgi Lozanov working at the University of Sofia during the Communist regime, because as a therapist he worked from intuition, following subtle indications that emerged from interactions. Healing victims of the regime, and obliged to use hypnosis for the worst cases, he sought to find a means to bring profoundly traumatised patients 'back to life'. What he developed through very delicate suggestion was a way of resuscitating the very essence of life – and it was the polar opposite of hypnosis, which in his experience drains away the life force. To banish the damaging implication of 'sick' people who needed 'help', he gave his therapeutic method the new goal of teaching a foreign language, and it was at that point that he discovered its extraordinary efficiency: not only did the trauma vanish but the learners learned English incredibly fast! Word spread, the government rushed in to seize the benefit of his work for the glory of Communism and a research institute was built.

The logic that Lozanov lived by is that which applies to the psychological dimension, that is subatomic and, therefore, in many ways the polar opposite of the Cartesian. To give an example, the fundamental Cartesian principle of contradiction no longer applies: things can be both A and not-A. Thus, in his teaching there are always two separate levels of effect for the teacher to negotiate: that which is conscious and that which is unconscious. If I, as a teacher of Italian, say 'Italian is easy', my student is unconsciously aware (a) that I am lying, and (b) that if he is finding Italian difficult, then that means he must be stupid!

The learning equivalent of the subatomic is what Polyani famously referred to as *The Tacit Dimension* (1967), considered by many educational thinkers to be the major stream of human learning (e.g. Claxton 1997), but largely ignored in education because it results only in 'passive' learning. Lozanov as a therapist knows that his patients respond far more powerfully to unconscious than to conscious stimuli. Why? Quantum biologists claim that 95 per cent of our mental process is unconscious; only 5 per cent is registered consciously (Lipton 2005). The complexity of Lozanov's method is due to a lifetime's research into the hidden language and territory of the unconscious, in particular the nebulous area where it meets the conscious, which he calls the 'para-conscious'.

SP aims to create the internal conditions to spark the 'bottom-up' learning of the tacit dimension, which, because it is unconscious, can occur 'in parallel' (I register sight, sound, touch, smell, movement, etc. simultaneously) rather than serially, one-thing-at-a-time. The infinitely greater volume of parallel process results in proportionately wider and more complex learning – an effect noted by Krashen (1981) and Asher (1977) in their 'acquisition' approaches, which resulted in very durable and plastic learning but did not solve the passivity problem. Learning parameters are the *opposite* of conscious learning: the conscious mind needs to narrow so as to focus down on individual items (our concept of 'concentration'), whereas the unconscious needs to remain wide open, that is in mental relaxation. Lozanov therefore focuses on learner receptivity, rather than on the material studied, and uses music, games and other complex means of relaxation to mediate a state of mind in which a vast quantity of material can be absorbed easily, effortlessly and without fatigue.

There are two more steps in this process, again imported from psychotherapy: incubation (supporting the unconscious as it does its work of recreating language) and elaboration (drawing the results up to conscious awareness), which will be illustrated later. But because there was no between-paradigm language available to him (and as a therapist, he has always been far more interested in results than explanations), because he was dependent on the funding of a government he opposed, and which restricted access to his work, Lozanov has frequently been misunderstood, misinterpreted and misrepresented. Miraculously, he is still working, based in Vienna, with an international training facility centred in Wales.

In the West we have favoured left-brain learning (Hannaford 1997) and have regarded the right brain as academically rather useless, because prior to Roger Sperry's exploration of hemispheric difference in the 1960s, we thought of the mind as a Cartesian logic-producing machine: the more logical it was, the better its quality. That tendency has endured because, since the right is not conscious, it cannot provide immediate answers for exam questions. Although it is dominant in the acquisition process, we tend to dismiss it in classrooms because of its passive nature. But Lozanov, like Krashen and Asher, targets the passive because it is more complex and voluminous than the active conscious mind. Iain McGilchrist's (2009) consummate study of brain hemisphericity explains the interaction between right (the master) and left: all new information enters through the right in a global way, is passed to the left for analysis and organisation, and goes back to the right for a final assessment. In normal day-to-day functioning both work perfectly together, a balance that is rarely honoured in today's classroom, due to what McGilchrist sees as the extreme left hemispheric polarisation that has been occurring in the Western world since the advent of Cartesian rationalism.

What Lozanov noticed in his therapeutic and medical practice is that when the whole organism is activated and encouraged to work in its natural way, not only is the person happier and the body healthier, but the mind can open to a state similar to that described by Csikszentmihalyi in *Flow, The Psychology of Optimal Experience* (1990). Our current epidemic of learning disorders in schools might suggest that when this natural process is suppressed, as it traditionally has been (lamented by Shakespeare, Blake and Wordsworth, as well as John Abbott 2010), we not only suppress human genius but cause a multitude of psychological and physical ills.

Lozanov's master teacher Evalina Gateva could intuitively create such 'quantum conditions' by surrounding her students with a cobweb of suggestions of security. There are teachers who can naturally do the same, but I was not one. I had to understand the concept before I could begin to work on upholding quantum possibility: for example, the trust, ease and suspension of disbelief needed to maintain fluid intersubjectivity. Once I realised that each part must be determined by the nature and purpose of the whole, I understood why it was that any exercise of mine that did not flow from the text or had been planned for grammatical purpose only, could collapse the whole delicate structure and puncture the confidence of the entire group. I spent difficult but rewarding hours reflecting on the many times I 'got it wrong' and the reasons behind my errors – and indeed this is Lozanov's own major recommendation for teacher development.

The overall aim of Suggestopedia is to hold the learner in a *state* in which the mind is optimally relaxed and fully expanded. For this reason art, with its suggestion of the search for the ideal, is a valuable tool. To feel this effect yourself, just look deeply at any one of Turner's sea or landscape paintings. When his teachers complain that their students are not learning, Lozanov's first suggestion will be to *double* the volume of the text – because this knocks the conscious mind out of action. Play (in the sense of just playing a game as opposed to doing an exercise) is one way of avoiding the storm of limitations and negative expectations that descend unconsciously when we labour to learn in classrooms: nobody judges or criticises your performance in snakes and ladders! Transform an exercise into a game and (provided you get it right) it will invite instead a confident expectation of fun and effortless success.

Lozanov called his method 'Suggestopedia' because *suggesting* rather than telling avoids the negative consequences of imposing control on organic/human process simply by giving the learner the power to choose for himself. McGilchrist's (2009) work on hemispherity is relevant here because the 'natural' approach engages the right hemisphere, which responds in an emotional and holistic way, whereas the left hemisphere is devoid of emotion and reacts rationally (and this is what is supposed to be targeted in today's government-controlled classrooms). Lozanov uses a variety of approaches to enhance learner autonomy; these are effectively tailored for the right hemisphere, although he himself never speaks of hemispheres. An example is the experience of success in suggestopedic learning. When this happens for the first time (new words tumbling out of one's mouth, unintended, and sometimes forming perfect sentences), it brings with it an extraordinary feeling of self-actualisation, knowing that learning has come entirely from inside, unaided, not in any way imposed by someone else. Students are very strongly affected by this experience, which is usually unlike any formal learning that they have previously known.

We now turn to the implications for text writing and grammatical presentation of the ideas expressed above. Remember that Dr Lozanov is essentially a therapist, who works through intuition and observation, constantly adjusting his method and ideas in response to situations and events. Although a highly educated man with more than one doctorate, he rejects all theorising (mine included) because abstract concepts *fix a reality* where he wishes to preserve fluidity and are not as precise as they purport to be since they have to be interpreted from within the (different) beliefs of each person who uses them. But for the reasons explained above, I continue with some reference to theory. I find it useful to refer to the work of Assagioli (1968), whose thinking was similar to Lozanov's and equally 'before its time': for example, he observed that whilst the conscious mind opens to that which makes logical sense and closes to that which is inconsistent with its beliefs, the non-conscious, like the rest of nature, is governed by the pleasure principle. As today's advertisers understand very well, colour, form, beauty, comfort and intimations of things we desire are magnets to the mind.

16.2 The Lozanov cycle

Lessons are considered in terms of a cycle: first comes the presentation, when learners absorb the material in three different ways, carefully orchestrated. The first, an informal, dramatised introduction to the vocabulary of the text, is followed by two formal but very different 'concerts', when the teacher reads the text aloud in synchrony with a piece of music. These 'input' sessions spark an unconscious 'incubation' process in each student that will continue throughout the course. Input can be completed in one long session, depending on circumstances, but it needs to be followed by at least one night's break. Then the 'elaboration' of the text begins, at first a decoding and then a freer and more creative session, as described below. Each lesson cycle follows this structure, but there will be one or more 'recapitulation' days to consolidate grammar, and the course finishes with the students planning, writing and delivering their own group performance. Each student takes on a new personality and name, framed in the target language, for the duration of the course. The teacher also takes on roles from time to time and mirrors fluidity of personality, changing as learning advances: being at first an authority figure to define and support the group interaction and set parameters of safety, gradually fading into the background as students gain in confidence and knowledge, and finally retreating to a back seat to let them take over. This results in a 'dismissal' of the teacher that always came as a surprise to me, bringing both relief (when I succeeded) and forlornness.

16.3 An example of the lesson cycle

Text: a comedy in 8–10 acts (1 act per cycle). Cycle 8–10 hours, parcelled as appropriate. Learners (L) choose a name and profession in the target language and develop the role as the course proceeds.

16.3.1 Presentation

1. Teacher (T) introduces the story of the act, using target grammatical structures and vocabulary. 'Passive' learners (Ls) listen, intervening only if they want to.
2. First concert: T distributes the text (1,000–2,000 words), plus translation at beginner level, then reads the whole act aloud to the accompaniment of classical music. Ls listen, read and follow the translation. Classical music conducive to emotion and with language-like structure – both of which assist memory.

3. Second concert: T reads again to accompaniment of Baroque music. Ls listen, eyes often closed, relaxed. Baroque music conducive to inner calm, clarity and order, optimal conditions to integrate and access understanding.

16.3.2 Elaboration

Activation of target structures and vocabulary. E1 involves Ls reading aloud, translation, occasional grammatical demonstration. E2 freer activities: games, drama, songs. VARIETY to reactivate items in different ways for memory and understanding.

The dialogue is written in column form, as in Figure 16.1, with language presented in sense units, which makes it easier to learn. Key words may be underlined or emphasised in colour, to stamp them into the memory. A grammatical feature is picked out and examples of it are listed in the right-hand column, again to mark it in the memory. Translation is used at beginner level, provided in a single column clipped over the grammar column, never printed in the text (this would be a suggestion that learning is difficult), and discarded as soon as students are confident enough to manage without it.

Since suggestopedic learning is based on text absorption, it is essential that all the grammatical structures chosen for emphasis or exposition are contained in the text. Texts need to be available electronically, so that they can be changed and adapted for different circumstances, but books or paper texts are used in the classroom, ideally including high-quality coloured illustrations (see the section on the aesthetic principle).

The text is also full of cue words or phrases to trigger activities and 'spontaneous' grammatical presentation (for example, when in the first elaboration we chorus the phrase 'on the fourth floor' from my text, this is my cue to run through a quick routine on ordinal numbers – as if the idea had just popped into my head and was not a planned piece of linguistic work). The students realise this, and enter the game, unconsciously knowing that they are also learning to learn. Everything must always be interrelated, an effect peculiar to Lozanov, discussed later in the section on grammatical presentation.

16.4 Language

The target structures and vocabulary are worked into a natural, flowing dialogue. The more fluid and melodious it sounds, the more vivid in imagery and poetic the language, the better it will penetrate the (nonconscious) mind. Simplicity implies ease, and texts should delight the

Figure 16.1

THE TEXT	
is a play in 8–10 acts, each complete in itself.	
The cast mirrors	
an ideal suggestopedic learning group –	
8 or more extraordinary people,	
equal in humanity	equal in . . .
if not in material status,	
involved in some way in the arts	involved in . . .
(to allow for artistic metaphors,	
high aesthetic content,	allow for . . .
underlying search for self-realisation).	search for . . .
The plot typically involves	
a situation which brings together	
geographically scattered people.	
It is important that the situation	
not be too 'far-out' because	
the intention is to show	
that high-voltage living	intend to . . .
is only a small step,	
an adjustment of mind,	
from where we are now.	
Mythical worlds appeal to writers	appeal to . . .
but may impose a dissociative framework.	

ear: just like the plays of Pinter and the poems of Blake. But, to be sure of engaging the subcortical brain so as to keep the action in the right hemisphere, there is also a need for high emotional content. Metaphors and images appear wherever possible to encourage global rather than analytical responses, symbols and archetypes to rivet attention at the unconscious level (water, trees, birds, animals, sun, moon, etc.), sensory words to stimulate sensori-motor learning, and a high concrete vocabulary to encourage imaging. Assagioli (1968), writing about language learning, also recommended galvanising the mind with wordplay, paradoxes, koans (apparently nonsensical word puzzles that require right hemispheric, inferential solutions), humour, tongue twisters, snatches of poetry, proverbs and sayings. In contrast with most methods, Lozanov's presents richness and complexity of structures from the start. Language is not limited to the structures which will be taught in that unit – so as to prime the mind for future learning and also present the language as a gestalt in all its variety and multiplicity (see the section on grammar, below).

A controversial issue in Lozanovian writing is the need for total 'positivity' at all times. 'Negativity' is avoided rather than denied (Lozanov also includes various other means of discharging negative emotion, particularly through music) because, *within this paradigm*, it is obstructive to learning: stress and anxiety tend to overactivate the left hemisphere whereas Lozanov aims to set the mind soaring high and free. Texts avoid gossip, malice (however enthralling), crime, accidents, disasters, manipulation in relationships and sex – because all of these things have the potential to invoke painful memory traces. Texts are peppered with symbols and suggestions of success – to prime the mind in this direction; everything is subtlety and sleight of hand. One can make an interesting comparison with Carl Rogers, who shared this distaste for didacticism. Rogers (1961) was one of the founding fathers of Humanistic psychology and brought its ideas into education, announcing provocatively in a widely attended public lecture at Harvard University in the 1950s that education was not only a waste of time but could be harmful to its recipients.

However, his alternative to lecturing was to send students off with a booklist to find out about the subject themselves, a solution they justifiably resented! For Lozanov, the subtle change from *telling* to *suggestion* is sufficient alone to enhance learner autonomy – without wasting their time or depriving them of the benefit of professional expertise.

Avoiding didacticism also lies behind Lozanov's insistence on aesthetic content. He shares the Socratic view of art as uplifting the mind, explaining that a work of art creates harmony amongst its various elements, which has the effect on perceivers of drawing their mind into a similar state (1978: 160–63). This supports a gestalt (right-hemispheric) rather than analytical (left-hemispheric) bias in perception. In his psychotherapy, long before he turned his attention to language teaching, he found that treating his clients with delicacy and respect predisposed them therapeutically to think and act in a similar way. He also found, in his research, that it is often sufficient to introduce into the text material *about* the artistic world, which has the effect of adjusting the mind in that direction. His own texts include poetry and, wherever possible, high-quality colour reproductions of paintings: Turner, Gainsborough, and so on, appear in his English teaching text *The Return*.

16.5 Grammar

Contrary to what is often believed about Lozanov's method, he is meticulous in grammatical presentation and insists that if a structure is omitted from overt presentation, it may never be learned. However, his methods of presenting are very different from the norm, aimed as they are at non- or para-conscious rather than conscious reception.

The major slot for overt grammatical presentation in the Lozanov cycle is in the first elaboration during the choral reading of the text. After the repetition of a certain sentence, there will be a momentary and apparently spontaneous (but carefully planned and prepared) focus on a grammatical item. This must:

(a) come from the text, so that the learner's mind remains focused on the drama rather than on the linguistic structure;
(b) be *brief* so that the learners do not get a chance to switch into analytical mode. Thus, it is never followed by an exercise or drill, which may occur at a later stage;
(c) be *incomplete* so that there is still material for the unconscious to puzzle over and work on; the mind is a compulsive pattern maker, positively stimulated by challenge.

Grammar never appears to be dwelt upon for its own sake, but to arise spontaneously as a textual puzzle. Questions about it are typically mirrored back to the asker, in a delicate and diplomatic way. The implication is first to leave it to the unconscious and secondly to work with each other, emphasising group autonomy. But if there is persistent request, assistance is given; the intention is to discourage, not distress.

Explanation is given in a demonstrative, physical way (kinaesthetic/ visual/auditory) and whenever possible includes visual display, such as a paradigmatic verb chart, which will engage the *right* hemisphere if presented as a pattern or 'whole picture' (as in the old-fashioned grammar books), with distinctions picked out in colour and/or underlining. The eye will then jump about as it needs to; each person can view in their own way. Lozanov never 'tracks' or blocks out text; this would break the pattern and stimulate the left hemisphere to lumber in with its slow, sequential process. Verbal explanation is always very short and elliptical so as to avoid activating the left brain.

Thus, everything is done in a way that preserves the gestalt; for example, information is never presented in a compartmental way but as part of a whole. All those old grammar books with page after page of tables would provide perfect material for the Lozanovian lesson if reproduced in colour. But old-fashioned teachers used to have students track through the text in a way that collapses the global sense of meaning; Lozanov, instead, presents a large quantity of material at speed with minimal comment. Posters appear on the wall in advance of the lesson to prime the mind, and stay briefly for consolidation.

Grammar is presented in the same whole-picture way, very different from the traditional graded approach to structures. In the case of modal verbs, for example, they are *all* introduced at once (and posters designed accordingly) so that it is immediately apparent that all conform to a single linguistic pattern, which, in the Lozanov context, is all that the learners need to be told. Semantics and order-of-simplicity are both subordinated to *form*. Lozanov tends to ignore semantics because meaning, inherent in the text, is something he expects the unconscious to discover for itself in the course of its complex, high-speed analysis of form. Again, the point is that finding meaning in this autonomous way boosts the learner's self-respect and autonomy, whereas to explain that which does not need explaining, gratuitously suggests learner inferiority.

There is no escaping the fact that some repetition will probably be necessary, even in the Lozanov context. But it has to be deeply disguised so as not to carry the usual implications of difficulty and learner inadequacy It can be slipped in during the second elaboration when learners are playing games, dramatising the text and asking questions. On the surface, this might seem similar to the communicative principle, but the emphasis is different; Lozanov seeks authenticity at the *process*, not just the linguistic, level. Learners have to have a reason to ask the question spontaneously (rather than just repeating it), so that on each occasion it genuinely springs 'from inside', preserving the natural bottom-up processing impulse.

Speed remains an issue at every stage of the lesson because as soon as the pace slows down, the left hemisphere will find something to worry about and focus attention on, and will take control of processing, thereby displacing the right. The atmosphere is laid-back but bustling, with many things happening at once. Puppets offer an active, indirect way of presenting grammatical information without didacticism, and can also stimulate imagination and add suggestion. Learners identify with puppets because they are free of the non-verbal messages that we living beings cannot help sending out unconsciously in our tones, expressions and gestures. The same is true of masks, which invite role play whilst at the same time providing a disguise for the shy and reluctant.

16.6 Conclusion

Since he is not a linguist and is more interested in psychological than linguistic issues, Lozanov has not written much about grammatical presentation, but his intent to retain globality has guided him to create a very distinct grammatical approach. To find the implied principles, I have teased them out from his text and activation notes. A great deal of work remains to be done in this direction, which makes it an exciting area for graduate studies and coursebook writing. The post-rationalist world is faced with the intriguing task of rediscovering and refining the rejected universe of 'passive learning', harnessing the power of that awareness which occurs below the conscious level, and learning how to work alongside the natural, organic, bottom-up processes.

References

Abbott, J. 2010. *Over Schooled and Under Educated*. London: Continuum.
Asher, J. 1977. *Learning Another Language Through Actions*. Los Gatos, CA: Sky Oaks Publications.
Assagioli, R. 1968. *Come Se Imparano le Lingue per l'Inconscio*, pamphlet available from the Istituto di Psicosintesi, Via San Domenico, Florence, Italy.
Claxton, G. 1997. *Hare Brain Tortoise Mind*. London: Fourth Estate.
Csikszentmihalyi, M. 1990. *Flow, The Psychology of Optimal Experience*. New York: Harper Perennial.
Hannaford, C. 1997. *The Dominance Factor*. Arlington, VA: Great Ocean Publishers.
Krashen, S. D. 1981. *Second Language Acquisition and Second Language Learning*. Oxford: Pergamon.
Lipton, B. 2005. *Biology of Belief*. Santa Rosa, CA: Mountain of Love/Elite Books.
Lozanov, G. 1978. *Suggestology and Outlines of Suggestopedy*. Gordon & Breach, New York.
McGilchrist, I. 2009. *The Master and his Emissary: The Divided Brain and the Making of the Western World*. New Haven: Yale University Press.
Polyani, M. 1967. *The Tacit Dimension*. New York: Anchor Books.
Rogers, C. 1961. *On Becoming a Person. A Therapist's View of Psychotherapy*. Boston, MA: Houghton Mifflin.

17 Access-self materials

Brian Tomlinson

17.1 Introduction

Nowadays a lot of self-access materials are available on the Web, as well as on computers and DVDs in self-access centres (see Chapters 12 and 13 of this volume). Some of these materials offer experience of language in authentic use and some set the learners authentic tasks. Nevertheless, the stereotypical image of self-access materials is still of practice exercises which enable the learners to work on what they need in their own time and at their own pace without reference to a teacher. Such materials attempt to achieve the desirable objective of learner-centred, learner-invested activity. Typically they are used to supplement (or even replace) classroom learning activities and usually they focus on providing practice in the use of specific language items or language skills which are problematic for the students. Thus, in an *ELTJ* article the authors asserted that:

> we remain convinced of the value of single-focus material for self-access learners who have been trying to identify their particular problems and who are keen to improve their ability in specific points of language. (Lin and Brown 1994)

The development of such materials and their attractive accessibility in learning centres or learning packages remains a positive feature of foreign language-learning pedagogy. However, the main strength of self-access materials has often been their main weakness too. In order to make sure that learners can work entirely on their own and still receive useful feedback, there has often been a limiting tendency to restrict the activities to those which can most easily be self-marked by the learners themselves. Thus, although there are notable exceptions, most self-access materials still consist of controlled or guided practice activities which use cloze, multiple choice, gap-filling, matching and transformation activities to facilitate self-marking and focused feedback. Such activities can usefully contribute to the development of explicit declarative knowledge (i.e. conscious knowledge of the forms, meanings and systems of the language). But their predominance has meant for many learners that their experience of self-access materials has been restricted to basically closed activities requiring a narrow left brain focus and little utilisation of prior personal experience, of the brain's potential learning capacity or of individual attributes or inclinations. It has also meant that opportunities have been lost to help learners to develop procedural knowledge of the language (i.e. knowledge of how it is actually used to achieve intended effects) and also that self-access materials have made little contribution to the development of implicit knowledge (i.e. knowledge acquired subconsciously). So much more could be achieved through the medium of self-access if only we could stop worrying about answer keys and self-marking. And maybe then more students would be enticed to spend more time in self-access centres and more time at home gaining experience of the language they are learning.

Ironically, in order to achieve ease and reliability of self-marking, many self-access materials designed to individualise learning have in fact treated learners as though they are stereotypical clones of each other. The prevailing learning styles for many of the materials are analytical, visual and independent. This is fine if you happen to be a learner who likes to focus on discrete bits of language, who likes to see the language written down and who is happy to work alone. In other words, if you are a studial learner, then self-access is for you. But then if you are a studial learner you probably fit the stereotypical image of the 'good language learner' (see Ellis 1994: 546–50) and you are making good progress anyway; because, let's face it, most coursebooks and lessons are designed for you. But what if you are an experiential, global, kinaesthetic learner (i.e. you like to learn by doing and you prefer to respond to the overall meaning of language which you encounter rather than to decode bits of it)? Then there is not much in most learning centres for you. And yet you probably need the extra opportunities to compensate for the unprofitable time you have had to spend engaged in form-focused, analytic activities in the classroom.

The narrowing tendency described above has been reinforced by the economy-led demand for cost-effective open learning in institutes of higher education in the UK (for example, some of the new universities currently stipulate that 10–15 per cent of courses be delivered through 'open learning'). Of course, in order to be cost-effective, open learning has to be closed enough not to require the participation of teachers during or after student activities. Self-marking keys are cheaper and more reliable than teachers, and thus closed activities rule.

Searching through the literature on learner autonomy and self-access language learning (e.g. Benson 2006; Cotterall 1995; Gardner and Miller 1999) reveals that most of the books and articles focus on how to help learners become autonomous, how to set up a self-access centre and how to motivate learners to make use of self-access centres. Very few of them focus on developing self-access materials which will engage learners cognitively and affectively. This is true, for example, of the Innovation in Teaching 1998–2009 website (http://innovationinteaching.org/autonomy_bibiliography.php) which cites 1,700 recent books, articles and chapters on learner autonomy, and also of a recent edition of Self-Access Language Learning (http://www.cityu.edu.hk/elc/HASALD/), the Web newsletter of HASALD (Hong Kong Association of Self-Access Learning and Development). There are materials developers and institutions, however, who have reacted against the tendency to restrict self-access materials to narrowly focused practice activities. For example, Littlejohn (1992) considers ways of giving self-access learners greater freedom and of stimulating them to take initiative and to be creative. Gardner and Miller (1999) advocate the use of authentic materials, of providing a variety of types of materials to cater for different learning styles, of guiding learners to contribute to the development of their own self-access materials and of making use of activities in self-access centres which promote learner enjoyment. McGrath (2002: 149) considers ways of making use of authentic materials in self-access centres, of making use of technological advances and of developing materials which 'go beyond familiar closed formats'. McDonough and Shaw (2003: 216) point out the 'danger in providing too much that is related to classroom work: the materials become "further practice" or "follow up activities" rather than allowing the students to explore and learn new things by themselves'. Mishan (2005) focuses on the importance of helping self-access learners respond to authentic texts. And Cooker (2008) draws attention to the widening role that authentic materials, graded readers and drama-based language-learning materials can play in a self-access centre. She also makes a plea for self-access materials to 'have the ability to interest and engage learners, to be meaningful and challenging and to have a sustained positive impact' (2008: 129), and she stresses the value of stimulating self-access learners to respond to affectively and cognitively engaging texts. Cooker's own self-access centre at Kanda University in Japan is a model of good practice in that it provides a great variety of materials to the learners, most of which aim to provide meaningful exposure to English in use and to stimulate personal responses to it. However, it is true to say that many institutions still restrict their self-access learners mainly to closed practice activities with answer keys.

What I would like to advocate is not the replacement of closed self-access activities (after all, the best time for individual language practice is when you are alone) but their supplementation by genuinely open activities which require learner investment of both the mind and the heart and which provide opportunities for the broadening and deepening of experience as well as for the acquisition of the target language. Such activities I shall distinguish by the descriptive label of access-self activities.

416

17.2 Principles of access-self activities

Access-self activities should:

1. Be self-access in the conventional sense of providing opportunities for learners to choose what to work on and to do so in their own time and at their own pace.
2. Be open-ended in the sense that they do not have correct and incorrect answers, but rather permit a variety of acceptable responses.
3. Engage the learners' individuality in the activities in such a way as to exploit their prior experience and to provide opportunities for personal development.
4. Involve the learners as human beings rather than just as language learners.
5. Require a personal investment of energy and attention in order for learner discoveries to be made (as recommended in Tomlinson 1994a, 2007 and as exemplified in Bolitho and Tomlinson 2005).
6. Stimulate various left- and right-brain activities at the same time and thus maximise the brain's potential for learning and development (as recommended in Lozanov 1978 and by Hooper Hansen 1992, 1999 and in Chapter 16 in this volume).
7. Provide a rich, varied and comprehensible input in order to facilitate informal acquisition (as recommended, for example, in Krashen 1981), as well as providing opportunities for selective attention to linguistic or pragmatic features of the discourse (as suggested by Bolitho *et al.* 2003, Schmidt 1990, Tomlinson 1994a).

In other words, I am recommending a more humanistic approach to self-access activities which aims to develop both the declarative and the procedural knowledge of the learners, as well as making a positive and broadening contribution to their education. For recommendations for humanising language learning see Tomlinson (2003a) and for a debate about the pros and cons of humanistic approaches see Arnold (1998) and Gadd (1998).

17.3 Features of access-self materials

1. The materials provide extensive exposure to authentic English through purposeful reading and/or listening activities.
2. Whilst-reading listening activities are offered to facilitate interaction with the text(s).
3. The post-reading/listening activities first of all elicit global, holistic responses which involve interaction between the self and the text (Tomlinson 2003b).

4. The focus of the main responsive activities is on the development of such high-level skills as imaging, inferencing, connecting, interpreting and evaluating.

5. There are also activities which help the learners to fix selective attention in such a way that they can discover something new about specific features of the text and thus become aware of any mismatch between their competence and the equivalent performance of target language users.

6. Production activities involve the use of the target language in order to achieve situational purposes rather than just to practise specific linguistic features of the target language. These activities offer involvement in various types of personal expression (e.g. analytical, aesthetic, imaginative, argumentative, evaluative).

7. The learners are given plenty of opportunities to make choices which suit their linguistic level, their preferred learning styles, their level of involvement in the text and the time they have available.

8. Whereas self-access activities are typically private and individual, access-self activities include the possibility of like-minded learners working together without reference to a teacher. That way the learners are able to choose between the tailor-made benefits of private work and the opportunity to pool resources and energy with fellow learners.

9. Feedback is given through commentaries rather than answer keys. The commentaries give the learners opportunities to compare their responses to those of the material developers and of other learners. They can be consulted at the end of the activities to gain summative feedback or during activities in order to help learners to modify or develop their responses as they proceed through the unit (as recommended in Dickinson 1987 and exemplified by Bolitho and Tomlinson 2005).

10. Learner training is encouraged through activities which involve the learners in thinking about the learning process and in experiencing a variety of different types of learning activities from which they can later make informed choices in determining their route through the access-self materials.

11. Suggestions for individual follow-up activities are given at the end of each unit.

17.4 Suitable texts for access-self materials

There are many types of text which can provide a base for access-self activities. What is common to them all is that they have the potential to engage the learners both cognitively and affectively (Tomlinson

2003a, 2003b, 2010). My own preferred genre is narrative whether it be in the form of novels, short stories, plays, poems, oral stories or songs (as used, for example, in Tomlinson 1994b). I find that narratives which engage the reader in interaction with characters, events and themes which are meaningful to them have the potential to utilise and develop personal experience as well to provide 'positive evidence' for language acquisition. And, as Ronnqvist and Sell (1994) say in discussing the value of literature in language education for teenagers, 'the reading of literary texts in the target language gives genuine and easily available experience in the pragmatics of relating formal linguistic expression to situational and socio-cultural contexts'. Of course, in order for this potential to be realised, the learners have to want to interact with the text and therefore have to be provided with a wide choice of texts to choose from. It has certainly been my experience that 'providing the learners have some say in the choice of texts and are not forced to "study", then literature can motivate even the most reluctant learners because of its appeal to their humanity' (Tomlinson 1994b). Other genres and text-types with similar access-self potential are newspaper reports, editorials and articles, television and radio news broadcasts, advertisements, magazine articles and television discussion and documentary programmes. One of the obvious advantages of narrative, though, is that it can be written for any level of learner without any loss of authenticity.

17.5 An example of a unit of access-self material

Below is an example of a unit of access-self material based on extracts from *My Son's Story* (Gordimer 1991). It is designed for self-access use in a Learning Centre but could easily be adapted for a self-access period in the classroom or for a homework book. Note in particular the use of open-ended, holistic activities, the possibility of group work and the use of a commentary which gives possible responses rather than answers as well as making use of previous learners' responses to the activities.

You could actually do the activities and experience what they involve or you could read through the materials and try to connect them to learners whom you know. Either way it would be useful if you could then evaluate the materials. Ask yourself whether they put into practice the principles of access-self materials as outlined above and whether they would appeal to your learners. If you like the materials, you could adapt them for use with your learners and you could also write other similar materials for use with your learners. If you do, please write and let me know what the learner responses are.

Ideas for materials development

An example of access-self material
Samples of modern literature
Sample 1 – *My Son's Story*

Introduction

This is one of a series of units which is based on modern literature and which is designed for learners who are at an intermediate level or above. Each unit introduces you to extracts from a book and aims to give you access to that book in such a way that will help you to develop your language skills and to acquire new language. It is also hoped that the extracts and activities will give you an interest in the book and that you will go on to read the book for yourself.

Try the unit and if you get interested in it, carry on and do most of the activities (you don't have to do them all). If you then want to read the book for yourself, take it out from the library. If you don't want to read the book, do another of these sample units and see if you want to read that book instead.

You can do this unit by yourself or you can work on it with other learners if you prefer.

Activities

1. You're going to read the beginning of a novel called *My Son's Story*. The novel begins:

   'How did I find out?
   I was deceiving him.'

   Think of different possible meanings for this beginning of the novel and then write answers to the following questions:
   (a) Who do you think 'I' might be?
   (b) What do you think the discovery could be?
   (c) Who do you think 'him' might be?
   (d) What do you think the deception could be?

2. Read the first paragraph of the extract from *My Son's Story* on page 1 of the Text Sheet [see Figure 17.1] and then answer questions 1 (a–d) again.
3. Check your answers to 2 above against those on page 1 of the Commentary [see page 422].
4. Read all of Extract 1 from the novel on pages 2–3 [see Figure 17.1] of the Text Sheet and try to picture in your mind the people and the setting as you read.

   If you found the extract interesting, go on to question 5. If you didn't find it interesting, choose a different Sample from the box.

5. Draw a picture of the narrator's meeting with his father. Don't worry about the artistic merit of your drawing (you should see my attempt); just try to include the important features of the scene.

6. Compare your drawing of the meeting with the drawings on page 1 of the Commentary [see page 425]. What do all three drawings have in common? What are the differences between the drawings?

7. If you're working individually, pretend you're watching a film of *My Son's Story* and act out in your head the meeting between the narrator, his father and Hannah. Try to give them different voices. If you're working in a group, act out the scene together.

8. Compare your scene with the suggested film script for the scene on page 2 of the Commentary [see page 425–6].

9. Imagine that the narrator is talking to his best friend the next day and that he's telling him about the meeting with his father. Write the dialogue between the two friends.

10. Compare your dialogue with the suggested dialogues on page 3 of the Commentary [see pages 426–7].

11. Write answers to the following questions:

   (a) Why do you think the narrator is so disturbed by the encounter with his father?

   (b) How old do you think the narrator was at the time of his encounter with his father and Hannah? Why?

   (c) Who does 'us' refer to in 'Cinemas had been open to us only a year or so'?

   (d) Explain in your own words the meaning of 'the moment we saw one another it was I who had discovered him, not he me'.

   (e) Why do you think his father opened the conversation by saying, 'You remember Hannah, don't you –?' Why did he not ask him why he was not studying?

   (f) When had the narrator met Hannah before? Why did he not recognise her when he first saw her outside the cinema?

   (g) What does the narrator mean by, 'And the voice was an echo from another life'?

   (h) What does the narrator's description of Hannah tell you about his attitude towards her?

   (i) Why do you think the narrator mentions that his father was wearing 'his one good jacket'?

   (j) What does the narrator mean when he says he was 'safe among familiar schoolbooks'?

12. Compare your answers to 11 with the suggested answers on pages 3–4 of the Commentary [see pages 427–8].

13. Find examples in the text of the use of the past perfect tense. For each example say why you think the writer used the past perfect instead of the simple past.
14. Compare your answers to 13 with the suggested answers on pages 4–5 of the Commentary [see pages 428–9].
15. Later in the novel, the father asks his son to go on his new motorbike to Hannah's house to deliver an important parcel to her.

   (a) Write the dialogue in the scene in which the father asks the son to deliver the parcel.
   (b) Imagine that you are the narrator. Write the scene from the novel in which you deliver the parcel to Hannah's house.

16. Compare your answers to 15 to the answers on pages 5–6 of the Commentary [see pages 429–30]. These are answers which were written by other learners.
17. Read Extract 2 from the novel on page 2 of the Text Sheet in which the narrator goes to Hannah's house on his motorbike [see Figure 17.1].

   If you'd like any further feedback on any of the written work that you've done in this unit, put your name on it and put it in the Feedback Box.
18. If you're still interested in the story, take the novel, *My Son's Story*, from the library shelf. Write down what you think the significance is of the illustration on the front cover.

   Read the novel in your own time and then, if you wish, talk about it with one of the other students who's already read the book (their names are on the back cover). Add your name to those on the back cover.

(Adapted from Tomlinson 1994b. *Openings*)

Samples of modern literature
Sample 1 – *My Son's Story*
Commentary

3. (a) 'I' is the narrator of the story. He or she was a pupil in a senior class at the time of the story and was about to take exams.
   (b) That his or her father had been to the cinema with a woman. Maybe the father was having an affair.
   (c) Probably the father.
   (d) The narrator had pretended he or she was going to a friend's house to study but had gone to the cinema instead.

6. Look at the two drawings below of the meeting between the narrator and his father. How are they similar to each other and how

Figure 17.1   Extracts from **My Son's Story** *by Nadine Gordimer*

Extract 1

How did I find out?

I was deceiving him.

November. I was on study leave—for two weeks before the exams pupils in the senior classes were allowed to stay home to prepare themselves. I would say I was going to work with a friend at a friend's house, and then I'd slip off to a cinema. Cinemas had been open to us only a year or so; it was a double freedom I took: to bunk study and to sit in the maroon nylon velvet seat of a cinema in a suburb where whites live. My father was not well off but my parents wanted my sister and me to have a youth less stunted by the limits of an empty pocket than they had had, and my pocket money was more generous than their precarious position, at the time, warranted. So I was in the foyer waiting to get into a five o'clock performance at one of the cinemas in a new complex and my father and a woman came out of the earlier performance in another.

There was my father; the moment we saw one another it was I who had discovered him, not he me. We stood there while other people crossed our line of vision. Then he came towards me with her in the dazed way people emerge from the dark of a cinema to daylight.

He said, You remember Hannah, don't you—

And she prompted with a twitching smile to draw my gaze from him—for I was concentrating on him the great rush of questions, answers, realizations, credulity and dismay which stiffened my cheeks and gave the sensation of cold water rising up my neck—she prompted, Hannah Plowman, of course we know each other.

I said, Hullo. He drew it from me; we were back again in our little house across the veld from Benoni and I was being urged to overcome the surly shyness of a six-year-old presented with an aunt or cousin. What are you going to see? he said. While he spoke to me he drew back as if I might smell her on him. I didn't know. They managed to smile, almost laugh, almost make the exchange commonplace. But it was so: the title of the film I had planned to see was already banished from my mind, as this meeting would have to be, ground away under my heel, buried along with it. The Bertolucci—an Italian film—it's very good, he said, delicately avoiding the implications of the natural prefix, 'We thought. . .' She nodded enthusiastically. That's the one to see, Will, he was saying. And the voice was an echo from another life, where he was my father giving me his usual measured, modest advice. Then he signalled a go-along-and-enjoy-yourself gesture, she murmured politely, and they left me as measuredly as they had approached. I watched their backs so I would believe it really had happened; that woman: with her bare pink bottle-calves and clumsy sandals below the cotton outfit composed of a confusion of styles from different peasant cultures, him

(cont.)

Figure 17.1   (cont.)

in his one good jacket that I had taken to the dry-cleaners for him many times, holding the shape of his shoulders folded back over my arm. Then I ran from the cinema foyer, my vision confined straight ahead like a blinkered horse so that I wouldn't see which way they were going, and I took a bus home, home, home where I shut myself up in my room, safe among familiar schoolbooks.

Extract 2

I went on the motorbike. I had it by then. They gave it to me for my birthday. He said to me with that smile of a loving parent concealing a fine surprise, you can get a licence at sixteen now, can't you. So I knew he was going to buy me a bike I never asked for it but they gave it to me. With the latest, most expensive helmet for my safety; he must have had to promise my mother that.

I went with the helmet and chin-guard and goggles hiding my face. You can't see the place from the street, where he goes. Dogs at the gate, and a black gardener had to come to let me in; I suppose they wag their tails for someone who comes often, is well known to them by his own scent. There was a big house but that's not where he goes. She lives in a cottage behind trees at the end of the garden. Maybe there's even a private entrance from there I didn't know about, he didn't like to tell me. All open and above-board through the front entrance.

He must have told her, she was expecting me. Oh it's Will, isn't it—as if the helmet and stuff prevented her from recognizing me, from remembering the cinema that time. It also playfully implied, determined to be friendly, that I was rude, not taking the helmet off. So I did. So she could see it was me, Will, yes. I gave her whatever it was he'd sent me with. It was a package, books or something, he told me 'Miss Plowman' needed urgently.—You're the family Mercury now, with that wonderful machine of yours—off you go, son, but don't tear along like a Hell's Angel, hey.— A perfect performance in front of my mother.

This was where he came. It must be familiar as our house to him, where we live now and where we lived when we were in Benoni, because our house is where we are, our furniture, our things, his complete Shakespeare, the smells of my mother's cooking and the flowers she puts on the table. But this isn't like a house at all; well, all right, a cottage, but not even any kind of place where you'd expect a white would live. The screen door full of holes. Bare floor and a huge picture like spilt paint that dazzles your eyes, a word-processor, hi-fi going with organ music, twisted stubs in ashtrays, fruit, packets of bran and wheat-germ, crumpled strings of women's underthings drying on a radiator—and a bed, on the floor. There was the bed, just a very big wide mattress on the floor, covered with some cloth with embroidered elephants and flowers and bits of mirror in the design—the bed, just like that, right there in the room where anybody can walk in, the room where I was standing with my helmet in my hand.

So now I know.

are they similar to your drawing? How are they different from each other and how is each one different from yours?

Go back and change any features of your drawing that you want to and add some extra details if you wish.

8. Here is one possible film script for the scene. How is it similar to and different from yours? Obviously there are many possible interpretations.

   The son is standing in a queue in the foyer of a new cinema complex. He looks at the posters on the wall and then at his watch. People start to come out of a door across the foyer. At first he looks at them without much interest but then he notices his father coming out of the door with a white woman. He looks surprised and annoyed. His father sees him and looks guilty.

The son and the father stand where they are whilst people walk between them. Then the father and the woman walk towards the son. When the father gets close to the son he gestures towards the woman and speaks to the son.

Father: *You remember Hannah, don't you ...*
Woman: (smiling at the son) *I'm Hannah Plowman. Of course we know each other.*
Son: (after hesitating for a while) *Hello.*
Father: (moving away slightly from the son) *What are you going to see?* (The father and the woman smile at the son. The son doesn't answer.)
Father: *The Bertolucci – an Italian film – it's very good. We thought ...*

(The woman nods enthusiastically.)

Father: *That's the one to see, Will.*

The father signals for the son to go along and enjoy himself. The woman murmurs something politely and the two of them then walk away from the son.

The son watches their backs moving out of the cinema and down the road. Then suddenly he runs away from the cinema in the opposite direction.

9. This is a creative writing exercise and therefore has many possible 'answers'. Compare your dialogue with the two versions below. How is yours similar to and different from each one?

(a)

Tom: *Heh, what's wrong Will?*
Will: *Nothing. Well nothing much.*
Tom: *What?*
Will: *It's my dad. He's having an affair.*
Tom: *Who with?*
Will: *A white woman. A do-gooder white liberal.*
Tom: *Wow! Are you sure?*
Will: *I caught them together at the cinema yesterday.*
Tom: *Maybe they're just friends or...*
Will: *No way!*
Tom: *Or they're working on something together?*
Will: *I know. I could tell.*
Tom: *Are you going to tell your mother?*
Will: *What do you think? I can't.*

Tom: *Yeah. You're right. C'mon forget it. It won't last. Let's do some revision.*

Will: *OK. Let's try the English Lit.*

(b)

Will: *Guess what?*

Tom: *What?*

Will: *My dad's got a girl friend.*

Tom: *Yeah. What's she like?*

Will: *Middle-aged ... clumsy... white.*

Tom: *White?*

Will: *Yeah. Well bits of her are pink.*

Tom: *Why?*

Will: *The sun of course.*

Tom: *No. I mean why her?*

Will: *I don't know. She's some sort of a liberal, a social worker.*

Tom: *On our side, eh?*

Will: *She's not on my side. That's for sure. C'mon. Let's do some work.*

11. Possible answers are:

(a) Probably because he had held his father in great esteem and he was shocked to find that he was not the perfect father after all. The father had deceived the son.

(b) Probably about 18. Because he was in a senior class at school and was preparing for an important examination.

(c) It refers to non-whites.

(d) Although he had been caught deceiving his father he immediately realised that his father's deception was much bigger and that his father was aware of that.

(e) Probably because he didn't want to antagonise his son and he wanted to pretend that the relationship with Hannah was as innocent as it was the last time they had met.

(f) One interpretation is that it was when he was six years old. Obviously she had changed and probably he could not at first connect his father's 'lover' with his father's colleague or acquaintance.

(g) It could be that he is thinking of the time when he was growing up 'in a little house across the veld from Benoni' when his father often gave him good advice. Or it could be that 'another life' refers to the time before this encounter when he respected his father and his advice – the implication being that now he doesn't respect his father.

427

(h) Obviously it communicates a negative reaction. He picks on unattractive features and uses emotive words (i.e. 'clumsy': 'confusion'). He suggests that she's trying to be something that she really is not (e.g. the sunburn on her calves: the clothes borrowed from cultures which she doesn't belong to).

(i) It suggests that his father had made a special effort to look good whilst Hannah had not. It also reminds him of how he'd taken the jacket to the cleaners for his father, presumably because it was needed for an important occasion and because he was proud of his father.

(j) His world had suddenly changed and his security had been threatened. He needed to be somewhere which hadn't changed and which didn't threaten him.

13. (i) 'Cinemas had been open to us only a year or so; ...'

To stress the period of time rather than the particular time. To stress how short this period was and how relevant it was to the point of time in the narrative.

(ii) '... it was I who had discovered him ...'

Possibly to stress that there was no time in which the son was guilty in comparison with the father. Right from the moment of recognition it was the father who was guilty.

cf. '... it was I who discovered him' (= I saw him and then realised he was guilty).

(iii) '... the title of the film I had planned to see ...'

To stress that the plan (although very recent) was now in the past and was irrelevant now.

cf. '... the title of the film I planned to see ...' (= He still intended to see it).

(iv) 'I watched their backs so I would believe it really had happened: ...'

Possibly to stress that the incident was now in the past and he wanted to make sure that it was true that his father was having an affair. Possibly he was thinking of the future, when remembering the visual details would convince him it was true.

(v) '... his one good jacket which I had taken to the dry-cleaners for him many times ...'
Possibly to stress that such acts were now definitely in the past and to emphasise his emotional involvement in the memory.

cf. '… which I took to the dry-cleaners …' (= It leaves open the possibility that he might do so again).

The above examples seem to suggest that perfect tenses indicate more involvement of the speaker than simple tenses. The speaker seems to be more subjective when using perfect tenses and to be drawing attention to what is salient to him. Look for other examples in newspapers and books to see if this subjectivity is typical of the use made of perfect tenses.

15. (a) Below is one student's dialogue. How is yours similar to it and different from it?

> Father: *Will? Do you fancy a ride on your bike?*
> Will: *Where to?*
> Father: *To deliver an important parcel for me. I daren't send it by post.*
> Will: *Where to?*
> Father: *To Hannah Plowman's house.*
> Will: *Do I have to?*
> Father: *No.*
>
> *(Long pause in which Will looks at his father. His father looks away.)*
>
> Will: *All right. Where is it?*
> Father: *Here's the parcel. And here's a map to show you how to get there.*
> Will: *OK. Give them to me.*
> Father: *Don't forget to wear your helmet.*

(b) Below is one student's scene. How is yours similar to or different from it?

I got off the bike across the road from her house. I took my helmet off and then tidied my hair in the mirror. Then I was annoyed with myself. What did it matter what I looked like?

I crossed the road hoping nobody would see me. There were some black kids playing at the end of the street. But they didn't bother about me. Trust her to live away from the other whites.

The house was small like the ones that black servants lived in. But hers needed painting and seemed to be falling down. The bell didn't work, so I knocked on the door. After a while she opened it and stood blinking into the sun. She was barefoot and wore only an African cloth.

Then she recognised me and asked me to come in. I saw into a room where my father must often have been and shook my head. I pushed the parcel at her, turned and ran. I heard her shout. 'Will. Will, come back!' just before I roared off down the road towards the frightened black kids without my helmet on.

17.6 Conclusion

The example demonstrated above shows how it is possible in self-access material to:

- give learners the responsibility of deciding what and how much to do (e.g. Introduction to Sample 1 and Activity 4);
- ask open-ended questions (e.g. Activities 1 and 11);
- encourage experiential reading (e.g. Activities 4 and 18);
- use previous learners' answers for comparison and feedback rather than imposing teacher answers (e.g. Activities 6 and 16);
- make use of creative drama (e.g. Activities 7, 8 and 9);
- set open-ended activities (e.g. Activities 5, 7, 9 and 15);
- make use of creative writing (e.g. Activities 9 and 15);
- ask 'think' questions (e.g. Activity 11);
- use extended texts for language awareness discovery work (e.g. Activity 13);
- provide opportunities for teacher feedback (e.g. Activity 17).

In addition, the sample unit shows how it is possible to engage the learner and to achieve depth of processing in self-access materials by activating both affective and cognitive responses and by respecting and challenging the learners. In my view, this is what all learning materials should be trying to do, and especially those which are designed to appeal to self-access learners who want something different and richer than what is conventionally offered in the classroom.

References

Arnold, J. 1998. 'Towards more humanistic language teaching'. *ELT Journal*, 52(3): 235–42.

Benson, P. 2006. 'Autonomy in language teaching and learning'. *Language Teaching*, 40: 21–40.

Bolitho, R., R. Carter, R. Hughes, R. Ivanic, H. Masuhara and B. Tomlinson. 2003. 'Ten questions about language awareness'. *ELT Journal*, 57(3): 251–59.

Bolitho, R. and B. Tomlinson. 2005. *Discover English.* 3rd edn. Oxford: Macmillan.

Cooker, L. 2008. 'Self-access materials'. In B. Tomlinson (ed.), *English Language Learning Materials: A Critical Review.* London: Continuum.

Cotterall, S. 1995. 'Developing a course strategy for learner autonomy'. *ELT Journal*, 49(3): 219–27.

Dickinson, L. 1987. *Self-Instruction in Language Learning.* Cambridge: Cambridge University Press.

Ellis, R. 1994. *The Study of Second Language Acquisition.* Oxford: Oxford University Press.

Gadd, N. 1998. 'Towards less humanistic English teaching'. *ELT Journal*, 52(3): 223–34.

Gardner, G. and L. Miller. 1999. *Establishing Self-Access: From Theory to Practice.* Cambridge: Cambridge University Press.

Gordimer, N. 1991. *My Son's Story.* London: Penguin Books.

Hooper Hansen, G. 1992. 'Suggestopedia: a way of learning for the 21st century'. In J. Mulligan and C. Griffin (eds.), *Empowerment Through Experiential Learning.* London: Kogan Page.

1999. 'Learning by heart: a Lozanov perspective'. In J. Arnold (ed.), *Affect in Language Learning.* Cambridge: Cambridge University Press.

Krashen, S. 1981. *Second Language Acquisition and Second Language Learning.* Oxford: Pergamon Press.

Lin, L. Y. and R. Brown. 1994. 'Guidelines for the production of in-house self-access materials'. *ELT Journal*, 48(2).

Littlejohn, A. P. 1992. 'Why are ELT materials the way they are?' Unpublished PhD thesis. Lancaster: Lancaster University.

Lozanov, G. 1978. *Suggestology and Outlines of Suggestopedy.* London: Gordon and Breach.

McDonough, J. and C. Shaw. 2003. *Materials and Methods in ELT*, 2nd edn. Oxford: Blackwell.

McGrath, I. 2002. *Materials Evaluation and Design for Language Teaching.* Edinburgh: Edinburgh University Press.

Mishan, F. 2005. *Designing Authenticity into Language Learning Materials.* Bristol: Intellect.

Ronnqvist, L. and R. D. Sell. 1994. 'Teenage books for teenagers: reflections on literature in language education'. *ELT Journal*, 48(2): 125–32.

Schmidt, R. 1990. 'The role of consciousness in second language learning'. *Applied Linguistics*, 11(2): 129–58.

Tomlinson, B. 1994a. 'Pragmatic awareness activities'. *Language Awareness*, 3&4: 119–29.

1994b. *Openings.* London: Penguin.

2003a. 'Humanizing the coursebook'. In B. Tomlinson (ed.), *Developing Materials for Language Teaching.* London: Continuum.

2003b. 'Developing principled frameworks for materials development'. In B. Tomlinson (ed.), *Developing Materials for Language Teaching.* London: Continuum.

2007. 'Using form focused discovery approaches'. In S. Fotos and H. Nassaji (eds.), *Form-Focused Instruction and Teacher Education: Studies in Honour of Rod Ellis*. Oxford: Oxford University Press.

2010. 'Engaged to learn: ways of engaging ELT learners'. In J. Mukundan (ed.), *Readings on ELT Materials V*. Petaling Jaya. Pearson/Longman.

Comments on Part E

Brian Tomlinson

The chapters in this section offer very different views on materials development but have many things in common. One thing in particular that they have in common is their concern that different types of learners and different preferred styles of learning should be catered for in language-learning materials. An analysis of any current global coursebook will reveal that it favours the analytic learner rather than the experiential learner (Masuhara *et al.* 2008; Tomlinson *et al.* 2001), that it caters for the visual learner more than it does for the auditory learner and that hardly any provision is made for the tactile or kinaesthetic learner. Yet it seems that more learners are experiential than analytic and that the preferred mode for most learners is the kinaesthetic (Oxford and Anderson 1995). It is not difficult to work out why coursebook materials typically favour the analytic learner. The school cultures which the teachers, learners, publishers and textbook writers come from encourage and reward those who are primarily analytic. The learners who succeed in these cultures are those who can focus on discrete chunks of information, who can analyse and categorise, who can memorise and retrieve consciously, who are systematic and sequential in the ways that they learn. Most teachers, writers and publishers have been successful in such cultures; most learners expect to learn languages in the same analytical ways that they have been made to learn other subjects at school; and most parents and administrators want languages to be learned in an analytic way which rewards effort and application and teaches the values of order and conformity. And it does not help when language acquisition researchers categorise the good language learner as someone who uses the appropriate learning strategies effectively, who monitors themselves and others, who pays attention to form and to meaning, who practises the language and who is aware of the learning process (Ellis 1994: 546–50). In other words, the good language learner is someone who is flexible but who learns the language primarily by focusing attention on aspects of it. And, of course, such a learner is identified as a good learner by teachers who are following a primarily analytic course and is rewarded by language examinations which feature tasks which are primarily analytic too. In addition, it is much easier to write and design a book which requires analytic responses and it is not easy to write and sell one which caters for the kinaesthetically inclined. But, as the chapters in this section demonstrate, it is possible to design materials which facilitate experiential learning and it is possible to cater for different learning styles by providing a variety of approaches, by providing opportunities for choice and by helping learners to take responsibility for their own learning. This, of course, does not mean that materials should stop trying to cater for analytic learning styles; it means that they should cater for other less language-focused styles too.

The stressing of the need to provide opportunities for learner choice is another of the common links between the chapters in this section and, of course, is one of the ways of catering for a diversity of preferred learning styles and modes. The problem for materials developers is how to offer useful choice to learners in such a way that they can make informed rather than purely intuitive decisions (see Maley 2003, Tomlinson 1996, 2003 and Chapter 15 in this volume for further suggestions). This must involve encouraging learners to sample different potential learning routes and helping them to understand the objectives, principles and typical procedures of each of these routes. This risks the danger of becoming a course on language acquisition; but, if done experientially (e.g. an activity followed by learner reflection on and evaluation of the activity), it can give the learners a greater repertoire of learning styles and strategies, it can help them to make informed choices of routes and activities and it can help them to become more aware of the learning process (a characteristic identified by most researchers as being typical of the good language learner, and one which does not necessarily inhibit experiential learning). We really do need to give our learners more respect and responsibility and to predetermine less of their decisions for them.

One of the surprising things about the chapters in this section is that none of them really stresses the potential role of the teacher's book in helping to cater for choice (and in contributing to teacher development too). At the moment teacher's books which accompany coursebooks receive little investment of time and energy in developing their contents and their design (because they do not sell many copies). They tend to provide just answer keys and obvious advice and are geared towards the inexperienced teacher. As a result they are underused and their potential is under-exploited. If student books consisted basically of a large bank of texts and visuals to select from, teacher's books could include many different suggestions for activities which teachers and learners could choose from. If these activities were attractively designed and made photocopiable, then the teacher's book could become essential and profitably expensive: and everybody could gain.

Perhaps the most significant link between the chapters in this section is that none of them is proposing anything radically new, but all of them are advocating approaches which are not commonly used by mainstream materials. The potential value of experiential learning, of peripheral learning, of engaging the senses and emotions in the learning process, of whole-person approaches, of catering for different learning styles, of offering responsibility and choice to learners is supported by considerable research and is substantiated by the experience of teachers and learners all over the world. Yet very few current global coursebooks have made more than token efforts to incorporate these approaches (Masuhara *et al.* 2008; Tomlinson *et al.* 2001). It would be difficult to persuade the consumers to buy a book which would conspicuously differ from their expectations, it would not be easy to consistently engage the emotions of learners without risking giving offence, and it would be a demanding task to provide cost-effective choice. But I believe it would be possible to develop a global coursebook which could cater for experiential learners, for analytic learners and for learners who, like myself, prefer to encounter language first of all in purposeful and engaging use but later enjoy analysing the 'text' to find out how the language was used. It would also be possible in the same book to provide activities involving visual, auditory, tactile and kinaesthetic responses and to offer choices both of major routes and of specific activities. Such a book could be extremely valuable to learners and teachers all over the world and could become a commercial success too. I have been advocating such a book for the last 30 years and I understand the reluctance of the commercial publishers to risk costly investment in a book whose differences from the norm might deny it face validity. But I am still hoping that one of these days such a book will be used in classrooms throughout the world.

References

Ellis, R. 1994. *The Study of Second Language Acquisition*. Oxford: Oxford University Press.

Maley, A. 2003. 'Creative approaches to writing materials'. In B. Tomlinson (ed.), *Developing Materials for Language Teaching*. London: Continuum.

Masuhara, H., M. Haan, Y. Yi and B. Tomlinson. 2008. 'Adult EFL courses'. *ELT Journal*, 62(3): 294–312.

Oxford, R. L. and N. J. Anderson. 1995. 'A crosscultural view of learning styles'. *Language Teaching*, 28: 201–15. Cambridge: Cambridge University Press.

Tomlinson, B. 1996. 'Choices'. *Folio*, 3(1): 20–3.
    2003. 'Humanizing the coursebook'. In B. Tomlinson (ed.), *Developing Materials for Language Teaching*. London: Continuum.
Tomlinson, B., B. Dat, H. Masuhara and R. Rubdy. 2001. 'EFL courses for adults'. *ELT Journal*, 55(1): 80–101.

Conclusions

Brian Tomlinson

I would like to end this book by highlighting certain messages which seem to have been communicated throughout the book and to suggest ways in which we can gain from them.

We should be proud but not complacent about the progress made in materials development

We have reached a situation in which high-quality materials are available throughout the world to help learners to learn languages. These materials have taken advantage of recent developments in technology and of our recently increased knowledge of how languages are learned (Tomlinson 2011). But many learners still fail to achieve a satisfactory level of communicative competence and many teachers and learners are still not happy with the materials they are using. We must not sit back and say that what we have is good enough, but rather continue to strive towards the development of materials which give even more learners the chance of satisfaction and success.

We need to find out more about the outcomes of existing materials

There has been very little research into the actual learning outcomes of language-learning materials. Publishers have been understandably reluctant to conduct longitudinal and expensive research into the effects of books which they have already published and, also understandably, they are likely to keep whatever research they do confidential. Academics have been wary of undertaking research which would require massive expenditure of time and resources and which would involve great difficulty in controlling the variables in order to reach any conclusive results. But are we really being responsible and professional when we judge the effectiveness of a book by the number of copies it sells? Or by its popularity judged by responses to questionnaires? Or by a general impression that most of the activities in it 'work'? We need to (and could) find out more about the actual learning outcomes of types of materials if we really want to help those learners who currently fail. Recently more and more postgraduate students are conducting their research projects on materials development (Tomlinson and Masuhara 2010), but not many of them are conducting longitudinal research focusing on the effects of particular types of materials. We could help and encourage more students to focus their research on the learning effects of materials and we could undertake more ambitious projects in which consortia of experts actually investigate the long-term effects of different types of learning materials on comparable groups of learners.

We need to find out more about what learners and teachers want from language-learning materials

Many of us are frequently guilty of saying things such as, 'What most learners want is ...' or, 'What teachers really want is ...'. But do we really know? I have not seen any research which convinces me that teachers and learners actually want what they are being given by the commercially published materials they are using. (For example, do they really welcome the presentation, practice, production approach of the majority of global coursebooks on the market?) Nor have I seen any research which demonstrates their dissatisfaction. But I really would like to know what they want and I think that we really ought to make greater efforts to discover reliable and valid information about the sort of materials they really want to use. Such research requires cooperation between different types of experts and it requires the sort of funding which could only really be provided by a consortium of universities and publishers working with their own agendas but also towards a common goal.

We need to find out more about how we can develop more effective materials

Providing learners and teachers with the materials they want could be extremely useful, but it would not be enough. We do not know what the most effective types of materials are for learners in different types of situations and what the learners want might not always necessarily be the most effective materials for them. For example, a class of 80 unmotivated university students of engineering might want an easy book of practice exercises which can help them prepare for their compulsory English examination without requiring much investment of time, energy or attention. But a book of communication activities offering choice and involvement might be more useful to them. We just do not know.

What we need is not only reliable and valid information about what teachers and learners want and about the actual learning outcomes of current materials but also about what effects could be achieved by new types of materials. We need to innovate and experiment if we are really to find out how we could make language-learning materials more effective. But why should publishers take risks when livelihoods are at stake? Why should ministries commit precious funds to projects which might not succeed? And why should learners risk failing to learn from experimental books? If only a large university (or group of universities) would cooperate with a publisher to produce and trial experimental materials, we might increase our knowledge about what contributes to the effectiveness of language-learning materials.

We need to make more use of what we know about language learning in the development of materials

If we are to develop more effective materials, then we need to incorporate features into the materials which we know can facilitate language learning (see Tomlinson 2010 and Chapter 1 in this volume). In Chapter 1 in this book I have mentioned many such features. Of these I would particularly like to see more use made in materials development of what we know about the value of permitting a silent period at the beginning of learning a language or of learning a new feature of it, of what we know about the value of engaging emotions in the learning process and of what we know about the value of offering opportunities to personalise and localise materials.

We need to find out more about how the target language is actually used and to apply this new knowledge to the development of materials

As the chapters in Part A reveal, we are finding out more about how languages are actually used and this new knowledge is already being applied to the development of textbooks. But, of course, we need to go on finding out and applying. We need more knowledge about how languages are actually used in specific situations (e.g. when conducting business, when giving commercial presentations, when being questioned by the police), we need more knowledge about how grammatical principles (e.g. economy) are actually applied to language use in different situations and we need more knowledge of the patterns and norms of interaction between proficient non-native speakers from different backgrounds. We also need to find out to what extent exposure to reality is more or less valuable to learners than exposure to simplified samples illustrating idealised norms.

We need to find ways of developing materials which are flexible enough to offer choices and to cater for a variety of wants and needs

This need has been expressed many times in this book already (e.g. my Comments on Part E), so I will just say that this is another area where we need actual information rather than subjective impressions. What are the effects of materials offering choice compared to the effects of materials offering no choice? How can we offer choice without increasing the processing load? Can we identify those learners who are likely to benefit from being offered choice and those who might gain from a more directed course? We need to know.

We need to find ways of using textbooks to contribute to teacher development

This is a need identified by Canniveng and Martinez (2003), by Popovici and Bolitho (2003), by Tomlinson (2003) and by Tomlinson and Masuhara (2004), and a need which is being addressed on textbook projects in countries where most teachers are untrained and are often reluctant to experiment with new approaches. In my experience of contributing to teacher development and curriculum development in England, Indonesia, Japan, Nigeria, Oman, Singapore, Vanuatu and Zambia, for any materials to contribute positively to teacher development they must not be imposed, they must invite and facilitate reflection, evaluation and adaptation by the teachers, and they must involve teachers in the development and trialling of the materials (Al-Busaidi and Tindle 2011). These factors are being considered as important in many local projects but could also be taken into account in the commercial development of global coursebooks.

We need to find ways of making the most effective use of the new technologies available to us as developers and users of language-learning materials

It is obvious that the new technologies available, for example through the mobile phone, through phone and video conferencing and through the Internet, offer interactivity not only between learner and materials but between learner and other learners, learner and tutor and learner and proficient user. This should offer far more opportunities for exposure to language in use, for noticing how the language is used and for producing language for communicative purposes. But we need to know exactly what the potential learning outcomes are and how best they can be achieved.

We need to find ways of helping commercial publishers to take advantage of new developments in methodology without risking financial loss

This, I think, is our most urgent need if we are to really improve the effectiveness of the materials which learners use. In the current economic climate, and given the massive costs of global coursebooks and the unprofitability of most supplementary materials, we cannot expect publishers to be experimental and innovative. They need to produce what they can expect to sell whilst, as Frances Amrani points out in Chapter 11, striving as much as they can to ensure that their materials are of value to their users. But is this enough? If the publishers are not going to experiment, who is? And if we do not experiment, how do we make progress? The answer has got to lie in more pooling of expertise and resources so that we can help publishers to find out which innovations might be well received and ultimately profitable. And we have got to help publishers to conduct more radical experimentation without the risk of financial disaster. MATSDA would very much like to be involved.

We need to find ways of bringing together researchers, teachers, writers and publishers so as to pool resources and to take advantage of different areas of expertise in order to produce materials of greater value to learners of languages.

All the messages above are calling out for greater collaboration between institutions with different types of resources and expertise in relation to the development of L2 materials. What we would really like to do in MATSDA is to find ways of helping to bring together experts in language acquisition, in research methodology, in language data collection and analysis, in language pedagogy, in materials writing, in materials design and in materials production and distribution. Only by pooling resources will we ever be able to answer some of the questions which we need to ask if we are to really increase the effectiveness of the materials which we produce.

I am looking forward to receiving approaches from institutions for MATSDA to help to arrange joint research projects aiming to inform materials development and I am looking forward to editing in the future a book reporting on the outcomes of such research.

References

Al-Busaidi, S. and K. Tindle. 2010. 'Evaluating the impact of in-house materials on language learning'. In B. Tomlinson and H. Masuhara (eds.), *Resesarch in Materials Development for Language Learning: Evidence for Best Practice*. London: Continuum.

Canniveng, C. and M. Martinez. 2003. 'Materials development and teacher training'. In B. Tomlinson (ed.), *Developing Materials for Language Teaching*. London: Continuum.

Popovici, R. and R. Bolitho. 2003. 'Personal and professional development through writing: the Romanian textbook project'. In B. Tomlinson (ed.), *Developing Materials for Language Teaching*. London: Continuum.

Tomlinson, B. 2003. 'Materials development courses'. In B. Tomlinson (ed.), *Developing Materials for Language Teaching*. London: Continuum.

2010. 'Principles and procedures of materials development'. In N. Harwood (ed.), *English Language Teaching Materials: Theory and Practice*. Cambridge: Cambridge University Press.

2011. 'Materials development'. *Language Teaching*.

Tomlinson, B. and H. Masuhara. 2003. 'Simulations in materials development'. In B. Tomlinson (ed.), *Developing Materials for Language Teaching*. London: Continuum.

2010. *Research in Materials Development for Language Learning: Evidence for Best Practice*. London: Continuum.

Recommended reading

For further reading on materials development in second language teaching the following books are recommended.

Byrd, P. 1995. *Materials Writers Guide*. Rowley, MA: Newbury House.
Cunningsworth, A. 1984. *Evaluating and Selecting EFL Teaching Material*. London: Heinemann.
    1996. *Choosing Your Coursebook*. Oxford: Heinemann.
Fenner, A. and D. Newby. 2000. *Approaches to Materials Design in European Textbooks: Implementing Principles of Authenticity, Learner Autonomy, Cultural Awareness*. Graz/Strasbourg: European Centre for Modern Languages.
Graves, K. 1996. *Teachers as Course Developers*. Cambridge: Cambridge University Press.
Harwood, N. (ed.). 2010. *English Language Teaching Materials: Theory and Practice*. Cambridge: Cambridge University Press.
Hidalgo, A. C., D. Hall and G. M. Jacobs (eds.). 1995. *Getting Started: Materials Writers on Materials Writing*. Singapore: SEAMEO Language Centre.
Johnson, K. 2003. *Designing Language Teaching Tasks*. Basingstoke: Palgrave Macmillan.
McDonough, J., C. Shaw and H. Masuhara. In press. *Materials and Methods in ELT: A Teachers Guide*. London: Blackwell.
McGrath, I. 2002. *Materials Evaluation and Design for Language Teaching*. Edinburgh: Edinburgh University Press.
Menon, S. and J. Lourdunathan (eds.), 2009. *Readings on ELT Materials IV*. Petaling Jaya: Pearson Malaysia
Mukundan, J. (ed.). 2003. *Readings on ELT Material*. Sedang: Universiti Putra Malaysia Press.
    (ed.). 2006. *Readings on ELT Materials II*. Petaling Jaya: Pearson Malaysia.
    (ed.) 2008. *Readings on ELT Materials III*. Petaling Jaya: Pearson Malaysia.
    (ed.) 2010. *Readings on ELT Materials V*. Petaling Jaya: Pearson Malaysia.
Renandya, W. A. (ed.) 2003. *Methodology and Materials Design in Language Teaching: Current Perceptions and Practises and their Implications*. Singapore: RELC.
Richards, J. 2001. *Curriculum Development in Language Education*. Cambridge: Cambridge University Press.
Sheldon, L. E. (ed.). 1987. *ELT Textbooks and Materials: Problems in Evaluation and Development*. ELT Documents 126. London: Modern English Publications and the British Council.
Tomlinson, B. (ed.) 1998. *Materials Development in Language Teaching*. Cambridge: Cambridge University Press.
    (ed.) 2003. *Developing Materials for Language Teaching*. London: Continuum.

Recommended reading

(ed.) 2007. *Language Acquisition and Development: Studies of First and Other Language Learners*. London: Continuum.

(ed.) 2008. *English Language Teaching Materials: A Critical Review*. London: Continuum.

Tomlinson, B. and H. Masuhara. 2004. *Developing Language Course Materials*. Singapore: RELC Portfolio Series.

2011. *Research in Materials Development for Language Learning: Evidence for Best Practice*. London: Continuum.

Index

Index

Index